A Future for the News

A Future for the News

What's Wrong with Mainstream News Media in America and How to Fix It

Edited by Jim A. Kuypers

ROWMAN & LITTLEFIELD
Lanham • Boulder • New York • London

Published by Rowman & Littlefield
An imprint of The Rowman & Littlefield Publishing Group, Inc.
4501 Forbes Boulevard, Suite 200, Lanham, Maryland 20706
www.rowman.com

86-90 Paul Street, London EC2A 4NE

Copyright © 2024 by The Rowman & Littlefield Publishing Group, Inc.

All rights reserved. No part of this book may be reproduced in any form or by any electronic or mechanical means, including information storage and retrieval systems, without written permission from the publisher, except by a reviewer who may quote passages in a review.

British Library Cataloguing in Publication Information Available

Library of Congress Cataloging-in-Publication Data

Names: Kuypers, Jim A., editor.
Title: A future for the news : what's wrong with mainstream news media in America and how to fix it / edited by Jim A. Kuypers.
Description: Lanham : Rowman & Littlefield, 2023. | Includes bibliographical references and index.
Identifiers: LCCN 2023044303 (print) | LCCN 2023044304 (ebook) |
  ISBN 9781538180228 (cloth) | ISBN 9781538180235 (paperback) |
  ISBN 9781538180242 (ebook)
Subjects: LCSH: Journalism--Objectivity--United States. | Mass media--Objectivity--United States. | Journalism--United States. | Mass media--United States.
Classification: LCC PN4888.O25 .F88 2023 (print) | LCC PN4888.O25 (ebook) | DDC 071/.3--dc23/eng/20230921
LC record available at https://lccn.loc.gov/2023044303
LC ebook record available at https://lccn.loc.gov/2023044304

*To
Cindy L. Blitzer
for the best of reasons*

Contents

Acknowledgments ix

Introduction: Problems in the Mainstream News and How to Fix Them 1
Jim A. Kuypers

Chapter 1: Trust in the News: Newsroom Attempts and Failures and the Promise of Helpful Technology 13
Michael Horning

Chapter 2: Objectivity and Anti-Objectivity in Journalism 31
William Max Knorpp

Chapter 3: Digital Dissonance: Rebuilding Trust in News in an Age of Misinformation, Filter Bubbles, and Bias 53
John Gable and Adriel Warren and Contributions by Isaiah Anthony and Julie Mastrine

Chapter 4: Debate in Journalism Curriculum as a Solution to Ideological Normativity 69
Ben Voth

Chapter 5: A Renewal of Journalistic Credibility through the Ancient Religious Tradition of Jubilee 87
Stephen D. Perry

Chapter 6: Apples and Bananas: The Necessity of Differentiating Facts and Opinion for Democracy-Nurturing Fact-Checking 107
Alex Christy and Brent Baker

Chapter 7: Guardians of the Galaxy: How the Media Stumbles When It Seeks to Protect Historically Underserved and

Marginalized Communities, and Never More So than When
Reporting on the Relationship between Blacks and Jews   129
Abe Aamidor

Chapter 8: Solving Media Deserts Requires Going beyond Mapping
News   147
Michelle Ferrier

Chapter 9: The Problem-Solving Solutions Journalism Model:
Treating News Audiences as Problem Solvers in Solutions
Journalism   171
Serena Miller, Soo Young Shin, and Jennifer Cox

Chapter 10: Media Monopolies and News Making: An Analysis of
How Media Conglomeration Affects the Marketplace of Ideas   195
Cayce Myers

Chapter 11: Reporting on Low Voter Turnout Is a Self-Fulfilling
Prophecy   215
Katherine Haenschen

Chapter 12: Democracy-Destroying Practices of the American
Mainstream News Media and Their Potential Solutions   231
Jim A. Kuypers

Index   259

About the Contributors   273

Acknowledgments

I thank my family for their unreserved and continual support of my writing. It is with gratitude that I mention Virginia Tech for paying my salary and also funding library services such as interlibrary loan and Ebscohost, all absolutely necessary to the completion of this project.

I also wish to acknowledge the chapter authors in this volume. Their hard work and professionalism are greatly appreciated. Additionally, thank you to the professional team at Rowman & Littlefield Publishers: Natalie Mandziuk, Yu Ozaki, Aiden Brown, and Anna Keyser.

Introduction

Problems in the *Mainstream News and How* to Fix Them

Jim A. Kuypers

Even with the rise of alternative news media and the ubiquitous nature of social media complicating news production and delivery models, there is broad consensus among Americans as to what constitutes "mainstream news media." Interestingly, this consensus runs strong with both those who do and who do not receive their news from a particular outlet, with even Republicans and Democrats agreeing on which outlets are included (thus outlets such as ABC News, Fox News, CNN, the *New York Times*, the *Wall Street Journal*, and the *New York Post*).[1] And it is with this common understanding of the phrase that the authors in this book write. What is also generally agreed upon by Americans is that the mainstream news media is a ghost of its former self, in a state of grievous disrepair, and in danger of collapse. For only a few instances, consider that in 2016 Gallup reported that only 17 to 23 percent of Americans rated journalists high or very high in ethical standards.[2] In 2018, a multiparty survey found that 72 percent of Americans believed that "'traditional major news sources report news they know to be fake, false, or purposely misleading.'"[3] In 2022, Gallup reported that a mere "16% of Americans have a great deal/quite a lot of confidence in newspapers, and that only 11% have some the degree of confidence in television news."[4] And by 2023, Rasmussen found that an amazing 59 percent of voters agree that the news media are the "Enemy of the People."[5] These are but a few examples of the hundreds of surveys and studies pointing to the same conclusion: the mainstream news media in America is on a downward spiral leading to its own destruction. It is mired in low credibility, low trust, low confidence, and even disdain.

There are many reasons for the state the mainstream news media finds itself in today, many of which have a long history.[6] Most Americans, around

81 percent, find that the news media are "critical" or "very important" to the proper functioning of our government and yet are also concerned about the "great deal" or "a fair amount" of political bias in news coverage. Of note is that about 84 percent of Americans place the blame for divisions (racial, social, political) squarely in the hands of the news media yet also say that the media could help solve these same problems.[7] These concerns are, however, only part of the difficulties facing the mainstream news media. Structural changes, emerging competition from alternate sources, lack of viewpoint diversity, a move away from objectivity as the standard, the embrace of social responsibility as a raison d'être for reporting, consolidation, and others plague the institution. All of these combine to create a challenging environment in which producers of the news must work. There are ways to restore trust and credibility with the American people, however, and that is the purpose of this book. Each chapter takes as its charge a problem faced by the mainstream news and provides a solution or set of possible solutions for news media practitioners and at times consumers (reporters, editors, owners, readers, viewers) to enact to help reestablish the mainstream news to a true position of trustworthiness with the American people, to help maintain a strong American republic. For there is no doubt that a free and trusted press is essential to the proper functioning of any government founded on true democratic principles. As Walter Cronkite said, "Freedom of the press is not just important to democracy, it is democracy."[8] But freedom also assumes responsibility to news consumers, and it is clear that the expectations of American news consumers are quite different from the expectations of those producing the news, as seen from the earlier survey results. It is commonly accepted that the healthier a nation's press, the better educated citizens are to participate fruitfully in the governing of their nation, state, town, etc., and so the healthier that nation's democracy. And thus this book, each chapter of which takes a particular problem facing the mainstream press today and offers a workable solution to that problem—solutions that can help restore the health of the American news media.

In "Trust in the News: Newsroom Attempts and Failures and the Promise of Helpful Technology," Michael Horning notes how public trust in journalism has been in steady decline for decades, citing in particular a precipitous drop from 72 percent of Americans in 1972 saying they had a "great deal or fair amount of trust" in the news media only 32 percent in 2016. The reasons for this are many, and Horning suggests that an increasingly partisan public that gravitates toward news that fits their ideology, as well as journalists who are increasingly seen as partisan and injecting their biases into stories, are among the major contributing factors.

Although some have suggested that journalists can combat this decline in trust by being more transparent about their journalism, Horning argues that the term "transparency" itself is often ambiguous and encompasses a wide variety of practices in journalism—from creating biographies of journalists' credentials to developing technical standards for online reporting such as linking to primary sources. Others have suggested that by rejecting a notion of objective reporting that news audiences will once again begin to trust journalists. Horning points out the flaws with each consideration and, moving beyond these ineffective practices, offers the suggestion that journalists should use twenty-first-century tools for twenty-first-century journalism. Specifically, he notes that a "number of technological advances in computing techniques such as crowdsourcing and natural language processing are leading to the development of a variety of tools designed to help people evaluate the quality of information" to which they are exposed. Specifically, he offers suggestions on how third-party applications could be developed to help audience members make judgments about the quality and trustworthiness of the news they consume. Such endeavors, Horning reasons, will not only allow journalists to receive actual perception feedback about their stories from those who consume them, but also that audiences will be able to learn how to evaluate the quality of the news they consume on their own.

Traditional notions of journalism have held that objectivity is a necessary practice to ensure ethical and productive journalism. William Max Knorpp, in "Objectivity and Anti-Objectivity in Journalism," delves deeply into these concepts, writing that although objectivity is ordinarily thought to be a crucial component of truth-seeking activities in areas such as science, scholarship, law, and, importantly to this chapter, journalism, it is under siege in popular and semipopular discussions of these endeavors. In journalism in particular, reporters and editors are now often told, from both inside and outside of their profession, that objectivity is both impossible (as in beyond the epistemic capacities of human beings) and even bad (in ways that range from boring to racist). Knorpp points to surveys showing that as journalists move further away from popular notions of objectivity, their credibility with the public declines (something also noted by a majority of authors in this book).

As a trained philosopher with a keen interest in matters journalistic, Knorpp offers a unique perspective on this issue. Philosophers, of course, have seemingly focused more attention on objectivity than anyone else, and using their efforts to assess the contemporary concerns raised in journalism circles provides a distinctive and practical opportunity to apply the insights and lessons learned from one discipline to another. To do this, Knorpp begins by offering clarification about objectivity's actual nature. Knowing objectivity's nature can help clear away some of the weakest arguments in the dispute, starting with the "perfection argument," which posits the conclusion that objectivity is impossible. Knorpp convincingly refutes such arguments and then turns to concerns central to the notion of objectivity in journalism: Is the ideal of objectivity inherently racist, does it illicitly favor the status quo, and does it turn journalists into mere stenographers? Mixing this with consideration of some common journalistic codes of ethics, he points out seeming contradictions between codes and practices and argues that several of their provisions are virtually equivalent to requirements of objectivity. He concludes by suggesting practical ways of improving journalists' thinking about objectivity and their contributions to the public discussions on this issue.

So many polls from noted agencies such as Gallup, the Knight Foundation, Rasmussen, and Pew show a steady decline in the confidence Americans have for the mainstream news media, much of which is linked to perception of bias. In "Digital Dissonance: Rebuilding Trust in News in an Age of Misinformation, Filter Bubbles, and Bias," John Gable and Adriel Warren explore the rapidly declining trust in the American news media, the prevalence of filter bubbles ("a term coined by Internet activist Eli Pariser that describes the intellectual isolation that can occur when technology companies use algorithms to feed users information and content that they will like, based on their interests, location, past searches, click history, and more"), and the increase of partisan polarization. Drawing upon numerous national surveys, including the Reuters Institute for the Study of Journalism, the authors share that of forty-six countries around the world, the United States ranks last in news trust, with just 26 percent saying today that they trust the news most of the time.

With this dangerously low starting point in mind, Gable and Warren examine the roots of this distrust, arguing that changes in the news industry have created partisan filter bubbles driven by financial incentives. This revenue-driven journalism, they reason, promotes clickbait and sensationalism that often misconstrues an accurate representation of the news, making news less balanced and contributing to bias. Next, they move to examining how media bias exacerbates political polarization, filter bubbles, and unbalanced news. Without balanced news, they argue, filter bubbles become cyclical instances of confirmation bias that deepen ideological and political divides. They conclude by offering a unique solution to this problem—the AllSides Media Bias Chart™ and media bias ratings, which combat hidden media bias by revealing the political leanings, ownership, and funding of major news outlets. Of note is that AllSides uses a patented methodology to rate bias, including expert editorial reviews and blind bias surveys that are designed to reveal the average judgment of Americans, not just one elite group. Thus, by combining expert analysis with surveys of Americans, Gable and Warren argue that AllSides provides robust bias ratings that empower readers to think for themselves. Their chapter concludes with a call to action for news organizations to reliably provide more objective and balanced news by regularly measuring their content in a robust, credible manner.

Ben Voth takes a different approach to recovering credibility in "Debate in Journalism Curriculum as a Solution to Ideological Normativity." In this chapter, Voth enlarges our understanding of a journalistic loss of credibility, taking for his starting point a situation noted by most of our chapter authors, that American journalism faces an acute credibility crisis with the American public. He points out that traditional major newspaper outlets such as the *New York Times*, the *Washington Post*, the *Los Angeles Times*, and the *Dallas Morning News* are perceived by readers to be reactionary toward widespread public interests as well as the Republican Party. Highlighting the bedrock principle of a free press, Voth notes that although the press has freedom to report as it sees fit, audience perceptions of biased reporting result in loss of credibility and audience share, ultimately damaging the republic.

Voth's solution to this dilemma capitalizes on the inherent civil right of freedom of the press, which is imperative for the future of an American republic operating with democratic principles. What better way for repairing this, then argues Voth, than to institute debate across the curriculum for journalists while in training. He defines debate as an intuitive critical thinking instructional practice that encourages the thoughtful consideration and expression of opposing points of view. After reviewing many positive aspects of such a program, Voth offers a practical way of implementing this for journalism schools, specifically, to adapt themselves to the public expressions and values representative of an objective Overton window. In brief, this involves understanding the range of acceptable and reviewed opinions as including the full range of the one hundred US senators without defining a significant percentage of senators as "extremists." Debate curriculum for journalism majors can expose undergraduate students to a relatively unmodified range of political opinions grounded in public political choices rather than critical theory curriculums that presuppose political outcomes or critique assumptions in a manner concurrent with the censorship of ideas. Through such a program, Voth argues that "instruction will likely reverse the spiral of cynicism rooted in . . . distrust of journalism and restore the American ideal model of a free press."

Stephen D. Perry takes an entirely different approach to the restoration of journalism's credibility in "A Renewal of Journalistic Credibility through the Ancient Religious Tradition of Jubilee." He begins his chapter by summarizing what numerous studies of the contemporary news media have found: that as journalists and news outlets move further away from a classic notion of objectivity to greater partisanship, their credibility with much of the public in America, and even the world, plummets. But what is objectivity? In order to understand this concept, Perry points out that one must rely on often unstated underlying assumptions about how objectivity is measured; yet as American society has become increasingly postmodern or even meta-modern,

Americans *seem* to have lost a shared underlying value system on which all reporters generally agree. In order to reestablish a foundation from which journalists can report on and critique current events, a new perspective is necessary, especially one that can overcome the fractured and contentious nature of American politics today. Perry offers for consideration the ancient principle of a jubilee year, which was taught to the nation of Israel, as a model from which reporters can pull ancient wisdom that critiques both the right and the left in America.

Perry introduces how the jubilee year can be fruitfully applied to controversial issues often covered by reporters (immigration, family, debt, charity, race, crime, economics, and so on), minimizing the risk of charges of political bias. Moreover, he demonstrates how the principal of jubilee balances the collectivist versus individualist orientations of American society and the notions of socialism with those of capitalism. It also, in terms of financial wealth, challenges any system of enduring "haves" and "have nots" in society. The principles of jubilee also, according to Perry, present objective foundations on which some of the main institutions of government that are linked either to left or right politically can be challenged by the press, thus rehabilitating the watchdog role of the press. He concludes his chapter by presenting how journalists can use this idea of jubilee to construct narratives that restore objectivity and credibility to the mainstream news media.

Closely linked with issues of credibility is news media fact-checking, which has always been an important task for journalists, and one that Americans especially saw during the 2016 presidential race. Since that time, however, there have been increasing concerns from large percentages of the population that fact-checking serves not so much the needs of the people but the needs of the press. In "'Apples and Bananas': The Necessity of Differentiating Facts and Opinion for Democracy-Nurturing Fact-Checking," Alex Christy and Brent Baker argue that in recent years there has been a shift in how the news media sees its role in society. Although journalists still cling to the label of objectivity, they do so with a modified definition of that term. Instead of it meaning nonpartisanship, or not taking sides, it is morphing into demonstrating a commitment to facts. As a result, they argue, Americans have seen the proliferation of professional fact-checking; however, this new industry has been plagued by the same issue found in traditional forms of journalism today: lack of trust.

Christy and Baker note that from being completely wrong, to playing games with semantics, to expert shopping, to misleadingly using statistics, to poor case selections, and often a combination of these elements, fact-checkers have often taken sides in contentious debates by confusing their opinions for facts. After providing numerous instances of such behaviors, the authors show

how they can explain the lack of trust Americans have for "fact-checkers," and perhaps also why large percentages of Americans do not trust professional fact-checkers' assertions about political issues. Importantly, they point out, when fact-checkers develop a partisan reputation, even that which they fact-check correctly will be viewed with skepticism. Although the authors do show how distrust of professional fact-checking predates the Trump presidency, they catalog the mainstream news media trend to dismiss any conservative criticism as just another "Trumpian" influence in the war to discredit journalists. Christy and Baker note that such a stance acts to enervate any fruitful assessment of fact-checking challenges, which results in only making the situation worse. The solution to bad fact-checking, they posit, is good fact-checking, and this begins with a healthy respect for the difference between truth and opinion. The authors conclude with several practical suggestions for how the industry could reestablish itself as a nonpartisan entity.

Thus far we have looked primarily at issues related to confidence in and the credibility of the media. Abe Aamidor takes a different approach in his chapter, examining how the news media exacerbates racial tensions. As noted earlier, Americans feel that the news media is largely responsible for racial divisions in America, and in his chapter, "Guardians of the Galaxy: How the Media Stumbles When It Seeks to Protect Historically Underserved and Marginalized Communities, and Never More So than When Reporting on the Relationship between Blacks and Jews," Aamidor notes that allegations of media bias (from the left and the right) often focus on how reporters present representation of minorities, ethnic groups, and protected classes in America. Some of the representations critics question, which Aamidor presents as examples of "poor representation," include an alleged emphasis on crime reporting and absentee fathers in inner-city neighborhoods that further negative stereotypes of Black Americans; labeling immigrants at America's southern border as "illegal" or "undocumented," thereby further stigmatizing them; and even articles that engage in "fat shaming."

Other claims, Aamidor notes, alleging that the media are sacrificing objectivity on the altar of diversity, equity, and inclusion, have only increased in recent years. He notes that such claims are usually contested, although evidence supporting the original claims, such as the "mainstreaming" policy of Gannett, do exist. The Gannett policy, simply stated for instance, is for journalists to consciously add more minority expert sources to comment on the news and add more diversity by including minority voices in any story where feasible. Aamidor notes anecdotally that mainstreaming now seems common throughout the media, and that all these claims and counterclaims are part of the culture wars, including charges of "liberal bias" in the news and the age-old debate over advocacy journalism. With this as his starting point, Aamidor adopts an apolitical definition of bias and argues that, in general, the mainstream media do look for ways to improve the representation of minorities, certain ethnic groups, and protected classes (either de jure or de facto), either as compensation for historically negative reporting or as part of the current push for diversity, equity, and inclusion. However, he demonstrates how such practices lead to serious contradictions in reporting, particularly when these groups and protected classes are in conflict with each other. Taking as his case study the reporting on Blacks and Jews when in conflict with each other, Aamidor offers a cogent insight into the contradictory reporting practices of the press when addressing interracial conflict and then offers insight into practices that will allow for both respectful and accurate reporting on racial and ethnic groups.

In "Solving Media Deserts Requires Going Beyond Mapping News," Michelle Ferrier examines a different type of problem, one involving the lack of news in many American communities. With the rapid changes in news delivery, production, and corporate consolidation, among others, there are places, primarily in America's rural communities, where many lack adequate news resources, a phenomenon called by some "media deserts." Ferrier's life in Appalachia provided the proving ground for several experiments using the media deserts methodology, ones in which she was able to develop "innovations in mapping and modeling the changing media ecosystem." She shares the results of these experiments here, taking into account a holistic view of the channels, locations, and ways in which geography intersects with communication issues, such as broadband access in our rural communities. She shares how the infrastructure, content, ownership, and other structures impede the growth of local news in rural and other marginalized communities. In short, Ferrier shares details of the Media Deserts Project, "a research effort to map and model the ways in which many of our rural and even urban communities have been impoverished over the past decade by the lack of fresh, daily local news and information." In sharing her findings in this chapter she not only provides results of the project but also presents a template for others to go into media deserts and make positive changes. In this sense, her chapter focuses on the possible and concludes with examples of possible positive outcomes for increasing the presence of nascent news entities.

Serena Miller, Soo Young Shin, and Jennifer Cox look at an area of growing interest among journalists, a solutions-oriented form of reporting that could potentially help recover audiences soured on what they view as overly negative news or skeptical because of what they perceive to be biased news. In "The Problem-Solving Solutions Journalism Model: Treating News Audiences as Problem Solvers in Solutions Journalism," these authors write that the "news media's generation of public outrage toward societal events motivates some people to act, but the news media should be wary because audiences also describe the news media as harmful, intolerable, and negative . . . contributing to readers feeling overwhelmed, distrustful, apathetic, and disempowered when faced with issues of geographic and humanitarian concern." Although audience members often want to act to help solve problems, they can be overwhelmed to the point of taking no action. Standard norms of reportorial practice discourage reporters from offering solutions, especially when one considers that traditional news organizations have avoided offering solutions to challenges facing society due to concerns with perceptions of bias. Miller, Shin, and Cox argue, however, that the benefits of a solutions-oriented approach outweigh any perceived disadvantages, and they assert that the news media should continue to report on problems facing society, taking into consideration what is "among the strongest predictive concepts that explains whether people positively act" when faced with negative news or events: perceived self-efficacy. By taking this into account, and adding to their reporting the additional component of problem-solving efficacy, the news media could offer audiences opportunity to engage more fully with the news and with their communities.

The authors base their explanation of how this might work on the extended parallel processing model (EPPM), which is rooted in the fear message appeals and protection motivation literature. This model posits that communicators (in our case, journalists) should provide both *threat* and *efficacious* information if they care about fueling positive and healthy responses to negative news such as tragedies, risks, and crises. Although the recent solutions journalism movement emphasizes straight reporting on solutions, journalists using a solutions-oriented approach could enact more than a solutions frame. They could envision their audience members as capable problem solvers by providing enough information to help them decide on their own whether a solution makes sense for their community. The approach bypasses the current and enervating approach of having an expert evaluate the solution's success and disseminates knowledge associated with the solution. The sources try to persuade others (the news audience) of the solution's value, which actually acts to encourage audiences to be *reactive* to a situation rather than *active* toward enacting a solution. Thus, the current, and passive, approach encourages audiences to scan environments and react rather than participate in the solution. Miller, Shin, and Cox conclude their chapter by suggesting practical approaches to a more active solutions-oriented approach that encourages both individual and collective efficacy.

In some ways looking at viewpoint diversity in the news media, Cayce Myers, in "Media Monopolies and News Making: An Analysis of How Media Conglomeration Affects the Marketplace of Ideas," examines how media consolidation has impacted the quality of the news and also shares ideas about how the negative aspects of this situation can be mitigated. Using both legal and historical analysis in his chapter, Myers explores the increased conglomeration of ownership of US mainstream media companies, focusing in particular on American media laws, (specifically federal statutes), Federal Communications Commission (FCC) regulations, and antitrust application, from the 1930s until the present—all of which led to increased media consolidation. He begins with the nascent media regulations of the 1930s and then moves into the rise of conglomeration that began shortly following the ending of World War II. Myers forcefully argues that the development of American media monopolies was facilitated through the promulgation of federal laws and FCC regulations, such as the Telecommunications Act of 1996 and FCC cross-ownership rules in the 2000s. Moreover, he demonstrates how during the twentieth century the federal government's gradual relaxation of ownership rules facilitated the growth of media monopolies.

Myers also covers the important area of US antitrust law as it relates to the mainstream news media, paying particular attention to the unique application of the Sherman Antitrust Act to media companies. An important discussion in the chapter focuses on how antitrust issues concerning social media are presenting themselves today. This includes how recent antitrust issues against the big four Big Tech companies (Amazon, Apple, Meta [formerly Facebook], and Google) may be harbingers for new diversification of digital ownership in the 2020s. All of this, of course, has bearing upon how the news is produced and its impact on the marketplace of ideas, particularly in a political context. With this in mind, Myers presents contemporary criticism of the impact concentrated media ownership has on news production, the rise of fake news, and the homogenization of information. He concludes his chapter by presenting legal solutions to address the impact of concentrated media ownership in the United States.

Focusing on an issue central to America's participatory democracy—voting—Katherine Haenschen discusses in "Reporting on Low Voter Turnout Is a Self-Fulfilling Prophecy" how contemporary reportorial practices act to exacerbate low voter turnout. This is something that remains a persistent problem in America outside of presidential elections, with even congressional midterm elections often falling below the 50 percent participation mark; local elections often see but single-digit participation. Drawing on empirical research across the social and behavioral sciences, she argues that by reporting on low turnout, the media is paradoxically creating a self-fulfilling prophecy in which their very coverage results in people not voting. In short, Haenschen argues that the mainstream news media makes this situation worse by the manner in which it reports on low turnout, through what she describes as its creation of "descriptive norms of nonparticipation." In her chapter she argues that the news media needs to refrain from reporting on low voter turnout (a *descriptive* model of reporting) and instead begin to emphasize the *injunctive* norm of doing one's civic duty, as well as covering the impact of elected offices to individuals' daily lives and profiling community members who are voting and helping to administer elections.

Finally, in "Democracy Destroying Practices of the American Mainstream News Media and Their Potential Solutions," Jim A. Kuypers shares how the American news media historically has operated from the libertarian model of news production, yet from the late 1950s into today has been incorporating ever more elements of social responsibility into its reportorial practices. Kuypers shows that to an ever increasing degree news reporters are focused on interpreting rather than presenting the news, and he argues that this practice, coupled with the ideological makeup and growing advocacy interests of journalists and editors, is beginning to move the American press away from a social responsibility model to something completely unknown in the history of the American republic, something fundamentally damaging to the democratic ideals and functioning of that republic. Moreover, this movement is correlated with ever increasing negative views of the press, with trust in the mainstream news at historical all-time lows. His chapter looks at this trend and positions it within the context of the recent pandemic and the 2020 American presidential election and offers suggestions for not only the American press but also any country seeking to have a robust and free press system that strengthens participatory republics operating on democratic principles.

Together, these chapters represent a strong voice both pointing out deficiencies in the mainstream news media and in offering viable solutions to these deficiencies. Viewed collectively, they offer an overview of the major challenges facing the American mainstream news media from numerous perspectives, thus offering a rich insight into the nuances of the situation. Moreover, they collectively provide thoughtful solutions, often unique, to help fix what is going wrong. Forceful in pointing out the bad, thoughtful in presenting practical solutions, each chapter seeks to help the mainstream news media reform to thereby recover its trusted place in the proper functioning of the American republic.

NOTES

1. Elisa Shearer and Amy Mitchell, "Broad Agreement in U.S.—Even Among Partisans—On Which News Outlets Are Part of the 'Mainstream Media,'" Pew Research, May 7, 2021, https://www.pewresearch.org/short-reads/2021/05/07/broad-agreement-in-u-s-even-among-partisans-on-which-news-outlets-are-part-of-the-mainstream-media/.

2. Jim Norman, "Americans Rate Healthcare Providers High on Honesty, Ethics," Gallup, December 19, 2016, https://news.gallup.com/poll/200057/americans-rate-healthcare-providers-high-honesty-ethics.aspx.

3. John Concha, "Poll: 72 Percent Say Traditional Outlets 'Report News They Know to Be Fake, False, or Purposely Misleading,'" *The Hill*, June 27, 2018, https://thehill.com/homenews/media/394352-poll-72-percent-say-traditional-outlets-report-news-they-know-to-be-fake-false.

4. Megan Brenan, "Media Confidence Ratings at Record Lows," Gallup, July 18, 2022, https://news.gallup.com/poll/394817/media-confidence-ratings-record-lows.aspx.

5. "Media Still 'Enemy of the People,' Most Voters Say," Rasmussen Reports, May 23, 2023, https://www.rasmussenreports.com/public_content/politics/biden_administration/media_still_enemy_of_the_people_most_voters_say.

6. See, for example, Jim A. Kuypers, *Partisan Journalism: A History of Media Bias in the United States* (Lanham, MD: Rowman & Littlefield, 2014).

7. Megan Brenan and Helen Stubbs, "News Media Viewed as Biased but Crucial to Democracy," Gallup, August 4, 2020, https://news.gallup.com/poll/316574/news-media-viewed-biased-crucial-democracy.aspx; and Knight Foundation, "Gallup/Knight Poll: Americans' Concerns About Media Bias Deepen, Even as They See It as Vital For Democracy," Knight Foundation, August 4, 2020, https://knightfoundation.org/press/releases/gallup-knight-poll-americans-concerns-about-media-bias-deepen-even-as-they-see-it-as-vital-for-democracy/.

8. Walter Cronkite, "Walter Cronkite Quotes," Azquotes, accessed June 5, 2023, https://www.azquotes.com/author/3422-Walter_Cronkite.

Chapter 1

Trust in the News

Newsroom Attempts and Failures and the Promise of Helpful Technology

Michael Horning

It is no secret that for many years now public trust in journalism has been on a decline. However, in the most recent years, those numbers indicate a public that has been deeply skeptical of the US media. Gallup Polling, which has tracked trust in the media since the 1970s, has noted that 72 percent of Americans reported a "great deal or fair amount of trust in the media" in 1976. That number dipped to an all-time low of 32 percent in 2016 and has continued to stay in that 30 to 40 percent range in recent years.[1] Gallup's picture, however, is perhaps incomplete, given that the concept of "trust in news" is an umbrella term that covers a wide variety of types of news. For example, to simply gauge general levels of trust does not fully help us understand whether publics distrust national news more than local news. This single measure also does not help us understand if that mistrust is directed at all of the news or certain segments of the industry such as broadcast television news.

Research from Pew provides some additional clarity to that question. Although in general trust across both local news and national news has declined over the years, local news organizations have consistently been seen as more trustworthy, with 84 percent of Democrats and 66 percent of Republicans saying they have "a lot" or "some" trust in the local news. Where the real numbers have shown a significant decline has been in metrics that capture trust in national news. Democrats have remained relatively consistent in their expressed levels of trust. In 2016, 84 percent said they had "a lot" or "some" trust in the news, and that number dropped a bit by

2021 to 78 percent. However, the real decline in trust has been among both Republicans and Independents. In 2016, 70 percent of Republicans expressed trust in national news, but by 2021 those numbers had fallen to only 35 percent. Similarly 76 percent of the Independents said that they have "a lot" or "some" trust in 2016, but that dipped to 58 percent in 2021.[2]

These findings do not bode well for an industry that is going to need to find innovative ways to attract audiences in the near future. A number of indicators suggest that both traditional newspapers and television audiences have and will continue to lose audiences. One report found that on average at least two newspapers close a week in the United states, and between 2008 and 2020 newspaper employment fell by 26 percent.[3] Meanwhile, cable television news has faced its own challenges. While general trends suggest that audiences are moving away from cable and opting for streaming services, even more troubling for cable news is that they are no longer attracting young audiences. One study found major news networks such as CNN, Fox, and MSNBC now have an audience with the average age of sixty.[4]

It is true that these data points do not give a full picture of what the future holds. Younger demographics may indeed move toward traditional sources as they age, and in general all news audiences have been moving away from newspaper and television mediums for some time and getting their news from social media.[5] However, there are some indicators that younger demographics are not just flocking to mainstream news sources. One study has found that Gen Z and millennials are less likely to seek out news on social media and instead tend to "bump into it." The same study also found that the type of news typically consumed by this demographic is of the soft (for example, entertainment, lifestyle, etc.) news variety rather than hard news, which is often focused on politics and corruption.[6] In addition, one other study noted that when younger audiences read news content, their top sources are a mixed bag of mainstream and nontraditional news sources such as Buzzfeed, Facebook, X, or Google News.[7] Taken together, the preponderance of research suggests that new media face an uphill battle to attract audiences.

Modern-day journalism has tried to solve this problem using two dominant approaches. One group argues that if news engages in greater transparency practices, this will lead to greater levels of trust. The other group, somewhat counterintuitively, argues that journalists should replace their goals of being objective in reporting with the goal of telling the truth. Journalists should, in other words, start to take sides on issues where they feel there is settled debate, and they should begin to advocate for those causes or for those individuals that support their values. In this article I examine the inherent flaws in these two approaches and argue that they are not only shortsighted but that they will likely create more challenges for the industry rather than solutions. As a result, I argue that these current solutions are at best going to have little impact on audience trust and at worst going to alienate audiences further, leading further to the decline in media industry jobs. Given the media's failure to come up with any real solutions, I argue that twenty-first-century journalism should provide audiences with third-party tools that allow their own newsrooms and the audiences the ability to analyze the quality of journalism for themselves. For journalists, such tools could aid in self-reflection about the limits of their own reporting. For audiences, such tools could improve their critical abilities to analyze media.

WHY DOESN'T THE PUBLIC TRUST THE MEDIA? IT'S THE BIAS, STUPID

If you ask most people today what they want out of journalism, their reasons for a declining trust are relatively clear. Nic Newman and Ryan Fletcher conducted a study that examined audiences' attitudes toward the news media in nine countries. In their survey of over two thousand participants they found that the most significant reason people gave for not trusting the media was that they felt that journalism today has too much bias. In that study respondents felt that journalism bias often came in the form of journalists privileging certain political and commercial agendas over others.[8] Another study supported by the Society of Professional Journalists went more in depth on this topic. In several interviews Mandy Jenkins found that people often picked up on both the implicit and explicit biases that they saw in news stories. Individuals noted that they felt the news now mixed too much opinion with their facts. They expressed a feeling that the media attempted to frame events in certain ways in order to influence how the audience thought about those events. Other respondents felt that the media often focused more on portraying people in a negative light and less on the substance of what they were doing at the time. As one interviewee put it, "Journalists seem powerful to ordinary citizens . . . they control how people's stories are told to the public . . . and who is cast as the hero or the bad guy. Those decisions can have favorable or destructive consequences for the people they are reporting about. And yet, journalists seem to dole out those benefits or damages pretty cavalierly."[9]

In the same reports, other participants mentioned that they felt that key facts were left out of stories that did not provide the whole picture, and others felt that the news privileged sensational language over factual reporting in order to increase clicks and shares.[10] A 2016 study by the American Press Institutes seems to also verify some of these concerns. In that study, the majority of Americans said that in order for them to trust the news it had to be accurate, fair, and transparent. When one looks further into how these values were described, people thought of accuracy, balance, and transparency in terms of getting the facts right and providing diverse viewpoints or through providing more details about how the journalist gathered or reported the story. Journalists have keyed in on some of these concerns using two approaches. The first has been to advocate for more transparency practices in the newsroom.

DEFINING NEWS TRANSPARENCY

What constitutes transparency in a newsroom varies widely depending on the organization discussing it. The concept often encompasses a number of practices in journalism from creating biographies that list journalists' credentials to developing technical standards for online reporting such as linking to primary sources. For example, the American Press Institute calls transparency "showing your work so readers can decide for themselves why they should believe it."[11] A Knight News Foundation report said that the "media should develop industry wide, voluntary standards on how to disclose the ways they collect, report and disseminate the news."[12] The Radio Television Digital News Association (RTDNA) has an entire policy section dedicated to "independence and transparency." Their definition includes "explaining editorial decisions . . . owning errors . . . [and] attribution" of sources.[13] There is obviously no clear agreement from organization to organization on what transparency actually is. Some seem to see it in terms of providing more context for a story, while others seem to advocate for peeling back the curtain during editorial meetings and letting the audience see how a story is made.

Academic literature that has tried to help clarify the concept of transparency has actually seemed to muddy the water more. Kalyani Chadha and Michael Koliska somewhat vaguely describe transparency as greater openness in journalism and being honest with sources about what the story is about. They also suggest that transparency includes journalists providing a rationale for how they approach a story.[14] Kelly McBride and Tom Rosenstiel argue that transparency is the practice of showing how the reporting is done and giving insight into how journalists make decisions when they make stories.[15] Stephanie Craft and Tim Vos argue that there are two strategies journalists can employ. They can practice disclosing both journalistic processes and disclosing any biases or motivations that lead to the story coverage.[16] Meanwhile, Michael Karlsson separated transparency into two types: disclosure transparency and participatory transparency.[17] One involves the practices of journalists and the other involves soliciting feedback on a journalist's performance. Karlsson finds journalists engaging in some very rudimentary practices that they identify as transparent such as providing updates to stories or linking to original documents or sources.

If we try to read between the lines, it seems that transparency is an emerging philosophy in journalism that seems to assert that if audiences are just provided with more arguments that show why a journalist is correct, this should solve the problem. Those arguments may come in the form of providing more information (for example, information about the journalist, or links to original sources) or through providing some type of context that helps the audience arrive at the conclusion that this newsroom made the right choices in terms of why and how it covered the story.

How Citizens and Journalists Feel About Transparency

Given that there are so many varied definitions of journalism, it is also not surprising that citizens and journalists also differ in whether they think transparency is an effective practice for improving trust. Momen Bhuiyan and his colleagues used a qualitative approach to ask citizens about a variety of transparency practices. Their findings indicated that citizens valued the use of embedded documents and shared concerns about the use of anonymous sources in stories. They also wanted to know more about how journalists selected certain facts over others. As a result, they concluded that the use of some transparency practices would be welcomed by audiences. The same study found that journalists were in agreement that transparency would be improved by providing more internal documents but shared some skepticism about providing the public with too many insights into how stories were developed. In another study, transparency was seen as an attempt to make journalists more approachable. Matthias Revers found that some journalists were being encouraged to use social media to share more about their personal lives in an attempt to humanize them. Journalists have mixed feelings about such transparency practices. Some felt that this made stronger connections between their readers, while others saw it as a breach of journalistic norms.[18] Similarly, Rebecca Nee found that newsroom managers thought of transparency as being more authentic. This means writing in a less formal way and being more approachable and accessible.[19] In another study, Peter Gade concluded that journalists felt that "while there has been a great deal of discussion and commentary about the importance of transparency, journalists in this study did not perceive that their managers are giving transparency much priority."[20]

Does Transparency Work?

So although journalism still seems to think of transparency as an aspirational idea, so far it seems that the industry as a whole has yet to settle on any clear conceptualization of what transparency looks like. Some seem to think of it as a concrete practice reflected in new digital practices while others seem to have this vague notion of being "buddy-buddy" with the public. It is also quite clear that not all journalists see these practices as either useful or helpful in establishing their credibility. So what does the empirical literature say about transparency practices? Several surveys and experiments have been conducted to tease out exactly what transparency approaches work, but that too has seen mixed results, and most have indicated that transparency will not have a major impact on perceived levels of trust.

Michael Karlsson and Christer Clerwall looked at what they called "disclosure transparency" (for example, linking to content, letting readers know when errors were made) and "participatory transparency" (for example, allowing audience comments, publishing news generated by citizens) practices. The survey results showed the public were more interested in disclosure practices than participatory practices, but the researchers noted that both practices were only seen as moderately helpful in improving trust in journalism.[21] A second study that used experimental methods found that transparency practices have led to increased evaluations of the credibility of a news story and greater intentions to engage with the news.[22] In Alexander Curry and Natali Stroud's experiment, the researchers provided respondents with a news story that contained, among other items, additional reporter information, a label (for example, news, analysis, opinion), footnotes to original sources, and information about how the story was written. Compared to their control condition, they found these features improved the story's credibility, but the effects were fairly small. This led the researchers to conclude that transparency features can be helpful, but the effects may not be the full solution for improving perceptions of trust in the media. The researchers then conducted three separate experiments to see whether the use of a "transparency box" would improve perceptions of the credibility of the news. This box provided readers with notes next to the story that explained how and why journalists were doing the story. Although they did find that the use of a transparency box could impact perceptions of credibility, again these effects were minimal. This led the authors to conclude that transparency practices are "not a panacea for lagging news outlet credibility perceptions."[23] One other study tried to tackle the transparency question by providing labels attached to a news story. In this study, participants were provided with a label about the type of news they were reading. The label indicated that the content was either news analysis, opinion, sponsored, or no label. They concluded that the use of such labels had no impact on transparency.[24] Michael Koliska also explored the impact of transparency features on audience trust in a separate experiment.[25] Participants were provided a variety of features. Some of those features provided information about the story itself (source cures) and the author (message cues). In this study they too found that these did not significantly impact whether the audience saw the media that produced that content as more trustworthy. Taken together, the studies suggest that the use of transparency as it is currently being practiced will at best have minimal effects on audience levels of trust in the news.

It should be said that this is not a full critique of these practices so much as an objective assessment of their likelihood of success. Further, there may be more work to be done in this area that suggests that transparency could be useful in some contexts. For example, much of what has been done has often looked at the impact of transparency features on news that was assumed to be true, and it may be that people respond differently to news that they already find credible than to news that they are skeptical of. In addition, some of this research was conducted in countries where trust in news is much higher than in the United States, so generalizability to US populations here is limited. It is also difficult to gauge the effect of a transparency feature in a one-off experiment. Longitudinal studies may demonstrate that the effects are incremental. At best, the current research suggests that transparency practices as they are currently conceptualized will not be the magic bullet that brings readers back to the fold. Transparency practices' effects will be minimal at best when it comes to influencing a person's perceptions of that news organization's trustworthiness.

IF WE ARE MORE BIASED, THEY WILL COME

Although efforts to restore trust through transparency seem to be at least an idea that moves in the right direction, a more mind-boggling solution has argued that journalists can be perceived as more trustworthy if they do away with objectivity in their reporting altogether.[26] In his 2021 interview with NYU journalism professor Ezra Klein, Jay Rosen said, "Objectivity creates a huge attack surface for the enemies of the press to do their work. . . . And that's a big attack surface, which the right wing has used very effectively to generate distrust in the news media."[27] Rosen's comments are part of a growing effort to push newsrooms away from the tradition of being objective in a news report. According to Leonard Downie and Andrew Heyward, the thinking goes that such practices lead to what they say is a "'both-sides-ism'—a dangerous trap when covering issues like climate change or the intensifying assault on democracy."[28] In their recent report produced by the Walter

Cronkite School of Journalism at Arizona State University, titled "How to Produce Trustworthy News without 'Objectivity,'" the authors support this position using a number of quotes from former journalists. For instance, they quote the editor-in-chief of the *San Francisco Chronicle*, Emilio Garcia-Ruiz, who states, "Objectivity has got to go." Garcia-Ruiz goes on to say that younger journalists see objectivity as a failed concept and are instead "willing to share their lived experiences to call out bullshit, despite their status in the newsroom."[29] In the same report, Julia Wallace, a professor and former editor of the *Atlanta Journal-Constitution*, said, "Objectivity was wrong, a failed concept." Kathleen Carroll, the former executive editor of the Associated Press, also stated that objectivity seems to be a standard set by "white, educated, fairly wealthy guys."[30]

Statements such as this are illustrative of the growing disconnect that is taking place between at least some journalists and the public. On the one hand, we see journalists pushing for apparently the right to be more biased in their reporting, while the public says such existing biases are part of the problem. Instead of journalism looking inward and asking itself the hard question of whether that public might be raising legitimate concerns, this effort seems to say, "damn the torpedoes, full speed ahead." Such a mindset will not only leave many journalists stranded and alone on the rocky shoals of unemployment, it will alienate audiences further as it relegates journalism to nothing more than a propaganda machine for its pet causes that it deems true. In the book *The Problem of Equity in Journalism: What's Fair*, BBC correspondent Fergal Keane explains this tendency in journalism quite succinctly. He writes, "I am increasingly struck by the reluctance of journalists to question their own motives. Too many in our ranks are infected with the self-importance and spurious notions of moral superiority. We demand from others that they be open and accountable and yet erect stockades when asked to discuss our own mistakes."[31] It is this notion of superiority, this feeling that journalists are somehow the sole arbiters of truth that society rejects.

One of the more deeply unsettling observations that can be made from the various statements shared earlier is that this camp of journalism argues that they are seeking truth yet simultaneously conclude that such "truth" can only emerge from those who have a certain class, political orientation, race, or status. This is in fact the opposite of truth seeking. It is simply advocacy disguised as a form of journalism. Jay Rosen claims that the enemies of the press are the right wing, so clearly they will not provide any useful truth for journalism. Emilio Garcia-Ruiz's truth emanates from some fuzzy lived experience of journalists—which may actually be just an opinion and not truth at all. It also suggests that some lived experiences might be more valid than others—a slippery slope indeed. Meanwhile, Kathleen Carroll's statement clarifies what truth journalists should seek even further. It should be the truth of people who are "non-white, non-educated, and poor." Journalists who push for such an agenda may win some individuals over to their form of journalism, but in the long run, they will lose massive amounts of credibility.[32]

The underlying assumption that motivates advocates who want to do away with objectivity is that they have arrived at the false conclusion that journalists are always best situated to determine what is true in the events they cover. It takes an incredible amount of hubris on the part of a journalist to imagine that he or she is the sole arbiter of truth. The late journalist and media critic Walter Lippmann tackles this problem head-on in his book *Public Opinion*.[33] In his reflections on what is news, Lippmann notes that news is at best an imperfect record of a "signalized event." In other words, it is a report of something that took place because that event is of interest to the public. In a recent interview with the BBC, Elon Musk attempts to describe this dilemma when he is asked about his motivation for opening up X (formerly known as Twitter) to more controversial speech. He said:

> I mean very often when I see an article about something that I know a lot about, and I read the article and it's like if they get a lot wrong, sort of the best interpretation is that this is someone who doesn't really understand what's going on in industry. [The journalist] has only a few facts to play with and has to come up with an article now. It's going to be, you know, it's not going to hit the bullseye.
>
> Generally this is how I explain this to others. If you read an article about something you know about, how accurate is that article? Now imagine that is how essentially all articles are. They're an approximation of what's going on, but not an exact situation. So if somebody is actually let's say in the fray or like an expert in the field and was actually there, and then writes about their experience of being actually there, I think that actually in a lot of cases is going to be better than a journalist because the journalist wasn't there.[34]

Both Lippman and Musk point to the same dilemma every journalist faces when covering a story: journalism should strive to accurately reflect the events as they took place, and that story should capture the things that were said; however, that news story never fully captures the entirety of the event. It is like Plato's shadow on the wall; it is a reflection of the truth, but at best it is a glimpse of it. That is because the event itself is often more complex than the story. A news event has a history and a backstory, and those who are participants in the event have lived through and understand it more deeply and have felt and thought about those experiences to a degree that the reporter can never accurately portray. This dilemma has been documented by other researchers as well. In their analysis of embedded coverage of reporters during the 2003 Iraq War Jim A. Kuypers and Stephen Cooper noted that coverage by journalists often did not adequately reflect the complexity of those events, but instead journalists often privileged certain news frames over others.[35]

Because of all of this, any news story written about an event is at best a poor reflection of the truth because it lacks a good deal of nuance and context. Any journalist who is honest knows that when he or she reports on any event, whether it would be a debate on policy or on COVID-19, there are numerous factors that influence our understanding of that event. What is "true" about that event is often contested and defined by political elites, public relations practitioners, and experts who eagerly assist the journalist in telling his or her version of the story. As Lippmann explains, the press can and should certainly push toward the truth, but "if the newspapers, then, are to be charged with the duty of translating the whole public life of mankind, so that every adult can arrive at an opinion on every moot topic, they fail. . . . It is not possible to assume that a world, carried on by division of labor and distribution of authority, can be governed by universal opinion in the whole population."[36] Journalists who think they can somehow be the ultimate truth tellers who help the world arrive at a consensus on our understanding of issues are not even telling the truth to themselves. By positioning themselves as some type of final say-so in public matters that are so often hotly contested, they are no longer acting as journalists but are in fact just pawns in the larger social, political, and economic debates that take place frequently in our society. To engage in such behaviors is to do something less than journalism.

TWENTY-FIRST-CENTURY TOOLS FOR TWENTY-FIRST-CENTURY JOURNALISM: SOLUTIONS FOR JOURNALISM

Modern journalism has tried to increase public trust using two major approaches. The former has been to make the journalistic process more transparent, while the latter has argued that a more partisan press would at least improve trust among certain audiences. Both solutions seem painfully ignorant of current research that shows strong links between declining trust and the perceived rising levels of bias in the news. The first approach—providing additional news transparency—will likely fail, because at its core, it still asks an audience to trust that the journalist is being truthful in the transparency process. Michael Karlsson calls this an attempt to "reduce one leap of faith by asking for another."[37] It asks audiences, for example, to trust that a journalist is documenting the right sources. It assumes that somehow through building more pseudo-interpersonal connections, that audiences will relinquish any skepticism about a given story. The second solution is dismissive of the research altogether. At best, it may draw certain demographics to certain news organizations, but it will fail to attract ideologically diverse audiences, and in that sense, it fails a key mission of journalism to provide a public forum for democratic discourse.

So how does journalism get out of the dead-end roads of transparency and advocacy? Part of that solution may be of a more technical nature. A number of new research trajectories in the field of computer science may one day afford opportunities for both journalists and the public to take a more objective and comprehensive look at the level of fairness and objectivity in a given piece of news coverage. Specifically, two areas—crowdsourcing and natural language processing—are leading to the development of a variety of tools designed to help people evaluate the quality of information. These computer-generated techniques have impacted everything from our day-to-day interactions with chatbots and virtual assistants to the ways that we receive content on social media. We see these techniques applied in reviews of products on Amazon.com and we rely on them to give us feedback about traffic flows in Waze maps. I firmly believe that the institution of journalism should embrace these technological innovations because these very tools that aid us in our thinking in almost every aspect of our lives are the very tools that can make journalism better.

A good first step to improving the quality of journalism in the twenty-first century would be to support the development of a nonprofit organization that encourages and supports the building and aggregation of third-party tools designed to help audiences evaluate the quality of a piece of news. Such organizations have precedent in history. Though it did not serve the exact same mandate, a third-party endeavor to improve the quality of journalism was the very recommendation of the Hutchins Commission report on the Freedom of the Press in 1947.[38] It took almost thirty years for that vision to come to fruition, and in 1973 an independent council consisting of professional journalists and citizens was developed to address problems in journalism. The National News Council (NNC) set out to try to help mediate claims of bias or unethical practices in news reporting. The goal of the commission was similar to today—to improve the quality of news so that citizens found the reporting trustworthy. It was, however, not well received on the part of journalists, and the experiment ended in 1984.[39]

Today some countries have found some success with similar NNC endeavors, but they have often been accused of placing too much favor on newsrooms and spending less time hearing about audience concerns. Nevertheless, nonprofit endeavors expanding on NNC core values (NNC 2.0, as it were) may help to secure journalists' credibility in the future. The concept of third-party oversight, or a group of individuals watching the watchdogs, could improve the quality of journalism; it could be a source of public trust, and at the same time it could combat the growing tide of misinformation on the internet. Where the original NCC commission fell short is that it relied largely on a few select elites, both citizens and journalists, to navigate concerns that the public had for journalistic reporting. It was wholly accepted neither by journalists nor by citizens. However, new tools developed in the computer sciences that use both crowdsourcing and natural language processing could lead to more public engagement with the journalistic process and ultimately improve the quality of news.

A second step in the right direction would look at how emerging tools and techniques in journalism could be applied the improve the field of journalism. One computer science approach that could be useful is the development of crowdsourcing tools to identify bias and misinformation in news. In his book *The Wisdom of Crowds*, James Surowieki shows how collective groups of everyday people can often set out to do tasks that are remarkably intelligent.[40] In the book, he documents a number of examples where individuals come together to accomplish tasks, and in using their collective intelligence, they are able to often find better solutions than experts. This is in part due to the diversity of thought that is often the result of large groups of people working on complex tasks. This notion of collective intelligence has spawned an entire area of research in computer science known as crowdsourcing and more recently has been used as a tool to provide individuals with more balanced perspectives on social media.

For example, in 2023 X launched something that it called Community Notes into its feed. The goal was to create a "better and informed world by empowering people on X to collaboratively add content to potentially misleading posts."[41] The entire enterprise is conducted using a crowdsourced technique where individuals sign up to rate posts on a number of different quality markers. For example, content could be flagged if it is misleading, contains a factual error, has outdated information, or is missing an important context. The entire project is also transparent in that individuals can download the content being analyzed and see how it was analyzed to determine for themselves whether they feel that the analysis was fair. Such practices are in line with several recent studies that have found that crowdsourcing techniques can be one solution to policing misinformation and poor-quality news. One study that conducted an experiment comparing the analysis of professional fact-checkers to a group of laypeople with balanced political views found that laypeople were just as good at analyzing content as professionals.[42] A second study, which experimented with extracting the stated concerns about a story from the "reply" sections of a news post, also found that when readers saw these comments it could have a positive effect by helping users evaluate the credibility of a piece of news.[43] Work conducted in crowdsourcing by Paul Resnick and his colleagues also looked at how crowdsourcing could influence consensus around misinformation. In their study they combined groups of crowdworkers with different types of ideological bias and tasked them with evaluating whether an article contained misinformation. They found that these groups were not sometimes better than journalists at assessing a piece of news and that the combination of political biases in the crowdsourced groups often reduced partisan disagreements about the news being evaluated.[44]

Such techniques may be part of the solution for improving the quality of journalism in the future. Crowdsourcing techniques could improve journalism in at least two ways. First, crowdsourcing can provide journalists with feedback about what the public sees as incomplete, unclear, or inaccurate in their reports. While journalists may not at first like the idea of such critiques, if journalists had at their disposal such analysis of their writing prior to publication, their content might be improved or they might be able to anticipate reporting practices that may need further explanation. In short, crowdsourcing techniques could provide valuable feedback for journalists before the story ever goes to print. Second, crowdsourcing techniques like those currently practiced by X may be one way for audiences to learn to evaluate the quality of a news source for themselves. In this sense, crowdsourcing could help in improving media literacy. If the public had crowdsourced tools that helped them see where others raised concerns about a story, they may be better consumers of the news. Such tools may help audiences make clearer distinctions between quality reporting and what has been popularly called fake news.

A third avenue of reform lies within a second field of computer science known as natural language processing (NLP); it may also provide clues into how the language of news helps to shape our understanding of world events and how that language may contain biases. NLP is a growing area of artificial intelligence research that uses algorithms to analyze texts similarly to how humans would analyze them. It accomplishes this by using a set of algorithms that can analyze and extract surface and underlying meanings from texts. Some algorithms can extract various themes and topics from a text. Other analyses can identify emotional words or words that express bias or negativity.

Several studies using NLP have already shown how it can be a valuable tool for journalism. In my own work with colleagues, we have used NLP to show how the language of news organizations has become increasingly polarized over the past decade.[45] From those studies, we have found biases in news prevalent across the ideological spectrum. Other research has been able to analyze the content of news stories in order to identify information that might be missing.[46] Such tools could be useful in helping audiences see when a reporter or a person pretending to be a reporter leaves out a valuable piece of information. Other work is still in its infancy stages, but it has successfully used NLP to detect the use of biased words in news.[47] These tools may have obvious uses for citizens seeking more balanced content, but they may also be useful for journalists interested in reflecting on their own word choices and how they are perceived by their audience. In addition, one of the more challenging aspects of detecting bias in news is being able to detect how the selection of word choices and other characteristics of language frame the ways that we understand news. Fred Morstatter and his colleagues at the USC Information Sciences Institute have begun to make first steps toward that goal by developing tools that extract frames from news stories.[48]

NLP is still a relatively new field of research, and most of those tools currently underway rarely make themselves out of the university labs where they are developed. Nonetheless, this research holds some opportunities for a third party to support the development of such tools to empower both journalists and citizens with the ability to analyze news themselves. It is true that NLP is only as good as the algorithms that analyze the content, and so future work is still needed to refine and improve those algorithms if they are to be accepted by audiences. It is also true that publics may not be willing to trust the analysis of an algorithm at all, and so additional work must be done to create transparency practices in those algorithmic structures so that publics can examine them for themselves for concerns that they might have.

CONCLUSION

Clearly there is no one-size-fits-all solution to improving public trust in journalism. If that trust is to ever turn around, solutions will no doubt come from several innovative directions that journalists are willing to explore. That may include educating the public better about the important work journalists do, as well as helping journalists consider how their own biases can be mitigated by considering the multiple viewpoints of their audiences. At the same time, some solutions for journalism may come from outside of journalism itself. In her classic work *The Printing Press as an Agent of Change*, Elizabeth Eisenstein traces the rise of a reading public, the fall of the Catholic Church, and the advancement of the scientific method all to the invention of the printing press.[49] This "new technology" of the day became the means by which information could become mass-produced and thus distributed easily to a much wider set of audiences. It was the printing press that created the idea of the "mass audience," and those who embraced that new technology—religious reformers, scientists, and journalists—built the foundations for lasting changes in their respective fields. Today journalism faces another era of change, and it remains to be seen whether it will have the courage to embrace new norms and those new technological tools and innovations that could once again improve the field of journalism for the better.

NOTES

1. Gallup Inc., "Americans' Trust in Media Remains Near Record Low," Gallup.com, October 18, 2022, https://news.gallup.com/poll/403166/americans-trust-media-remains-near-record-low.aspx.

2. Jeffrey Gottfried and Jacob Liedke, "Partisan Divides in Media Trust Widen, Driven by a Decline among Republicans," *Pew Research Center* (blog), accessed March 29, 2023, https://www.pewresearch.org/fact-tank/2021/08/30/partisan-divides-in-media-trust-widen-driven-by-a-decline-among-republicans/.

3. Gianna Melillo, "Two Local Newspapers Close Every Week in the US," *The Hill* (blog), June 30, 2022, https://thehill.com/changing-america/enrichment/arts-culture/3542521-two-local-newspapers-close-every-week-in-the-us/; Mason Walker, "U.S. Newsroom Employment Has Fallen 26% Since 2008," *Pew Research Center* (blog), accessed April 9, 2023, https://www.pewresearch.org/fact-tank/2021/07/13/u-s-newsroom-employment-has-fallen-26-since-2008/.

4. Jeremy Barr, "Can Cable News Win over Young Viewers? At MSNBC, a 40-Year-Old New President Is Going to Try," *Washington Post*, May 24, 2021, https://www.washingtonpost.com/media/2021/05/24/msnbc-rashida-jones/.

5. Naomi Forman-Katz and Katerina Eva Matsa, "News Platform Fact Sheet," *Pew Research Center's Journalism Project* (blog), accessed April 9, 2023, https://www.pewresearch.org/journalism/fact-sheet/news-platform-fact-sheet/.

6. Eric Young, "Fatigue, Traditionalism, and Engagement: The News Habits and Attitudes of the Gen Z and Millennial Generations," The Media Insight Project, Associated Press–NORC Center for Public Affairs Research, n.d., https://www.americanpressinstitute.org/wp-content/uploads/2022/08/MIP-Report-Release-1-Final-8.29.pdf.

7. "Millennials & Teens' 20 Top News Sources," *YPulse* (blog), accessed April 9, 2023, https://www.ypulse.com/article/2016/08/29/millennials-teens-20-top-news-sources/.

8. Nic Newman and Richard Fletcher, "Bias, Bullshit and Lies Audience Perspectives on Low Trust in the Media" (Reuter's Institute for the Study of Journalism, 2017), https://reutersinstitute.politics.ox.ac.uk/sites/default/files/2017-1/Nic%20Newman%20and%20Richard%20Fletcher%20-%20Bias%2C%20Bullshit%20and%20Lies%20-%20Report.pdf.

9. Mandy Jenkins, "The News We Believe News, Disinformation and the Audience They (Mostly) Share," Society of Professional Journalists: Project Disconnect, September 2019, https://zombiejournalism.com/wp-content/uploads/2020/11/Project-Disconnect-Final.pdf.

10. Jenkins.

11. "Journalism as a Discipline of Verification," *American Press Institute* (blog), March 29, 2023, https://www.americanpressinstitute.org/journalism-essentials/verification-accuracy/journalism-discipline-verification/.

12. "Crisis in Democracy: Renewing Trust in America," The Aspen Institute, February 2019, https://csreports.aspeninstitute.org/Knight-Commission-TMD/2019/report.

13. RTDNA, "Code of Ethics," June 11, 2015.

14. Kalyani Chadha and Michael Koliska, "Newsrooms and Transparency in the Digital Age," *Journalism Practice* 9, no. 2 (2015): 215–29.

15. Kelly McBride and Tom Rosenstiel, *The New Ethics of Journalism: Principles for the 21st Century* (Thousand Oaks, CA: CQ Press, 2013).

16. Stephanie Craft and Tim P. Vos, "The Ethics of Transparency," in *The Routledge Companion to Journalism Ethics*, edited by Lada Trifonova Price, Karen Sanders, and Wendy N. Wyatt (New York: Routledge, 2021), 175–83.

17. Michael Karlsson, "Rituals of Transparency: Evaluating Online News Outlets' Uses of Transparency Rituals in the United States, United Kingdom and Sweden," *Journalism Studies* 11, no. 4 (2010): 535–45.

18. Matthias Revers, "The Twitterization of News Making: Transparency and Journalistic Professionalism," *Journal of Communication* 64, no. 5 (2014): 806–26.

19. Rebecca Coates Nee, "Creative Destruction: An Exploratory Study of How Digitally Native News Nonprofits Are Innovating Online Journalism Practices," *International Journal on Media Management* 15, no. 1 (2013): 3–22.

20. Peter J. Gade et al., "Management of Journalism Transparency: Journalists' Perceptions of Organizational Leaders' Management of an Emerging Professional Norm," *International Journal on Media Management* 20, no. 3 (2018): 168.

21. Michael Karlsson and Christer Clerwall, "Transparency to the Rescue? Evaluating Citizens' Views on Transparency Tools in Journalism," *Journalism Studies* 19, no. 13 (2018): 1923–33.

22. Alexander L. Curry and Natalie Jomini Stroud, "The Effects of Journalistic Transparency on Credibility Assessments and Engagement Intentions," *Journalism* 22, no. 4 (2021): 901–18.

23. Gina M. Masullo et al., "The Story behind the Story: Examining Transparency about the Journalistic Process and News Outlet Credibility," *Journalism Practice* 16, no. 7 (2022): 1300.

24. Cynthia Peacock, Gina M. Masullo, and Natalie Jomini Stroud, "The Effect of News Labels on Perceived Credibility," *Journalism* 23, no. 2 (2022): 301–19.

25. Michael Koliska, "Trust and Journalistic Transparency Online," *Journalism Studies* 23, no. 12 (2022): 1488–1509.

26. Kathryn Towey, "How to Produce Trustworthy News without 'Objectivity,'" *Cronkite News Lab* (blog), January 26, 2023, https://cronkitenewslab.com/digital/2023/01/26/beyond-objectivity/.

27. "Transcript: Nicole Hemmer Interviews Jay Rosen for 'The Ezra Klein Show,'" *New York Times*, November 12, 2021, sec. Podcasts, https://www.nytimes.com/2021/11/12/podcasts/transcript-ezra-klein-show-jay-rosen.html.

28. Towey, "How to Produce Trustworthy News without 'Objectivity.'"

29. Towey.

30. Towey.

31. Robert H. Giles and Robert W. Snyder, *What's Fair?: The Problem of Equity in Journalism* (New York: Routledge, 2000).

32. Towey.

33. Walter Lippmann, *Public Opinion* (New York: Harcourt, Brace and Company, 1922).

34. Elon Musk, BBC Interview at Twitter Headquarters, April 12, 2023, https://www.youtube.com/watch?v=IflfP4XwzAI&t=2926s. Transcribed and edited for clarity by the chapter author. Note: Musk's statements have been lightly edited for clarity.

35. Jim A. Kuypers and Stephen D. Cooper, "A Comparative Framing Analysis of Embedded and Behind-the-Lines Reporting on the 2003 Iraq War," *Qualitative Research Reports in Communication* 6, no. 1 (2005): 1–10.

36. Lippmann.

37. Michael Karlsson, "Dispersing the Opacity of Transparency in Journalism on the Appeal of Different Forms of Transparency to the General Public," *Journalism Studies* 21, no. 13 (2020): 1808.

38. The Commission on Freedom of the Press, *A Free And Responsible Press* (Chicago: The University of Chicago Press, 1947), http://archive.org/details/freeandresponsib029216mbp.

39. Erik Ugland, "The Legitimacy and Moral Authority of the National News Council (USA)," *Journalism* 9, no. 3 (2008): 285–308.

40. James Surowiecki, *The Wisdom of Crowds: Why the Many Are Smarter than the Few and How Collective Wisdom Shapes Business, Economies, Societies, and Nations* (New York: Doubleday, 2004).

41. "About Community Notes on Twitter | Twitter Help," accessed April 24, 2023, https://help.twitter.com/en/using-twitter/community-notes.

42. Jennifer Allen, Antonio A. Arechar, Gordon Pennycook, and David G. Rand, "Scaling up Fact-Checking Using the Wisdom of Crowds," *Science Advances* 7, no. 36 (September 2021): eabf4393, https://doi.org/10.1126/sciadv.abf4393.

43. Md Momen Bhuiyan et al., "NudgeCred: Supporting News Credibility Assessment on Social Media Through Nudges," *Proceedings of the ACM on Human-Computer Interaction* 5, no. CSCW2 (2021): 1–30.

44. Paul Resnick, Aljohara Alfayez, Jane Im, and Eric Gilbert, "Searching for or Reviewing Evidence Improves Crowdworkers' Misinformation Judgments and Reduces Partisan Bias," *Collective Intelligence* 2, no. 2 (2023): 26339137231173410.

45. Xiaohan Ding, Michael Horning, and Eugenia H. Rho, "Same Words, Different Meanings: Semantic Polarization in Broadcast Media Language Forecasts Polarity in Online Public Discourse," in *Proceedings of the International AAAI Conference on Web and Social Media* 17 (2023): 161–72.

46. Brian Keith, Michael Horning, and Tanushree Mitra, "Evaluating the Inverted Pyramid Structure through Automatic 5W1H Extraction and Summarization," *Computational Journalism C+ J* (2020).

47. Jan-David Krieger, Timo Spinde, Terry Suas, Juhl Kulshrestha, and Bela Gipp, "A Domain-Adaptive Pre-Training Approach for Language Bias Detection in News," in *Proceedings of the 22nd ACM/IEEE Joint Conference on Digital Libraries*, JCDL

'22 (New York: Association for Computing Machinery, 2022), 1–7, https://doi.org/10.1145/3529372.3530932.

48. Fred Morstatter Liang Wu, Uraz Yavanoglu, Stephen R. Corman, and Huan Liu, "Identifying Framing Bias in Online News," *ACM Transactions on Social Computing* 1, no. 2 (June 27, 2018): 5:1–5:18, https://doi.org/10.1145/3204948.

49. Elizabeth Eisenstein, *The Printing Press as an Agent of Change: Communications and Cultural Transformations in Early Modern Europe* (Cambridge; New York: Cambridge University Press, 1979).

Chapter 2

Objectivity and Anti-Objectivity in Journalism

William Max Knorpp

Questions about objectivity arise naturally in and about many truth-seeking endeavors. Science is generally regarded as our most successful such endeavor, and its success is commonly attributed to the rationality and objectivity of its methods and practitioners. The analogy between journalism and science is obvious, and it is no surprise that questions about objectivity loom large there as well. *Journalistic objectivity* is an idea that I would think resonates with everyone—even those who ultimately reject it. Currently, discussions of objectivity seem to be of particular interest, as evidenced by prominent contributions to it in the first few months of this year alone, including (to name just three) the Cronkite School of Journalism's *Beyond Objectivity*[1] and two major discussions in the *Columbia Journalism Review*, Wesley Lowery's "A Test of the News: Objectivity, Democracy, and the American Mosaic,"[2] and A. G. Sulzberger's "Journalism's Essential Value."[3] The first of these, in particular, has influenced this chapter.

I should confess at the outset that I come to this question from the discipline of philosophy, so might be seen as a kibitzer at best or, worse, an interloper. I have a true interest in journalism, but it is the interest of an outsider. My formal experience is limited to a brief stint as a journalism minor and a little associated work on the student paper. (I worked the library beat. My big story was something like "Library Gets Ten New Copiers.") I realize that I am inserting myself into a decades-old conversation among journalists and scholars thereof—an intimidating prospect, and one that I have tried to approach with due respect. My position is particularly precarious given that I incline to think that philosophy should keep itself separated from more practical subjects, for the good of both. However, I also think that philosophers can occasionally be of assistance if they stick close to the ordinary, commonsense worldview and merely offer advice on the validity of arguments and the clarification of concepts. That is what I have tried to do here.

The centerpiece of my discussion concerns what I call *the impossibility argument against objectivity*, and the most important version of that argument, which I call *the perfection argument against objectivity*, is roughly: *perfect objectivity is impossible, therefore objectivity is impossible*. This argument manifests itself in various forms and is probably the most common argument in discussions of objectivity. Evaluation of this argument requires us to explicate the concept *objectivity*. I argue that, when we do so, we see that objectivity does not require perfection but, rather, admits of degrees. Therefore the perfection argument is invalid (or unsound, depending on how we reconstruct it).

Once we see our way past the perfection argument, it becomes easier to address related, less prominent criticisms of journalistic objectivity, including Hunter S. Thomson's argument that objectivity is possible only in the simplest matters, and the argument that journalism should aim at truth not objectivity. So in this chapter I discuss challenges to journalistic objectivity, focusing on the perfection argument and its invalidity. I also consider some confusions about the allegedly merely terminological argument for rejecting the word "objectivity," but not the concept nor the associated ideal. In the penultimate section I ask what it is that opponents of journalistic objectivity hope to achieve. Finally, I conclude by recommending that we reject the main proposals of journalistic anti-objectivists, but also at least identify at least one point of agreement.

PROBLEMS IN JOURNALISTIC OBJECTIVITY TODAY

It is no exaggeration to say that journalism is facing a crisis with respect to objectivity. From the outside it is deluged with accusations that it routinely deviates from the ideal of journalistic objectivity, producing news coverage that is systematically biased. From the inside, it faces energetic and radical challenges, especially from younger journalists who bridle at restrictions on their public political expression and activism and who often reject the ideal of objectivity tout court, arguing, inter alia, that objectivity is impossible, that journalism should rather aim at truth, that talk of objectivity merely serves to conceal bias (that is, that journalistic "objectivity" is mere pseudo-objectivity), and that the very term "objectivity" has become corrupted. I address especially these latter arguments shortly, beginning with what I consider the central arguments against the ideal of objectivity.

IMPOSSIBILITY AND PERFECTION

Sometimes ideas and arguments lurk in the background of a debate, unarticulated or poorly so, addressed only obliquely or superficially. Such arguments can influence debates from the shadows, as we might say. It is important to bring such arguments forward, into the light, articulating them fully and evaluating them directly.

Here are a few versions of the main argument I want to consider, as they appear in the literature:

- Humans are not objectivity-driven machines.[4]
- There is no view from nowhere.
- Objectivity is binary: one is either objective or one is subjective.[5]

Each of these claims commonly functions as an abbreviated implicit argument against the ideal of objectivity; each is a version of what I call *the perfection argument (against objectivity)*, itself a version of a more general objection, *the impossibility argument (against objectivity)*. Such arguments sometimes manifest themselves as mere casual dismissals, supercilious references, or "argument" by "scare quotes."

Before addressing the perfection argument directly, I will back up a step and address the more general type of argument of which it is a species.

The most general form of the argument I will discuss is the impossibility argument. Appearing in various forms, it is perhaps the most common argument against the ideal of objectivity, and often appears in an abbreviated form:

(OI) Objectivity is impossible.

This basic idea is often expressed less directly:

- There is no such thing as objectivity.
- *True* objectivity is impossible.
- Objectivity is a myth (or a fiction or an illusion).[6]
- Objectivity is unattainable.
- Objectivity is an impossible standard.[7]

Such assertions are commonly premises in an implicit argument:

(OI) Objectivity is impossible.
Therefore: We are not obligated to be objective.

The leading principle is the principle philosophers call *Ought implies can*—more familiar in its contraposed form: *Cannot* implies *not ought*. If it is not possible for me to do x, then I am not obligated to do x. (This does not mean that if I cannot do x then I am under an obligation *not* to do x, a stronger claim that is not true.) It would be absurd to suggest that I am under an obligation to single-handedly cure cancer or colonize and terraform Mars. (Conceivably I am obligated to do *something* toward these goals, but that is a different claim—I am not obligated to *accomplish* them.) The argument can be reconstructed like so:

(OI) Objectivity is impossible.
We are not obligated to do the impossible.
Therefore: We are not obligated to be objective.

Some object that I have an obligation to *strive* to attain certain impossible goals. I doubt this, especially when I *know* the goal is unattainable. It would be irrational for me to strive to stop the attack on Pearl Harbor. If objectivity is really impossible, then striving for it can only be good by accidentally conducing to some unrelated good.

Ought implies can is too plausible and fundamental to be called into question in this context. But what of the first premise? Why do people find *that* claim alluring? I will consider two arguments for (OI)—one less important and one more important. I will address the former first.

DEFINITIONAL AND CONCEPTUAL OBJECTIONS

One way to argue for (OI), the proposition that objectivity is impossible, is to argue that the very term "objectivity" (or concept *objectivity*) is incoherent. Steven Maras quotes Hunter S. Thompson: "With the possible exception of things like box scores, race results, and stock market tabulations, there is no such thing as journalistic objectivity. The phrase itself is a contradiction in terms."[8] Michael Kinsley argues that "objectivity is a muddled concept."[9] Julia Wallace calls it a "failed concept,"[10] though in neither case is it *entirely* clear that these are genuine incoherence claims. Stephen Engelberg, editor-in-chief of ProPublica, says, "Objectivity is not even possible. . . . I don't even know what it means."[11] One might object that one who does not know what a word means cannot know that its referent is impossible. But that is uncharitable. "I don't even know what that means" does not mean *I have never bothered to look up the word*. It is a way of saying, roughly: *The word does not mean anything coherent*. Which does not mean that the word has simply never been given a meaning; it means that the term cannot be *coherently* defined—generally because the associated concept is incoherent. (When I was in philosophy graduate school this was, perhaps, our favorite criticism: *I don't even know what that means.*) The most charitable and plausible interpretation of Engelberg's objection is:

> The term "objectivity" is not coherently definable.
> *Therefore*: Objectivity is impossible.

I am willing to grant the validity of the argument—but is the premise true? The question brings us to just where we need to be.

WHAT OBJECTIVITY IS

The philosopher Thomas Nagel, often cited in discussions of journalistic objectivity, is worth quoting at some length here:

> Objectivity is a method of understanding. It is beliefs and attitudes that are objective in the primary sense. Only derivatively do we call objective the truths that can be arrived at in this way. To acquire a more objective understanding of some aspect of life or the world, we step back from our initial view of it and form a new conception which has that view and its relation to the world as its object. In other words, we place ourselves in the world that is to be understood. The old view then comes to be regarded as an appearance, more subjective than the new view, and correctable or confirmable by reference to it. The process can be repeated, yielding a still more objective conception.[12]

Though Nagel's concerns are more theoretical than mine, his points are applicable. In our epistemic endeavors, we can become more objective by "stepping back" from, "rising above," or "setting aside" our initial beliefs, attitudes, inclinations, judgments, inferences, and the like. This commonly involves coming to see those things as themselves objects of scrutiny. We often acquire beliefs or form judgments more or less automatically, involuntarily, finding ourselves with them rather than deliberately accepting them. But we can be, and often are, more autonomous and deliberate. We question the beliefs, judgments, etc. we find ourselves with, subjecting them to rational scrutiny, often forming new ones, not only about their objects but about those beliefs and judgments themselves and about their relationships to their objects. Are they accurate? Warranted by the evidence? Do they represent the truth, at least so far as can be ascertained? Often I come to see my initial beliefs and judgments as consequences of facts about *me*—presuppositions, antecedent beliefs, personal preferences, biases, idiosyncrasies, tribal commitments, etc.—rather than facts about the objects of those beliefs and judgments. Jones asserts that p, and I react derisively, judging p to be ridiculous. But in a cooler moment, I realize that my judgment about p is actually a consequence of the fact that I dislike Jones personally. Realizing this, I am likely to reconsider p. As Nagel puts it: "Thus objectivity allows us to transcend our particular viewpoint and develop an expanded consciousness that takes in the world more fully."[13]

Such transcendence is effected not only by "stepping back" but also by consciously emphasizing certain epistemically relevant factors and deemphasizing others. If I say that Smith is objective about some matter, I mean something like: Smith is reasonably dispassionate and rational about the subject. He tends to bracket or deemphasize his own preferences and predilections, to attend to and emphasize the actual evidence available to him, and to apportion belief in accordance with the strength of that evidence. Thus the ability to be objective is importantly dependent on the ability to set aside or resist the effects of *subjective* influences on cognition. There is no canonical list of these subjective factors, but they include idiosyncrasies, prejudices, biases, preferences, passions, tribal and ideological allegiances, wishful thinking, and the like. If I believe Greene will win, and believe it because I want him to, my belief is more subjective; if I believe Greene will win and believe it because he is ahead in the polls, my belief is more objective. Sulzberger articulates basically the same ideas with a specifically journalistic focus (while generally avoiding the term "objectivity" in favor of "independence"):

> Independence asks reporters to adopt a posture of searching, rather than knowing. It demands that we reflect the world as it is, not the world as we may wish it to be. It requires journalists to be willing to exonerate someone deemed a villain or interrogate someone regarded as a hero. It insists on sharing what we learn—fully and fairly—regardless of whom it may upset or what the political consequences might be. Independence calls for plainly stating the facts, even if they appear to favor one side of a dispute. And it calls for carefully conveying ambiguity and debate in the more frequent cases where the facts are unclear or their interpretation is under reasonable dispute, letting readers grasp and process the uncertainty for themselves.[14]

Objectivity is related to generality and universalizability—for example, with the application of uniform standards across similar cases. One mark of the partisan is the application of double standards—more permissive standards to favored ideas, individuals, or groups and more stringent standards to disfavored ones. We often speak of this aspect of objectivity as *fair-mindedness, even-handedness, impartiality*. The familiar table-turning test is a method of achieving greater objectivity by checking for uniformity of standards and their application. Even children recognize the reasonableness of such tests, and we often introduce the idea of objectivity to them in the form of the Golden Rule.

By this point, it should be clear that it is actually rather difficult to separate objectivity from reason. Nicholas Rescher makes roughly this point in *Objectivity: The Obligations of Impersonal Reason*: "Objectivity calls for putting one's idiosyncratic predilections and parochial preferences aside in forming one's beliefs, evaluations, and choices. It is a matter of proceeding in line not with one's inclinations but with the dictates of impartial reason."[15] If this is, as I suspect, correct, critics of objectivity—journalistic or otherwise—must carry a heavy burden of proof indeed, as to be against objectivity is tantamount to being against reason.

The above hardly constitutes a tight definition of objectivity—but this is the kind of characterization often required for difficult concepts. It is not pithy, but it seems to constitute a rebuttal of the charge that the term "objectivity" and the associated concept are meaningless, undefinable, or incoherent. This positions us to address the most influential version of the impossibility argument.

IMPOSSIBILITY ARGUMENTS: PERFECTION ARGUMENTS

The most common type of impossibility argument against the ideal of objectivity turns on the denial of the possibility of perfect objectivity. Stated clearly:

Perfect Objectivity Argument (POA) Perfect objectivity is impossible; therefore objectivity is impossible.

Normal people rarely put arguments in textbook form, but philosophers do it obsessively, and it can be helpful, and I will not resist the urge:

[POA]
Perfect objectivity is impossible
Therefore: Objectivity is impossible.

The logical form of POA is:

[POÁ]
Perfect x is impossible
Therefore: x is impossible.

This argument form is deductively invalid, as we see via the following counterexamples, each of which seems to have a true premise and a false conclusion:

Perfect friendship is impossible.
Therefore: Friendship is impossible

Perfect remorse is impossible.
Therefore: Remorse is impossible.

Perfect physical fitness is impossible.
Therefore: Physical fitness is impossible.

We can also apply the argument to the preferred replacement for objectivity suggested by the authors of *Beyond Objectivity*:

Perfect trustworthiness is impossible.
Therefore: Trustworthiness is impossible.

This is a standard method (called *modeling*) of demonstrating the invalidity of an argument by demonstrating the invalidity of its form. What it shows here is that statements of the form *x is impossible* do not follow from statements of the form *perfect x is impossible*.

But this should come as no surprise. The world is a world of imperfection, and humans not the least. If imperfect things were to disappear from the universe nothing would remain. Borderline cases and matters of degree are everywhere. And human epistemic matters are matters of approximation.

Is this the end of POA? Can we just move on? No. POA is best interpreted as enthymematic, presupposing the following implicit premise:

(OPO) Only perfect objectivity is objectivity.

Analogous implicit premises cannot save the other arguments, as all of them are clearly false:

- Only perfect friendship is friendship.
- Only perfect remorse is remorse.
- Only perfect physical fitness is physical fitness.
- Only perfect trustworthiness is trustworthiness.

Why does OPO seem plausible when none of the others do? Because, unlike in the other cases, there is a prima facie plausibility to the claim that perfection is a necessary condition for objectivity. Though both arguments below are valid, only the first seems like it may possibly have true premises:

[POA2]
Perfect objectivity is impossible.
(OPO) Only perfect objectivity is objectivity.
Therefore: Objectivity is impossible.

[PFI]
Perfect friendship is impossible.
Only perfect friendship is friendship.
Therefore: Friendship is impossible.

PFI's second premise will find few defenders. Imperfect friendship—all the friendship there is—is obviously still friendship. But POA does have defenders precisely because many people find OPO plausible, commonly because they find the following proposition plausible:

(OMP) "Objective" just means *perfectly objective*.

This constitutes a crucial defense of the perfection argument against objectivity: perfection is built into the very definition of the word "objectivity" (or we could also say into the very concept *objectivity*.)

But objectivity is *not* a perfection concept, (OMP) is false, and (OPO) is not true by definition—nor is it true at all. If the account of objectivity sketched earlier is at all right, then objectivity—like almost every other real property or characteristic—comes in degrees. Nagel concurs: "Though I shall for convenience often speak of two standpoints, the subjective and the objective, and though the various places in which this opposition is found have much in common, the distinction between more subjective and more objective views is really a matter of degree."[16]

When we set aside or rise above our initial beliefs and judgments, we do this to a greater or lesser degree. Under ordinary conditions, when we speak of objectivity, we are not speaking of perfect objectivity but of something like *sufficient or admirable degrees of objectivity*. Just as when we speak of something being reliable we are not saying that it is perfectly so, but sufficiently or unusually so, or something similar. My car is reliable, but not perfectly so. My house is comfortable—not perfectly. My TA is diligent—to a laudable, yet imperfect degree. Similarly, we easily speak of a person being more objective about finances than he is about politics, of referees being more objective than fans, of judges being more objective than litigants. None of these ways of speaking would make sense if perfection were built into the very definition of the word "objective" (or the concept *objective*). But they do make sense. Which means that OMP (discussed earlier) is false. Ergo [POA2], though valid, is unsound, and [POA] is invalid.

Once we see why the clearly formulated core of the perfection argument is invalid (or unsound, depending on the reconstruction), we can easily see that it remains invalid in its many often unclearly stated variations and modifications. Consider again Greenwald's "humans are not objectivity-driven machines."[17] Whatever else this means, it is intended to convey the idea that humans are incapable of perfect objectivity, and the point of saying this is to convince the reader to conclude that objectivity is impossible (at least for us). And that is just the perfection argument. This interpretation is confirmed by his next few sentences: "We all intrinsically perceive and process the world through subjective prisms. What is the value in pretending otherwise?" There are hints and suggestions of other ideas here too. But once we can recognize the perfection argument amid the foliage, and once we know why that argument fails, we have understood most of what there is to understand about the overall argument. The same can be said of many other such arguments, explicit and implicit.

BIRD'S-EYE, GOD'S-EYE

The perfect objectivity argument is a straw man. The ideal of objectivity need not be perfectly realized in order to be epistemically useful. What we actually seek is not perfection, nor the "view from nowhere," nor to become the God's-eye view, nor what Hilary Putnam called a "no-eye view,"[18] nor what Emerson called the "transparent eyeball."[19] What we seek is ordinary, achievable degrees of objectivity—a bird's-eye view, not a God's-eye view.

If Greene is accused of swindling Browne on a land deal, we want to know what happened. That will require an account of relevant facts, including, probably, Greene's side of the story and Browne's, summaries of police reports, accurate accounts of antecedent verbal or written agreements, surveyor's reports, bank records, eyewitness accounts, and the like. We neither need nor want an account that abstracts away from all human interests and points of view. We are not interested in the fact that some philosophers have argued that land cannot be owned. Nor in the fact that, *sub specie aeternitatis*, theft may be nothing more than an idiosyncratically human idea, based on mere preferences of our primate progenitors. We do not care that God, if he exists, might not care about such trivialities nor that, from a perfectly objective perspective, the universe may be a moral void. We just want to know what happened—in ordinary senses of *what* and *happened*. We want to know the ordinary, relevant facts that ordinary, interested humans would want to know if they cared about the incident—but did not care in exactly the way that the parties involved care. We are not interested in bringing our entire worldview into question. In fact, to do so would almost certainly be a profound mistake. If I am hungry, what I need is food, not philosophical reflection on the possibility that death may not be so bad. Philosophy is interesting, and there is value in bringing our worldview into question—but not when interferes with the more pressing business of life.

And if Scoop Smith reports on the alleged land swindle, we do not need her to exhibit superhuman, godlike objectivity, we do not need her to eschew all human interests, preferences, or biases, we do not need her to file a report from nowhere, nor from everywhere all at once. We just need her to be objective—disinterested, dispassionate, neutral—enough to get the facts straight. And that means: the ordinary, relevant facts. She may have a normal array of human prejudices and preferences, as long as none are so strong that she cannot set them sufficiently aside to give us the straight dope about the relevant matter. Vague gestures at perfection, at points of view that are not points and from which there's no view—these are all distractions from what is, at its core, a fairly simple idea: we want accurate news of the world, and in order to get that reliably, we need information conduits that keep distortion to a reasonable minimum.

The ideal of journalistic objectivity does not require acceptance of this proposition:

Journalists should exhibit godlike objectivity.

It requires something more like a *rejection* of this proposition:

Journalists are never obligated to constrain their subjectivity in any way.

We are not choosing between (a) godlike perfection and (b) ordinary, reasonable standards of neutrality and fair-mindedness. Rather, we are choosing between (b) ordinary, reasonable standards of neutrality and fair-mindedness and (c) unbridled opinion and editorializing.

THOMSON'S ERROR: DIFFICULTY AND IMPOSSIBILITY

A kind of claim that deserves special attention here is represented by a Hunter S. Thomson quote we have already seen: "With the possible exception of things like box scores, race results, and stock market tabulations, there is no such thing as journalistic objectivity." This is a distant relative of the impossibility argument: objectivity is possible with respect to simple matters, impossible with respect to complex ones.

Pace Thompson, this is unlikely to be true. The difference in complexity among "Who won the 2017 men's NCAA basketball championship?," "What were the main causes of World War II?," and "What was the Russiagate hoax?" is a matter of degree. There seems to be no in-principle difference among them, and so no reason to believe that objectivity is possible in one of these cases but impossible in at least one of the others. How a party voted on a bill, which country is ahead in the hypersonic arms race, why we are experiencing inflation, whether our culture is in decline—none of these crosses some line past which objectivity is impossible. Thompson is making a common error: confusing difficulty with impossibility. As matters become more complicated, important, and emotional, it can become more difficult to be objective about them. We might even suggest that our ability to be objective begins to fail us as we begin to need it most. But there is all the difference in the world between the following two claims:

[i] Objectivity is impossible beyond the simplest matters.
[ii] Objectivity becomes more difficult as matters become more complex.

The latter claim seems to be true, the former false.

TRUTH NOT OBJECTIVITY

Critics of objectivity often argue, plausibly, that the primary aim of truth-seeking endeavors, like journalism and science, is, well, *truth*. More precisely: its discovery and transmission. So, it is argued, we should aim at truth, not objectivity. I will call this argument *Truth Not Objectivity*:

(TNO) Journalists should not aim at objectivity, they should aim at truth.

We should not allow ourselves to be distracted by philosophical questions about the nature of truth. As in the rest of this chapter, I stick as closely as I can to the ordinary, commonsense worldview. We cannot make any progress if we ascend to the level of philosophical argument, or if we try to bring everything into question at once. Accordingly, I will stick to the most ordinary, uncontroversial conception of truth. Aristotle is commonly taken to articulate that conception in this passage: "To say of what is that it is not, or of what is not that it is, is false, while to say of what is that it is, and of what is not that it is not, is true."[20] Truth is thus, roughly, accurate representation.

If I say, "Missouri is west of Virginia," I speak truly. If I say, "Virginia is west of Missouri," or "Missouri is not west of Virginia," or similar things, I speak falsely. A similar conception of truth is: correspondence to the facts. We need not try to get too precise about such things here; the ordinary concept of truth, like most other ordinary concepts, is rather imprecise. But that's not a problem for our purposes.

TNO is represented, for example, in *Beyond Objectivity*: "The Journalist's job is truth, not objectivity. It is getting close to reality, notwithstanding that we all have biases and passions."[21] It also seems to appear in the Keller-Greenwald discussion in a slightly different form, when Greenwald claims that "ultimately, the only real metric of journalism that should matter is accuracy and reliability."[22]

To say that an account is accurate is to say that it is true, and to say that it is reliable is to say that it is ordinarily true. So this is a version of TNO.

But TNO seems confused. Though the journalist's ultimate aim does seem to be finding truth, objectivity is a critically important *means* to that end. By striving to suppress interfering subjective factors, by allowing the evidence to have its full effect on our thinking, we find the truth more often than if we do not do those things. Saying that the journalist's job is finding truth, rather than achieving objectivity, seems rather like saying that the student's job is learning rather thanstudying, or that an NBA player's job is winning championships rather than playing well. It would be ridiculous to advise someone that he should not be concerned to find a good career but rather to make good money. Such advice may not be incoherent, but it is at least terrible. Unless, perhaps, one thinks one has a better suggestion—*forget about a good career, kid; just play the ponies*.

We might object to this, however, by noting that truth simpliciter is not really the aim of journalism nor of inquiry generally. Suppose A punches B and B punches A back, but I only report that B punched A. My report is true but incomplete and misleading. A more objective report would include both facts and their order of occurrence. This is a reason to think that truth alone is not sufficient even if we could get it—and so objectivity is more than a mere means to truth. This objection does not save TNO, of course. If correct, it undermines both TNO *and* the objection to TNO articulated earlier. But in either case, TNO fails.

REJECTING THE WORD: OBJECTIVITY AND "OBJECTIVITY"

Very commonly, journalists and others who initially seem to oppose journalistic objectivity turn out merely to oppose "objectivity" (the word). Some do this implicitly, some explicitly, sometimes it is not clear which they are doing. Implicit nominal rejections often seem accidental and involve arguments of the form *We should abandon objectivity in favor of x*—where x just turns out to be objectivity by another name. And, unsurprisingly, because many of the arguments we are considering can be mixed and matched, sometimes we encounter claims that seem to have one foot in the perfection argument and one in a merely terminological concern, as Keller's "I avoid the word 'objective,' which suggests a mythical perfect state of truth."[23]

Beyond Objectivity advocates "a fresh vision . . . that replaces outmoded objectivity with a more relevant articulation of journalistic standards." But that vision includes "restoring a belief in the value of fair, fact-based reporting"—"trustworthy news" that is "free of bias."[24] The difference seems merely terminological.

Wesley Lowery provides us with an interesting case. In an earlier publication, "A Reckoning over Objectivity, Led by Black Journalists," he writes:

> Those of us advancing this argument know that a fairness-and-truth focus will have different, healthy interpretations. We also know that neutral "objective journalism" is constructed atop a pyramid of subjective decision-making: which stories to cover, how intensely to cover those stories, which sources to seek out and include, which pieces of information are highlighted and which are downplayed. No journalistic process is objective. And no individual journalist is objective, because no human being is.
>
> Instead of promising our readers that we will never, on any platform, betray a single personal bias—submitting ourselves to a life sentence of public thoughtlessness—a better pledge would be an assurance that we will devote ourselves to accuracy, that we will diligently seek out the perspectives of those with whom we personally may be inclined to disagree and that we will be just as sure to ask hard questions of those with whom we're inclined to agree.[25]

Batya Ungar-Sargon makes what seems to me to be the right point in response:

> This is a good ideal. The problem is, this ideal that Lowery suggests we replace objectivity with is itself objectivity. When journalists promise to be objective, we're never promising to never feel a certain way about a subject; we're promising to be aware of those feelings and do our best to counteract them in our reporting. We aren't promising never to betray a personal bias but rather promising to do exactly what Lowery rightly suggests: challenge our personal biases by seeking out others who disagree with us.[26]

Subsequently, Lowery seems to retreat to the merely terminological argument, claiming this is what he always intended:

[Defenders of journalistic objectivity]cast themselves as defenders of a sacrosanct value suddenly fallen out of favor. This is all a ruse. The principle of fact-based reporting has not been attacked. There is no serious or sustained argument being leveled against "standards" or a methodical process of verification. This so-called "war on objectivity" has been about the *corruption of the term itself* and its *misapplication*. Neither I nor others have argued against open, empathetic inquiry.[27]

The interpretive task here is somewhat complicated by intrusions by both the perfection argument and the *truth not objectivity* argument. But it seems clear that objectivity per se was Lowery's initial target, whereas his targets in the latter passage are (a) the *term* "objectivity" and (b) *pseudo-objectivity*, that is, the false pretense of objectivity that he thinks has corrupted the term. In my recommendations below I agree with Lowery about the problem of pseudo-objectivity but disagree with his terminological point.

CRITICS OF OBJECTIVITY AND THEIR AIMS

We have thus far come at these issues in a more bottom-up way, looking at particular arguments directed against the traditional ideal of journalistic objectivity—or thereabouts. But at this juncture, before I advance recommendations about how to move beyond what we could call a crisis of objectivity, it is helpful to take a more top-down view and ask: What changes are those skeptical about journalistic objectivity proposing?

We have just discussed the most conservative of the major relevant changes: the proposal to merely abandon the word "objective" without abandoning the ideal of objectivity. This proposal is commonly paired with a proposal about a replacement term (for example, "neutrality," "independence"). Of course this, being a merely terminological proposal, is not actually an anti-objectivist one. On the other end of the spectrum is the radical suggestion to actually abandon the ideal of objectivity. As we have seen, these very different recommendations are often confused or conflated. Often it simply is not clear *what* is being recommended. *Beyond Objectivity* ends with recommendations, some of which are inscrutable—for example, "Strive not just for accuracy, but for truth." Perhaps even more puzzlingly:

> What we hope ties these guidelines together is our own core belief that journalism must address the needs and aspirations of our increasingly diverse society more effectively than it has in the past.
>
> That means striving to reach not only an audience, but all audiences, and no longer with one-size-fits-all, traditionally white male "objectivity," a journalistic

concept that has lost its relevance. It means avoiding replacing that with some new rigid orthodoxy, which could also impede accurate and fair reporting. It means building a newsroom that reflects the communities it serves and embraces diversity to provide strong, more accurate, and responsible journalism.[28]

This may express a rather conservative goal of rejecting (a certain specific type of) pseudo-objectivity—"traditionally white male objectivity"—in order to embrace genuine objectivity—roughly fair, accurate, responsible journalism. But then the title of the report, as well as its clearly anti-objectivity tone, are baffling and misleading. A better title would have been, for instance, *Toward Objectivity*. And what is it that has "lost its relevance"? Objectivity? Or "white male subjectivity" (allegedly) masquerading as objectivity? Neither reading quite allows all of the passage to make sense. And, of course, one wonders: if pseudo-objectivity is the concern, why not reject *all* pseudo-objectivity, that is, all bias masquerading as objectivity? For example, what about progressive bias, thought by many to be extremely prevalent?

Other proposals appearing in *Beyond Objectivity* and elsewhere include rejecting "both-sides," or "he-said/she-said" reporting, which some argue is a consequence of an objective (or pseudo-objective) model of journalism.[29] A related suggestion is to replace the ideal of objectivity with that of "moral clarity."[30] These suggestions appear in *Beyond Objectivity* in particular interviews, though not in the report's official recommendations. A representative one is provided by Mark Fisher of the *Washington Post*, who describes disagreement "between younger folks who want to practice journalism that matches their personal views and older folks who want to maintain traditional standards of fairness and rigor," with younger journalists "seeking more advocacy for their views of the correct side in stories. They want to infuse stories with the language of the reporter. They say we should not be reflecting both sides, but what they see as reality. They object to objectivity as morally bankrupt."[31] Ted Glasser clearly expresses a version of this "younger" view: "Journalists need to be overt and candid advocates for social justice, and it's hard to do that under the constraints of objectivity."[32] These younger journalists also oppose restrictions that their employers often place on their public expression of opinions, especially on social media, and their political activism. Although this last point may seem to be of lesser importance, I suggest, below, that it may be of more significance than it seems to be.

CONCLUSION/RECOMMENDATIONS

Finally, I offer the following recommendations:

Recommendation 1: Reject the proposal to abandon journalistic objectivity.

First, do no harm. Contra *Beyond Objectivity* et al., journalism's problem is not an excess of objectivity but an insufficiency thereof. The arguments we considered earlier purporting to show that objectivity is impossible were invalid. (Other arguments exist, of course. But I believe they fare not better; at any rate, they are beyond the scope of this chapter.) In fact our best evidence indicates that we are often capable of being substantially objective much of the time—objective enough to suppress at least our most distorting biases, at least long enough to produce reasonably accurate accounts of the facts, at least much of the time. And we know that we are better at discerning and reporting the truth when we strive for higher degrees of objectivity. That this is often difficult does not entail that it is always impossible. And the fact that we do not always live up to the ideal does not mean that it should be abandoned. I can do no better here than to quote Sulzberger:

> As with scientists, doctors and judges, it is far better to have journalists imperfectly striving for independence [his term for *objectivity*] backed by a defensible process than choosing not to bother because total independence can never be fully achieved. "Failure to achieve standards does not obviate the need for them. It does not render them outmoded. It makes them more necessary," wrote Mary Baron, former executive editor of the *Washington Post*. . . . "And it requires that we apply them more consistently and enforce them more firmly."[33]

To acquiesce to the currently fashionable proposal to abandon the ideal of journalistic objectivity would be to take a giant stride in exactly the wrong direction. That proposal must be rejected.

Recommendation 2: Reject the proposal to abandon the term "objectivity."

It would certainly be less damaging merely to abandon the term "objectivity," while maintaining the substance of the ideal of objectivity, than it would be to abandon the substance of the ideal. There are serviceable alternatives, as we have seen (for example, Keller's "impartial"; Sulzberger's "independent"). However, I recommend against this proposal. Attempting to give up the word while maintaining the ideal is an unstable option. First, as we have seen, it is often difficult for people to distinguish clearly between merely giving up the word and actually giving up the ideal. This should be unsurprising because the word "objectivity" represents *objectivity*; it is natural to think that rejecting the word means rejecting the concept. And "mere" terminological changes are seldom actually *mere* in contexts such as this. It is now common to introduce linguistic change as the first step in a push for conceptual change. This is the real idea underlying Orwell's fictional Newspeak. "Gender," for example, initially seemed to be nothing more than a synonym for "sex." Later, however, we found that it served to introduce a radical new set of concepts, substantive propositions, and arguments. Linguistic change can serve as a foot in the door. I suggest resisting it.

Recommendation 3: Strengthen/revitalize journalism's commitment to objectivity.

Though this is, perhaps, implicit in recommendation 1, I think it is worth making explicit: ideally, journalism would not merely refuse to abandon the ideal of objectivity but would strengthen its commitment to it. We know that admirably objective journalism is possible—indeed, we know it is done quite often. I suggest that more of it would be better. One important route to that is strengthening commitment to and realization of the ideal. I realize this is likely more easily said than done. And I have few suggestions how to effect it. But I do have one practical suggestion that I believe is important enough that I represent it as a separate recommendation 4.

Recommendation 4: Energetically address the problem of pseudo-objectivity.

I agree with critics of journalistic objectivity that pseudo-objectivity is a significant problem—as, I believe, should anyone who accepts the ideal of objectivity and takes it seriously. One version of this concern—one pervading, for example, *Beyond Objectivity*—is that what currently passes for objectivity is a disguised form of white male subjectivity. A well-known objection from the other end of the political spectrum is that journalism is rife with liberal or progressive bias. To some extent we can ignore specifics and perhaps reach agreement about this general proposition: pretending to more objectivity than you actually exhibit is a serious—perhaps the most serious—error that one can commit if one aspires to be (and be regarded as) a reliable source of information. Though being objective is preferable to merely being candid about one's biases,[34] the latter is preferable to pseudo-objectivity. Unless the problem of pseudo-objectivity is mitigated, journalism may be forced to abandon the ideal of objectivity and accept the less ambitious ideal of being candid about biases.[35]

My suggestion is that journalistic organizations devote significant resources to the empirical investigation of their own deviations from objectivity, honestly reporting on the results, and adjusting their coverage accordingly. It is likely that such investigations and evaluations would best be conducted with the help of external, independent organizations. I expect that the prospect of such an assessment would be anxiety provoking, even (or perhaps especially) for our most prestigious news organizations. But a commitment to the ideal of objectivity is not without its difficulties.

Recommendation 5: Weaken restrictions on journalists' extrajournalistic expressions of opinion

I am inclined to agree with younger journalists who chafe at restrictions their organizations place on public expression of opinions, for instance, on social media.[36] In this respect, I am significantly more radical than even *Beyond Objectivity*, which recommends against this course of action.[37] Such restrictions apparently aim, in large part, at maintaining news organizations' *reputation* for objectivity. But such policies seem to conceal concerns rather than address them. Most of us would prefer to know about journalists' strong political commitments because such commitments sometimes clearly influence reporting. Though it is the quality of the journalistic output that matters most, most readers would prefer to be informed about journalistic conflicts of interest, be they personal, financial, or political. However, in extreme cases, as when the objectivity of an organization's reporting is already in doubt, journalists' off-the-clock expression may well be of interest. So it seems that both journalists and their readers have an interest in protecting the freedom of the former's extracurricular expression. And news organizations with confidence in in their journalists' objectivity, judiciousness, and diversity of opinion would seem to have little to fear from such expression. So the only news organizations that should fear such expression would seem to be those who believe their reporters to be systematically biased to such a degree that it would harm their reputation should this be known. Loosening restrictions on such expression, then, would have the added advantage of incentivizing the hiring of more objective, more judicious journalists with a wider range of opinions.

Beyond Objectivity suggests that it is the same cohort of young reporters who both (a) bridle at restrictions on extracurricular expression of opinion and (b) push for the freedom to include opinion in straight news stories. But, as I have probably made clear, I believe serious news organizations must regard (b) as nonnegotiable. This makes loosening restrictions on extracurricular expression an obvious way to relieve some of the pressure younger journalists feel to express their political beliefs, and seems to be a reasonable compromise.

NOTES

1. Leonard Downie Jr. and Andrew Heyward, *Beyond Objectivity: Producing Trustworthy News in Today's Newsrooms* (Walter Cronkite School of Journalism and Mass Communication, Arizona State University, 1993), https://cronkitenewslab.com/wp-content/uploads/2023/01/Beyond-Objectivity-Report-3.pdf.

2. Wesley Lowery, "A Test of the News: Objectivity, Democracy, and the American Mosaic," *Columbia Journalism Review*, April 25, 2023, https://www.cjr.org/analysis/a-test-of-the-news-wesley-lowery-objectivity.php.

3. A. G. Sulzberger, "Journalism's Essential Value," *Columbia Journalism Review*, May 15, 2023,
https://www.cjr.org/special_report/ag-sulzberger-new-york-times-journalisms-essential-value-objectivity-independence.php.

4. Bill Keller, "Is Glenn Greenwald the Future of News?" *New York Times*, October 27, 2013, https://www.nytimes.com/2013/10/28/opinion/a-conversation-in-lieu-of-a-column.html.

5. Charlotte Wien, "Defining Objectivity within Journalism," *Nordicom Review* 26, no. 2 (November 2005): 4.

6. Conor Friedersdorf, "Stop Forcing Journalists to Conceal Their Views from the Public," *The Atlantic*, October 30, 2011.

7. Matthew Ingram, "What Comes After We Get Rid of Objectivity in Journalism?" *Columbia Journalism Review*, July 2, 2020. https://www.cjr.org/the_media_today/what-comes-after-we-get-rid-of-objectivity-in-journalism.php/.

8. Steven Maras, *Objectivity in Journalism* (Malden, MA: Polity Press, 2013), 70.

9. Michael Kinsley, "The Twilight of Objectivity," *Slate*, March 31, 2006, https://slate.com/news-and-politics/2006/03/how-opinion-journalism-could-change-the-face-of-the-news.html.

10. Downie Jr. and Heyward, *Beyond Objectivity*, 10.

11. Downie Jr. and Heyward, *Beyond Objectivity*, 9.

12. Thomas Nagel, *The View from Nowhere*, revised edition (New York: Oxford University Press, 1989), 4.

13. Nagel, *The View from Nowhere*, 5.

14. Sulzberger, "Journalism's Essential Value."

15. Nicholas Rescher, *Objectivity: The Obligations of Impersonal Reason* (Notre Dame, IN: University of Notre Dame Press, 1997), 3.

16. Nagel, *The View from Nowhere*, 4–5.

17. Keller, "Is Glenn Greenwald the Future of News?"

18. Hilary Putnam, *Reason, Truth and History* (New York: Cambridge University Press, 1981), 50.

19. Ralph Waldo Emerson, "Nature," in *The Essential Writings of Ralph Waldo Emerson* (New York: The Modern Library, 2000).

20. Aristotle, *Metaphysics*, 1011b25, trans. Richard McKeon (New York: Random House, 1941), 749.

21. Downie Jr. and Heyward, *Beyond Objectivity*, 9.

22. Keller, "Is Glenn Greenwald the Future of News?"

23. Keller, "Is Glenn Greenwald the Future of News."

24. Downie Jr. and Heyward, *Beyond Objectivity*, 1.

25. Also quoted by Batya Ungar-Sargon, *Bad News: How Woke Media Is Undermining Democracy* (New York: Encounter Books, 2021), 194.

26. Ungar-Sargon, *Bad News*, 194.

27. Wesley Lowery, "A Test of the News: Objectivity, Democracy, and the American Mosaic," *Columbia Journalism Review*, April 25, 2023, https://www.cjr.org/analysis/a-test-of-the-news-wesley-lowery-objectivity.php.

28. Downie Jr. and Heyward, *Beyond Objectivity*, 36.

29. Downie Jr. and Heyward, *Beyond Objectivity*, 7, 9.

30. See Downie Jr. and Heyward, *Beyond Objectivity*, 36; Masha Gessen, "Why Are Some Journalists Afraid of 'Moral Clarity'?" *The New Yorker*, June 24, 2020, https://www.newyorker.com/news/our-columnists/why-are-some-journalists-afraid-of-moral-clarity.

31. Downie Jr. and Heyward, *Beyond Objectivity*, 10–11.

32. Zadie Winthrop, "Should Journalists Rethink Objectivity?," *Stanford Daily*, August 20, 2020.

33. Sulzberger, "Journalism's Essential Value."

34. As Greenwald suggests in Keller, "Is Glenn Greenwald the Future of News?"

35. That model of journalism is unlikely to succeed given that it merely trades the ordinary problem of objectivity for the problem of being objective about one's biases. Unfortunately I cannot pursue that problem here.

36. Downie Jr. and Heyward, *Beyond Objectivity*, 21–22. See also Friedersdorf, "Stop Forcing Journalists to Conceal Their Views from the Public."

37. Downie Jr. and Heyward, *Beyond Objectivity*, 30.

Chapter 3

Digital Dissonance

Rebuilding Trust in News in an Age of Misinformation, Filter Bubbles, and Bias

John Gable and Adriel Warren
Contributions by Isaiah Anthony and Julie Mastrine

In the wake of the invention and widespread adoption of the printing press, the written word emerged as a force to be reckoned with—a double-edged sword capable of disseminating transformative ideas and corrosive falsehoods alike. Within this realm of boundless potential, much like our present digital age, some found an avenue to unleash deceptive narratives and sensationalism that fueled chaos with unprecedented speed and reach. Over time, as subsequent generations better understood how to harness the technology, the printing press propelled notions central to the fabric of modern society, such as freedom, democracy, liberty, and equality.

Previous generations grappled with the issue of misinformation, bias, and sensationalism, but none developed a comprehensive methodology equipped to tackle the complex challenges of our current digital era. The early pioneers of the internet thought that widespread access to other perspectives would foster global connectivity, and it clearly did, though some warned of some negative consequences, which it clearly had.

This chapter delves into the unsettling erosion of trust in news media—a consequence of increased bias and misinformation propelled by major shifts in technology that changed how we communicate with each other as a society. It also explores the dilemmas confronting news consumers today as they strive to navigate a treacherous landscape in search of reliable, accurate information. As the lines between truth and falsehood blur, the very foundations of our democratic society are at stake, but amid this crisis lies the potential for a transformative solution. Drawing upon cutting-edge research, critical insights, and visionary perspectives, we propose a forward-thinking approach that has the potential to restore news media, empower discerning readers, and reinvigorate our democratic society.

In the pages that follow, we first provide some important historical considerations; second, we discuss the rapid rise in bias and decline in audience trust; third, we discuss the notion of journalistic filter bubbles; fourth, we review two major flawed solutions to the bias challenges facing the press today; and finally, we conclude by offering a new approach to fix the bias problem.

HOW WE GOT HERE

Broadly speaking, the news industry has transformed significantly from the 1960s to the present due to technological advancements, altering consumer behavior, and business models. Computers, satellite technology, and the internet revolutionized news production and distribution, enabling global reach and instant reporting but reducing the significance of local news. Digital platforms and social media allowed news consumption anytime and anywhere, leading to a decline in print circulation and a shift toward digital advertising revenue models. This resulted in a twenty-four-hour news cycle, revenue-driven reporting, and partisan news outlets, contributing to sensationalism, polarization, and eroding trust in mainstream news organizations. The internet also promoted citizen journalism, diversifying voices but raising concerns about credibility and journalistic standards.

In the 1980s, mergers and acquisitions surged in the news industry, driven by global business trends and relaxed media ownership rules. Consolidation aimed to save costs and reduce competition but raised concerns about editorial independence, viewpoint diversity, and news quality. Television's rise diminished print newspapers, leading to fewer news sources and mainstream outlets monopolizing the industry. The shift from print newspapers to the immediacy of television changed not only the delivery method of news but also the content itself. This period witnessed the emergence of the twenty-four-hour news cycle, meeting consumer demand for constant news access. Market segmentation became crucial for advertisers, which influenced news content by catering to specific audiences to boost revenue. As a result, audiences became trapped in filter bubbles. This fragmentation resulted in a polarized media landscape driven by revenue-driven publications and marked by a decline in trust in mainstream news organizations.

In his book *Amusing Ourselves to Death* (1985), Neil Postman described the ways in which news content would be shaped by the shift in medium from print to the immediacy of television, which lends itself to sensationalism and emotionalism.[1] He would later issue a warning about the ways in which technology could shape society and culture in *Technopoly* (1992).[2] These texts were crucial in forming the basis for what is now AllSides Technologies, a company founded by John Gable, who in 1997 feared the internet may train people to discriminate against each other in news ways.[3] These predictions came true. As internet usage grew, societies began to think more in terms of metaphor—putting people into different ideological groups. Despite several advantages of the internet, it has largely trained people to reject any ideas or opinions that disagree with their own. Polarization, breakdown of civility, and misinformation became the by-products of a revolutionary new technology, eroding trust in the news and sowing discord among people.

DECLINING TRUST IN NEWS

In 2022, the Reuters Institute conducted the Digital News Report,[4] an extensive survey that explored the opinions of 93,000 news consumers across forty-six markets and six continents. The United States saw the fourth-largest decline in consumers' general interest in news. Research indicates a rise in selective news avoidance since 2019, with 42 percent of US respondents actively avoiding news media. Respondents cited several reasons for this avoidance, including the overwhelming political emphasis in the news, the negative impact on mood, and concerns about bias or untrustworthiness.

Alarmingly, trust in news also declined in twenty-one markets, with the United States ranking dead last. Only 26 percent of US respondents reported having trust in the news. Another crucial study that exposes the decline in trust is the American Views report by the Knight Foundation in partnership with Gallup, which revealed that in 2017, those that had a negative view of the news slightly surpassed those with a positive view. In 2022, that negative perception has more than doubled.[5] The investigation into this plummeting trust has explored issues related to credibility and transparency in reporting. A 2022 Gallup study found that only 34 percent of Americans trust the media to report "fully, accurately, and fairly," a statistically insignificant two points higher than the lowest-ever recorded trust score.[6] Although fair, accurate, and objective reporting is important to journalistic integrity, this may not be sufficient to garner what is referred to as emotional trust. The concept of emotional trust is defined by consumers' confidence in a news organization's underlying intentions. Emotional trust, then, is built upon the news organization as a civic entity and not solely upon individual stories or articles. This idea is supported by a recent Pew Research Center survey, which revealed 88 percent of people agreed that an important factor to consider in the trustworthiness of a news article is the news organization that publishes it, while only 66 percent agreed that it is important to consider the journalist who did the reporting.[7]

The decline of trust in the news underscores the importance of news organizations maintaining high standards of journalistic integrity in their reporting. Although many organizations have these standards in place, they may not reliably follow those guidelines or are not seen to do so. American Views 2022: Part 2 reports that "the public's declining trust in national news organizations does not appear to be indicative of a lack of capability to deliver reliable information. Instead, Americans perceive negative intent in these outlets' reporting." This study found that half of Americans believe that news organizations intentionally mislead their audiences. Additionally, only 23 percent of Americans believe that national news organizations have the best interest of their audience in mind.[8]

PARTISAN BIAS DRIVES LACK OF TRUST IN NEWS

What Americans want from their news sources and what they are getting is starkly different. The Pew Research Center found that 76 percent of news consumers in the United States want "balanced, unbiased news." Additionally, the study found only 9 percent of respondents "don't see much bias" in their news. This data indicates that an overwhelming majority of news consumers not only perceive bias in the news but also desire to avoid it.[9] Widespread frustration with major media producers injecting bias into reporting was a focal point of Donald Trump's successful 2016 campaign. In demonizing major media outlets that published negative coverage of him, Trump tapped into an existing sentiment among the American public: The belief that the corporations entrusted to inform the public were increasingly using their power to craft narratives aligned with their interests, both economic and political.

As a result of Trump's attacks on traditionally liberal media outlets such as CNN and MSNBC, these outlets dug further into their bias. In reaction, both these outlets took "sharp left turns during Trump's presidency,"[10] becoming more biased while framing themselves as beacons of light defending viewers from the threat of a despotic leader. CNN and other outlets received a ratings bump during the Trump administration, a result of increasingly catering to a smaller demographic on the left at the expense of moderate audiences. Fearing their livelihood was under attack, left-leaning viewers diligently watched CNN for the latest updates on the Trump administration. CNN and other outlets met this demand by feeding scared viewers a nonstop IV drip of fear and panic. In the aftermath of the Trump administration and the start of the Biden presidency, a problem arose for liberal outlets such as CNN. The panic had subsided, the threat was gone, and viewers were no longer motivated to incessantly tune in to the channel. Ratings dipped, and the network realized that in catering to the left-leaning audience and framing the opposition as a demagogue force for that past half-decade, they had lost the trust of a large politically centrist demographic. The desire to regain this trust led Warner Media, the CNN parent company, to shake up leadership at the network and bring in a new CEO focused on regaining the truth of moderate news consumers as well as nonmoderate consumers seeking balanced news.

Other outlets, such as Fox News and Newsmax, have had similar stories.

The relentless pursuit of profits or the devotion to a partisan agenda often blurs the boundary between news organizations functioning as profit-driven enterprises and their responsibility as guardians of public service. It is no secret that biased and partisan news content serves as a cash cow, leaving 75 percent of Americans convinced that most news organizations are primarily motivated by financial gain rather than serving the public good. Among those who place high emotional trust in the media, a mere 24 percent agree that news organizations prioritize the public interest. When trust in the news media is diminished, skepticism about the motivations of these organizations follows. A staggering 78 percent of those with low emotional trust struggle to discern the facts amid a perceived deluge of bias in national news coverage. The disconcerting trend of perceiving news as biased has been steadily on the rise since 2017, leaving news consumers questioning the integrity of the information they receive.[11]

BIAS POLARIZES AND LIMITS
THE MEDIA LANDSCAPE

The increasing partisan divide in news media fuels this broken relationship between consumers and news outlets. News outlets drive revenue by publishing news that appeals to their target audience, often positioning themselves as a bastion of truth amid an increasingly biased media landscape. These tactics discourage consumers from engaging with news content from a diverse array of perspectives. This has contributed to an ever narrowing, increasingly polarized news media landscape.

Researchers at AllSides.com have been studying this phenomenon and its effect on news consumption. In a recent study,[12] AllSides analyzed website traffic data for the sixty news outlets on the AllSides Media Bias Chart™ from June to August 2022, focusing on page views rather than individual visitor numbers. The AllSides Media Bias Chart™ categorizes over sixty major news outlets based on their bias, designated as either Left, Lean Left, Center, Lean Right, or Right. Among the top ten most visited news websites, only two were Center outlets: BBC News and Forbes. Lean Left was the most common rating, including the *New York Times*, the *Guardian*, Yahoo! News, and the *Washington Post*. Fox News and *Daily Mail* represented the right, while CNN represented the Left. There were no Lean Right outlets represented. These top ten outlets received twice as many site visits as the other fifty-four reviewed outlets combined. Although CBS News and the Daily Wire find success in television and social media, they do not receive as much online traffic as the *New York Post*. This suggests that only a few outlets have a significant influence on news viewership, regardless of bias. Between June and August 2022, Center and Lean Left outlets accounted for over half of site visits, giving the left side an advantage. In July, Left and Lean Left outlets received about 375 million more site visits than Lean Right and Right outlets. Sixteen Lean Left outlets had the highest share, followed by fourteen Left outlets, eleven Center outlets, nine Lean Right outlets, and fourteen Right outlets.

One possible explanation for the Lean Left/Lean Right imbalance is that journalists themselves tend to hold more liberal beliefs. A 2014 poll found that only 7 percent of journalists identified as Republicans, compared to 28 percent identifying as Democrats and 50 percent identifying as Independents.[13] Around half of American registered voters believe journalists try to convey their own viewpoints, with a notable partisan divide. Journalists will always have to make subjective decisions about which voices to highlight and what information to cover.

Whereas giving each side fair and equal attention is viewed by the public as a key principle of traditional, trustworthy journalism, recent political polarization in our country has led to a mindset that some viewpoints are so flawed or misinformed that they do not deserve a platform in the press whatsoever. Some journalists feel a responsibility to refrain from amplifying what they consider false narratives or harmful ideas. This extends beyond the typical concerns of false equivalency, such as giving a "fair shake" to genocidal regimes or flat-earthers. Because a viewpoint might be seen as one that represents the views of a certain political side or agenda, biased journalists may deem it unfit for mention in their work—further fueling the divide.

BIASED JOURNALISM FUELS FILTER
BUBBLES AND CONFIRMATION BIAS

The fueling of filter bubbles and confirmation bias is made apparent in a recent study by the Pew Research Center, which found that over half of US journalists say they believe that every side does not always deserve equal coverage.[14] There is a major gap between what the public thinks and what journalists think on this issue too—76 percent of US adults think that journalists should always strive to give every side equal coverage. Julie Mastrine, director of Media Bias Ratings at AllSides, explored this phenomenon in depth. The idea that some perspectives do not deserve to be covered because they are "wrong" or "bad" can lead to one-sided, biased news, in which perspectives the journalist does not agree with are omitted. When a journalist does not cover all relevant sides, bias by omission occurs. It is closely related to slant, which occurs when journalists tilt their coverage by highlighting one particular angle (or downplaying another angle). It can include cherry-picking voices or data to support one side, ignoring another perspective, or burying alternative views at the end of the article where they are less likely to be read.

Of course, the issue of which sides to include in journalistic writing is not that simple. Journalists will generally include views that are within the Overton Window—the range of views that are considered acceptable in a society—which is why pieces advocating for slavery or arguing the earth is flat do not get much, if any, coverage. Societies will always consider some perspectives as dangerous. The problem arises when views that many Americans share or perspectives on ongoing, unresolved issues are omitted from news pages.

Journalists are tasked with recognizing which views are truly extreme or on the fringes while making sure they are not unfairly silencing legitimate voices worthy of being heard. Complicating matters further, just because a view is on the fringes does not necessarily mean it is wrong or unworthy of being heard and explored—the idea that cigarettes and sugar were bad for your health used to be "fringe views." More subtly, journalists also have to decide what information or evidence is relevant to a story, and their political bias may cause them to deem some things irrelevant that others would find relevant. Without balance on important issues, journalists do a disservice to the reader, who will not have enough information to make their own decisions and may grow to resent media institutions who consistently exclude their point of view.[15]

Furthermore, this type of biased journalism can lead to a type of confirmation bias in which reporters and news consumers search for stories or information that supports preexisting beliefs about politics, society, or the world at large. This cycle makes it easy to reject information that calls those beliefs into question. The issue of confirmation bias in news consumers is compounded by the mechanisms of the modern digital ecosystem. Digital platforms such as Twitter (now X) and Facebook, as well as search aggregates such as Google and Bing, are designed to herd users toward content the platform determines they find agreeable. This has proven to be a reliable model to increase user engagement on platforms, but it produces a landscape ripe for the spread of misinformation and results in an ill-informed user. Algorithmic content filtration systems employed on apps such as TikTok, Instagram, and others incessantly track the user's decisions—logging what type of content grabs their attention, what type of content they ignore, and more. The platform then uses this information to design a content feed best suited to increase time spent on the platform. The consequence of constant content filtration is the prevalence of filter bubbles—a term coined by internet activist Eli Pariser that describes the intellectual isolation that can occur when technology companies use algorithms to feed users information and content that they will like, based on their interests, location, past searches, click history, and more.[16]

FILTER BUBBLES LIMIT THE SCOPE OF UNDERSTANDING

Filter bubbles are unhealthy for both personal psychology and democracy/politics at large because they shut out alternative viewpoints, which ultimately inhibits critical thinking and promotes misinformation. When audiences do not see information, data, or ideas that might challenge their existing views, the cycle of confirmation bias can continue. Audiences not only have a harder time finding information that challenges their views, they also will be less practiced at digesting new information and integrating it into their worldview or belief system. When people only have their views reinforced and never encounter alternative perspectives, the more polarized they become in their thinking, skewing their perception of reality and increasing the spread of misinformation, distrust, paranoia, and depression. Filter bubbles cause people to believe that there is only one answer, which robs them of the ability to decide for themselves and makes them less tolerant of other perspectives. In this way, filter bubbles can fuel political polarization, bias, hatred, or negative beliefs about other groups or ideas, and even violence.

Regardless, both right-wing and left-wing outlets build loyal customer bases with highly partisan reporting because it pays: people keep coming back to hear what they want to hear. Filter bubbles are also reinforced by our social circles, geography, and media bias. A study from the University of Colorado found that "people's attitudes become more extreme after they speak with like-minded others." When we surround ourselves only with people who agree, we are much less likely to entertain an opposing viewpoint.[17] Ultimately, this hyperpartisanship in the news media changes the ways in which people relate to one another. A 2020 study by Beyond Conflict illustrates this change:

> When polarization in the United States becomes more about identity than disagreement on issues, it becomes toxic. Increasingly, Americans who identify themselves as either Democrats or Republicans view one another less as fellow citizens and more as enemies who represent a profound threat to their identities, creating a form of American sectarianism. Toxic polarization, like violent sectarianism in many parts of the globe, distorts our view of reality. This leads people to underestimate what they have in common and creates a vision of the world that is defined by a destructive "Us vs. Them" mentality. . . . Once we adopt the lens of "Us vs. Them," a range of unconscious psychological processes take root that accelerate toxic polarization and distort the ways we see one another and understand the world around us. When this mindset develops, compromise with the other side is viewed as weakness or betrayal, and their gain is seen as our loss.[18]

Group polarization resulting from filter bubbles and bias accelerates the problem of misinformation. Group polarization occurs when individuals with similar viewpoints or beliefs become more extreme in their opinions due to their interactions with one another. Misinformation that aligns with preexisting beliefs can exacerbate this process, as individuals are more likely to accept and share information that confirms their biases. In turn, the filter bubbles created by this cycle of confirmation bias create an atmosphere in which misinformation thrives. Similarly, biased, partisan news outlets contribute to the spread of misinformation through reporting tactics (such as clickbait and sensationalism) that seek to reach and make money from a target audience.

FILTER BUBBLES AND BIAS FUEL MISINFORMATION

The distinction between misinformation and bias is often less clear than commonly assumed. Studies have shown that misinformation can contain elements of truth, which contributes to their rapid and broad reach. Moreover, determining what is objectively "true" is often a complex task that even AI or impartial observers struggle to confidently conclude.

For example, the phrase "the election was stolen" was often used in reference to the 2020 Trump-Biden election. If one defines "stolen" solely in terms of election fraud, then claiming the election was stolen would be unfounded. While changes in election processes across nearly every state may have increased the potential for undetectable fraud, studies and research have found no substantial evidence of fraud that could alter the presidential election results. Therefore, stating as an undeniable fact that the election was "stolen" based on this narrow definition would be false. Conversely, if one broadens the definition of "stolen" to include a wide range of illegal or illicit actions, there are indeed several issues that arise. One example is the censorship of news related to Hunter Biden's laptop, which contained controversial information that could have influenced the election outcome. Despite the laptop being in the possession of the FBI for about a year before the election, its contents only became public close to Election Day. A false narrative that claimed these events were a Russian plot led to the censorship and restriction of free speech on an unprecedented scale. Twitter (now X) and Facebook, which serve as channels for communication among average citizens, labeled this information as likely false to prevent its spread throughout the public sphere. Although circumstances surrounding this issue are more complex, it nonetheless indicates an unfair and illicit manipulation of public opinion.

Furthermore, ignoring or hiding information or perspectives can actually cause people to harden their beliefs. Research at Duke University on vaccine hesitancy reinforces this point, finding the best way to reduce hesitancy is through "effective, respectful communication and trust-building."[19] When the media fails to represent the perspectives or address some concerns of some people it is supposed to reflect, it erodes trust in the news. The manipulation of facts can also serve as a means of deception. By selectively emphasizing facts that align with a particular viewpoint while disregarding conflicting evidence, individuals can effectively mislead others into adopting false beliefs or influence them toward desired conclusions. The subjective interpretation of the same facts can also further complicate matters.

One particularly powerful example of "truth" with dramatically different interpretations happened during the coverage of BLM protests. A study presented findings regarding the prevalence of peaceful and violent demonstrations during the summer protests of 2020.[20] One faction asserted that 93 percent of the protests maintained a peaceful nature, leveraging this statistic to bolster their narrative.[21] Conversely, the opposing side highlighted the 550 instances of violent demonstrations to support their narrative. Both sides represented factual information in different ways.[22]

FLAWED SOLUTIONS

Solutions to Misinformation: "Ministry of Truth"

Ironically, the solutions most often voiced to address misinformation caused by digital mechanisms suffer from the same polarization as the media platforms themselves. One side argues for a ministry of truth—that technology companies, or a governmental body, should have a more hands-on approach, changing algorithms in order to expose people to different ideas and perspectives and issuing and enforcing determined truths on particularly volatile topics while silencing viewpoints determined to be misinformation. Historically, this is supported more from the political left, a political ideology that tends to hold greater trust in government and higher belief in the efficiency of centralized, public institutions. They are also more likely to turn to a single or group of "mainstream" media sources that align with their perspectives.

In this model, a centralized, trusted group trained with the skills needed to make accurate determinations could thoughtfully define or clarify information for the rest of society. In times of crisis when there is increased demand for accurate information and an increased opportunity for bad actors to spread misinformation, some might understandably seek the guidance and ease of this model to cut though the noise and deliver unquestioned verdicts. The problem arises when centralizations of power, especially as they grow more extreme, foster corruption and internal decay. Typically, this manifests in a government-controlled institution that issues verdicts and decrees determining the "accepted truths" of the society, while working to censor and erase information that contradicts or challenges the established truths. This group of course gets to decide what the truth is and may choose incorrectly or deliberately pick beliefs that support their own agendas or control, whether factually true or not. And by suppressing opposition, those false truths are far more permanent, enduring far longer than they would in a more open society.

Highly centralized governments propped up by singular ideology do not face enough internal friction or effective external input to maintain the institution's sharpness. An overreliance on loyalty to the people inside the institution and separation from the people the institution is supposed to serve leads to growing incompetence or worse. Those outside the institution, the consumers of the proclaimed truths, are also taught to not think independently, as thinking independently could challenge the institution. Over time, the people lose agency, feeling less in control of themselves and their minds. The pressure to adhere to the established truths squashes individualism and diminishes critical thinking.

The way to combat misinformation is not to silence dissent but to elevate it and hold it against established notions. Silencing critics serves only to validate their criticism, whereas acknowledging and addressing concerns demonstrates to people that public interest and well-being are important. Consider the long-term outlook of the ministry of truth model. Sooner or later—usually sooner—this system becomes corrupted, creating an even worse environment where established sources mislead people in the interest of preserving power and even credible, uncorrupted information is no longer trusted. People rightly revolt against this, but that often leads to the opposite option: information anarchy.

Solutions to Misinformation: "Free-for-All"

The other side believes entities have no duty, and the government no right, to ensure that users ingest a variety of information and ideas. This option, most commonly associated with the political right, calls for an informational free-for-all. Others might call this anarchy, where the reins of language are let loose, and the burden falls on the individual to determine right from wrong, fact from opinion, and malice from altruism. In a perfect world, an open, competitive forum of ideas would lead to the elevation of the best choices and the proliferation of the most reliable information and sources. The free-for-all would provide individuals with the agency and responsibility to discern truth, accuracy, and the best course of action for themselves. Anarchy is good while it is ripe, but the rot can only be delayed so long. The lack of structure in this model historically leads to a similar outcome as the ministry of truth. From the first crop of institutions to emerge, a handful will rise above the competition, seize control of the landscape, and prevent any challengers or competition from arising.

The governing factors that determine what messages are amplified on the current internet are not validity, accuracy, or insight. Instead, economic incentives drive companies to prioritize incendiary, emotion-driven content. The technology corporations controlling the dominant platforms have learned what content keeps people engaged, and while they are within their rights to moderate content on their platform, the peoples' freedom to seek information free from predatory agents is not protected. The absence of rules, however, does not directly equate to more freedom. When done in accordance with the betterment of society, rules and regulations can ensure the protection of freedoms.

A NEW APPROACH: A BALANCED PLATFORM OF CREDIBLE INFORMATION AND DELIBERATION

Neither of these options promote the level or quality of discourse and information necessary for a healthy democratic society to thrive. What is needed is an open, balanced platform of information and discourse. Content moderation systems should not be concerned so much with the content itself but instead concerned with maintaining a balance in order to allow strong ideas, information, dissent, contradiction, and discussion to be elevated. Argument, disagreement, and concession are fundamental components of a healthy democracy. This enables society to address differences of opinion in a healthy, productive way. It is trendy to say the country is more divided than ever and is irreparably at odds. But is this truly because the people have independently dug into their views? Or have they been deprived of dissent, deprived of critical thought by institutions that care far more about the proliferation of their own success than the success of the republic?

Most popular media coverage of a story almost always leaves some important perspective out. People are not enabled to engage with good-faith arguments that contradict and challenge their viewpoints. They are only exposed to interpretations of those arguments by familiar voices that have modeled the opposing stance in such a way that allows it to be easily dismantled. People only see the weakest points of every argument they disagree with. The result is a crop of citizens not trained to critically think because they have been coddled by the institutions they rely on to be informed. When given the tools to engage with a balanced array of perspectives and thoughts, people are able to determine truth with greater accuracy than an appointed institution. Disagreement is not inherently divisive but a fundamental element of a healthy democracy that ensures all voices are heard and all factors are considered. Perspectives must be challenged. Established truths must be questioned. When we question what we believe to be certain, our understanding of the world is strengthened and deepened.

Although rebuilding trust in the media seems like an insurmountable task, efforts to mitigate the destructive effects of polarizing media and misinformation cannot be overlooked. A crucial step in this process is to create an atmosphere of transparency in the news, which contributes to a better-informed reader base. For this to happen, news media organizations would have to turn their attention from a short-term revenue-driven mindset and embrace public demand that news should be first and foremost a civil service. A long-term view establishes trust and loyalty that can translate into more paying subscribers and better financial returns.

Waiting for major media organizations to make these changes is not necessary to transform society. There is an ever growing demand for transparent, balanced news. Corporations such as AllSides are meeting this need by introducing new ways to consume news. There will always be demand for one-sided content, but there must also be alternatives that offer the necessary tools to address critical issues. Currently, such resources are lacking. AllSides and others have begun to fill this gap and facilitate real progress. By embracing these alternatives, we can heal divisions, reinvigorate our democracy, and empower individuals to actively engage with other perspectives and solve collective problems. When information and perspectives are balanced, respected, and presented fairly, division decreases, profits increase, and democracy flourishes.

NOTES

1. Neil Postman, *Amusing Ourselves to Death: Public Discourse in the Age of Show Business* (New York: Penguin Publishing Group, 1985).

2. Neil Postman, *Technopoly: The Surrender of Culture to Technology* (New York: Knopf Doubleday Publishing Group, 1993).

3. John Gable, "The Dark Ages of the Internet," AllSides.com, 2018, https://www.allsides.com/sites/default/files/The%20Dark%20Ages%20of%20the%20Internet.pdf.

4. N. Newman, *Reuters Institute Digital News Report 2022* (Reuters Institute for the Study of Journalism, 2022), https://reutersinstitute.politics.ox.ac.uk/digital-news-report/2022.

5. Knight Foundation and Gallup, Inc., *American Views 2022: Part 1*, Gallup, October 2022, https://knightfoundation.org/wp-content/uploads/2022/10/American-Views-2022-pt1.pdf.

6. Megan Brenan, "Americans' Trust in Media Remains Near Record Low," Gallup, October 18, https://news.gallup.com/poll/403166/americans-trust-media-remains-near-record-low.aspx.

7. Knight Foundation and Gallup, Inc., *American Views 2022: Part 2*, Gallup, February 2023, https://knightfoundation.org/wp-content/uploads/2023/02/American-Views-2022-Pt-2-Trust-Media-and-Democracy.pdf.

8. John Gramlich," What Makes a News Story Trustworthy? Americans Point to the Outlet That Publishes It, Sources Cited," Pew Research Center, June 9, 2021, https://www.pewresearch.org/short-reads/2021/06/09/what-makes-a-news-story-trustworthy-americans-point-to-the-outlet-that-publishes-it-sources-cited/.

9. Knight Foundation and Gallup, Inc., *American Views 2022: Part 2*.

10. Amy Mitchell, Katie Simmons, Katerina Eva Matsa, and Laura Silver, "People Around World Want Unbiased News," Pew Research Center, January 11, 2018, https:

//www.pewresearch.org/global/2018/01/11/publics-globally-want-unbiased-news-coverage-but-are-divided-on-whether-their-news-media-deliver/.

11. Eunji Kim, Yphtach Lelkes, and Joshua McCrain, "Measuring Dynamic Media Bias," *Proceedings of the National Academy of Sciences* 19, no. 32 (2022), doi: 10.1073/pnas.2202197119.

12. Knight Foundation and Gallup, Inc., *American Views 2022: Part 2*.

13. Joseph Ratliff and Clare Ashcraft, "Are Conservative or Liberal Media Outlets More Popular?" AllSides.com, December 6, 2022, https://www.allsides.com/blog/are-conservative-or-liberal-media-outlets-more-popular.

14. Hadas Gold, "Survey: 7 Percent of Reporters Identify as Republican," *Politico*, May 6, 2014, https://www.politico.com/blogs/media/2014/05/survey-7-percent-of-reporters-identify-as-republican-188053.

15. Naomi Forman-Katz and Mark Jurkowitz, "U.S. Journalists Differ from the Public in Their Views of 'Bothsidesism' in Journalism," *Editor & Publisher*, July 13, 2022, https://www.editorandpublisher.com/stories/us-journalists-differ-from-the-public-in-their-views-of-bothsidesism-in-journalism,234297.

16. Julie Mastrine, "Over Half of U.S. Journalists Don't Believe Both Sides Deserve Equal Coverage." AllSides.com, July 14, 2022, https://www.allsides.com/blog/over-half-us-journalists-don-t-believe-both-sides-deserve-equal-coverage.

17. Eli Pariser, *The Filter Bubble: How the New Personalized Web Is Changing What We Read and How We Think* (New York: Penguin Publishing Group, 2022).

18. Jessica Keating, Leaf Van Boven, and Charles M. Judd, "Partisan Underestimation of the Polarizing Influence of Group Discussion," *Journal of Experimental Social Psychology* 65 (2016): 52–58.

19. "America's Divided Mind: Understanding the Psychology That Drives Us Apart," BeyondConflict.org, June 2020, https://beyondconflictint.org/wp-content/uploads/2020/06/Beyond-Conflict-America_s-Div-ided-Mind-JUNE-2020-FOR-WEB.pdf.

20. Susan Gallagher, "The Many Faces of Vaccine Hesitancy," Duke Global Health Institute, April 21, 2019, https://globalhealth.duke.edu/news/many-faces-vaccine-hesitancy.

21. "Demonstrations and Political Violence in America: New Data for Summer 2020," The Armed Conflict Location & Event Data Project, September 3, 2020, https://acleddata.com/2020/09/03/demonstrations-political-violence-in-america-new-data-for-summer-2020/.

22. Lois Beckett, "Nearly All Black Lives Matter Protests Are Peaceful Despite Trump Narrative, Report Finds," *The Guardian*, September 5, 2020, https://www.theguardian.com/world/2020/sep/05/nearly-all-black-lives-matter-protests-are-peaceful-despite-trump-narrative-report-finds; and Jake Dima, "Study: America Hit By Roughly 550 Violent Demonstrations in Three Months," *Daily Caller*, September 5, 2020, https://dailycaller.com/2020/09/05/550-violent-demonstrations-riots-three-months/.

Chapter 4

Debate in Journalism Curriculum as a Solution to Ideological Normativity

Ben Voth

In fixing any problem, the clear identification of the problem can be as challenging as implementing the solution that may hopefully follow such analysis. Our national American civic system faces many problems, and in this era of the twenty-first century, hyperpartisanship appears to be profound. Presidential elections 2000, 2016, and 2020 were bound by very close elections that demonstrated high political passions, narrow close results, and an array of legal and civil struggles over the winner. In the midst of it all, voter participation was at record levels in 2020. Nonetheless, the particular problem of partisanship is real and well acknowledged. Its application to the broader praxis of journalism is important in clearly identifying a problem in journalism. Partisanship within the professional field of journalism is a problem. It is a problem at a definitional level because a code of journalistic ethics dictates that such behavior not be indicated by journalistic writing.[1] To be specific, an anti-Republican ethic so pervades the field of journalism that while the percentage of journalists who openly identify as Democrat has grown, the number who publicly identify as Republican is now statistically insignificant. A 2022 survey of 1,600 journalists found that from 2013 to 2022, the percentage of journalists identified as Democrat in their politics grew from 21 percent to 36 percent, and the number of journalists identified as Republican fell from 7.1 percent to 3.4 percent. In 1971 when the survey first asked such an affiliation question, the ratio was 35 percent Democrat and 25 percent Republican. The Republican number has fallen to less than 5 percent: 25 in 1971, 19 percent in 1982, 16 percent in 1992, growing to 18 percent in 2002, back down to 7.1 percent in 2013, and 3.4 percent in 2022. A clear reactionary force has closed the ideological mind of journalism. A pedagogical correction is needed within journalism instruction to correct this problem. To this end, this chapter will document the problem of partisanship and explain a pedagogical solution in the form of debate in the classroom.

PARTISANSHIP AS A PROBLEM

As many experts acknowledge that partisanship permeates an array of professional fields including journalism, it is intuitive and somewhat comforting to hypothesize that there are two reciprocal communities of partisans who are damaging the professionalism of their field and that with an appeal to bipartisan approaches to the craft of journalism the problem will fade. This is an unsatisfactory solution and one that has been given serious attention and effort. To fix the problem of journalism ethics, the problem must be clearly identified, and for many years, this identification is made murky by the bipartisan appeal. Journalism should be seen as a public service that provides audiences with reasonably accurate information from which an array of civil rights will allow the American public to exercise "government of the people, by the people, and for the people." Ideally, from a constitutional perspective, that is what the First Amendment guarantee of "free press" is aiming to achieve—the accomplishment of an informed electorate that American civic founders deemed necessary to prevent the collapse of the republic; however, the accuracy of information produced by journalism is hampered by a reactionary political atmosphere that diminishes public interest in news and creates a dangerous reliance on sensationalism and emotional responses among the public.

The honest problem in journalism that ought to be acknowledged and needs to be seen clearly in order to pursue a solution is to recognize that journalism in the United States is largely captive to a reactionary political view that Republicans, conservatives, and especially Republican presidential candidates are an exceptional civic threat.[2] This political group is held as a profound danger to the public in the area of civics, and they require special rhetorical dispensations such as "fact-checking," "misinformation" labels, and cautionary terminologies that presume falsity from many of these political figures in these ranks. This is a difficult logic to absorb and accept. An anecdote may be a useful beginning to this difficult assessment of the problem.

As a debate coach, my primary interest in journalism is to gather the accurate information journalists provide and marshal it into affirmative and negative debate cases for debaters to use in public demonstrations of controversy.

While serving as director of debate at a state university in Ohio in 2004, a journalism faculty colleague ask me if I would give a lecture to her fall editorial journalism class. We were fairly close friends, so I agreed rather readily. She then clarified my purpose, saying, "I know you might not be inclined to do this, but I would really like you to spend most of the time explaining the Republican point of view in the 2004 election." I recognized the compromise to the general bipartisan ethic we all know should prevail in classrooms. She confessed to me that for the semester, despite her best intentions, she had favored the Democrats in her discussion of controversies the students could write editorials about in the class. Hearing her earnest explanation, I agreed and I also agreed to read all twenty-four of their current election editorials in mid-October 2004. I began my lecture to the class explaining that I read all twenty-four essays and thought they were quite good—well organized, researched, and supported in their conclusions. I noted that they might find something interesting about a pattern apparent in reading their essays: twenty-three of the essays endorsed John Kerry—the Democrat for President—and one essay endorsed Ralph Nader—a more left-leaning consumer advocate for president. Not one student wrote an essay endorsing the incumbent Republican President George W. Bush for president. They all looked around the room at each other rather shocked. There was clearly a sense that surely someone should have written such an essay, but by some mystery, this had not happened. This anecdote is I believe illustrative of the larger national problem. We are pretending that our self-rationalizations surrounding ideological preferences are not damaging the vital public sphere of fair debate. In almost twenty years since that incident, neither the ongoing data on this question nor my own experiences in academia suggest that this problem is retreating and being reduced. Are there examples of extreme right-wing journalists and bias against the left and/or Democrats? I do think there clearly are, and I think that hurts the goal of accurate information. That is not, however, useful to solving the larger problem of a preponderance of journalists exerting a reactionary ethic toward Republican politicians and a deeper sense of conservative politics they perceive at work below the public texts of these politicians. In fact, the failure to acknowledge this disposition likely drives dangerous overreactions on the right. If we could honestly acknowledge this, we could begin to fix the problem. As I write this, I remain unsure whether academic professionals can acknowledge this; however, there are journalists who have acknowledged this problem rather bravely; for example, multiple Emmy award–winning journalist Bernie Goldberg makes among the strongest historical cases for this thesis.[3]

The Hill editorially noted this, citing a 2021 Pew Research study, in which it was revealed that the partisan divide in journalistic trust between Democrats and Republicans has more than doubled since 2019 in regard to news coming from social media.⁴ This means that a long acknowledged problem is in fact accelerating as Republicans conclude that journalism as a national practice deserves very little public trust. Only 19 percent of Republicans report they have at least "some trust" in social media journalism. General trust in national and local media is at 35 percent for Republicans and 78 percent for Democrats. This 43 percent gap has grown markedly since 2016 when a 70/83 differential yielded a gap of only 13 percent.⁵

A 2022 survey of more than 1,600 journalists found that partisan identification with Democrats is increasing and declining precipitously for Republicans:

> Compared with 2013, the percentage of full-time U.S. journalists who claim to be Democrats has increased 8 percentage points in 2022 to about 36 percent, a figure higher than the overall population percentage of 27 percent, according to a 2022 *ABC News/Washington Post* national poll. This is the third highest percentage of journalists saying they are Democrats since 1971.
>
> Journalists who said they were Republicans continued to drop from 18 percent in 2002 and 7.1 percent in 2013 to 3.4 percent in 2022. This figure is notably lower than the percentage of U.S. adults who identified with the Republican party (26 percent according to the poll mentioned earlier) in 2022. About half of all journalists (51.7 percent) said they were Independents, which is about 12 percentage points above the figure for all U.S. adults (40 percent). Overall, U.S. journalists today are much more likely to identify themselves as Independents rather than Democrats or Republicans—a pattern similar to 2013.⁶

Nearly 22 percent of surveyed journalists felt there was a greater need for political diversity in their newsroom—falling behind racial diversity slightly as the second most urgent lack of diversity among those surveyed. This small percentage is striking given that Republican affiliation among journalists was at a record low 7.1 percent in 2013 and that the percentage of Republican journalists is now less than half that in 2022 with 3.4 percent. Thus an almost 50 percent drop in nine years, and even the political category of "other" political affiliation was much larger at 8.5 percent. As the smallest political identification category and trending aggressively lower over the past twenty years, it is evident that ideological marginalization is occurring and the journalistic field is not representative of the political affiliations held in the public. This is a serious problem for accurate information being conveyed on controversial topics.

Journalists have tremendous power in determining which news events, which candidates, and which issues are to be covered in any given day. Often what they fail to do is as important as what they do. Journalists represent the essential praxis of a civil right known as "freedom of press." A free press should account for political arguments as they are presented in the public sphere. That rhetorical accounting exerts major influence upon the success or failure of political campaigns. A serious problem both for candidates and election consumers is the potentially reactionary views of the press. If the press favors one ideology over the other, then it is not free. That freedom is the ideal that the First Amendment envisions. Ideological captivity is not unusual as an American or global phenomenon. Abundant surveys suggest that print media do favor the major political party of Democrats over the major political party of Republicans, even as more than 70 percent of the public believes the press should give equal coverage to both sides of a political contest. Of note, though, is that fewer than half of current American journalists agree with that premise according to a 2022 survey offered by Pew Research,[7] with that conviction declining even more the younger the journalist is. Despite low convictions among journalists, strong majorities of Americans, over 65 percent among Democrats and Republicans, believed that journalists should give equal coverage to both sides. Of note is that in a 2020 survey done by Knight, only about 27 percent of Democrats felt journalists were biased "a great deal of time," whereas in sharp contrast, 68 percent of Republicans felt this way.[8] Public trust of journalism is declining and the opportunities for new journalists to correct these concerns can be a strategic opportunity for all political campaigns. The number of print newspapers in the United States has fallen from near 2,000 in 1970 to less than 1,300 in 2018.[9] Major newspapers such as the *Chicago Tribune*, the *New York Times*, and the *Wall Street Journal* have suffered readership declines in the past decade. These newspapers nonetheless exert important influence on the agenda-setting processes of daily campaign communication, and cultivation of relationships is important regardless of rhetorical problems such as ideological captivity that may interfere with campaign messaging. They can factor into powerful choices including who becomes president of the United States.[10] Public distrust of the media can become its own political force, as observable in the 2016 presidential election. Despite apparent negative coverage of candidate Trump in the fall of 2016, with some studies suggesting over 90 percent at times,[11] the public was drawn toward him in the political upset he scored against longtime political figure Hillary Clinton. One Harvard *Shorenstein* study documented an ironic path wherein journalists strongly favored Trump during the primaries and then turned sharply against him in the fall season leading to the election. Coverage was exceptionally positive for Hillary Clinton in October 2016.[12]

These examples should suffice to provide evidence that there is a partisanship problem in the mainstream news media. The real question is: What can be done about it?

THE SOLUTION: DEBATE-DRIVEN JOURNALISM CURRICULUM

Journalists need to understand, be able to communicate, and ultimately analyze the various political arguments in existence in the United States and even worldwide. As noted in the problem section, like many other professional endeavors, the ethics urging nonpartisanship have succumbed to a pattern of partisanship that makes the American public unwilling to read journalistic products. This problem is at record levels. The primary polarization of American politics is witnessed in presidential races that take place every four years. Since at least Richard Nixon, Republicans complain consistently and in ever greater numbers that journalists actively disfavor them in coverage that provides both the agenda setting of election coverage but also regimes of "fact-checking" that typically disfavor Republican presidential candidates such as George W. Bush and Donald Trump.

Apart from the problems of partisanship, homogeneity of thought can produce a phenomena known as "group think," and what some also call "confirmation bubbles." In group think, individuals lose the underlying abilities associated with critical thinking and crave a cycle of affirmation found in agreement with the group. This cycle limits the discovery of solutions beyond the comfort zone.[13] The survey mentioned earlier about journalist affiliations noted that an increasing number of journalists seek a greater intellectual diversity in their ranks and a growing apprehension about this problem.[14]

Because the presidential races tend to feature two candidates from the parties of Democrats and Republicans, they represent an inherent reductionism of the American political spectrum. A better and more varied indication of the Overton window for American politics is the US Senate. The US Senate is composed of one hundred representatives popularly elected by all fifty states. Each state is equally represented with two senators. With that in mind, students of political debate should be comfortable discussing all one hundred senators with equanimity. This is particularly useful in 2023 because the Senate is nearly evenly divided between Republicans and Democrats with regard to membership. None of the one hundred senators should be deemed "extremist" or unsuitable for fair consideration in argument because the public considered this individual in a public political contest representing tens of thousands if not millions of American voters. This is inherently not a fringe view. Reconstituting political thinking to accept that there are at least one hundred distinct views of American politics across more than two major political parties can help establish the new norms for political discussion going forward. A high percentage of US presidents end up being drawn from senatorial ranks—seventeen thus far out of forty-six. It is worth noting that even in rare instances where senators are not members of the two major parties—such as Senator Bernie Sanders of Vermont—these individuals have won a popular ballot that merits respectful political argument rather than presumptive dismissal or pejorative labeling by journalists.

UNDERSTANDING DEBATE AS A CRITICAL THINKING SOLUTION

Debate is a unique pedagogy designed to increase critical thinking and diminish the problems noted previously with partisan attachment. Critical thinking involves the consideration of multiple points of view and a desire to know what the better alternatives are for the future. Debate instructs students in argumentation and has demonstrated values in improving critical thinking. Debate across the curriculum—such as in journalism—is empirically successful in working in various educational contexts. Between 2013 and 2017, Wiley College, a historically Black college implemented debate across the curriculum. The results were startling and positive. While national test scores in critical thinking were declining, Wiley critical thinking scores rose dramatically. Wiley saw nearly 20 percent increases in critical thinking scores in an era where state rivals such as University of Texas at Austin and University of Texas at Dallas saw 1 to 2 percent declines in critical thinking scores.[15] These results are important in an era where race relations are an important political frustration and common basis for overheated conversations that tend to allow partisanship to overwhelm the power of conversation and critical thinking.

In a debate-centered curriculum, journalism students would ideally be exposed to two complementary learning exercises: (1) extemporaneous speeches and (2) debates. In the extemporaneous speech assignment, a class of twenty journalism students would work with their professor to brainstorm twenty-five topics of controversy that would be typed onto a document viewed on the classroom projection. Topics might concern an impending election, environmental policy, court issues, military engagement, or any number of public controversies. One such topic might be: The United States should reduce the use of the death penalty. In explaining the assignment it is useful to explain that students performing these speech topics may take any side they wish and in fact they must express some preference for a side after five minutes of preparation. A simple three-point style should be explained as possible: (1) pro opinion, (2) con opinion, and (3) the student's personal opinion. In the pro segment of the speech, the journalism student giving the speech would explain the arguments for reducing the death penalty. In the second con opinion segment of the speech the student would explain the arguments against reducing the death penalty. The third and final segment of the speech would offer the student's personal perspective on the matter in light of the two sides.

Students can brainstorm a list of current event controversies and then be allowed forty-eight hours to study that list and be sure they understand the basic parameters of the provided topics. On the day of performance, students will one at a time draw three topics out of a cup that contains all twenty-five of the original topics on a strip. They will choose one topic of the three that they want to prepare a speech on. Using only a blank note card, students can rotate into the hallway and sit at a desk for five minutes while another student is giving their speech. Ten students can perform in a fifty-minute class and almost twenty can perform in a seventy-minute class. Students should prepare three points on their note cards and evidence is not required in the three- to four-minute speech about the current event. Instructors should provide one-minute time signals with a preference for the speech to be at least three minutes in length and indicative of good organization, delivery, and argument. At the end of the speech, the instructor can ask for a volunteer to draw again, and typically this will approximate the five minutes each student is given in the hallway to prepare an extemporaneous speech.

This learning exercise clarifies the two sides of public controversy while also providing insight into how classmates provide different viewpoints. This builds a better relationship with public attitudes about public controversy that presently the public perceives as misunderstood by journalists. Debriefing this exercise can enable the journalism professor to seek observation and analysis of apparent ideological biases shown in the collective student performances. This initial class activity can build toward the larger activity for the end of the class. Students can be divided into teams of three and perform a World School style of debate where each side gives four short speeches in favor of their side in the debate (affirmative or negative). Students may choose topics from the original mix of extemporaneous topics created earlier. Students should also produce evidence briefs suitable to providing expert testimony in one or two instances of each speech. The evidence briefs can be used to supplement or even replace the oral performance component by emphasizing writing as argument. Much like a legal brief in court, journalism students should be able to write evidence-based editorials for and against a debate topic. In the most robust rhetorical environment, students would prepare debate briefs and present them orally. One team member will give an additional closing speech to end the debate. A hypothetical match might appear in the manner shown in table 4.1.

Resolution: The United States should increase gun control legislation.

Affirmative	Negative
Four-minute opening remarks	Four-minute opening remarks
Two-minute cross-examination by opponent	Two-minute cross-examination by opponent
Three-minute opening speech	Three-minute opening speech
Three-minute opening speech	Three-minute opening speech
Three-minute closing remarks	Three-minute closing remarks

These speeches will alternate back and forth beginning with the affirmative and ending with the negative. Students can be allowed to use laptops while the instructor stresses that when not reading evidence, debaters should make as much audience eye contact as possible. Students should effectively interpret and compare their evidence to opponents. These two assignments of extemporaneous speaking and debates can emphasize several key aspects of journalism while at the same time emphasizing the fundamental civic of fairness and equal opportunity to present sides in public controversy. It essentially illustrates the difference between propaganda and free speech. In circumstances of freedom of speech like that spelled out as a civil right in the First Amendment, journalists and advocates witness competing viewpoints offered in public oral advocacy. Text boxes at the end of this chapter are provided to help journalism faculty implement the curriculum described here.

Debate as curriculum represents an important and necessary answer to the dilemma of closed societies. We must develop a pedagogical discipline of listening that is not closed. We must recognize the profound instability of knowledge lest we become intoxicated with the "knowledge is power" maxim that makes us ready to rid the world of its "fools." Debate is empowering and humbling in a concurrent manner that offers a good educational step forward to remedying the risks of genocide. Some of life's most important lessons can be learned losing a debate such as: "I was not listening. I was too sure of myself. I was not respectful enough of my opponent." The costs are not so high that recovery and growth are impossible. In fact, the genuine stakes of debate will motivate the journalism student more than the challenges of rote memorization or recitation of rules and procedures. This will give the journalist the important empathy for competing voices.

As previously noted, debate across the curriculum was used at an HBCU (historically Black college or university)—Wiley College—to improve critical thinking outcomes on their campus. Wiley is an important historical antecedent to debate because the school in many ways immortalized debate as an American pedagogy during the 1930s. Melvin Tolson—portrayed by Denzel Washington in the Hollywood film *The Great Debaters* (2007)—inspired the great debater James Farmer Jr. to pursue the end of racial segregation through the nonviolent means derived from debate.[16] In 1968, Farmer made an important point about the necessity of debate during eras of political frustration. When asked about political rival Stokely Carmichael's invocation of "burn baby burn," Farmer made this salient response:

> Well, I think Mr. Carmichael is wrong there. I think that there must be voices that say this is not the way, obviously. What we need now is not destruction—we need buildings. The slogan should not be "Burn baby burn" but "learn baby learn" and "build baby build."
> We've had enough of destruction. We've had enough of violence . . .
> We should understand that the black community is not monolithic, nor is the white community monolithic. There are many voices, there are many leaders, there is much debate and dialogue, discussion and disagreement in the black community; and that's as it should be.[17]

Debate has throughout American and even global history proven capable of building the young minds necessary for proper civics. In the exceptional and even violent frustrations of the 1920s where the KKK became exceptionally powerful, young Black men and women were learning how to debate and argue and implement a range of social and political changes that were fiercely resisted between 1941 and 1970. Because those eras involved greater levels of violence than we presently encounter, we should not flinch from pursuing debate as a journalistic training tool to diminish the partisan deformity of a central civil right known as freedom of the press.

DEBATE AND STRENGTHENING JOURNALISM

The debate across the curriculum model used at Wiley College between 2013 and 2017 produced a number of important and measured learning outcomes critical to our analysis on how to improve journalism:

Learning Outcome 1—Compile and analyze empirical and expert evidence from diverse media to support a logical claim. This learning outcome assesses the students' ability to research, gather, and utilize evidence. Basic information literacy is a cornerstone of debate and was assessed in each implementation of a debate activity. Students averaged 75.2 percent of the possible 20 points in every implementation, demonstrating proficiency in information literacy.

Learning Outcome 2—Draw conclusions by evaluating an argument to determine the veracity of the evidence and the logic of the idea. The second learning outcome focuses on evaluating the logic of the ideas presented. The ability to identify parts of an argument, logical fallacies, and weighing the strength of the overall argument is important in the evaluation of an argument. Students demonstrated proficiency in this leaning outcome as demonstrated by the average score of 79.6 percent.

Learning Outcome 3—Demonstrate knowledge and application of a well-formulated argument that uses evidence to support their position. This learning outcome assesses the ability of students to create counterarguments against presented arguments. Students averaged 78.89 percent in this area, demonstrating proficiency.

Learning Outcome 4—Recognize opposing viewpoints and utilize research evidence to champion their position through the exchange of verbal questions and answers. Students are able to refute opposing viewpoints and answer questions about their positions as demonstrated by the average of 80.83 percent.[18]

Each of these outcomes is important to the need to fix ideological normativity in the newsroom and is not about providing different ideologically grounded reporters but providing the training necessary for them to see beyond their own ideology to be able to better report on those who have a different ideology than their own. The learning outcome regarding "diversity of media" information will help journalists gather information that goes beyond their Democratic Party comfort zone. Learning outcome 2 regarding objectivity helps promote a value that is in decline among newsroom practitioners and corrects a trend toward ideological subjectivity. Learning outcome 3 helps with differentiating between opinion and fact in writing news articles and editorials. Learning outcome 4 showed the greatest strength in the learning cohort at Wiley. This is important to help the opposing viewpoint of Republicans gain more recognition in the preparation of journalists. As previously noted, Wiley students experiencing this curriculum for four years saw a critical thinking score (based upon the *College Learning Assessment* test) go from an average of 809 to 960. This 150-point improvement came at a time when CLA scores were declining nationwide. Debate instruction is a proven tool for improving critical thinking, and this lies at the heart of a goal to improve the ideological mix of thinking in American newsrooms.

The other important impact of debate training is the potential to take small voices individually and make them larger. In the case of the average American newsroom, a tiny minority of journalists are Republican. They are as already noted marginalized. Debate empirically strengthens marginalized voices and helps them exert greater social influence and ultimately greater political outcomes. In the area of racial minorities, key Black leaders including Barbara Jordan, James Farmer Jr., Malcolm X, Martin Luther King Jr., Medgar Evers, and James Meredith all received debate training in college that formed them for strong leadership outcomes. Many of these Black contemporaries argued with each other in the public sphere about how best to achieve ideal political outcomes. They did not all agree about how to stop anti-Blackness in America, but the larger panorama of arguments and discursive complexity improved society as a whole for all individuals.

Major powerful figures in the American presidency emerged from collegiate training in debate, including Woodrow Wilson, Calvin Coolidge, and Richard Nixon. Calvin Coolidge was an exceptionally reserved individual who was so socially awkward that he was rejected at Amherst by every single fraternity.[19] After completing a successful in-class debate against the football captain, he became interested in political leadership. He wrote about this new interest to his father. Ultimately, the quiet Coolidge became one of the most active presidential speakers in US history.[20] In this respect, debate instruction is a force multiplier that can fix rhetorical problems with small investments that reap large dividends within individuals often held at social margins.

Jürgen Habermas's elusive communication competence[21] is found in the teaching of debate so global publics are able to apprehend and resist propaganda denying the humanity of fellow human beings. Proper and ethical journalism respectful to all sides is a key component of communication competence as a social practice. The low discursive complexity of a world without debate breeds violence, injustice, and ultimately genocide. These are broader ramifications to specific solutions sought in the imaginative world of public debate. We must build, more broadly, a pedagogy of debate that disseminates discursive complexity. In this new pedagogy, the individual tendency to shrink and be silent in the face of discrimination and crimes diminishes, and the bravery and courage common to efforts to stop the worst of human harms rises.

Discursive complexity is defined as the capacity of individuals and/or groups to consider and express multiple points of view.[22] The gatekeeping functions of journalism alongside agenda setting make their role in the formation of discursive complexity critical. For Habermas, a Frankfurt School theorist, American society held an ideal of free speech and free expression that forms the basis of his notion of communication competence. The ability of individuals to communicate should be the proper basis of individuals rising and falling within society—rather than material determinations like those feared in socialist critiques of political power. Broad instruction in argumentation represents an ideal in disseminating and maintaining discursive complexity and holding the problem of propaganda at bay. A critical theory based upon communication rather than materiality is the key to a brighter American future and a strong global signal to journalists around the world trying to open closed societies. A communication critical theory examines the ideological distortions dominating the public sphere and closing the Overton window in a manner that trends communication practice toward propaganda rather than debate and argumentation.[23]

The current ideological makeup of journalists ensures that with regard to Republican and conservative political viewpoints, a rhetorical environment of propaganda now exists. As I told young journalists in 2004, "When Republicans speak to you about their interests, it is as familiar to you as someone speaking French." From the standpoint of newsrooms composed of 3.4 percent Republicans, it is unlikely that those partisan interests can be accurately conveyed. This requires aggressive pedagogical correction and meets a need that journalists themselves observe and attest to in surveys.

CONCLUSION

Surveys of American journalists show clearly that Republicans are drastically underrepresented[24] and that the public is precipitously losing trust in journalism on a basis of political ideology.[25] This is a critical problem for the United States, because journalists are the essential practitioners of a core civil right known as "freedom of the press" in the First Amendment. Without dissemination of political viewpoints represented across a range of public opinions like those found in the US Senate, conditions of low discursive complexity[26] and propaganda are likely to prevail—leading to public frustration and even desperate acts of political violence. To repair this problem, it is necessary and useful to implement a debate-oriented curriculum where journalists practice speaking and arguing opposing sides of current controversies. This pedagogy was used in locations such as the HBCU Wiley College in Marshall, Texas, with tremendous positive effects.[27] Such instruction will likely reverse the spiral of cynicism rooted in Republican distrust of journalism and restore the American ideal model of a free press.

ADDITIONAL MATERIALS

Although these examples are primarily for oral presentations, they can be modified for the assessment of written arguments (editorials) as well.

POTENTIAL TOPICS FOR DEBATE—SAMPLE LIST

Is the death penalty justified?
Should assault weapons be allowed?
What should be done about mass shootings?

Should the United States have mandatory service?
Should organ donation be mandatory?
Should the United States ban ICE?
Should abortion be legal?
Should we keep improving AI technology?
Should the Dalai Lama face further repercussions?
Should Biden run again?
Should taxes on the top 1 percent be increased substantially?
Is income inequality a pressing issue?
Should we have UBI?
Should recreational marijuana be legal?
Should we allow transgender competition in sports?
Should SMU students be able to carry firearms on campus?
Should animal testing be banned?
Will BRICS displace the United States as the dominant global force?
Should we dismantle the UN peacekeeping force?
Should the United States continue military aid to Ukraine?
Should other nations be encouraged to increase aid to Ukraine?
Should cancel culture apply to comedians?
Are Saudis using sports washing to cover up human rights abuses?
Are books better than television?
Should the Supreme Court limit the use of affirmative action in admissions?
Should SMU increase recruiting of DFW area students?
Is AI bad for education?
Should remote work be encouraged?

EXTEMPORANEOUS SPEECH EVALUATION FORM

<u>Introduction</u>   <u>5 pts.</u>   <u>Comments</u>
  1. Caught audience attention
  2. Overview of points
  3. Offered a clear thesis

<u>Organization</u>   <u>10 pts.</u>
  1. Signposting
  2. Proper use of pauses
  3. Discernible pattern or connection between main points

Body_____15 pts.
   1. Evident use of prep time
   2. Adapted difficult explanations
   3. Avoided rambling
   4. Filled main points equally
   5. Used notes effectively
   6. Answered the question

Delivery_____15 pts.
   1. Maintained eye contact
   2. Utilized hand gestures
   3. Comfortable speech rate
   4. Time _____ (3–4 mins.)

Conclusion_____5 pts.
   1. Reviewed points of analysis
   2. Increased emphasis

   3. Ended speech with a memorable point

DEBATE RUBRIC AND EVALUATION FORM

Resolution: _____
Affirmative _____ Negative
First affirmative name: _____ First negative name: _____
   1 2 3 4 5 Delivery 1 2 3 4 5
   1 2 3 4 5 Organization 1 2 3 4 5
   1 2 3 4 5 Evidence 1 2 3 4 5
   1 2 3 4 5 Refutation 1 2 3 4 5

Second affirmative name: _____ Second negative name: _____
   1 2 3 4 5 Delivery 1 2 3 4 5
   1 2 3 4 5 Organization 1 2 3 4 5
   1 2 3 4 5 Evidence 1 2 3 4 5
   1 2 3 4 5 Refutation 1 2 3 4 5

Third affirmative name: _____   Third negative name: _____
                1 2 3 4 5 Delivery 1 2 3 4 5
                1 2 3 4 5 Organization 1 2 3 4 5
                1 2 3 4 5 Evidence 1 2 3 4 5
                1 2 3 4 5 Refutation 1 2 3 4 5

Decision: [vote for affective or negative] _____
Reason for decision: Why did one side win?

NOTES

1. Joe Matheson, "Chapter 8: Current Codes of Ethics Render High Professional Standards That Endure, and Should," in *Ethical Journalism: Adopting the Ethics of Care* (Abingdon, Oxon: Routledge, 2022), https://doi.org/10.4324/9781003140337.

2. "American Journalists under Attack," *The American Journalist*, 2022, https://www.theamericanjournalist.org/post/american-journalist-findings; Jeffrey Gottfried and Jacob Liedke, "Partisan Divides in Media Trust Widen, Driven by a Decline Among Republicans," *Pew Research*, August 30, 2021, https://www.pewresearch.org/short-reads/2021/08/30/partisan-divides-in-media-trust-widen-driven-by-a-decline-among-republicans/; David Barker and Adam B. Lawrence, "Media Favoritism and Presidential Nominations: Reviving the Direct Effects Model," *Political Communication* 23 (January–March 2006): 41–59; Thomas E. Patterson, "Research: Media Coverage of the 2016 Election," Shorenstein Center, Harvard University, September 7, 2016, https://shorensteincenter.org/news-coverage-2016-general-election/; Curt Nichols, "The Presidential Ranking Game," *Presidential Studies Quarterly* 42, no. 2 (2012): 296; Joseph E. Uscinski and Arthur Simon, "Partisanship As A Source Of Presidential Rankings," *White House Studies* 11, no. 1 (2011): 5, https://www.joeuscinski.com/uploads/7/1/9/5/71957435/partisan_bias_in_rankings.pdf; Ben Voth, *The Centennial of the Modern American Presidency: The Presidential Rhetoric of Woodrow Wilson, Warren Harding, and Calvin Coolidge* (Lanham, MD: Lexington Books, forthcoming fall 2023).

3. Joe Concha, "The Media Trust Gap Between Conservatives and Liberals Continues to Grow," *The Hill*, September 6, 2021, https://thehill.com/opinion/healthcare/570916-the-media-trust-gap-between-conservatives-and-liberals-continues-to-grow/.

4. Gottfried and Jacob, "Partisan Divides."
5. Gottfried and Liedke, "Partisan Divides."
6. "American Journalists Under Attack."
7. Naomi Forman-Katz and Mark Jurkowitz, "U.S. Journalists Differ from the Public in Their Views of 'Bothsidesism' in Journalism," Pew Research, July 13, 2022, https://www.pewresearch.org/fact-tank/2022/07/13/u-s-journalists-differ-from-the-public-in-their-views-of-bothsidesism-in-journalism/.

8. "American Views 2020: Trust, Media and Democracy: A Deepening Divide," Knight Foundation, November 9, 2020, https://knightfoundation.org/wp-content/uploads/2020/08/American-Views-2020-Trust-Media-and-Democracy.pdf.

9. Amy Watson, "Number of Daily Newspapers in the United States from 1970 to 2018," Statista, June 10, 2021, https://www.statista.com/statistics/183408/number-of-us-daily-newspapers-since-1975/.

10. David Barker and Adam B. Lawrence, "Media Favoritism and Presidential Nominations: Reviving the Direct Effects Model," *Political Communication* 23 (January–March 2006): 41–59.

11. Thomas E. Patterson, "News Coverage of the 2016 General Election: How the Press Failed the Voters," Shorenstein Center, Harvard University, December 7, 2016, https://shorensteincenter.org/news-coverage-2016-general-election/.

12. Patterson, "Research: Media Coverage of the 2016 Election."

13. Roger von Oech, *The Creative Contrarian: 20 "Wise Fool" Strategies to Boost Your Creativity and Curb Groupthink* (Hoboken, New Jersey: Wiley-Blackwell, 2021).

14. "American Journalists under Attack."

15. Christopher Medina, Sean Allen, Drake Pough, and Ben Voth, "Debate as Pedagogical Empowerment at HBCUs in the United States," in *Debate as Global Pedagogy: Rwanda Rising* (Lanham, MD: Lexington Books, 2021), 90–93.

16. Ben Voth, *James Farmer Jr.: The Great Debater* (Lanham, MD: Lexington Books: 2017).

17. James Farmer Jr., April 16, 1968, TV Interview, Transcript; James Leonard Jr. and Lula Peterson Farmer Papers, Dolph Briscoe Center for American History, The University of Texas at Austin, Austin, Texas, Box 2R635.

18. Medina, Allen, Pough, and Voth.

19. Amity Shlaes, *Coolidge* (New York: Harper, 2013).

20. President Coolidge gave more major addresses than any US president except Ronald Reagan. Lyn Ragsdale, *Vital Statistics on the Presidency: George Washington to Barack Obama*, fourth edition (Thousand Oaks, CA: CQ Press, 2014).

21. Jürgen Habermas, *Communication and the Evolution of Society* (Boston: Beacon Press, 1979).

22. Ben Voth, "Discursive Complexity," in *The Rhetoric of Genocide: Death as a Text* (Lanham, MD: Lexington Books, 2014).

23. George H. Talbot, "Widening the Overton Window—While Avoiding Defenestration," *Clinical Infectious Diseases* 70, no. 11 (2020): 2442–43, https://doi.org/10.1093/cid/ciz990.

24. "American Journalists Under Attack."

25. Gottfried and Liedke.

26. Voth, "Discursive Complexity."

27. Medina, Allen, Pough, and Voth.

Chapter 5

A Renewal of Journalistic Credibility through the Ancient Religious Tradition of Jubilee

Stephen D. Perry

We live in a world full of networks where groups form in defense of or in opposition to various components of the social structure. These groupings may find commonality in ideas that could be political, religious, generational, geographic, or could be based on any number of other criteria. Protocols of communication are established in these networks, and those protocols determine who can be admitted into the "club" in question. Those rules may be negotiated, but the more entrenched a group becomes, the less variation is allowed in the rules of inclusion.[1] News has long had entrenched rules for objectivity, but it seems we have entered a day in which to understand news objectivity, we must rely on often unstated underlying assumptions about how objectivity is measured. As society has become increasingly postmodern or even meta-modern, we have lost an underlying value system on which all reporters generally agree. In order to reestablish a foundation from which journalists can critique current world events, it is difficult now to rely on the multitude of post-Enlightenment value systems that people fight over. With this in mind, in this chapter I turn to the ancient principle of a jubilee year, which was taught to the nation of Israel but was never practiced, as a model from which reporters can pull ancient wisdom that critiques both the right and the left in America.

The jubilee principle can be applied to controversial issues often covered by reporters: immigration, family, debt, charity, crime, economics, and so on. The principle of jubilee balances the collectivist versus individualist orientations of society, and the notions of socialism with those of capitalism. It challenges any system of enduring "haves" and "have nots" in society. The principles of jubilee also present objective foundations on which some of the main institutions of government that are linked either to left or right politically can be challenged by the press, thus rehabilitating the watchdog role of the press.

ENTRENCHED JOURNALISM

Journalists as a group have become entrenched, but they have become entrenched into camps where little variation from the camps' protocols is accepted by either the segmented audience or the news directors and network powers. Democratic pluralism requires multiple power foci, which allows opposing interests to not only exist but also to be able to organize. When the number of journalistic entities are few, and their numbers are decreasing due to the commodification of news and its delivery models, that results in the "progressive elimination of alternatives for opposing interests."[2] But where alternative voices exist—at the national level—the voices have aligned with specific audience segments to create a system that allows people to avoid cognitive dissonance and hear news that largely reinforces preexisting beliefs. This catering to ideological viewpoints also leads to more commentary and opinion programming and less factual news content, further shielding ideologically aligned viewers from diversity in the conclusions that may be drawn from the news that is presented.[3]

The commodification of news noted earlier leads to processes that help make the news more profitable. Thus, rules are established that lead to coverage of the sensational, the stars, the sinful, sports, and many other things that may not be important for democracy or decision-making, but these things begin to be thought of as what news is. The processes become unofficial rules that journalists internalize and seek out as a priority in their news production process. These rules, then, brought on by a system that prioritizes a profit before public interest, tend to limit the diversity of ideas and voices regardless of the individual diversity of the journalists.[4] This is the result of news routines, where journalists act individually but think collectively. The routines and rules they follow make their work more efficient, and the journalists also find safety in the continued practice of routines.[5] Yet some scholars have argued that routines in news may have contributed to a loss of trust and the distortion of journalistic credibility.[6] This may not be solely the fault of journalists and their organizations, but the routines themselves are targeted for exploitation by politicians and public relations experts and even shrewd manipulators of news to the extent that some intentionally spread disinformation.[7]

In order to restore trust and credibility to journalism, one possible contribution to that effort could be having journalism that operates based on different routines. Those who exploit routines of journalism would have more difficulty if the routines were not so similar across outlets. One current difference is the presence of commercial versus noncommercial outlets, but the minimal news competition from noncommercial venues in the United States has not made this difference effective. And because even noncommercial outlets need revenue, the resulting news is still driven by financial models of carving out a niche audience. Most audiences are carved out of political niches. The audience will either lean liberal or conservative, left or right in the United States at least. Two possible nonpolitical ways to attract audiences would be to base the audience's attraction to a news source on an audience's religious commitments or on the outcome of scientific findings. Certainly, there are sources that do this to an extent such as the Christian Broadcasting Network's news program, CBN News (www2.CBN.com), and the Environmental News Network (www.ENN.com). These are not devoid of politics and can even take a political angle in their news, seeming to side with a political party, bringing into question journalistic credibility in those venues as well. But because the audience for religiously based paradigms for news may provide the largest potential for financial success, in this chapter I propose an alternative to politically oriented news routines that might help reestablish journalistic credibility if fully enacted by weakening the influence of political echo chambers.

A PROPOSED SOLUTION OF JUBILEE

Due to these systemic ways of thinking that lock the public as well as the subset of journalists into similar paradigms, one way of breaking out of that mold is through turning to non-American, non-Western models that include elements of wisdom that are outside our preconceived biases and party-oriented orthodoxies. Of course, such an outside framework would be likely to be avoided by those audience members seeking ideological reinforcement. But that might not necessarily be so. For example, if there was a way for the playbook of the Chicago Bears to be a guide for journalists rather than the Republican or Democratic playbooks, you would get fans of the Bears, regardless of the party to follow that news. There would be a different alignment of beliefs that would provide cognitive resonance from a different source, making any political dissonance palatable, or at least worthy of discussion, because the readers and viewers would have a set of common values on which they can agree while they simultaneously may debate tangential issues to that commonly held value system.

Although a sports team's playbook is unlikely to work, another playbook can. Susan Emmerich studied the use of a knowledge source culturally aligned with the worldview of a fishing community in the Chesapeake Bay and demonstrated how to help align the beliefs of these people, who made their living from the Bay's resources, with those of environmental scientists who were fighting to gain compliance in sustainable fishing. She did this by approaching the environmental concern in a way that was aligned with the faith of the watermen. This required finding a different source of knowledge than that accepted by the scientists, but one that helped lead to cooperation between the watermen and the environmentalists. That source was the Bible.[8] One of the factors influencing the acceptance of a change in one's worldview is to seek ways that "the premises on which the worldview of the receptor is based are similar to those of the advocate."[9] In this chapter, therefore, I advocate that a news network that appeals to an audience where the worldview of a group of "receptors," that is, the news audience, is based on grounds different from partisan politics might attract viewers willing to consider different points of view. Those points of view, however, would need to be friendly to a worldview that is held in common on a different plane, the plane of faith. And because faith is so broad and varied, I recommend here focusing down on a faith teaching that is narrow enough to correlate it with a system by which society might function, the teaching of jubilee, which will be explained shortly.

The number of US adults claiming Christianity as their primary faith has declined precipitously from the 1970s and before to its 2020s state with between 63 percent and 70 percent now claiming Christianity as their religious basis.[10] But an additional 1 to 2 percent share the Jewish scriptures, which are incorporated into the Christian Bible. Appealing, then, to the non-Western origins of scriptures shared by at least these two major religions of the world should provide that the premises of the values presented from news that orients its concerns toward issues addressed therein would appeal to and find alignment with an audience in a way that might free journalists from the politically polarized model.

THE LAW OF JUBILEE

One specific teaching found in the Hebraic scriptures is the law given to the Jews to hold a year of jubilee. It is perhaps the most overt teaching about a system of government that should be valued by Jews and Christians. This principle of jubilee is not a new idea for solving modern dilemmas. It has been used by scholars in fields other than journalism to position academic research through new ways of thinking. Michael Hudson, for example, discusses debt forgiveness through the lens of jubilee. It seems, however, he uses jubilee as more of an excuse for the discussion than through the full overview of what is articulated in jubilee.[11] Others have advocated the jubilee concept for returning lands to Indigenous peoples, including a 2007 report from the United Nations.[12]

Another area in which jubilee has been used to advocate for change is in the criminal justice system. Some argue that incarceration is like slavery, and having a year of jubilee would free affected people, and in this argument, it would affect people of color most, addressing other economic, community, and relational harms.[13] An organization named Jubilee USA appeals to the teaching of jubilee in its efforts to bring together various religious groups to support debt cancellation by richer nations for the benefit of poor countries and their citizens.[14] Finally, Gary Roberts introduces the principles of jubilee while assessing the tenets of conscious capitalism and allows for a practical solution that differs in literal application but maintains fidelity to the principle of jubilee to help the poor in a modern context.[15]

So what is jubilee? The teaching is found in the Torah and the Bible in the book of Leviticus, chapter 25. The teaching was given to Moses concerning the nation of Israel and how property should be regarded. A year of jubilee was to occur every fifty years, or no more than twice in an adult's lifetime. It required the canceling of debts, return of property to the original owner's family, a year's vacation from farm labor, and the freedom of people from servitude—with exceptions.

Jubilee deals in a rudimentary level with foreign relations but mostly deals with values, nationalism, and wealth and its pursuit. One must look at underlying layers of meaning and purpose to apply the jubilee principle to modern society, but in doing so, the ideas can inspire a journalist to perhaps ask different questions and to think outside the box. It addresses current topics that journalists would face, even beyond those other organizations have discussed as noted earlier, like crime, charity, debt, family, reparations, and immigration. Let us walk through the three broad topics one at a time, starting with values. It will become clear that they are interlinked. As each is discussed, I will try to explain how it might change the journalist's approach to the craft.

VALUES

First the jubilee teaching assumes that the highest value is not overly individualistic, but individualism is influenced by the importance of the collective. The value of collectivism is not foreign to democracy. In democracies people understand that the common good is of high value, though for some, common good is achieved when each person seeks his or her own best interest and the interests balance out so that everyone gets something that they want.[16] Perhaps more common today is the concern for the interests of minorities and marginalized or disenfranchised groups whose interests are overshadowed by those of the majority group. This overshadowing cannot be eliminated without intentional effort for the majority to vote or act against their own interests. So in either case, both individualistic and collectivist values can be identified in democratic societies, even though individualism is usually portrayed as the highest value in the West and collectivism is the higher value in Eastern cultures.[17]

The jubilee system values the collective. Verses 14 and 17 instruct the Israelites not to take advantage of each other. In verses 35–37, Jews are admonished to treat their fellow Jew as someone who belongs or like an honored guest. They were not to charge them interest if they needed to borrow money. They were to not profit from their fellow Jew but to instead feed them at cost. Businesses in the form of real property could provide an income that belonged to the family, not just an individual (verse 10), at least in the long term. The notion of the business was important enough that if someone had to sell a property—one's means of earning future living—a "nearest relative" should redeem the property or buy it back from the new owner in order to keep it in the family.

Obviously, this is a collectivist approach, but it is not universally collectivist. Families supported their own clans as a priority even within the Jewish nation. But then fellow Jews came second and were to be treated as important partners in business. In a corporate environment we might think of them as "shareholders" of the business, with the immediate family holding the most shares and more distant members of the population holding fewer shares but still being part owners. Of course, those "fellow Jews" were the leading shareholders in their own families' businesses, so in some way each family unit was seeking its own best interest, and in so doing each supported the collective Jewish interest. It was the non-Jew, or the immigrant class, who was to be the "employee," which was most likely an indentured servant (or slave in most translations) in status (verses 39–46).

There is a fair amount of contrast between jubilee and today's political emphases. A conservative-leaning political philosophy would value seeing people endeavor toward the personal accumulation of wealth, relying on the wealthy and even the middle class to philanthropically support socially beneficial institutions that help the less fortunate. For this group, it is important that people be motivated to "pull themselves up by their own bootstraps," or to at least give more of a "hand up rather than a hand out." The more liberal-leaning person tends to characterize wealth accumulation as greed and values the state reaching in to even out a wealth gap through taxation and social programs, not trusting that philanthropy is enough to provide for the common good. This group sees different economic situations not as something that has been earned, but as the result of unfair systems that favor some groups over others, giving them a chance to be the economic winners and, thus, undeserving of their material advantage.

Journalism and the Appeal to Values

To explore how these principles might help a journalist engage this value system that is neither "right" nor "left" in the political spectrum but instead might offer solutions outside of political advantage, we can first see that understanding the balance between individual values and collective values can point the journalist toward the questions that would challenge whomever they would interview. On concerns about an ongoing or permanent upper class, a very individualistically focused view for those who support the right to perpetually pass down wealth, journalists can certainly probe for how the lower classes make the life of the upper class comfortable and how the upper classes could live without them, but they can also ask their sources if they believe in the ancient Hebraic idea that every so often the lower classes might need a second chance. Then a question of the redistribution of at least the means of earning income from society might be appropriate. Note this may not be the same as the distribution of disposable income but rather the redistribution of the engine that makes society prosper, but that could be open to other interpretations of jubilee.

Alternatively, what if the question revolves around how some people take advantage of others? Can those who benefit from credit card interest in the 20 to 30 percent range or those who benefit from payday or car title loan companies that charge 100s of percent interest be asked to simply loan other people money for nothing regardless of the risk to the original investment? Certainly, it might depend on what the money is for. But the journalist could question whether the value is on people instead of property, on family and clans and nation instead of personal possessions, the lender would be a person, a relative or a sponsor of some kind who values the person, not an impersonal system that will lend for any purpose for the right reward. Imagine the politician who claims to share a biblical worldview but who is being questioned on whether the policies he or she supports align with the principle of jubilee. The journalist could press on this by asking, "What policies would you support that would help achieve a society that more reflects the biblical teaching of jubilee?" Commentary from informed journalists and commentators could then follow, placing pressure on the political system toward rethinking some systems that many would argue are unjust or broken.

But let us reverse these scenarios. Jubilee helps the journalist conducting an interview with a socialist who argues that there should be no societal classes as well. The liberal-leaning person who initially thinks the jubilee system requires return of everyone's property and makes everyone equal in outcome, perhaps thinking socialism is the equivalent of jubilee, fails to dig deep enough. There is a psychological reason the reversion of the business land through distribution happens only every fifty years and on a predictable schedule. The journalist can point out, based on jubilee, that while there should be periods of resetting the distribution of ownership of the income-producing property, there would be no reason to redistribute such property if there was not an expectation that people would profit from it if they worked hard and managed it correctly. If there were to be no motive to work to improve one's own living conditions, the jubilee system would not work. Throughout the first forty years of the jubilee period those who are not likely to live to the next jubilee or even those who have a desire to build a successful enterprise will have a largely free-enterprise, capitalist system to work in. This is the motivation for people to build the wealth of the nation and perhaps even the family and tribe, and the removal of overall economic incentive would bring about economic decline.

Thus, the journalist can appeal to jubilee by asking why there is not a period that would inspire risk for reward through the potential for business success like there is in the jubilee, while still providing relief from greed and a perpetual rich class. The relief is both for those who are in the upper classes to come back to the pack and not become too self-important as well as for those who, through bad investments, poor choices, addictions, incarceration, or whatever need a second chance and need to be treated as people who have value because we all have the inalienable right to life, liberty, and the pursuit of happiness, a pursuit that must at some point be given a kick start for the downtrodden because we are all made in God's image as Christians claim.[18]

As a side consideration, if a jubilee actually happened, beyond the practice of identifying its principles to help invigorate journalism, it could be a boon to educational training. People could not rely on just owning an asset forever, but they would instead need the knowledge and skills that can be "owned" through education to manage the new resources they are given at jubilee. Thus, a journalist could emphasize that a redistribution of property should drive people to fully train themselves for use of that property in a successful manner, whether that is physical land property or the property of significant interest into a corporation.

Returning to the economic principles, you might question why I say this would happen through forty years instead of forty-nine years. The closer the nation would come toward the fiftieth year, the less motivation there would be to amass control of larger engines of the economy. Any land or business that would be returned to the general coffers for equalizing economic disparity would be worth less each year as time passed. In the Jewish law, someone buying a farm in the forty-second, forty-fifth, or forty-eighth year of the cycle had few years in which crops could be grown and profits made on the property of the business. Whether forty is the magic number or whether it is thirty-five or some other number, the truth is that with anywhere from the first to the twenty-fifth or thirtieth year of the jubilee cycle, many people would figure they would not want to run that business enterprise longer than the time to jubilee anyway. So the decline in value would be less steep. Once the time begins to seem like it is looming in the distance, the pure profit motive that some people embrace when running a business would certainly begin to decline, as the profits would be much more temporary. Many people run businesses for other motives too, so the looming redistribution of property would not end business production, but it would change the motives.

Other motives that spur people on to run businesses include self-realization and autonomy.[19] Others seek prestige or have social goals.[20] These motives that are other than financial would be elevated in the waning years of a period between jubilees. This should help the journalist to envision value in things besides financial profit. Certain types of enterprises might benefit particularly, such as the arts, not usually something that generates large profits except in the hit music or blockbuster movie sense. The efforts to innovate in business processes or in invention of products might be more motivated because failure in a financial sense does not come back on the entrepreneur once jubilee is reached, but success could result in someone grabbing a space in the history books for their invention. Also, the motivation to philanthropy would become greater during those last years, knowing that the more people do well, the better the overall redistribution of the business property would be. Jubilee brings a shift in the way of thinking about wealth, because each person or family succeeds as the nation succeeds. Journalists who seek to understand the jubilee thinking would have a mechanism from which to consider other motives beyond the financial in their reporting. CNBC or Fox Business channel conversations might have additional motivations beyond financial success as journalists approach the world with jubilee values.

NATIONALISM

Closely related to the collectivism value, enhanced by philanthropic motives brought on by the waning years of the jubilee is nationalism. In the jubilee framework immigrants did not have the rights of Jews. Those who understood the culture were trusted to protect it. There was no assumption that someone who immigrated—or perhaps had come as a captive after a war—would share the same value system and national pride. In order to maintain a nation or culture's uniformity, there seems to have been caution about the non-Jew. They could not let those who brought different worldviews, sets of expectations, and understandings of how the world should work have equal status with those who shared national values (also a concern in Deuteronomy 28: 43–44). This makes sense if you attribute importance to the need for a nation to work toward the same goal. Everybody needs to operate from the same playbook for maximum success.

This played out again in the form of business rights where every jubilee year the land would revert to the original family and clan that had owned it (verse 10). The non-Jew had no right to receive the property that was redistributed. Along these lines, those Jews who had become indentured laborers or slaves were to be released from their contracts of servitude and freed. They would again have a chance to start over in the family business as coowners of the land of their family and clan. The foreigners, on the other hand, were not freed from their contract, servitude, or slavery and were even treated ruthlessly (verses 39–43).

Of course, the focus on the land is also very nationalist. There is a teaching that the land is "sacred" in a literal sense for the Jewish people, but even without any covenant with God as Abraham experienced, every people group finds value in the land on which they have built a nation or a state or a village. So while jubilee as a teaching is given to a people who have conquered a land over the course of a few centuries (that is, no land is absolutely original to any group), at least within a nationalistic context there is a jubilee value that the land is sacred for the rights of the inhabitants who have labored on it for long enough to have existed there for a few generations.

Journalism and the Appeal to Nationalism

There are many aspects of nationalism that the journalist deals with, and immigration is probably chief among them. But so are school curricula, domestic production, natural areas, the use of natural resources, historical narratives, and even military conflict. Jubilee would be a challenge to the current culture around nationalism. There is no one size that fits all on who is patriotic in America, or probably any country, though the common perception would expect a conservative to be more nationalistic than a liberal voter. The conservative is probably more likely to fly a flag, wear a patriotic lapel pin, or believe in a concept referred to as "God and Country," but the liberal person also is more likely to endorse a flag than not, knows the words to the patriotic songs, and loves things that are part of Americana such as baseball and apple pie.

By appealing to jubilee, a journalist should recognize that it is important for a country to protect traditions and values that make people feel a sense of community. Just like supporting the businesses on Main Street is important for the life of a small town, the supporting of nationalistic successes helps a nation prosper. A journalist might ask why a person who is new to the nation should benefit from the work of the people who have labored for its success while they have not, and simultaneously ask what path should be established to help people earn the right to be part of the benefits of the nation. The jubilee recognizes that "slave workers," or those who were likely from a country that tried to oppose Israel and lost the battle or war, certainly should not benefit from the natural productivity of the nation they once tried to defeat.

However, once a person has become a citizen and the family has become part of the national fabric—think of the homesteader who tames a plot of land or the person who goes from penniless to prosperous through turning an idea into a successful business—those people have experienced the nation's challenges, costs, rewards, and values to a point that they eventually are no longer the outsider but the insider who has adopted the culture of the nation. An immigrant journalist could be among those with an eye to telling the nation's story, hearing from its people, and understanding the nation's heartbeat. So at some point all immigrants can become nationals. It would not be a question of race or ethnicity but a question of contributing to the fabric of the nation. They cease being more interested in their home nation's flag and more interested in their adopted homeland. Journalists would learn from jubilee that there is more to the nationalist principle than simply becoming a citizen. It is about embracing one's adopted land enough to pass it down to all succeeding generations of one's family.

This embracing of the land as well as a recognition that working, not necessarily as a team but at least as a league (insert your favorite sports league and teams here), would then inform questions about school curriculum and the teaching of national history, values, civics, sustainable resources, the beauty of the nation's national parks and green spaces, and economics. Neither the jubilee system nor any other valued way of balancing systems of economic distribution can endure across a long range of time beyond generations without a strong curriculum and understanding of why it was enacted. Democracy is not well liked by the loser. The economic system based on supply and demand was not well liked by the carriage maker or the buggy whip manufacturer once the automobile was invented. Similarly, the petroleum industry may not like supply and demand if electric vehicles replace gas power on the nation's roads.

Journalists should know that ignorance of national values could undercut the nation's adherence to a free press, a protection for the writing of unpopular and even hated ideas. Jubilee points to the importance of teaching and understanding of national values and public welfare. It should push the journalist to challenge voices who attempt to redefine core principles of the nation, such as freedom of the press or liberty, through redefinition and spin rather than through an evaluation of some revision of practices based in concepts of the public good. Ignorance of the full history and arguments behind the concepts that undergird a nation allow spin doctors to redefine rather than successfully argue and negotiate changes in a nation's core values. Jubilee is underscored by a value of making sure those who have a stake in the nation's future understand its institutions, values, and history, an educational role played as much by journalists as by schools.

Foreign policy coverage by journalists would also be influenced by jubilee. While this article will not attempt a full discussion on the subject, topics such as the influence of China on educational and economic institutions in a country would be much less likely to survive scrutiny under a jubilee line of nationalist thinking. Similarly, products made at home would have an additional level of attractiveness to buyers if the national economic resources were treated like the land that is redistributed during jubilee. Consumers would be aware that the future redistribution of the nation's productive resources would benefit them if those companies within the nation were stronger at the year of jubilee. Reliance on supply chains from international producers would diminish in favor of domestic supply chains. Journalists who write from the perspective of valuing the nationalist bent in jubilee would, thus, be considering the domestic public good.

WEALTH AND ITS PURSUIT

The aspect of jubilee that has been used most by those seeking different approaches to social science instruction deals with money. It is, it seems, human nature to spend beyond one's means. Perhaps that is through business investments—taking a risk to make it big or taking on student loan debt to develop employability—or perhaps it is through squandering wealth like the prodigal son (Luke 15:11–31) or the gambling addict.[21] In the year of jubilee all debts of the citizens, the Jews, were canceled and obligations were forgiven. Because of that, and because the jubilee was to happen on a regular basis, the value of business land decreased every year as the next jubilee approached, and the motive to loan money with interest did too because all debts were canceled in the jubilee year (Lev. 25:15–16). In Babylon the canceling of debts was at the pleasure of a king who typically did this to "establish justice" at the beginning of his reign.[22] Hudson and Charles Goodhart focus their economic arguments for debt cancellation on both jubilee principles and the frequent cancellation of debts by each new ruler who came to power. Because debt was owed to that ruler and not banks or ordinary citizens, they had the right to make such debt cancellation.[23]

Such an ad hoc canceling of debts to curry favor is easily welcomed by people. In the musical *Scrooge*, Ebenezer Scrooge tells the soup man Tom Jenkins that his debts are canceled as a Christmas present, and Jenkins launches into a song that says, "that's the nicest thing that anyone's ever done for me."[24] Such generosity is not forbidden by jubilee, but nor is it part of what makes the economic system dependable. It is, however, in the spirit of Leviticus 25:14 and 17, which both forbid people from getting rich off the misfortunes of others.[25] The regularity of the jubilee and the ability to plan for it were not just a free-for-all chance to spend and consume and then have one's debts canceled. There was a self-righting mechanism. It was a measured way to encourage people to not hold material possessions too close to their heart, yet it still allowed for a capitalistic spirit of entrepreneurship. There was both a chance for individual gain and a realization that the gain of each individual would ultimately help the whole of the nation through a redistribution process. In other words, this was not socialism, and it was not capitalism either, but shared aspects of both.

There was the chance for personal gain that was long term, however. Houses in the countryside were relatively short term, if half a century can be considered short term, as they had to be returned in the year of jubilee. Those are the houses where the business of agriculture was centered. But a house in a walled city was a permanent possession of the buyer and the buyer's descendants, but only if the prior owner or a relative did not buy it back within a year after its purchase (verses 29–30). In such cases, it was the permanent possession of the buyer until it was sold to someone else and a year had passed. Such a house may have indicated influence, safety, and wealth but would not have been using up productive agricultural business land.

Influence on Journalists and Wealth Questions

Journalists have many stories about people who pursue wealth to extremes, taking advantage of others in the process. People such as Bernie Madoff and the Ponzi scheme he ran that bilked investors of over $60 billion;[26] or Sam Bankman-Fried, the failed CEO of FTX, a cryptocurrency exchange, who was alleged to have fraudulently used investors' money for influence, real estate, and high-risk investments and lost billions of dollars in the process.[27] But even stories of credit card interest rates rising or banks raking in record profits due to supply chain issues[28] result in questions that jubilee principles could inform. Rather than sticking to party-dominated talking points, a steady belief system like jubilee allows a journalist to probe through principles presented here.

In addition to stories on taking advantage of others, stories of large tracts of land being bought up by various people such as Bill Gates[29] or business entities with connections to other countries[30] or by other countries such as China[31] would be a concern for journalists within a jubilee framework, though that land would return to others through redistribution someday. The value of the land would be connected only to the business value for the remaining years and would likely maintain the mindset of a family farm. Instead, in the modern farm land rush world, people are buying land more than one thousand miles from where they live, and whether they choose to farm it, build on it, or make it a wildlife refuge will be totally based on the whims of people with no family or experiential connection to that land.[32] A journalist thinking about this from a jubilee mindset can see the many aspects of these land purchases that may be profitable for the individual, but not for society, and could probe about it with sources and write up reports from that mindset. In so doing, the framework is not a partisan divide article but an article based in a belief system that money is only about the ability to generate further productive benefit for society, as would be the case with agricultural land of Israel thousands of years ago.

But the journalist is not limited to the direct observations of jubilee. Whole systems of crime and taking advantage of others might be derailed in a jubilee-type regulatory environment. A PSA for a TV program called *Trafficked* showed the host interviewing a black market participant about why he did not report on the evils of the system in which he operated. He said, "It's about the money." The love of money has long been referred to as the "root of all kinds of evil" (1 Timothy 6:10). Maybe money, as noted earlier, should not be revered so much as a value by journalists. Certainly, that would be in the spirit of Jubilee.

Modern Application of Property Redistribution

Maybe playing out the jubilee scenario in the modern time should be reexamined. What if rather than only farmland as the major business platform we looked at Wall Street in the modern day. What if stock market assets were the thing that was redistributed? We would have to ask ourselves whether people would invest in businesses if the ownership would eventually be transferred. A jubilee approach would certainly make stock purchase about the P/E ratio, price compared to earnings, rather than about growth stocks that are banking on long-term profits. This might reduce the corporate behemoth as the focus of investing. Lots of small companies might be more desirable instead of a few large mega companies, the oligopolies that exist in many industries such as energy, telecommunication, automotive, media, pharma, etc. The executive officers who control the shares of the corporations would change, meaning that the leadership could be voted out by new shareholders, though strong performance would certainly make someone more likely to remain in control through the will of the shareholders broadly, rather than through the will of a couple of large shareholders and mutual fund managers who are able to influence corporate control.

Commodities would probably need to be part of the redistribution scenario too. If people cannot gain control of companies, they would move to commodities. This is even a closer connection to the notion of redistributing the land during jubilee. Oil, gold, platinum, silver, or any other precious mineral like those used in battery production would require redistribution. During World War II the United States controlled the allotment of fuel, controlled ownership of gold and silver, and even engaged in collecting greases and cooking oils. Thus, there is some precedent where people could not own a commodity just because they had the money even in modern America.

But jubilee is not about preventing people from having some wealth, as was permitted in the case of the houses owned inside a walled city. The purpose was to give the means of production and the tools with which to prosper to everyone. Therefore, people would certainly try to store wealth in items of value. Art, historical objects, collectibles, recreation or sports gear, etc. might be things that people would "park" their wealth in. Because those things do not allow for the generation of productive essentials for living, those would seem to be outside the scope of concern for a jubilee mindset. In fact, the replacing of stocks and commodities with arts and collectibles might serve as a huge boon for the visual arts to flourish. After all, there are only so many paintings by van Gogh, Monet, or Renoir, or, if nationalism values extended into the arts, the Remington bronzes, Tiffany lamps, and Georgia O'Keeffe paintings. So more people would have a chance to produce art that would be purchased for its long-term value if people were unable to place as much value in controlling the engine of business.

There are many other aspects of pursuing wealth that jubilee values would change. Journalists covering issues of retirement income or support for the elderly or disabled might consider how jubilee principles factor in. People retiring in the jubilee year would be returning valuable business instruments, be it land or stocks, to the common coffers for redistribution. Their retirement would then be based on the redistribution. But someone retiring at mid-jubilee cycle with twenty-five years to go before a redistribution would not have the benefit of the redistribution. If that person had not saved up or if the government did not provide a retirement program, that person's net worth at that time would determine what they would have to live on. Because family relationships are much more important in a jubilee system (verses 10 and 25–27), perhaps a journalist would emphasize the family's responsibility more than the government's. Certainly, jubilee influenced journalism would ask different questions on these points.

The principle of a sabbatical from work is also addressed under jubilee teaching (Verses 11–12). Was that idea in the Hebraic scriptures primarily for the benefit of the people or was it a rest for the land? Perhaps it was both. It was the idea that there is benefit in the redirection of one's focus away from constant production. In the jubilee principle, people would survive on the produce that grew on the leftover vines or the plants that came up naturally from the prior years—the untended vines. After all, everyone took a simultaneous sabbatical from work. Imagine the universities, banks, grocery stores, gas stations, plumbing repair shops, etc. all shutting down business for a full year. It seems hard to imagine a replacement for the complex system nowadays unless you live off the grid somewhere, and even then, the work of hunting, harvesting, etc. for subsistence is seemingly endless.

A jubilee journalist would have a struggle with a direct twenty-first-century comparison with the sabbatical problem, and I would leave it to such people to bring various ideas to the forefront on this. But certainly from a pursuit-of-wealth angle, the emphasis on sabbatical is a challenge to the constant pursuit of wealth. At least, then, the journalist can question workaholism and the rat race mentality of the current style of life proffered in the media and on the news for Americans. Improved mental health, education, family relations, and sustainability practices may be among the advantages of providing people and the land with a sabbatical season.

DISCUSSION/IMPLEMENTATION

In an age of politically polarized news sources that are energized by the niche audiences networks must appeal to, finding a different shared worldview that meshes with a range of the audience based on a nonpartisan common ground can facilitate discussion of ideas and values that may cross the political spectrum. Rather than continuing their news consumption in an echo chamber, Christian and Jewish constituencies in America might follow journalists who appeal to the revealed worldview in this non-Western wisdom of antiquity that is common to their religious backgrounds. Although it is unlikely and not necessarily advised to rigorously institute the ancient teaching of jubilee in a sudden fashion, it does provoke opportunities to dig into values that challenge both political parties' fervently held stances, and whether or not that results in systemic changes to politics would be a separate concern from that of how this can aid journalism.

Journalism can only shed its addiction to the financial rewards that come with pandering to echo chamber–hungry audiences if they have an alternative that supports their financial needs. Turning to a different plane of reasoning might appeal to journalists and editors who seek to have more freedom from the political narratives of the various political parties. Implementing a jubilee-informed journalism mode would seem likely to attract a bipartisan audience of faith-based individuals. The ability to address issues through the lens of the non-Western ancient tradition of jubilee would help restore credibility and balance to journalism, and it would frustrate the ability of public relations practitioners and politicians to strategically use the routines of politically based news organizations in their favor.

Because in many parts of the country, Christians and Jews together would certainly account for two-thirds of the constituents in a politician's district, asking government actors to reflect on the wisdom of such religious traditions would allow the audience to hear answers to uncommon questions that still address issues of today. Rather than quickly tuning out a politician or a news anchor who fails to toe the preferred party line, if questions and the resulting answers were evaluated from a principle that is valued but is distinct from political mantras, perhaps the audience would be willing to entertain the resulting discussion and debate. And hopefully that debate would be able to exist without the ad hominem attacks and un-fact-checked claims that are so common in berating the other side in current journalism and politics in America.

The proposal here is only theoretical as there is no field test or case study that can be examined. We can only turn to Emmerich's success in helping change the minds of the fishing community in the Chesapeake Bay through appealing to a religious plane instead of a scientific plane to generate changed behavior to environmentally friendly practices. Perhaps in this age of digital news some entity will choose to invest in an experiment that reflects the ideas in this treatise, but unfortunately, it can only be presented as a theoretical or philosophical approach until that occurs. Still, this is a necessary step as scholars seek remedies for journalism's decline as an entity that credibly serves as a government watchdog. Thus, I would challenge a journalism entrepreneur to embrace the spirit of jubilee or some other wisdom that would appeal to the potential audience. The recommendation of appealing to wisdom far removed from contemporary politics as a basis seems essential to allow for a return to journalism that reports objectively.

In the emerging democracies of the former USSR, hopes for democracy withered into denunciations of corruption as elites (holdovers from the former communist system) used what were once state-owned assets and profited from them during the rapid privatization. Throughout the democratic world, ordinary citizens criticized unrepresentative institutions and bureaucrats who dominated such institutions.[33] Hope for democracy in the United States similarly is withering as each side castigates the other and seeks ultimate power advantages rather than the public welfare and the common good. Systems of thinking like the jubilee teaching that value the common good in new ways help shed light on the shortsightedness of either party's current mantras and hopefully would help drag government actors back to the table of negotiation and compromise to produce a working governmental system that abhors being a house divided against itself even while maintaining robust discussion and debate on ideas.

NOTES

1. Manuel Castells, "Network Theory: A Network Theory of Power," *International Journal of Communication* 5 (2011): 15.

2. Jeanne Fox, "Deviant Voices: News Agency Coverage of Controversial Public Figures (2012–2022)" (PhD diss., Regent University, 2023), 18–19.

3. Markus Prior, *Post-Broadcast Democracy: How Media Choice Increases Inequality In Political Involvement And Polarizes Elections* (Cambridge: Cambridge University Press, 2007).

4. Fox, "Deviant Voices," 24; David Michael Ryfe, "The Nature of News Rules," *Political Communication* 23, no. 2 (2006): 203–14.

5. Ryfe.

6. Phillip Williams and Stephen D. Perry, "Journalism and Sources: Dealing More Carefully with the Devil We Know," *Better Journalism* 1 (2023): 1.

7. George Bovenizer, "Fanning the Fake News Flames: The Impact of Emotion and Image Appeal on the Acceleration of Disinformation," *Better Journalism* 1 (2023): 52.

8. Susan Drake Emmerich, "Faith-Based Stewardship and Resolution of Environmental Conflict: An Ethnography of an Action Research Case of Tangier Island Watermen in the Chesapeake Bay" (PhD diss., University of Wisconsin–Madison, 2003).

9. Susan Emmerich, "Fostering Environmental Responsibility on the Part of the Watermen of Chesapeake Bay: A Faith and Action Research Approach," Redeemingreason.org, n.d., http://www.redeemingreason.org/archives/papers/emmerichs.pdf.

10. "How U.S. Religious Composition Has Changed in Recent Decades," Pew Research Center, September 13, 2022, https://www.pewresearch.org/religion/2022/09/13/how-u-s-religious-composition-has-changed-in-recent-decades/; Jeffrey M. Jones, "How Religious Are Americans?" Gallup News, December 23, 2021, https://news.gallup.com/poll/358364/religious-americans.aspx; PRRI Staff, "The 2020 Census of American Religion," PRRI, July 8, 2021, https://www.prri.org/research/2020-census-of-american-religion/.

11. Michael Hudson, ". . . *and forgive them their debts: Lending, Forclosure and Redemption from Bronze Age Finance to the Jubilee Year* (Dresden: Islet-Verlag, 2018); Michael Hudson and Charles Goodhart, "Could/Should Jubilee Debt Cancellations Be Reintroduced Today? If Not, What Alternative Measures of Debt Relief and

Redistribution Might Be Possible?" *Economics: The Open-Assessment E-Journal* 12, no. 2018-45 (2018): 1-25.

12. United Nations, "Report of the United Nations Permanent Forum on Indigenous Issues," Sixth Session (E/C.19/2007/10) (New York: United Nations, 2007).

13. M. Alexander, *The New Jim Crow: Mass Incarceration in the Age of Colorblindness* (New York: The New Press, 2010).

14. Jubilee USA Network, "The Jubilee Story," n.d., paragraphs 1-6, https://www.jubileeusa.org/the_jubilee_story.

15. Gary Roberts, "Conscious Capitalism from a Christian Worldview Lens," in *The Spirit of Conscious Capitalism: Contributions of World Religions and Spiritualities*, ed. M. Dion and M. Pava (London: Springer Nature, 2022), 133-42.

16. Walter Lippmann, *Public Opinion* (New York: Penguin, 1984).

17. Jang Kang, Stephen D. Perry, and Seok Kang, "The Relationship Between Television Viewing and the Values Orientations of Japanese Students," *Mass Communication and Society* 2, no. 3-4 (1999): 147-61.

18. David C. Innes, *Christ and the Kingdoms of Men: Foundations of Political Life* (Phillipsburg, NJ: P&R Publishing, 2019), 9-11.

19. Marco Gelderen and Paul Jansen, "Autonomy as a Start-Up Motive," *Journal of Small Business and Enterprise Development* 13, no. 1 (2006): 23-32.

20. Dilani Jayawarna, Julia Rouse, and John Kitching, "Entrepreneur Motivations and Life Course," *International Small Business Journal* 31, no. 1 (2013): 34-56.

21. Lia Nower, Kyle R. Caler, Dylan Pickering, and Alex Blaszczynski, "Daily Fantasy Sports Players: Gambling, Addiction, and Mental Health Problems," *Journal of Gambling Studies* 34 (2018): 727-37.

22. Robert P. Gordon, "Leviticus," in *The International Bible Commentary with the New International Version*, ed. F. F. Bruce (Grand Rapids, MI Zondervan, 1986), 210-11.

23. Hudson and Goodhart, 1-25.

24. Ronald Neame (Director) and Robert H. Solo (Producer), *Scrooge*, Paramount, 1970, based on Charles Dickens, *A Christmas Carol in Prose: Being a Ghost Story of Christmas* (1843).

25. Gordon, 210.

26. "Bernie Madoff: Disgraced Financier Dies in Prison," BBC.com, April 14, 2021, https://www.bbc.com/news/business-56750103.

27. Rob Garver, "Fraud Charges Unsealed in Arrest of Crypto Magnate Bankman-Fried," VOA News, December 13, 2022, https://www.voanews.com/a/fraud-charges-unsealed-in-arrest-of-crypto-magnate-bankman-fried-/6875521.html.

28. Peter Hobson, "Big Banks to Rake in Record Profits from Commodities This Year," Reuters, September 9, 2022, https://www.reuters.com/business/finance/big-banks-rake-record-profits-commodities-this-year-2022-09-09/.

29. Gates owned almost 270,000 acres of farmland in February 2021. Hannah Weinberger, "Why Bill Gates Is Investing Big Time in Farmland Across Washington and the Country," NWPB News, February 17, 2021, https://www.nwpb.org/2021/02/17/why-bill-gates-is-investing-big-time-in-farmland-across-washington-and-the-country/.

30. Ariel Zilber, "Ron DeSantis Blasts China for Buying Up US Farmland: 'It's a huge problem,'" *New York Post*, July 25, 2022, https://nypost.com/2022/07/25/ron-desantis-blasts-china-for-buying-up-florida-farmland/.

31. Elirehema Doriye, "The Next Stage of Sovereign Wealth Investment: China Buys Africa," *Journal of Financial Regulation and Compliance* (2010): 23–31, https://doi.org/10.1108/13581981011019606.

32. Dan Charles, "Big-Money Investors Gear Up for a Trillion-Dollar Bet on Farmland," *Morning Edition*, July 30, 2020, https://www.npr.org/2020/07/30/892366385/big-money-investors-gear-up-for-a-trillion-dollar-bet-on-farm-land.

33. William A. Galston, "The Enduring Vulnerability of Liberal Democracy," *Journal of Democracy* 31, no. 3 (2020): 8–24.

Chapter 6

Apples and Bananas

The Necessity of *Differentiating Facts and Opinion* for *Democracy-Nurturing Fact-Checking*

Alex Christy and Brent Baker

In response to Donald Trump's 2016 victory, CNN International's Christiane Amanpour, whose show is simulcast in the United States on PBS, wrote, "Now, more than ever, we need to commit to real reporting across a real nation, a real world in which journalism and democracy are in mortal peril, including by foreign powers like Russia paying to churn out and place false news, and hacking into democratic systems here and allegedly in upcoming crucial German and French elections too."[1]

An appropriate response to Amanpour's article could be "Now?" Amanpour can claim that revulsion to facts is a recent Trumpian feature that threatens democracy, but the people she would need to convince most are unconvinced. For instance, many political moderates as well as conservatives do not hear a journalist such as Amanpour using "now" and think of Trump, they hear "now" and think of just the next Republican who is replacing a Democrat; so even if Jeb Bush had been elected president, they would have gone after him too. This response is not new to the 2016 election, because in their minds, in 2012, elite journalists went after Mitt Romney too. For example, Neil Newhouse was a pollster for the Romney campaign and in September of that year he created a sensation when he proclaimed, "We're not going to let our campaign be dictated by fact-checkers." Responding to Newhouse, Neil Brown at PolitiFact wrote, "This fact-check business, it turns out, makes some partisans very uncomfortable."[2] Romney's rival, President Barack Obama, also attempted to seize on not only Newhouse's remarks but the reaction to them: "Somebody was challenging one of their ads, they just—they made it up about work and welfare. . . . Every outlet said, 'this is just not true.' And they were asked about it and they said—one of their campaign people says: We won't have the fact checkers dictate our campaign. We will not let the truth get in the way."[3]

Other examples from the 2012 campaign show similar results. Arguing with Republican representative Peter King on whether Obama had a record of apologizing for the United States, CNN's Soledad O'Brien declared, "None of those speeches at all, if you go to factcheck.org which we check in a lot, they all say the same thing. They fact check this." After King replied that he did not care, O'Brien shot back, "There are fact checks. You may not care, but they're a fact checker. I'm reading the speeches." King's response was to declare the fact-checkers wrong: "No. Soledad, what I'm saying is any common sense interpretation of those speeches, the president's apologizing for the American position. That's the apology tour."[4]

Years later, conservative writer Jonah Goldberg objected to a PolitiFact article giving him a half-true rating for a claim about Obamacare by leading off his counterrebuttal, "I have little use for Factcheckers, though I have plenty of use for facts and I believe in checking them. The problem with the Factcheckers is that they seem to think they have an authority they did not earn to tell other journalists what the facts are. That's bad enough, but they almost invariably end up objecting not to untruths but to truths they don't like. That often makes them combatants, hiding behind their self-appointed status as referees."[5]

These remarks from Newhouse, King, and Goldberg all occurred before 2016. It is not credible to accuse the 2012 Romney campaign or Goldberg of being enamored with Donald Trump, yet fact-checking is as popular as ever because of the Trump phenomenon with some journalists going so far as to claim the two are directly related. In response to Trump, CNN initiated a marketing campaign called "Facts First" that featured an apple situated against a plain white background with a narrator explaining, "This is an apple. Some people might try to tell you that it's a banana . . . but it's not. This is an apple."[6]

However, journalists are not always the best apple pickers. Even in Amanpour's article and subsequent history, there are problems that a critic can point to in order to cast doubt on the efficacy of professional fact-checking. On the specific issue of "now" and Russian foreign interference in American politics, a journalist of foreign affairs such as Amanpour should know that such interference did not begin when Trump decided to run for president. For example, George Kennan's famous "Long Telegram" from 1946 contains multiple examples of Westerners being used by Moscow to promote Soviet interests.[7]

Additionally, Amanpour could criticize Trump for peddling fake news, but when Israeli prime minister Naftali Bennett appeared on her show in April 2022, she could not take that same criticism. When Bennett called her blaming recent Israeli-Palestinian tensions on Israel "a lie, simply lie," Amanpour shot back, "You cannot say that to me. You cannot tell me I'm lying."[8] Why not? If journalists are going to portray themselves as the bulwarks against fake news, they cannot portray themselves as above criticism, especially considering Amanpour omitted that tensions rose because ISIS terrorists murdered three Israelis.

LEANING LEFT/LEANING RIGHT INFLUENCES

Traditional discourse on political media bias has centered on issues such as framing, which explores how the very words journalists use to describe issues, events, and people are designed for political effect. For example, when discussing abortion, journalists will frequently refer to the issue as one of "women's rights" or "reproductive rights," which is exactly how Democrats frame the issue. They portray pro-life laws as "restrictive," but not pro-choice laws as "ghoulish" or other description pro-lifers might apply. Some of them are repulsed at the words "pro-life." These are more obvious types of bias. However, one form of bias that is considerably more difficult to detect is with fact-checking. There are many reasons for this: fact-checkers can be just as wrong as anybody else, they can play word games, end up confusing facts for opinions, and can manipulate numbers. Additionally, by keeping databases of politicians they can portray certain ones as more or less dishonest than they actually are, which can skew perceptions of candidates and causes.

As a case in point, the *Washington Post* shut down its presidential fact-checking database, which it created in 2017, one hundred days into Joe Biden's presidency on the grounds that it was no longer needed. Chief *Post* fact-checker Glenn Kessler tweeted that "maintaining the Trump database over four years required about 400 additional 8-hour days over four years beyond our regular jobs for three people. Biden is off to a relatively slow start but who knows what will happen. We will keep doing fact checks, just not a database."[9]

Before Kessler and the *Post* shut down the database, they conceded that one of the reasons why Trump told more mistruths than Biden was because Trump tweeted more, gave more interviews, and gave more speeches than Biden, a specious explanation at best. Kessler reported that Trump gave 183 general remarks, speeches, interviews, press gaggles, and press conferences in his first one hundred days in office while Biden gave 139. The *Post* gave Biden 78 misleading claims, or 0.56 per remark, while giving Trump

511 or 2.79 falsehoods per appearance.[10] Trump's cumulative numbers begin to look exceptionally bad only when it is considered that Trump opened himself up to additional criticism by giving more remarks, and that is before one considers the actual substance of the claim and corresponding check. However, such reporting of numbers does not take into account claims that were made but that were not checked, such as when Biden claimed to know what it is like to have "had a house burn down" when the truth is that the incident at issue was about a small kitchen fire.[11]

As another example, Senators Ted Cruz and Elizabeth Warren share a lot of similarities. Both were first elected in 2012, both consider themselves be leaders of an ideological grassroots movement, and both have run for president. Cruz has a law degree from Harvard and Warren has taught law at Harvard. Yet as of June 5, 2023, PolitiFact has checked the conservative Cruz 156 times with 105 "false," "mostly false," and "pants-on-fire" ratings: a rate of 67 percent.[12] Warren, on the other hand, has been checked 35 times with only six "false" or "mostly false" claims or a rate of 17 percent. She has yet to receive a "pants-on-fire" rating.[13] Like Biden, it is not as if Warren is above embellishing a story to make herself look good, as her Cherokee ancestry controversy proved. However, some people may still respond that conservatives are fact-checked more because they deserve it and the following sections will seek to address that criticism by showing faults with the specifics of fact-checking.

CASE SELECTION

The main problem with databases is not only what data gets put into them but how. Variables are supposed to be constant, but changing standards and definitions sometimes get in the way. In 2018, PolitiFact's Tom Kertscher checked a claim by Wisconsin governor Scott Walker, who was touting what he claimed to be record-low unemployment and a record high of people working. In a sentence that, on PolitiFact's website, included links to five previous articles, Kertscher wrote, "As we've noted repeatedly in previous fact checks, the economy is affected many factors, including national ones, and a governor plays an important—but limited—role in a state's economy." Later, when justifying the "half-true" rating, Kertscher reiterated this point, "Walker is correct on the two statistics. But his various reforms can only be considered to be a contributing factor, at most, given many factors that affect the state's economy."[14]

However, two years earlier, Dan Clark ran a fact-check, also in PolitiFact, of New York governor Andrew Cuomo's statement, "We created 800,000 new jobs, we cut the unemployment rate almost in half and today New York

State has more private sector jobs than it has ever had in its history." Clark noted that part of the reason New York would have more jobs is because the population has naturally increased, but did not include any reference to a "limited" role of the governor. Instead, Clark did a simple numbers check and rated claim "true."[15] There is no substantive difference between what Cuomo claimed and what Walker claimed, yet they received two different ratings, which brings into question the totally of PolitiFact's checks of the two men where the percentages suggest Cuomo was the more truthful one.[16]

During elections, politicians seek to define themselves and their opponents. In swing races, the one who can do this the best and the quickest is usually the one who is going to win. In 2020, Georgia senator David Perdue sought to define Jon Ossoff as a "socialist." PolitiFact gave him a "pants-on-fire" rating because, "Strictly speaking, however, the most narrow definition of socialism refers to 'governmental ownership and administration of the means of production and distribution of goods.'"[17] The "pants-on-fire" rating is extreme. PolitiFact's Tom Kertscher admitted in his article that socialism is viewed more positively in the Democratic Party than capitalism, but it is not Kertscher's definition they are thinking of when they answer that way. They are much more likely to associate socialism with Sweden than Venezuela, but that is not the totality of our point. A year later, Georgia passed a new election law that was labeled "Jim Crow" by President Joe Biden and others. When it came to fact-checking this claim, PolitiFact wavered, writing a long article that delivered no judgment, but the difference in treatment was easy to catch: "Some said Biden's rhetorical point was justified as a way of highlighting the dangers of backsliding from hard-won voting rights. Those who say the comparison is justified acknowledge that the Georgia law does not literally resemble Jim Crow in its particulars."[18] Clearly PolitiFact gave one politician a "pants-on-fire" rating for not using the *literal* definition of socialism, even when people who say they support socialism do not use that same definition, yet gave another politician, who argued that the means of using extremist, nonliteral rhetoric justifies the ends, a pass. These double standards diminish the credibility of fact-checkers and contribute to the distrust shown by many moderates, Republicans, and conservatives.

In August 2022, a Twitter (now X) user named "Freesus Patriot™" posted an image of a list of books that were supposedly banned by the state of Florida. It was shared by many prominent critics of Governor Ron DeSantis including American Federation of Teachers President Randi Weingarten, *The Atlantic* columnist Tom Nichols, and actor Mark Hamill. MSNBC host Katie Phang replied to Hamill, "we should start the BBC: the Booster Books Club and amplify these titles!" The problem was that the list was fake,[19] yet Snopes's Bethania Palma gave it a rating of "originated as satire."[20]

There were two main problems with this rating. First, Palma omitted a Freesus tweet that said, "I'm not going to say where this list came from due to protecting sources but if this list is wrong then I invite @RonDeSantisFL to publicly state the books on this list will not be banned in Florida & he intends to protect student's rights. I will take it down if he does." This tweet occurred the day before Freesus claimed it was satire. It is possible that this anonymous Twitter account got caught spreading fake news and was trying to cover its tracks after unexpectedly going viral. Furthermore, the Freesus only added "satire" to his bio after receiving pushback.[21] The second problem is the uneven application of fact-checking standards. The only reason Snopes has a satire label is because they previously sought to fact-check *The Babylon Bee*. The difference between Freesus and *The Babylon Bee* should be obvious as the latter is an open Christian and conservative version of *The Onion*. The infamous example is Snopes giving *The Babylon Bee* a "false" rating for a story about CNN using an industrial washing machine to spin the news.[22] That an intangible object such as the news cannot be physically spun by a washing machine is self-evident, and Snopes was eventually forced to change their label.[23]

This is yet another example where we have conservatives and liberals being treated differently by the same website. In response to the 2016 election and all the concerns over disinformation, social media companies, such as Facebook and Twitter, started to work with fact-checkers to get fake news off their sites. For professional satirists such as *The Babylon Bee*, these rules could impact their bottom lines as they lose out on clicks and therefore ad revenue. Was that article such a threat to democracy that it originally deserved a false rating? Yet either because of liberal presuppositions or being scarred from the many fights with *The Babylon Bee*, Snopes labeled something as satire even though it was far from clear that was the case.

A similar example happened in March 2023 in a case involving the Media Research Center's Facebook page, which was hit with a "missing context" label that also declared, "Independent fact-checkers say this information could mislead people." The claim was not even original MRC content but rather a clip of Home Depot cofounder Bernie Marcus telling Fox News's Neil Cavuto, while commenting on Silicon Valley Bank, "These banks are badly run because everybody is focused on diversity and all of the woke issues and not concentrating on the one they should, which is shareholder returns." The MRC appealed the ruling to the Associated Press's fact-checking department pointing out that Marcus, who is an accomplished professional and not a cable news crazy person, was giving his opinion and that neither Marcus nor the MRC explicitly claimed SVB collapsed because of woke policies.

Editor Barbara Whitaker sent the MRC a response that argued that while Marcus never explicitly said woke policies were to blame for SVB's failure, the context of the segment being about that failure implies he believes they were. Whitaker also told the MRC that "you say that this is his opinion, but this was a news segment not an opinion piece. There is nothing to counter-balance what he said, leaving the reader to think those policies led to the bank's failure, hence the rating." The MRC sent back another email pointing out that not having balance is a routine feature of discussions on CNN and MSNBC, after which Whitaker directed the MRC to AP's communications department. Not only did the AP have a double standard, but Whitaker's LinkedIn profile lists the Center for Counter Digital Hate on her Interests section, which placed the MRC on their Toxic Ten list in 2021, which raises serious questions about her status as an unbiased and dispassionate fact-checker in this case.[24]

There is a saying that in politics, perception is reality. This is not so much a statement on facts themselves as it is about people and causes. The problem professional fact-checking claims to remedy is that right-leaning America and left-leaning America increasingly no longer live in a shared reality. Yet the very nature of contemporary fact-checking only serves to further exacerbate this growing tension. Consider the *Washington Post* study that found that Donald Trump had 30,573 "false or misleading claims" during his four years as president.[25] Liberals look at that number and see a president who not just lies but cynically and obsessively lies, and to an extent that goes beyond the typical political spin, exaggeration, and misrepresentation. Conservatives see that number and wonder what the definition of "misleading" is. If it does include typical spin, exaggerations, and misrepresentations, then is Trump really that different from Democrat presidents?

In 2019 Trump invited Clemson University's championship-winning football team to the White House, where the dinner menu consisted of a vast assortment of fast-food options. Reacting to a tweet that quoted Trump saying "they bought '1,000 burgers' for Clemson. 'It was piled up a mile high,'" the *Washington Post*'s Phillip Bump wrote, "FACT CHECK: At two inches each, a thousand burgers would not reach a mile high."[26] Perhaps Bump was being sardonic, but to many it did not come across that way. It came across as just another hit job. If Bump was trying to match a humorous situation with humor of his own, the reason it failed was because sarcasm does not always translate well in print and other Trump critics did not respond with humor. For example, *Rolling Stone*'s Ryan Bort used the L-word, "He was also lying. In the video, Trump notes the White House brought in 300 hamburgers for the event."[27] Figurative language is a part of everyday life. People say "a mile high" when they mean "very tall" or use numbers such as a hundred, a thousand, a million, or a billion when they mean "a lot." In one sense it does not matter if this particular case is one of the 30,573 because it appears to confirm that Trump critics were nitpicking and sensationalizing in order to reach a large number while also not having a comparison to other presidents.

FACT-CHECKING FACTS

The challenges to good fact-checking mentioned earlier are compounded further when one considers the legion of instances when fact-checkers simply get it wrong. Let us consider several extended examples of this. In 2015, Republican senator David Perdue criticized President Obama for the state of the military, arguing that the country is "about to have the smallest Army since before WWII, the smallest Navy since WWI and the smallest Air Force ever." PolitiFact's April Hunt responded by giving Perdue a "half-true" rating, claiming he was correct about the Air Force but wrong the Army and Navy. Her check did make legitimate points about the Army by citing 2015 numbers against pre-9/11 numbers, but the check of the Navy was completely wrong. Hunt reported that 2019 estimates projected "a fleet of 234 battle force ships . . . which compares to 231 deployable ships" in 1915, two years before the United States entered World War I. The fact-checker's job should be to do this simple numbers comparison, but Hunt went a step further by attempting to provide political context: "And our allies and foes alike have kept their word to the 1922 Washington Naval Conference, which limits the world's navies by tonnage as a solution to an early arms race. In other words, the Navy has been small since World War I not because of any single administration decision but due to a nearly century-old disarmament accord."[28]

The trouble with fact-checkers introducing their political interpretations into the mix is that they reflect not facts but selective interpretation of new facts that the fact checkers wish to emphasize and that may not even be facts at all. In our present case, the Washington Naval Treaty was terminated in 1936, five years before Pearl Harbor and thirteen years before David Perdue was born. The state of the Navy is therefore not what it is because the government's hands are tied by an arms control treaty but because of conscious decisions political leaders, Republicans and Democrats, have made, and fact-checks like this seek to immunize them from legitimate criticism. In short, in this case, Perdue was exactly right about the Navy and Hunt was wrong.

One cannot deny, whether liking or disliking President Trump, that he was the subject of plenty of emotional but not necessarily level-headed analysis. Fact-checkers should be the dispassionate referees between truth and fiction, but when the progressive Jewish group Bend the Arc tweeted in July 2020, "The President of the United States is campaigning for reelection with a Nazi symbol. Again," *USA Today*'s fact-checking department failed in its mission, rating the claim "true." The Trump campaign prop in question was a rightward-facing eagle clutching a circular American flag, which was compared to a rightward-facing eagle clutching a wreath with an enclosed swastika. The original article even pointed out that "the eagle is still used as the coat of arms for Germany today, without the swastika." It goes on to point out differences between the Trump and the Nazi logos: "The American eagle is also a bald eagle, whereas the Nazi eagle is depicted as an all-black bird. Germany's federal eagle is depicted as a black bird with a red beak and talons."[29] The backlash to the *USA Today* ruling was swift. Just because the Nazis used the eagle as a symbol does not mean that the eagle is a Nazi symbol. While *USA Today* changed their ruling to "inconclusive,"[30] they gave credence to a hyperpartisan Reductio ad Hitlerum and the fact that they conceded in the original check was wrong, at best. At worst, they looked partisan because the original check did include information that seemed to debunk the reductionist claim by Trump's critics.

In another instance, on September 28, 2022, Hurricane Ian struck Florida's Lee County, causing great destruction; additionally, lives were lost and some tried to blame the state for not issuing an evacuation order. Defending the state and county response was Governor Ron DeSantis, who told CNN, "But you know, 72 hours, they weren't even in the cone," the cone being the storm's projected path. PolitiFact's Yacob Reyes gave DeSantis a "mostly false" rating. In his check, Reyes noted, "But one of the county's barrier islands, Cayo Costa—where the Category 4 hurricane made landfall—appeared inside the cone on each of eight advisories from Sept. 25." Reyes also included an enhanced image of a map showing Cayo Costa barely inside the cone.[31]

Reyes was correct that Cayo Costa, and therefore Lee County, was included in the cone, but it was just barely inside. However, it would be outrageous for a police officer to give someone a ticket for only going half a mile an hour over the speed limit, but that is essentially what Reyes did by including an island that is mostly a state park. The few homes that are on the island are vacation homes and off the electrical grid.[32] The rating should have been "mostly true." A "mostly false" rating comes across as insincere nitpicking of a possible 2024 presidential candidate who was up for reelection with two months to go until Election Day.

If professional fact-checkers want readers, and especially distrustful conservatives, to agree that the truth is under assault, it is imperative that they get their own facts straight. It does not do anybody any good for somebody to declare that it is wrong to say 2+2=5 if their rebuttal is that 2+2=3. Most people understand that politicians lie, spin, and tell half-truths devoid of context; if fact-checkers get their facts wrong, however, people will naturally ask if they are really fact-checkers at all.

SEMANTICS

Is tə-mā′tō or tə-mă″tō the correct pronunciation of "tomato"? All possible jokes aside, the correct answer is that it does not matter. However, in politics, partisans will attempt to take the most insignificant triviality and turn it into a gaffe or lie or use it to question somebody's character or intelligence. However, when fact-checkers do it, they will naturally end up looking like just another partisan actor. In 2016, NBC News ran a fact-check of a debate between Donald Trump and Hillary Clinton. The topic was President Obama's "red line" regarding the use of chemical weapons by Syrian dictator Bashar al-Assad and NBC quoted Trump as saying, "First of all, she was there as secretary of state with the so-called line in the sand, which . . ." The check also quotes Clinton's rebuttal, "No, I wasn't. I was gone." NBC ruled them both wrong, but their check of Trump was less convincing: "It was a 'red line' that President Obama drew on the use of chemical weapons in Syria, not a 'line in the sand.'"[33] NBC never bothered to explain the functional difference between a "red line" and a "line in the sand," probably because there is none.

Likewise, when Democrats were trying to pass the Freedom to Vote Act in early 2022, Senate Minority Leader Mitch McConnell spoke out in opposition: "It's a sprawling takeover of our whole political system." Into this debate entered PolitiFact's Amy Sherman, who wrote the bill "would set uniform policies for voting by mail and in person in federal elections, as well as various aspects of election administration, such as audits of results. The bill would mandate some policies that are already used in many states, such as same-day voter registration." To many, the federal government mandating certain policies certainly sounds like a takeover, but McConnell was still given a "false rating" because while the federal government would mandate certain policies, the states would still be in charge of the running of elections: "'takeover' is a mischaracterization, because it would still leave intact many election administration powers held by state and local officials."[34] At worst, McConnell could be criticized for bad word choice, but even that is a stretch. If somebody takes away your decision-making authority by forcing you to change a policy but leaves you to implement the changes, that can still be credibly described as a "takeover." If fact-checkers are going to check words, they must ensure that their definitions are correct or else they are simply taking sides, another problem to which we now turn.

CHOOSING SIDES

There are at least two sides to every policy argument, and newspapers, magazines, and TV shows have people whose job it is to give their opinions as to which is best. This is a different task than being a fact-checker, whose job is to ensure that people are following the proper definitions of the facts in a particular case, not providing judgments about the facts, which is the function of the reader to provide. For instance, if two politicians were talking about food, fact-checkers would need to check how they were using the terms "pizza" and "pineapple" but not provide commentary on whether pineapple pizza is good or not. However, fact-checkers will frequently become food critics and pronounce judgment on the perceived correctness of an opinion.

In the same way that some food critics would try to argue that some types of pizza are better than others, some fact-checkers try to argue that some opinions and the policies derived from them are better than others. The Associated Press's Calvin Woodward tried to make such a point in a 2011 fact-check of a Republican primary debate on the question of Iran's nuclear program. He quoted Mitt Romney as saying, "The president should have built [a] credible threat of military action, and made it very clear that the United States of America is willing, in the final analysis, if necessary, to take military action to keep Iran from having a nuclear weapon." This is clearly an opinion about a policy, and there are not straight facts to check. Although the degree to which President Obama had or had not made a "credible threat of military action" could be debated, it is not something within the realm of a fact-checker's job. Nonetheless, Woodward's fact-check argued, "It is an open question whether the U.S., stretched thin by two long wars and a massive debt is in a position to make a credible threat of war against Iran right now. . . . The U.S. certainly has military force readily at hand to destroy Iran's known nuclear development sites in short order. This is highly unlikely, however, because of the strategic calculation that an attack would be counterproductive and ultimately ineffective, spawning retaliation against U.S. allies and forces in the region, and merely delaying eventual nuclear weapons development."[35] It would not be unreasonable for President Obama to state that bombing Iran would be an unwise move that could lead to problems that Romney downplayed or completely ignored, but not for a fact-checker to do so. Although some predictions about the future are better than others, they are still just predictions, which are opinions, not facts, but more on this later.

After the Supreme Court overturned *Roe v. Wade* in summer 2022, abortion became more of a campaign issue than it had been previously. During that year's campaign, Republicans would often counter charges that they were radicals by arguing that Democrats were the real radicals for not supporting any restrictions. Into this controversy stepped *Washington Post* fact-checker Glenn Kessler, who noted that "Republicans defend their allegations by pointing to votes these candidates cast for the Women's Health Protection Act, a bill that would have restored the right to abortion enshrined in *Roe v. Wade*, the 1973 case recently overturned by the Supreme Court. The legislation includes exceptions for the health of the mother, which Republicans describe as a loophole that puts no limit on when an abortion can take place."

This would appear to be a relatively straightforward check, either the legislation does what Republicans say or it does not, but Kessler moved beyond this and wrote, "the GOP attacks are disingenuous at best. They imply that late-term abortions are common—and that they are routinely accepted by Democrats. The reality, according to federal and state data, is that abortions past the point of viability are extremely rare. When they do happen, they often involve painful, emotional and even moral decisions."[36] Kessler's check does not include a rating, but it nevertheless reads like an opinion piece. It provides data showing the rarity of late-term abortions as well as why a woman may seek to obtain one, but it does not actually fact-check the Republican claims. Because virtually all laws passed by pro-lifers have health of mother exceptions, it is reasonable to assume that if Democrats still refuse to vote for late-term restrictions then the Republican claims have merit. If there is an inconsistency between a Democrat's stated position and the text of legislation they say they support, it is not the job of the fact-checker to come in to explain this by claiming nuance.

EXPERT SHOPPING

One way that fact-checkers seemingly avoid the insertion of their own opinions into their checks and to enhance credibility when researching a claim is to ask experts for their take. When done well, this can lead to fair and insightful results. However, improperly applied, this can also lead to "expert shopping" where experts on one side are cited and experts on the other are ignored or discredited, leaving just an opinion with the added fallacious appeal to authority. To return to the Freedom to Vote Act–McConnell controversy, Sherman interviewed Ilya Shapiro of the Cato Institute, who agreed with McConnell's assessment, only to swiftly ignore it by citing other experts saying the opposite,[37] thus justifying the original "false" ruling we reviewed in the Semantics section and raising the question why Shapiro was even asked to comment if PolitiFact was not going to give his expert opinion the same level of credence as the pro-FVA voices.

In another example using facts surrounding the US Navy, a 2016 fact-check of a Republican primary debate by Glenn Kessler and Michelle Ye Hee Lee lamented that they were forced once again to repeat this "zombie claim" that earned a "three Pinocchio claim in the 2012 presidential election." Kessler and Lee conceded that ship count "is the lowest count since 1916," but noted, "A lot has changed in 100 years, including the need and capacity of ships." The duo went on to quote Navy Secretary Ray Mabus and provide some commentary of their own: "'That's [ship count] pretty irrelevant. We also have fewer telegraph machines than we did in World War I and we seem to be doing fine without that. . . . Look at the capability. Look at the missions that we do.' Plus, the Navy is on track to grow to just over 300 ships, approximately the size that a bipartisan congressional panel has recommended for the current Navy."[38]

The problem of citing the Democratic Secretary of the Navy as an authoritative source to rebut Republican attacks on his job performance should be self-evident. Beyond this, however, is the substance. In naval circles, this debate is known as capability versus capacity, and while such an academic subject may not seem to have an obvious Republican versus Democrat angle, as we have seen, Republicans are, to oversimplify, believers in capacity while Democrats believe in capability.

Although Mabus and the *Post* claim numbers are close to irrelevant, the best ship in the world does not do you any good if it is at the bottom of the sea, lacks reinforcements, is tied up in port for maintenance, or on the other side of the world. In 2022, the French Navy ran a simulation for a modern high-intensity battle that showed this is anything but a "zombie claim." The exercise saw eight out of twenty ships sunk or put out of action. The French Navy's key takeaway from the simulation was that "this format [of ships] would likely be insufficient in the event of a high-intensity conflict."[39] It is true that the US Navy has more ships than the French, but that is not the point. The challenges the United States face are different and larger in scale than those of France. The debate between capability and capacity is one as old as navies themselves and will continue to be debated well into the future. The only thing that will change is the technology; for the *Washington Post* to simply declare a multigenerational debate over is journalistic malpractice, to do so by quoting a partisan actor on one side is a public disservice.

Beyond technical policy questions, there are the moral ones, but behind the most emotional political topics is a debate much less exciting than the morality of a policy: the meaning of words. What is fair? What is a fetus? What is marriage? And for PolitiFact's Daniel Funke and Mariam Valverde and Representative Marjorie Taylor Greene, what is gender?

When Funke and Valverde ran this article in March 2021, Greene was frequently in the news. Democrats had recently removed her from her House committee assignments for "conspiratorial" tweets and statements she made prior to being elected, but these remarks were not about the 1969 moon landing being faked or how jet plane chemtrails are full of government-sponsored mind-altering chemicals. Instead, it was something any mainstream conservative would have said. Greene had a sign that read, "There are TWO genders: male & female. 'Trust the science!'" Funke and Valverde responded by writing, "However, public health agencies, doctors and biologists say science is clear: Gender identity goes beyond male and female." To back up their assertion they quote professor of biological science Ignacio T. Moore, "Sex is a biological term, gender is a social construct" and clinical assistant professor Jason Rafferty, "A person's gender identity may be masculine, feminine, a combination of both or neither, or it may shift over time."[40] Of course, the meanings of words change over time into something less literal, but they do not, or should not, change because of politics. The entire conservative argument is that this is politicized junk science, that gender is a synonym or euphemism for sex, and what Rafferty described is simply one's personality.

Writing about the concept of "verbicide" or "the murder of a word," C. S. Lewis argued that words have the tendency to end up being "useless synonyms for *good* or for *bad*."[41] Lewis's own idea of gender could be complicated[42] and would leave both Greene and her critics unsatisfied, but as for PolitiFact, they should have included information on the history of the word "gender" and how it relates to "sex," especially because the latter now has different connotations than the strictly scientific rather than just simply citing the other side as authoritative or to pronounce judgment on transgenderism. This should have been a fact-check about etymology, not biology or political ideologies. They also stumbled into a false dichotomy where if Greene was wrong, then Moore and Rafferty were necessarily correct, which is ironic considering that is what they accused Greene of doing. Considering all the controversies surrounding Greene, PolitiFact also should have considered checking a more mainstream conservative making the same claim, not one most people are predisposed to think of as controversial.

In response to progressive demands that Democrats add additional justices to the Supreme Court, Senator Ted Cruz declared in 2021, "You didn't see Republicans when we had control of the Senate trying to rig the game." PolitiFact's Louis Jacobson and Brandon Mulder rated this claim "false." They wrote, "Legal experts were unimpressed with Cruz's assertion that Republicans didn't 'rig the game' with the Garland and Barrett nominations." One of these experts was legal studies and political science professor Paul M. Collins Jr., who alleged the rejection of Garland "involved an effort to temporarily alter the size of the court to advance the agenda of the Republican Party." Legal historian Paul Finkelman labeled it "political manipulation" and law professor Emily Berman declared it to be "rigging the game."[43]

When it comes to Collins's claims, the key word is "temporarily," the progressive goal of expanding the Court from nine to thirteen—which just happens to be the number that would have given liberals a Supreme Court majority—would be permanent or at least until Republicans reexpanded it to fifteen or some other number as a form of retribution. Finkelman may be correct, but politicians acting like politicians is not "rigging," any more than voting down a cabinet nominee is "rigging," which also means Berman is simply wrong. Cruz's statement is true and while voting for Amy Coney Barrett in 2020, but not Merrick Garland in 2016, may be described as "hardball," such moves did not change the rules. Not confirming judicial appointments of the other party's president is not new as Republicans who remembered Robert Bork and Miguel Estrada were quick to point out. Senate Republicans used their constitutional prerogative of advice and consent to reject Garland and confirm Barrett while keeping the number of justices at nine.

In May 2020, amid the COVID-19 pandemic, President Trump tweeted in part, "Vaccine work is looking VERY promising, before end of year." Whatever the reasons behind Trump's prediction, he ended up being correct, but that was in the future. When he made the claim, NBC wrote, "experts say the development, testing and production of a vaccine for the public is still 12 to 18 months off, and that anything less would be a medical miracle."[44] Trump is obviously not a doctor, and NBC's sources—Stanley Plotkin, Paul Offit, and Walter Orenstein—are doctors, but the check raises important points about fact-checking predictions. Predictions are not factual assertions, they are opinions. Even if Trump ended up being wrong, that would not count as a falsehood. Certainly, some predictions are better than others, but fact-checking predictions requires checks of the facts used to form opinions, not the final opinion itself. It is one thing to predict the horse with the longest odds will win the Kentucky Derby, it is another to predict a horse that is not even in the race will win. In the NBC article, author Jane Timm wrote, "While technically possible, [Orenstein] added, it is unlikely."[45] The trio of doctors should feel no shame in being wrong about vaccine timetables, the key is to simply admit that and keep these types of opinions in the opinion section.

NUMBERS DO NOT TELL THE WHOLE STORY

Numbers, it has been said, do not lie. However, they can be cherry-picked to the point where the truth gets buried or distorted to further advance certain preferred narratives. Readers come to fact-checkers to learn about the pressing issues of the day, but knowing that the data used to back up the claim is wrong or misleading requires additional knowledge that the casual reader is unaware is missing. For example, in June 2022, NPR ran a story under the headline "7 Persistent Claims about Abortion, Fact-Checked." One of these claims was "there is big support for ending *Roe* in America." The word count of the article meant that this claim, like the others, was given only a two-sentence response, "According to the Pew Research Center's polls, 37% of Americans want abortion illegal in all or most cases. But an even bigger fraction—around 6 in 10 Americans—think abortion should be legal in all or most cases."[46]

This fact-check, along with polls showing broad support for *Roe*, was also a common talking point in the media and Democratic Party about how extreme Republicans and the Supreme Court were on the issue. However, most moderates and those leaning right might have different ideas of what "most cases" means. Furthermore, when you asked about specific abortion restrictions, different results followed. NPR cited Pew, but their May survey complicates NPR's check. For example, bans for six weeks and after came in with 51 percent opposed, 26 in favor, and 19 said "it depends." For fourteen weeks—the Mississippi law before the Court was a fifteen-week ban—the results were 41 percent opposed, 33 percent in favor, and 22 percent undecided. A twenty-four-week ban—roughly the *Casey* precedent—polled 29 opposed, 48 percent in favor, and 18 percent undecided.[47] A headline saying 40 percent of Americans oppose the Mississippi law is quite different than one saying 60 percent, and that also does not take into consideration that what the average Mississippian supports is not necessarily the same thing as what the average American supports. These numbers also call into question all the media assertions that Americans support *Roe*, because pre-*Dobbs* polling, such as this, showed they supported policies that *Roe* did not allow.

SUGGESTIONS FOR INCREASING ACCURACY AND CREDIBILITY

Throughout this chapter we in no way are arguing that fact-checking is an unimportant endeavor. Well done, it can add to the accuracy and credibility of the news media; done poorly, it has the opposite effect. In life, the truth is often difficult to grasp. Answering one question often only results in more questions. In politics this is made more difficult by people with agendas that are not always altruistic. Still, fact-checking is not a useless form of journalism, but humility is the first necessary prerequisite for any fact-checker. Everyone has a bias, including fact-checkers and journalists, few of which identify as Republican or conservative. We tend to give the benefit of the doubt to people we like while treating those we do not like with suspicion. We are inclined to say things are true because we want them to be true and false because we want them to be false. To prove our seriousness we tend to cherry-pick information to fit moral conclusions in an attempt to show we are critical thinkers who did not arrive at a predetermined conclusion.

For every argument, there is a rebuttal. The key is to try to analyze the rebuttal in as dispassionate a way as possible. The best way to do this is to remember that opinions are based on facts. Fact-checkers should avoid taking positions on policy questions—from moral questions such as abortion to technical ones such as naval force structure. They can define terms, but be careful not to wade into politicized language for politicians and activists will always describe what they want as good and what their opponents want as bad. They can verify numbers, but be wary of extrapolating arguments based on those numbers. Poll results are what they are, but poll questions are not always worded in such a way that key insights can be obtained. They need to be consistent. If they are going to rate Republican hyperbole as false, they must do the same for Democrats. They must recognize the difference between legitimate and illegitimate predictions. A prediction for the time line of the availability of COVID vaccines is not the same as predicting that the election will be stolen. Finally, they can also verify that certain events did or did not happen, "Did so-and-so really say . . . "

When fact-checkers stray from a straightforward telling of the facts, trust in them declines. Democracy, at its best, is about arguments, not personalities. We would like to think the side with the better arguments is the side that wins. For this to happen, we do need a shared conception of reality. The problem is that fact-checkers will often conflate their interpretation of reality with reality itself. It is a *fact* that Donald Trump won the 2016 presidential election, it is an *opinion* to say that because of him we live in a posttruth political space. It is another *opinion* that this is hyperbolic, that politicians have been lying since the beginning of time and will continue to do so until the end of time. Certainly, Trump did not help himself after the 2020 election, but history did not begin in November 2020. When journalists claim he told tens of thousands of lies or mistruths, such a staggering number will naturally raise eyebrows, not just for Trump, but also for those checking him.

Trump aside, this chapter made the deliberate choice to cover many fact-checks of Republicans before 2016 and cite conservatives who were not big fans of Trump to hopefully make the point that one does not need to embrace conspiracy theories about the 2020 election or COVID-19 being a hoax to believe that professional fact-checking has a problem. When fact-checkers sound indistinguishable from liberal columnists, people will treat them as such. Conspiracy theories arise out of the alure of possessing some form of forbidden knowledge and a sort of unprincipled contrarianism to the "official" narrative. Years of blown credibility by fact-checking legitimate debate, predictions, and just being wrong made fact-checking impotent. Wolves are real, but crying wolf is the quickest way to get people to disbelieve in wolves. While good fact-checking will not eliminate conspiracy theories, it will certainly help keep them on the fringe.

NOTES

1. Christiane Amanpour, "Journalism Faces an 'Exisential Crisis in Trump Era,'" CNN, November 23, 2016, https://www.cnn.com/2016/11/23/opinions/christiane-amanpour-journalism-in-trump-era/index.html.

2. Neil Brown, "You Can Handle the Truth," PolitiFact, September 12, 2012, https://www.politifact.com/article/2012/sep/12/you-can-handle-truth/.

3. Jake Tapper, "President Obama Quotes Romney Pollster Dismissing Fact-checkers," ABC, August 29, 2012, https://abcnews.go.com/blogs/politics/2012/08/president-obama-quotes-romney-pollster-dismissing-fact-checkers.

4. Peter King interview by Soledad O'Brien, *Starting Point with Soledad O'Brien*, CNN, September 17, 2012, Transcript, http://www.cnn.com/TRANSCRIPTS/1209/17/sp.02.html.

5. Jonah Goldberg, "Politihacked," *National Review*, February 15, 2015, https://www.nationalreview.com/corner/politihacked-jonah-goldberg.

6. Tucker Higgins, "CNN Takes on White House Over Fake News Criticism: Apples Are Not Bananas," CNBC, October 23, 2017, https://www.cnbc.com/2017/10/23/cnn-tweets-that-apples-are-not-bananas-as-president-slams-fake-news.html.

7. George Kennan, "The Charge in the Soviet Union to the Secretary of State," February 22, 1946.

8. Neftali Bennett interview by Christiane Amanpour, *Amanpour*, CNN International, April 20, 2022, Transcript, https://transcripts.cnn.com/show/ampr/date/2022-04-20/segment/01.

9. Glenn Kessler (@GlennKesslerWP), "Maintaining the Trump database over four years required about 400 additional 8-hour days over four years beyond our regular jobs for three people. Biden is off to a relatively slow start but who knows what will happen. We will keep doing fact checks, just not a database," Twitter, April 26, 2021, https://twitter.com/GlennKesslerWP/status/1386867954927738887.

10. Adrian Blanco, Glenn Kessler, and Tyler Remmel, "The False and Misleading Claims President Biden Made during His First 100 Days in Office," *Washington Post*, April 30, 2021, https://www.washingtonpost.com/politics/interactive/2021/biden-fact-checker-100-days/.

11. Linda Qiu and Michael D. Shear, "Biden, Storyteller in Chief, Spins Yarns that Often Unravel, Leading to Criticism," *New York Times*, October 14, 2022, https://www.nytimes.com/2022/10/10/us/politics/biden-exaggeration-falsehood.html.

12. "Ted Cruz," PolitiFact, accessed March 20, 2023, https://www.politifact.com/personalities/ted-cruz/.

13. "Elizabeth Warren," PolitiFact, accessed March 20, 2023, https://www.politifact.com/personalities/elizabeth-warren/.

14. Tom Kertscher, "Record-Low Unemployment and Record-High Number of People Working Due to Scott Walker's Policies?," PolitiFact, April 18, 2018, https://www.politifact.com/factchecks/2018/apr/18/scott-walker/record-low-unemployment-and-record-high-number-peo/.

15. Dan Clark, "New York Has More Private Sector Jobs than Ever Before," PolitiFact, July 22, 2016, https://www.politifact.com/factchecks/2016/jul/22/andrew-cuomo/new-york-has-more-private-sector-jobs-ever/.

16. Tim Graham, "PolitiFact Whacks Scott Walker: Facts Correct, But You're 'Half True' (Cuomo, He's 'True')," *NewsBusters*, April 19, 2018, https://www.newsbusters.org/blogs/nb/tim-graham/2018/04/19/politifact-whacks-scott-walker-facts-correct-youre-half-true-cuomo.

17. Tom Kertscher, "Ga. Sen. David Perdue's Claim that Jon Ossoff Is a Socialist Is Pants on Fire," PolitiFact, November 23, 2020, https://www.politifact.com/factchecks/2020/nov/23/david-perdue/ga-sen-david-perdues-claim-jon-ossoff-socialist-pa/.

18. Amy Sherman and Louis Jacobson, "Georgia's Election Law Sparks 'Jim Crow' Rhetoric, as Well as Pushback," PolitiFact, April 30, 2021, https://www.politifact.com/article/2021/apr/30/georgia-election-law-comparable-jim-crow-democrats/.

19. Alex Christy, "Snopes Labels Viral DeSantis Book Banning Disinformation 'Satire,'" *NewsBusters*, August 23, 2022, https://www.newsbusters.org/blogs/nb/alex-christy/2022/08/23/snopes-labels-viral-desantis-book-banning-disinformation-satire.

20. Bethania Palma, "Is This a List of 'Banned Books in Florida Schools and Libraries'?," Snopes, August 22, 2022, https://www.snopes.com/fact-check/florida-book-bans-schools-libraries/.

21. Alex Christy, "Snopes Labels Viral DeSantis Book Banning Disinformation 'Satire,'" *NewsBusters*, August 23, 2022, https://www.newsbusters.org/blogs/nb/alex-christy/2022/08/23/snopes-labels-viral-desantis-book-banning-disinformation-satire.

22. David Mikkelson, "Did CNN Purchase an Industrial-Sized Washing Machine to Spin News?" Snopes, March 1, 2018, https://www.snopes.com/fact-check/cnn-washing-machine/.

23. Mikkelson, "Did CNN Purchase an Industrial-Sized Washing Machine to Spin News?"

24. Tim Graham, "LAME! AP 'Fact Check' Slaps 'Missing Context' on Our Facebook Page Over SVB Bank Failure," *NewsBusters*, March 24, 2023. https://www.newsbusters.org/blogs/nb/tim-graham/2023/03/24/lame-ap-fact-check-slaps-missing-context-our-facebook-page-over-svb.

25. Meg Kelly, Glenn Kessler, and Salvador Rizzo, "Trump's False or Misleading Claims Total 30,573 Over 4 Uears," *Washington Post*, January 21, 2021, https://www.washingtonpost.com/politics/2021/01/24/trumps-false-or-misleading-claims-total-30573-over-four-years/.

26. Philip Bump, "President Trump's Extravagant, $3,000, 300-Sandwhich Celebration of Clemson University," *Washington Post*, January 14, 2019, https://www.washingtonpost.com/politics/2019/01/15/president-trumps-extravagant-sandwich-celebration-clemson-university/.

27. Ryan Bort, "Supreme Leader Donald Trump Lies About Volume of Fast Food Hamburgers," *Rolling Stone*, January 15, 2019, https://www.rollingstone.com/politics/politics-news/trump-fast-food-white-house-779128/.

28. April Hunt, "Sen. Perdue Overstates Real Reduction in U.S. Armed Forces," PolitiFact, May 4, 2015, https://www.politifact.com/factchecks/2015/may/04/david-perdue/sen-perdue-overstates-real-reduction-us-armed-forc/.

29. Will Peebles, "Fact check: Trump Campaign Accused of T-shirt Design with Similarity to Nazi Eagle," *USA Today*, July 11, 2020, https://web.archive.org/web/20200712002923/https://www.usatoday.com/story/news/factcheck/2020/07/11/fact-check-trump-2020-campaign-shirt-design-similar-nazi-eagle/5414393002/.

30. Peebles, "Fact Check."

31. Yacob Reyes, "Most of Florida's Lee County Wasn't in the Cone Three Days Before Hurricane, but Parts of It Were," PolitiFact, October 4, 2022, https://www.politifact.com/factchecks/2022/oct/04/ron-desantis/most-floridas-lee-county-wasnt-cone-three-days-hur/.

32. Laura Ruane, "Cayo Costa Island: Why It Stays Wild," *News-Press*, October 30, 2015, https://www.news-press.com/story/news/2015/10/30/cayo-costa-island-why-stays-wild-florida-development-tourism-state-park-beaches/74796712/.

33. NBC News, "Both Candidates Wrong in Syria War Spat," NBC, October 9, 2016, https://www.nbcnews.com/card/both-candidates-wrong-syria-war-spat-n663401.

34. Amy Sherman, "Why It's Wrong to Call the Voting Rights Bill a Federal Takeover," PolitiFact, January 24, 2022, https://www.politifact.com/factchecks/2022/jan/24/mitch-mcconnell/why-its-wrong-call-voting-rights-bills-federal-tak/.

35. Calvin Woodward, "FACT CHECK: Misfires on Iran, China in GOP Debate," Associated Press, November 13, 2011, https://www.masslive.com/politics/2011/11/fact_check_misfires_on_iran_ch.html.

36. Glenn Kessler, "The GOP Claim that Democrats Support Abortion 'Up to Moment of Birth,'" September 9, 2022, https://www.washingtonpost.com/politics/2022/09/22/gop-claim-that-democrats-support-abortion-up-moment-birth/.

37. Sherman, "Why It's Wrong to Call the Voting Rights Bill a Federal Takeover."

38. Glenn Kessler and Michelle Ye Hee Lee, "Fact-Checking the 12th GOP Debate," *Washington Post*, March 11, 2016, https://www.washingtonpost.com/news/fact-checker/wp/2016/03/11/fact-checking-the-12th-gop-debate/.

39. Martin Manaranche, "Feedback on French Navy High Intensity Exercise POLARIS," *Naval News*, May 31, 2022, https://www.navalnews.com/naval-news/2022/05/feedback-on-french-navy-high-intensity-exercise-polaris/.

40. Daniel Funke and Miriam Valverde, "What the Equality Act Debate Gets Wrong about Gender, Sex," *PolitiFact*, March 4, 2021, https://www.politifact.com/article/2021/mar/04/what-equality-act-debate-gets-wrong-about-gender-s/.

41. C. S. Lewis, *Studies in Words* (New York: HarpeOne, 2013), 7, Kindle. Emphasis in the original.

42. C. S. Lewis, *The Space Trilogy, Omnibus Edition* (New York: HarperCollins, 2013), 530, Kindle.

43. Louis Jacobson and Brandon Mulder, "Ted Cruz's Dubious Claim that GOP Didn't 'Rig' SCOTUS Confirmations," PolitiFact, April 27, 2021, https://www.politifact.com/factchecks/2021/apr/27/ted-cruz/ted-cruzs-dubious-claim-gop-didnt-rig-scotus-confi/.

44. Jane Timm, "Fact Check: Coronavirus Vaccine Could Come This Year, Trump Says. Experts Say He Needs a 'Miracle' to Be Right," NBC, May 15, 2020, https:

//www.nbcnews.com/politics/donald-trump/fact-check-coronavirus-vaccine-could-come-year-trump-says-experts-n1207411.

45. Timm, "Fact Check."

46. Jaclyn Diaz, Koko Nakajima, and Nick Underwood, "7 Persistant Claims about Abortion, Fact-Checked," NPR, June 24, 2022, https://www.npr.org/2022/05/06/1096676197/7-persistent-claims-about-abortion-fact-checked.

47. Pew Research Center, "America's Abortion Quandray," Pew Research Center, May 6, 2022, https://www.pewresearch.org/religion/2022/05/06/americans-views-on-whether-and-in-what-circumstances-abortion-should-be-legal/.

Chapter 7

Guardians of the Galaxy

How the Media Stumbles When It Seeks to Protect Historically Underserved and Marginalized Communities, and Never More So than When Reporting on the Relationship between Blacks and Jews

Abe Aamidor

Allegations of media dereliction often point to negative representation of minorities, ethnic groups, and other historically underserved and marginalized groups in America.[1] Examples of such poor representation include an alleged emphasis on crime reporting and absentee fathers in inner-city neighborhoods that traffic in negative stereotypes of African Americans,[2] labeling immigrants at the southern border as "illegal" or "undocumented," and/or emphasizing the immigration status of an arrestee for an unrelated crime, thereby further stigmatizing such folks,[3] and even stories that engage in "fat shaming."[4]

Yet counterclaims that the media are sacrificing objectivity on the altar of improved representation, including demands for more diversity, equity, and inclusion, have only increased in recent years.[5] Evidence supporting these claims include NBC's online news site that has separate categories reserved specifically for news about Blacks, LGBTQ+, Asian Americans, and Latinos (typically, articles are about abuses committed against these groups or uplifting stories about successes in the face of adversity), and the stated policy of Gannett, the largest newspaper chain in the country, which was an early proponent of "mainstreaming," meaning the practice of adding more minority expert sources to comment *on* the news and including more minority representation *in* the news such as in feature stories, health reporting, or simply "man in the street" interviews.⁶

The claims and counterclaims are part of the culture wars, of course, including charges of "liberal bias" in the news and the age-old debate over advocacy journalism. For purposes of this chapter, I take it for granted that, *in general*, the mainstream media do look for ways to improve the representation of minorities, certain ethnic groups, and protected classes, whether de jure or de facto, including sometimes seeking to refute or suppress negative content that might otherwise cause harm to such groups, either as compensation for past biased reporting or to improve representation. As just one example, early in the Black Lives Matter movement, there were numerous articles in the media seeking to refute claims that so-called Black-on-Black crime was much worse than comparable numbers for White-on-White crime (they were only marginally worse),⁷ but that often ignored the crime *rates* in the two communities, which was the real issue. When the FBI's Uniform Crime Report data for comparative known murder offenders is referenced, Blacks commit close to 50 percent more murders than Whites,⁸ while recent census data show that the "Black/African American, alone" category makes up 13.6 percent of the population while "White, alone" makes up 59.3 percent of the population.⁹

Another example might be the treatment of "DREAMERS," those immigrants brought to the United States, apparently illegally, while they were still young. Any stories about DREAMERS now often show them as earnest, all-American kids who are training for impressive careers in such fields as medicine and computer science.¹⁰

Yet such tendentious reporting, to the extent that it exists and however well-intentioned it may be, creates a real dilemma for journalists. For example, how does the media handle tensions when they exist *between* two protected groups, what is sometimes called "interminority racism"? This might include tensions between Black inner-city residents and Korean Americans operating businesses in their neighborhoods. How does the media respond to rising levels of HIV in both the Black community and among gay men who engage in unprotected sex¹¹ while at the same time trying to combat both homophobia and racism? Or how does the media report on the obesity epidemic: Is good health reporting being sacrificed in the current push for "body positivity" and "size acceptance"? Reports linking obesity to early death, for example, irrespective of any other medical diagnosis, are rare even though reliable government estimates put the number at approximately 300,000 annually,¹² or three times the number of annual opioid overdose deaths in recent years, which are widely reported in the media. The suspicion, again, is that representation is more important than actual reporting.

Yet the most fraught area for the media when reporting on minorities, ethnicities, or protected classes (getting stuck in the quicksand of identity politics) is when Blacks and Jews clash. This historic animosity came to the fore in late 2022 when Ye, the entertainer more commonly known as Kanye West, made statements that seemed to glorify Adolf Hitler and essentially accused "the Jews" of controlling Hollywood, not merely being influential there. Of all the traps the media has set for itself when acting to protect minorities and other groups from harm and to improve representation, none is more evident than when reporting on conflict between Blacks and Jews.

An old journalism ethic calls for reporting the news and "letting the chips fall where they may," which in this context means reporting the news without worrying about whom it helps or hurts. It is the view of this chapter that the media has largely abandoned such a principle when it comes to reporting on minorities, ethnic groups, and protected classes, whether de jure or de facto. I believe this is because the mainstream media has assigned itself a role not merely of combating racism, homophobia, xenophobia, and so on but of improving representation of various groups. Yet such a policy ultimately fails because some of the protected classes are themselves at each other's throat, which forces the media to choose between them or ignore the underlying tensions altogether.

In the remainder of this chapter, I examine this situation in four main parts: (1) Tensions, (2) We Blacks and Jews, (3) The Great Replacement Theory, and (4) Thoughts and Solutions.

TENSIONS

Reporting on the Jews remains problematic for the media. This may seem a surprising claim because stories about Holocaust survivors, as well as acknowledgment of the internationally recognized Holocaust Remembrance Day, are now routine, and Jews have been prominent in the media and entertainment industry for decades. Yet the rising tide of hate crimes against Jews, both in America and in Europe, were not commonly reported in the American mass media before the Tree of Life synagogue massacre in Pittsburgh in 2018 that killed eleven worshippers. And they were not much reported afterward even as they surpassed all other hate crimes based on race, religion, sexual orientation, or ethnicity in America except those committed against African Americans, according to the FBI's "Supplement to 2021 Hate Crime Statistics,"[13] the latest available as this chapter is being written. For example, more than 51 percent of all hate crimes *based on religion* were committed against Jews, more than all other hate crimes based on religion combined, even though Jews are only 2 percent of the US populations.

African Americans continue to be the largest target overall, however, with 2,229 incidents reported, or about 30 percent of all hate crimes based on race, ethnicity, or gender, according to the FBI's Crime Data Explorer.[14] Anti-White crimes accounted for 948 incidents, with lesser totals in descending order for antigay (male); anti-Asian; anti-Hispanic or Latino; and antilesbian, gay, bisexual, or transgender (mixed group). The FBI data cited here are based on data received from 11,883 of 18,812 law enforcement agencies in the country for 2021, so cannot be considered complete. Data on anti-Asian hate crimes were interpolated from a separate Department of Justice database, cited in the previous paragraph.

Before I turn to reporting on tensions between Blacks and Jews, which I have indicated is a priority in my analysis, it may be instructive to see how the media—again, in general—report on tensions between Blacks and Asian Americans, which have a history in this country that in part mirrors the Jewish experience, namely that are rooted in each group's alleged business practices in Black neighborhoods. Just as Jewish Americans in the past were criticized for doing business in Black neighborhoods without reinvesting in those communities, many Asian American (particularly Korean American) businesspeople have faced the same issues. Yet when Black and Asian American tensions have been acknowledged in the media the emphasis has been either on efforts of the two groups to work together to fight the racism that afflicts them both,[15] or they argue that any Black hostility is a result of anti-immigrant sentiment that Blacks have internalized and negative stereotypes of Blacks that Asian Americans have internalized, as well as economic competition that divide the two communities. Here is an excerpt from a recent report by *Vox*, not an obscure news site, that talks up the economic competition between the two groups while at the same time blaming reporting by others for any suggestion that there are underlying tensions between Blacks and Asian Americans:

> What also isn't new in times of anti-Asian sentiment is the focus on relationships between Black and Asian communities. Many of the attacks that have gained widespread attention have featured Black assailants and have threatened to inflame tensions between Asian Americans and Black Americans. While *Vox* found no evidence that Black Americans are predominantly responsible for this rise in attacks, or that they are particularly hostile to Asian Americans relative to the rest of the population, *the narrative of Black-Asian hostility is rooted in immigration and economic policies that have historically pitted these communities against one another.*[16]

Yet much of the tension between the Asian American and Black communities is, in fact, rooted in exactly what is behind much of Black anti-Semitism historically—many Blacks do not like other people making money in their community, then taking it home with them. For the media to acknowledge this, however, puts them at risk of making Asian Americans look bad, thereby violating a commitment to improve representation of *them*. To the credit of *Vox*, one source quoted in the same article cited earlier is quite candid about the parallels between Asian American and Jewish American businesses in Black neighborhoods:

> Edward T. Chang, a professor of ethnic studies at the University of California Riverside, explained the "middleman minority" theory, which helps further explain the tensions that arose at these Korean-owned businesses.
>
> "'Middleman minority' is a term derived from the historical experiences of Jews in Europe and Chinese in Southeast Asia and Asian Indians in Africa," Chang told Vox. "Middlemen minorities exist between dominant and subordinate groups in society and often hold professions heavily concentrated in the retail and service industries like grocery markets and liquor stores," he explained.[17]

The "middleman" is the businessman operating in Black neighborhoods, of course, and these often were Jews in major American cities, especially New York and Brooklyn, until the mid-twentieth century, but also Chicago, where I largely grew up, and other major metropolitan areas, while being largely replaced by Korean Americans as well as Arab Americans more recently. Besides being "middlemen" (which includes not being fully accepted by the dominant culture, yet not as low in the hierarchy as Blacks), the Jews could invoke "ethnic succession" in their defense. Ethnic succession is a theory that holds that groups lower on hierarchy move up both socioeconomically and into better neighborhoods as groups ahead of them move up, which is what opens up space for them. Mostly East European Jews around the time of the early twentieth century moved up this way as various mainstream American groups that were ahead of them moved up and sold their real estate holdings (and sometimes small family businesses) to the Jews. But when the Jews were ready to take a further step up the ladder the only group behind them were African Americans, who were cash poor. Hence, Jews may have moved out of the old neighborhoods but began renting out their old properties to Blacks, earning the sobriquet "slum landlords," and continued to operate small businesses (such as furniture stores, clothing stores and—yes—pawnshops) while commuting from afar. Asian Americans, as well as Arab Americans, were not much part of this ethnic succession scenario but opened up businesses simply as opportunities arose without necessarily ever having lived in the affected neighborhoods.[18]

Jewish Americans seem to infrequently own stores or rental property in Black neighborhoods today. The great African American writer James Baldwin wrote the groundbreaking essay on Jews doing business in Black neighborhoods in 1967 titled "Blacks Are Anti-Semitic Because They're Anti-White," which is easily searchable on the internet. In it, Baldwin writes of growing up in Harlem and watching Jewish landlords coming around weekly to collect the rent or having to buy on credit from Jewish store owners. He uses the word "hate" freely in the essay but also condemns social workers, police, and teachers regardless of race for the way they allegedly treated people in poorer African American neighborhoods, and he separately condemned more odious anti-Semitism among some other Blacks.[19]

Although there have been other prominent Black artists and leaders who were anti-Semitic, leading the charge against the Jews has been the leader of the current iteration of the Nation of Islam, which was originally founded in Detroit in 1930. The group drew upon certain Islamic principles but was not in fact part of the organized Islamic faith. It was racialist at its core, arguing that White people were the devil, and held certain other novel views, including the heretical view that its founder, Wallace Fard Muhammad, was the personification of God, and that Elijah Muhammad was his "messenger." Elijah Muhammad's son, Warith Deen Mohammed (sometimes spelled Muhammad), assumed leadership of the group after his father's death in 1975 and effectively disbanded it, distancing himself from the heretical beliefs inherent in the Nation of Islam, and he aligned himself and his followers with mainstream Islamic beliefs and practices. However, in 1977 a New York–based leader named Louis Farrakhan inaugurated a *new* Nation of Islam and accelerated his attacks on Jews, often singling out Hollywood for racism or blaming the slave trade primarily on Jews, as well as occasionally calling them vermin and termites and the like. I mention all this not as a history lesson but because mainstream media have frequently publicized Farrakhan, for better or worse, while largely ignoring the much more moderate, and more popular in terms of actual membership, Warith Deen Mohammed, the true heir to the Nation of Islam who saw the original movement for what it was and had the courage to take it toward mainstream Islam, as Malcolm X himself had done a year prior to his assassination. All that Farrakhan did was continue Malcolm X's earlier anti-Semitism while garnering the admiration of some leading Black artists and activists for his Black nationalism and—possibly—his outspoken anti-Semitism.

The media occasionally will credit Farrakhan for preaching self-reliance and entrepreneurship by Blacks,[20] but in so doing has almost completely forgotten the pioneering post–Civil War leader Booker T. Washington, founder of the Tuskegee Institute and author of *Up from Slavery*, a wildly popular book across the racial divide in the mid- and late nineteenth century. Washington also helped organize the National Negro Business League and preached self-reliance decades before Farrakhan, yet he was accused of being "the great accommodator" by critics to his left, including after his death in 1915.

The veritable suppression of Booker T. Washington's story, or that of Warith Deen Mohammed, even the early Black Panther leader and author of *Soul on Ice* Eldridge Cleaver, does suggest a corollary to my thesis that the media seeks to improve the representation of African Americans—the media (again, in the aggregate and on average) may have gone so far as to assign itself the right to choose just who are the authentic Black leaders, or perhaps the media is taking its cues from truly far-left Progressives who want nothing to do with a Booker T. Washington or Warith Deen Mohammed, and certainly not Eldridge Cleaver, who later renounced militancy, embraced Christianity, and joined the Republican Party.

WE BLACKS AND JEWS

Downplaying anti-Semitism by notable Black Americans continues, including the protection afforded Alice Walker, the Pulitzer Prize–winning author of the bestselling *The Color Purple*. What did Ms. Walker do? In 2018, she promoted a wildly anti-Semitic book in an interview in the *New York Times Book Review*. The book she touted, *And the Truth Shall Set You Free* by British author David Icke, claims that Jews *funded* the Holocaust in Europe as well as the Ku Klux Klan in America, among other accusations.[21]

Yet Walker had praised Icke's conspiracy theories years earlier, and in 2017, a year before the *New York Times Book Review* interview was published, she posted online a poem that repeatedly accused the Jewish Talmud of countenancing child intercourse, rape, murdering non-Jews, and of condemning Jesus to death, in other words, deicide. The Talmud is a collection of up to thirty-eight books, dozens of tractates, and thousands of pages, mostly commentary on mundane matters of Jewish law, that was written, edited, and interpretated over centuries, and parts of the collection can be viewed as written in the face of fierce anti-Jewish oppression, Jewish exile, and that Christ-killing charge. It was only after the *New York Times Book Review* interview was published, however, that a wider journalistic audience took note of Walker's anti-Semitic positions. Even at that, much of the coverage treated Walker delicately while generally focusing on David Icke, and the controversy quickly petered out.

Other current Black artists implicated in making strong anti-Semitic statements and advancing antisemitic conspiracy theories include rapper and producer Ice Cube and entertainer Nick Cannon.[22] Cannon later apologized for his indiscretion and said he would be learning more about anti-Semitism and the Holocaust going forward. But perhaps the most notable anti-Semitic Black artist in the twentieth century was the poet, playwright, and Black nationalist Amiri Baraka ("I got the extermination blues, Jewboys. I got the Hitler syndrome figured," being his most threatening meme, which you can find online). Shortly after the 9/11 terrorist attacks on the World Trade Center in New York City, he also wrote, "Who knew the World Trade Center was gonna get bombed / Who told 4,000 Israeli workers at the Twin Towers / To stay away that day / Why did [Ariel] Sharon stay away?"[23]

The Rev. Jessie Jackson, during his run for president in 1984, called New York City "Hymietown" and referred to Jews collectively living there as "Hymie." He linked his comments to an anti-Zionist, or anti-Israel, stance. Here is the full quote: "That's all Hymie wants to talk about is Israel; every time you go to Hymietown, that's all they want to talk about."[24] These terms are rather old-fashioned antisemitic slurs and hardly the most offensive, and it is clear Jackson was speaking in the context of Jewish support for Israel when Black activists already were much in the pro-Palestinian camp. The way the mainstream media reacted to the incident is what is germane to this chapter, however. A thorough and well-sourced report by the Institute for National Security Studies at Tel Aviv University found that although the remarks were made in January 1984, it was only the next month that the *Washington Post* reported on them, but in a small article in its back pages, and that the *Post* only later issued a "scathing" editorial calling on Jackson to explain his choice of words. Furthermore, it was discovered that several veteran journalists had heard Jackson make the remarks in real time but never reported on them at all.[25] This is all consistent with my thesis that mainstream media seeks to improve representation of protected classes but struggles when two protected classes are in conflict with each other, especially if the groups involved are Blacks and Jews.

Additional evidence suggesting that mainstream media stumbles when presented with evidence of possible anti-Semitism by Black or other minority activists emerged in the delayed reporting of anti-Jewish rhetoric within the 2019 Women's March that ultimately forced Linda Sarsour (an Arab American), Tamika Mallory (an African American and acolyte of Louis Farrakhan), and Bob Bland (a gay and lesbian rights activist) to step down from their leadership positions within the organization.[26]

Again, the purpose of this chapter is not to document anti-Semitism but to show how difficult it can be for the media to report on conflict between protected classes (whether de jure or de facto), and especially if the conflict involves Blacks and Jews. In the case of the three Women's March cochairs (who all later made statements denouncing anti-Semitism), the controversy seems not to have been covered by the mainstream media until *Tablet*, a Jewish-oriented publication, pointed out alarming statements made by the organizers.[27]

As part of my research for this chapter I came across the transcript of a curious NPR interview with Marc Dollinger, a self-professed Jew and author of *Black Power, Jewish Politics: Reinventing the Alliance in the 1960s*.[28] Near the top the interviewer, Leah Donnella, a biracial Jew, declares that "black nationalism" has been misconstrued as "black anti-Semitism." I immediately saw this claim for it what was, a false dichotomy, because a person can be both a Black nationalist and an antisemite, or one and not the other, or neither. It is not a question of "either or."

In the body of the Dollinger interview, the book author declares that virtually everything people think about Jewish support for the civil rights movement in the 1950s and 1960s is wrong. Everything? Two of the three civil rights workers murdered in Mississippi in June 1964 were Jewish; Thurgood Marshall's right-hand man at the NAACP Legal Defense Fund for many years was a Jew, Jack Greenberg; in the front line with Dr. Martin Luther King Jr. in the famous march from Selma to Montgomery on March 21, 1965, was Rabbi Abraham Joshua Heschel, a strong and well-known supporter of the civil rights movement at the time (yet who was essentially written out of Ava DuVernay's well-received 2014 movie *Selma*). Even Malcolm X conceded that Jews once had a leading role in the civil rights movement, though he still hated the lot of them. This hardly means all Jews were on board with civil rights for African Americans—that would be a myth—but I have to ask whom NPR was trying to please by turning history on its head?

THE GREAT REPLACEMENT THEORY

As much as I find most media subject to a self-imposed duty to improve representation for various groups, to protect them from harm, it is instructive to note how so many in the media were late to acknowledge that the "great replacement theory," which alleges there is a conspiracy to replace or beat down White people via immigration, is linked to extreme antisemitic narratives. But it was never a secret. Indeed, this fact was evident during the highly publicized "Unite the Right" rally in Charlottesville, Virginia, in August 2017 in which a prominent chant was, "The Jews will not replace us," meaning the Jews were engineering immigration policies for the purpose of controlling America indirectly. This was hardly emphasized in the media at the time, however. The rally was in part a protest against the removal of

Confederate monuments after the 2015 murder of nine African Americans in their church by a White nationalist in Charleston, South Carolina; the march included many Nazi and Confederate battle flags and was widely understood to be a neo-Nazi, White nationalist, and White supremacist rally. But the anti-Semitic nature of "great replacement theory" in America—it meant something a bit different in France a century ago, where the theory originated[29]—was not more widely acknowledged until statements were made by controversial former Fox News personality Tucker Carlson that *seemed* to endorse the theory, suggesting that the media, collectively speaking, was not so much interested in protesting anti-Semitism as it was in building a case against Carlson.

I have italicized *seemed* in the previous paragraph because I am not yet convinced that Carlson, whatever his other sins may be, really believes White people face some kind of existential threat in this country as do the hardcore "great replacement theory" types and, indeed, he has been explicit in saying that he is talking only about being overwhelmed at the ballot box, thereby affecting the political process. "Every time they import a new voter, I become disenfranchised as a current voter," Carlson said in one broadcast. "Everyone wants to make a racial issue out of it. Oh, you know, the white replacement theory. No, no, no. This is a voting rights question. I have less political power because they're importing a brand-new electorate. Why should I sit back and take that?"[30]

Anecdotal evidence supporting Carlson's disclaimer can be found in my personal experience as an undergraduate at the University of Chicago in the late 1960s, one of a handful of radical college campuses historically, though less so today. It was a standard position of New Left activists, including members of Students for a Democratic Society whom I knew, to call for full citizenship for migrant workers in the country as part of support for Cesar Chavez and the United Farm Workers, which I thought was entirely correct, but also more immigration from Central America for the specific purpose of moving the American political landscape to the left. Additionally, calls were made for more immigration from Arab countries to help change US foreign policy vis-à-vis Israel and the Palestinians. Compare this goal to the old Soviet practice of moving Russian-speaking citizens into the formerly captive Baltic States as well as Ukraine, of course, or the People's Republic of China's practice of moving ethnic Han Chinese into Buddhist Tibet and mostly Muslim Xinjiang province. Forcing a change in demographics is always a political tactic. In fairness, it must be acknowledged that Israel is following the same practice by moving hundreds of thousand Jewish Israelis into the partly occupied West Bank in recent decades.

By 2022, however, in the wake of the Tucker Carlson controversy, it has become more common to identify and explain "great replacement" theory in the media. Here's an excerpt from Reuters that is typical, this time in connection with the Buffalo, New York, Tops supermarket mass murders in May 2022: "The [great replacement] conspiracy theory fosters the belief that leftist and Jewish elites are engineering the ethnic and cultural replacement of white populations with non-white immigrants that will lead to a 'white genocide.' According to this belief, the cabal of political and business elites would be kept in power by the masses of indebted non-whites."[31]

Linking "great replacement" theory to anti-Semitism is now part of the media narrative, but attacking anti-Semitism may now also be a way to go after conservative and right-wing politicians and media, not as a way of actually protesting anti-Semitism. As an example, several media reports documented remarks made by House GOP candidate Carl Paladino, who in 2021 had called Hitler "the kind of leader we need today" and lauded the dictator's ability to mesmerize crowds.[32] Republican congresswoman Marjorie Taylor Greene (GA-14) has been widely condemned for comparing COVID-19 restrictions to treatment of Jews in Nazi Germany, and Donald Trump himself allegedly praised Adolf Hitler to his then–White House Chief of Staff John Kelly, allegedly saying, "Hitler did a lot of good things," though a Trump spokesman at the time vigorously denied he had ever said such a thing.[33] Either way, any politician who expresses any level of support for, or appreciation of, Adolf Hitler can be attacked by pointing out just what Hitler and the Nazis did to the Jews, which again suggests that the media—a generalization, to be sure—sometimes discovers anti-Semitism when it is convenient to use against other media elites or politicians deemed to be undesirable, but not necessarily because the media is protecting the Jews in the same way it seeks to protect other minorities, ethnic groups, and marginalized people.

A major problem for mainstream media in exposing anti-Semitism is that Jews, for the most part, do not fit the BIPOC template, that is, Black, Indigenous, and people of color. The highly publicized February 2022 controversy involving Whoopi Goldberg, cohost of the popular daytime ABC television show *The View*, who claimed the Holocaust was not about race because Jews are White, helps make the point. Editorial writers across the media landscape jumped on Goldberg's remarks, and she was suspended for two weeks, yet she was just expressing what many people, Blacks included, have long believed. It was at the core of what James Baldwin, quoted earlier, wrote about Jews.

THOUGHTS AND SOLUTIONS

There always is a danger when advancing any thesis to glom on to evidence that supports it, whether due to confirmation bias or "motivated research."

With literally hundreds, if not thousands, of sources to choose from, it is not difficult to find *something* that will support the thesis being advanced. Then there is the special problem of effectively weighting the influence of one media outlet over another. For my graduate thesis at Southern Illinois University–Carbondale I focused on the *New York Times* and its coverage of the Arab-Israeli conflict (as it was more commonly known at the time) because of the prominence of that newspaper. Today, with multiple media outlets covering the ongoing conflict, including many that are overtly partisan, it is challenging to know where one should look first. There are, of course, academic studies and treatises, but they often are either so narrowly focused as to be useless for drawing broader conclusions or they are themselves tendentious, meant to support one side or the other but not to educate or elucidate. Besides, I wanted to survey the media landscape on my own. And what I have discovered is that many in the media really have assigned themselves the role of improving representation of, and protection for, various groups, something that is not quite the same as liberal bias or advocacy journalism but more like making amends for past wrongs, either the media's own reporting or crimes by past oppressors (usually held to be a White heterosexual patriarchy at home and European imperialists everywhere, but that must wait for another study). What I have also discovered is that there is a hierarchy or ranking of protected classes, which shows up both in which groups get the most attention, as well as when one group is in conflict with another, but most strikingly when Black interests are seen in conflict with Jewish interests. Improving representation, righting historic wrongs, and protecting specific groups from harm may seem like a moral imperative to a new generation working in the media today, but it is not journalism. As evidence that even some in the so-called liberal media have been rethinking their role by 2022, one only has to look at the changes at CNN, what really was once "the most trusted name in news," and the demand by its former CEO, Chris Licht, to make the cable news network both less sensationalistic and less partisan.[34]

If I am correct in my analysis, then what suggestions can be made to correct or improve the news going forward? I would urge that opposing views and alternate hypotheses be included in every story. The Federal Communications Commission once had a "fairness doctrine" that mandated all licensed TV and radio stations offer airtime to opposing views whenever an editorial position was being advanced by the outlet. It is not a coincidence that partisan reporting increased after its demise in 1987, though surely the plethora of new cable and then online news sites allowed consumers of news to choose outlets that already were telling them what they wanted to hear.

Then there is the concept once known as "the quality control function of free speech and freedom of the press," per my thesis adviser, Stuart Bullion, at Southern Illinois University–Carbondale, something that was relevant to the liberalization of the former Soviet Union in its late stages. Communist and far-left doctrine never accepted that there is such a thing as a free press (A. J. Liebling's famous quote that "freedom of the press is guaranteed only to those who own one" summed up the belief neatly enough), but a more pragmatic approach accepted that criticism and opposing views in the media could be useful, even in state-controlled media. Imagine if Toyota refused to listen to engineers who said there was a design flaw in one of its cars, or refused to countenance feedback in the marketplace—it would not be the large car manufacturer it is today. Popular fact-checking news sites offer some of this quality control, but we are still left with the age-old problem of "Who judges the judges?"

Imagine how much better reporting of the recent COVID-19 pandemic would have been if mainstream media had not adopted a public service model, trying to tell us what is good for us, and instead had more frequently cited perfectly reputable scientists who questioned official policy on masking, lockdowns, and even the efficacy and risks involved with the new vaccines, or if the media had reported more fully on advanced, democratic countries such as Sweden, which did not follow our stringent policies on COVID-19 yet seem to have fared no worse than us. Imagine how much more clarity could have been brought to understanding the origins of the pandemic if the media were not so intent on proving that former President Trump was a racist when he contemptuously and unfortunately referred to SARS CoV-2, the virus that causes COVID-19, as "the China virus." Most in the media seemed to beat the drums for the claim that there was "no evidence" the virus emerged from a lab in Wuhan, China. In fact, there was no compelling evidence it came from anywhere else, either, if one were to play the same rhetorical game. What did exist was the Chinese government's refusal to allow any fully independent inquiry on its territory into the source of the outbreak—that was reported, yet most in the media accepted the unproven claim that the virus came via a Wuhan market. They just had to be agnostic on the issue, but generally were not.

Additionally, we may ask how the media is reporting on trans rights. For the most part "the lead" has been that trans boys and girls face discrimination, are more likely to die by suicide, and that gender, not biology, represents the "authentic" self. Some stories talk about "firsts" for trans people in the same way that they talk about "firsts" for Blacks and women in various fields. Transgender people, trans rights, and transphobia are all newsworthy, of course. But instead of merely acting to protect trans people and trans rights, better reporting would have included documented evidence of the harm that may come from hormone treatments and surgeries when gender transitioning.[35] This was largely left to conservative media and some independent scientists and columnists to raise red flags, but mostly the coverage has simply been to protect trans people.

I try to follow the Ukraine war from all sides. The pro-Russian online site I follow in America (RT.com), which is in fact Russian state media, is full of distortions and lies, including appeals to right-wing American populism, but also contains occasional wire stories or politically neutral features. Germaine to this chapter, however, is the fact that it does represent the Russian position on NATO expansion since the fall of the Soviet Union in 1991 and its suspicions about American support for Ukraine. What to do about those lies and distortions? It should be up to other media outlets, journalists, and their sources to cite authoritative sources in their rebuttals—that is the quality control function of free speech and freedom of the press again.

Nothing I have written here should suggest ignoring racism, Islamophobia, transphobia, anti-Semitism, and more. The media should continue to report on all of it, but not to the extent of downplaying misconduct within any of the groups or becoming so obsessed with representation that the news begins to look promotional. This may mean being harder on Black activists who are proven to be anti-Semitic, or harder on Israel for its continued occupation of parts of the West Bank or violence against Gazans, or about the continuing relationship between unprotected sex and AIDS[36] even if this might cause "harm" to the gay community. Absent any meaningful improvement in media performance, however, I can only recommend that consumers of news access multiple sources on any contentious news item or trend, that they challenge everything and everyone equally, and that they be prepared to take some serious heat if they reach unpopular conclusions.

NOTES

1. Katti Gray, "The Racial Divide on News Coverage," Knight Foundation/Journalism, September 25, 2020, https://knightfoundation.org/articles/the-racial-divide-on-news-coverage-and-why-representation-matters/.

2. Elizabeth Sun, "The Dangerous Racialization of Crime in U.S. News Media," Center for American Progress, August 29, 2018, https://www.americanprogress.org/article/dangerous-racialization-crime-u-s-news-media/; and Tracy Jan, "News Media Offers Consistently Warped Portrayal of Black Families, Study Finds," *Washington Post*, December 12, 2017, https://www.washingtonpost.com/news/wonk/wp/2017/12/13/news-media-offers-consistently-warped-portrayals-of-black-families-study-finds/.

3. Jonathan Kwan, "Words Matter: Illegal Immigrant, Undocumented Immigrant, Unauthorized Immigrant," Markkula Center for Applied Ethics at Santa Clara University, February 2021, https://www.scu.edu/ethics/focus-areas/immigration

-ethics/immigration-ethics-resources/immigration-ethics-blog/words-matter-illegal-immigrant-undocumented-immigrant-or-unauthorized-immigrant/.

4. Amanda Ravary et al., "Shaping the Body Politic: Mass Media Fat-Shaming Affects Implicit Anti-Fat Attitudes," *Personality and Social Psychology Bulletin*, April 14, 2019, https://pubmed.ncbi.nlm.nih.gov/30982402/ (subscription required).

5. Bernard Goldberg, "No Liberal Bias in the Media? Who Is Chuck Todd Kidding, Besides Himself?" *The Hill*, August 16, 2021, https://thehill.com/opinion/campaign/567748-no-liberal-bias-in-the-media-who-is-chuck-todd-kidding-besides-himself/; and "Gallup/Knight Poll. Americans' Concerns about Media Bias Deepen, even as They See It Vital for Democracy," Knight Foundation, August 4, 2020, https://knightfoundation.org/press/releases/gallup-knight-poll-americans-concerns-about-media-bias-deepen-even-as-they-see-it-as-vital-for-democracy/.

6. Tom Witosky, "Mainstreaming and Diversity Are Gannett's Core Values," Nieman Reports, accessed February 15, 2023, https://niemanreports.org/articles/mainstreaming-and-diversity-are-gannetts-core-values/#:~:text=Executives%20at%20Gannett%20define%20%E2%80%9Cmainstreaming,minority%20expert%20on%20the%20topic.

7. Camille Caldera, "Fact Check: Rates of White-on-White and Black-on-Black Crime Are Similar," *USA Today*, September, 29, 2020, https://www.usatoday.com/story/news/factcheck/2020/09/29/fact-check-meme-shows-incorrect-homicide-stats-race/5739522002/.

8. Crime in the United States, "Expanded Homicide Data Table: Murder Offenders by Age, Sex, Race and Ethnicity, 2019," https://ucr.fbi.gov/crime-in-the-u.s/2019/crime-in-the-u.s.-2019/tables/expanded-homicide-data-table-3.xls.

9. United States Census Bureau, "Quick Facts," accessed February 13, 2023, https://www.census.gov/quickfacts/fact/table/US/RHI225221.

10. Jeremy Raff, "DACA Med Students Face Uncertain Future," *The Atlantic*, September 2017, https://www.theatlantic.com/health/archive/2017/09/daca-med-students-face-uncertain-futures/538695/.

11. Centers for Disease Control and Prevention, "HIV and African American Gay and Bisexual Men," page last reviewed January 11, 2022, https://www.cdc.gov/hiv/group/msm/bmsm.html.

12. D. B. Allison et al., "Annual Deaths Attributable to Obesity in the United States," *JAMA* 282, no. 16 (October 27, 1999), 1530–38, https://pubmed.ncbi.nlm.nih.gov/10546692/; and Craig M. Hales et al., "Prevalence of Obesity and Severe Obesity Among Adults: United States, 2017–18," CDC, National Center for Health Statistics, last reviewed February 27, 2020, https://www.cdc.gov/nchs/products/databriefs/db360.htm.

13. FBI Releases Supplement to the 2021 Hate Crime Statistics, found June 1, 2023, https://www.justice.gov/crs/highlights/2021-hate-crime-statistics.

14. US Department of Justice, Federal Bureau of Investigation Crime Data Explorer, found June 1, 2023, https://cde.ucr.cjis.gov/LATEST/webapp/#/pages/explorer/crime/hate-crime.

15. Deepa Shivaram, "Amid Wave of Violence, Asian Americans, Black Communities Build Coalitions," NBC News, February 18, 2021, https://www.nbcnews.com

/news/asian-america/amid-wave-violence-asian-americans-black-communities-build-coalitions-n1258275.

16. Jerusalem Demsas and Rachel Ramirez, "The History of Tensions—and Solidarity—between Black and Asian American Communities, Explained," *Vox*, March 16, 2021, https://www.vox.com/22321234/black-asian-american-tensions-solidarity-history; emphasis added.

17. Ibid.

18. Nausheen Husain, "Chicago's Arab American Store Owners Face Reckoning in Wake of George Floyd Murder," *Chicago Tribune*, June 15, 2020, https://www.chicagotribune.com/news/breaking/ct-george-floyd-arab-american-businesses-chicago-20200615-uoyfmycn55eodfcjhhjfqnxepq-story.html; and Kyung Lah, "The LA Riots Were a Crude Awakening for Korean-Americans," *CNN.com*, updated April 29, 2017, https://www.cnn.com/2017/04/28/us/la-riots-korean-americans/index.html.

19. Homer Bigart, "Baldwin Leaves Negro monthly; He and Ossie Davis Protest *Liberator* Series on Jews," *New York Times*, February 28, 1967, https://www.nytimes.com/1967/02/28/archives/baldwin-leaves-negro-monthly-he-and-ossie-davis-protest-liberator.html.

20. Although this is not always the case. See, for example, the chapter on Louis Farrakhan's Million Man March speech in Jim A. Kuypers, *Press Bias and Politics: How the Media Frame Controversial Issues* (Westport, CT: Praeger, 2002).

21. Yair Rosenberg, "The New York Times Just Published an Unqualified Recommendation for an Insanely Anti-Semitic Book," *Tablet*, December 17, 2018, https://www.tabletmag.com/sections/news/articles/the-new-york-times-just-published-an-unqualified-recommendation-for-an-insanely-anti-semitic-book.

22. Cassie Da Costa, "The Disturbing Rise of Anti-Semitism Among Black Celebs," *The Daily Beast*, July 17, 2020, https://www.thedailybeast.com/the-disturbing-rise-of-anti-semitism-among-black-celebs-from-diddy-and-nick-cannon-to-ice-cube.

23. "Amiri Baraka, Black Poet Condemned as Anti-Semitic, Dies," *The Jerusalem Post*, January 10, 2014, https://www.jpost.com/jewish-world/jewish-news/amiri-baraka-black-poet-condemned-as-anti-semitic-dies-337808.

24. Gigi Anders, "'Hymietown,' Revisited," *American Journalism Review*, May 1999, https://ajrarchive.org/article.asp?id=370.

25. Eunice G. Pollack, review of *Black Antisemitism in America: Past and Present*, by Xose Bouzas and Hans Lucas, The Institute for National Studies, Tel Aviv University, June 1, 2022, https://www.inss.org.il/publication/black-antisemitism/.

26. Marissa Lang, "Women's March Replaces Three Original Leaders, After Anti-Semitism Accusations, with 16 Board Members," *Washington Post*, September 16, 2019, https://www.washingtonpost.com/dc-md-va/2019/09/16/womens-march-cutting-ties-with-three-original-board-members-accused-anti-semitism/.

27. Leah McSweeney and Jacob Siegel, "Is the Women's March Melting Down?" *Tablet*, December 10, 2018, https://www.tabletmag.com/sections/news/articles/is-the-womens-march-melting-down.

28. Leah Donnella, "Exploding Myths About 'Black Power, Jewish Politics," NPR, posted online June 4, 2018, and accessed November 2022, https://www.wcsufm.org/arts/2018-06-04/exploding-myths-about-black-power-jewish-politics.

29. Josh Kaplan, "The Antisemitic Roots of Great Replacement Theory," *The Jewish Chronicle*, May 20, 2022, https://www.thejc.com/news/world/the-antisemitic-roots-of-the-great-replacement-theory-1vaL2tdeopDe46v2yzpUUI.

30. J. Clara Chan, "Anti-Defamation League Head Calls for Tucker Carlson's for 'Anti-Semitic, Racist and Toxic' Commentary," *The Wrap*, August 9, 2021, https://www.thewrap.com/fox-news-tucker-carlson-anti-defamation-league-jonathan-greenblatt/.

31. "Explainer: What Is 'The Great Replacement Theory' and What Are Its Origins?" Reuters, May 15, 2022, https://www.reuters.com/world/us/what-is-the-great-replacement-what-are-its-origins-2022-05-16/.

32. William Vaillancourt, "GOP House Candidate Backed by Party Leadership Said Hitler Is 'The Kind of Leader We Need," *Rolling Stone*, June 9, 2022, https://www.rollingstone.com/politics/politics-news/carl-paladino-praises-hitler-1365057/.

33. Martin Pengelly, "Trump Told Chief of Staff 'Hitler Did a Lot of Good Things,' Book Says," *The Guardian*, July 7, 2021, https://www.theguardian.com/us-news/2021/jul/06/donald-trump-hitler-michael-bender-book.

34. Jon Lafayette, "New CNN Head Chris Licht Explains Plans for Network," *Broadcasting+Cable*, May 18, 2022, https://www.nexttv.com/news/new-cnn-head-chris-licht-explains-plans-for-network.

35. Carey Callahan, "Gender Identity Is Hard but Jumping to Medical Solutions Is Worse," *The Economist*, December 2, 2019, https://www.economist.com/open-future/2019/12/03/gender-identity-is-hard-but-jumping-to-medical-solutions-is-worse?utm_medium=cpc.adword.pd&utm_source=google&ppccampaignID=18151738051&ppcadID=&utm_campaign=a.22brand_pmax&utm_content=conversion.direct-response.anonymous&gclid=Cj0KCQiAxbefBhDfARIsAL4XLRqdVj28QdUQKVC0GJ4aD00bXZ4vHexn6chgWe6Mm7o6OAH_UnaOAcIaAhWfEALw_wcB&gclsrc=aw.ds.

36. "Health Issues for Gay Men and Other Men Who Have Sex with Men," Mayo Clinic Healthy Lifestyle Adult Health, accessed February 16, 2023, https://www.mayoclinic.org/healthy-lifestyle/adult-health/in-depth/health-issues-for-gay-men/art-20047107.

Chapter 8

Solving Media Deserts Requires Going beyond Mapping News

Michelle Ferrier

Former ProPublica manager and columnist Richard Tofel wrote in 2022, "There are two big trends in local news in America these days, one positive and one negative." In this column he examined "the news deserts problem" and its impact, he says, on the fissures between Americans.[1] The negatives include the decline in legacy "mainstream media"—such as content, reach, personnel, financials, and trust. For the positive, he points to the emergence of nascent news entities—hyperlocal online news sites, regional nonprofit start-ups, cooperative models, and other experiments. Tofel points to cities where these experiments have been playing out then asks, what of our rural communities? The answer to that question is complicated.

In 2011, at a gathering of journalists, technologists, and media workers in Brattleboro, Vermont, I began to explore the concept of "slow news." What were some of the needs of these emerging media deserts? How could better communication and journalistic practices help communities to grow and thrive? If we begin to think of news as food, we see direct parallels to the news and food systems. Residents need access to fresh, local news and information. And some of our current media products can be viewed as "junk food" that affect the well-being of individuals and communities.

The Federal Communication Commission asked researchers to examine that question in 2012, to determine the effects of internet and communication technologies on community news and information needs. As a journalism educator and scholar at several rural Appalachian higher education institutions, I lived and worked in the Virginia Highlands and in the northern reaches of the Appalachian mountain range in Ohio. I was living the rural experience Tofel describes and trying to find ways with my students out of our own media deserts of news and information. We created one of the first online-only campus news sites after 9/11 at www.ehcwired.com. I taught media entrepreneurship and building using new digital technologies. Students created and developed hyperlocal online news or media businesses. I became a researcher with the Communication Policy Research Network (CPRN), headed by the University of Southern California and the University of Wisconsin–Madison. Our network conducted research and literature reviews to inform Federal Communication Commission policy on community information needs. My research into emerging hyperlocal, online-only news sites and geographic information system-based visualizations sought to make visible the contractions and changes in the media industry in US communities. My dynamic modeling of the media ecosystem allowed me to bring awareness to the eroding media ecosystems or "media deserts" and help direct critical resources to communities most in need of fresh, local news and information. My hope was that through policy interventions at the federal level and entrepreneurship interventions at the local level, we could address the inequities in the media system.[2]

In *The Communication Crisis in America, and How to Fix It*, scholars including me and several others from the CPRN examined the state of America's local news. In the foreword, the editors describe the challenges plaguing journalism:

> Driven by changes in the contemporary cultural, political, economic, and technological environments, this special status [of journalism] has eroded dramatically over the past several decades, at great expense to the profession and the institutions of journalism. In the last three decades, more than 300 daily newspapers have closed, newspaper circulation has dropped by 35 percent, the number of professional journalists has declined by over 40 percent, and revenues are at the same level as 1950, when the population was half what it is today and the economy was one seventh its current size.[3]

Several national reports pointed to a dynamic and troubling media ecosystem. Newsgathering, reporting, dissemination, and reader engagement had changed as a result of changing technologies, changing business models, and changing attention from audiences and readers. The net effect has been a sharp erosion in meeting the community information needs of rural and urban communities alike. As newspapers cut and slashed personnel or closed completely through the economic downturn in 2008, they contracted their coverage on their perimeters and in their urban cores. Towns and communities across the United States have been impacted by the closure and consolidation of newspapers, layoffs of personnel, and new technologies being used by journalists like social media and streaming video. But what of the rural communities? What was the impact of this decline on rural communities? How and in what ways were these communities affected by the competing challenges facing communication in rural regions? Ownership of local radio stations consolidated in rural areas around right-leaning media organizations. Broadband access and last-mile challenges and lack of cellular coverage in rural geographies compounded the communication issues. Shifts across geography were happening on multiple levels in the media industry that left many geographies lacking robust local media ecosystems.

My life in rural Appalachia became the proving ground for several experiments and innovations in mapping and modeling the changing media ecosystem. The media deserts model was developed from my experiences in such "media deserts" in the Appalachian regions of the United States watching as local radio and local news became decimated by corporate consolidation and format changes. I had been mapping Tofel's question back then in 2008, at first collecting data on news and media layoffs and closures to begin to determine gaps in personnel and coverage. The goal of the media deserts project became to make visible the communication flows at the local level and to help communities develop solutions to their news and information needs. Then, I added emerging hyperlocal online news outlets, broadband and broadcast reach maps, and other layers to understand the erosion in news coverage. I used this mapping work to identify geographies for new entrepreneurial ventures and media start-ups; additionally, the models helped identify regions for deeper study using a variety of other digital ethnographic methods, knowledge and network maps, and communication audits.

I also wanted to examine a larger question than Tofel. What impact was technology, ownership, readership, paywalls, poverty, digital divides, and other infrastructure issues having on communities across the United States? How was information, news, community dialogue, and knowledge circulating in a community? The media deserts methodology takes into account a holistic view of the channels and locations and ways in which geography intersects with communication issues, such as broadband access in our rural communities. Or the ways in which media deserts can exist in urban areas where markers of income and race are used to geographically design coverage areas. I wanted to create a knowledge audit system for community learning, dialogue, and action. I wanted to question who and how knowledge is created, circulated, and codified at the local level. Knowledge management uses a variety of audit tools to assess organizational knowledge. I wanted to take a more holistic view, applying knowledge management assessment techniques to create a systems-level view of the US news and information landscape, with newspapers being one of many cultural knowledge producers in a local ecology. This narrative mapping uses data from many sources to create dynamic models. By layering and mapping these community narratives and data, we can visualize the data for patterns, gaps, and opportunities.

In the pages that follow, I describe the media deserts methodology and its use in analyzing US media ecologies. Second, I dig into an ethnographic study of media deserts in rural Ohio and my efforts to design for local news and information needs. I detail a variety of digital, ethnographic, and engagement strategies used in three geographies and their use in developing communication and news and information capacity. Third, I make visible our learnings about how to cocreate media oases in media deserts and what it means for how we grow media ecosystems for thriving communities.

MAKING MEDIA DESERTS VISIBLE

The Media Deserts Project is a research effort to map and model the ways in which many of our rural and even urban communities have been impoverished over the past decade by the lack of fresh, daily local news and information. Media deserts are defined as geographies lacking in fresh, daily news and information. Using circulation data of print newspapers; emerging

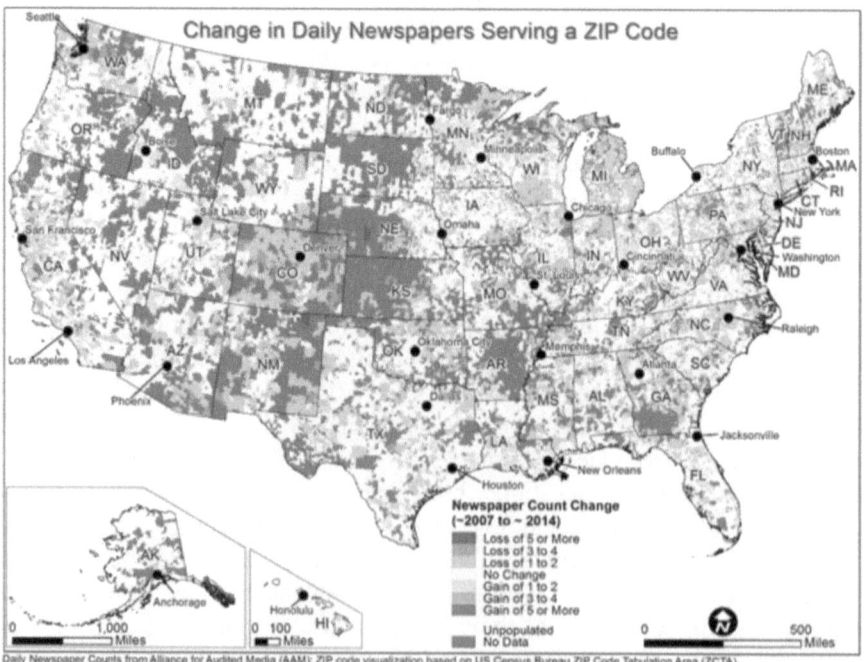

Figure 8.1. The Media Deserts Research Atlas change in newspaper counts at ZCTA level from 2007 to 2014.

hyperlocal, online news sites in digital networks; and broadband access data from the Federal Communication Commission, the Media Deserts Project maps and models the geographic and virtual spaces of a community, making visible the reach and penetration of existing media sources. The Media Deserts Project maps these changes using geographic information systems (GIS) down to the zip code level, so communities can design localized solutions (figure 8.1).

Using an ecological framework to model the communication systems at the local level, I used circulation data and ZCTA postal codes to map the geographic attributes and markers of newspapers in the United States. We used broadband maps to determine coverage. We added broadcast maps of radio and television to determine coverage areas. We added overlays of emerging hyperlocal online outlets. And census data.[4]

Visualizations, such as my media deserts maps, are designed to interrogate the changes to an environment over time and answer questions such as, "What characteristics constitute a healthy news ecology?" or "How can we measure the impact of the presence or absence of news on local economies and local residents to help them to thrive?" Some of this early mapping work in 2012, in North Carolina and Ohio, informed research for the Federal Communication Commission as part of their inquiry into media needs of the American public. We used Ferrier's mapping and modeling work to identify geographies where new online start-ups were growing, to find geographies in need of new entrepreneurial media ventures, and used GIS to map these media deserts, to identify underserved and underrepresented communities in the United States. Using census data, we could perform a geographic and spatial analysis of the demographic and economic conditions in the media deserts. The use of geospatial technologies is key to the growing importance of geography and digital technologies in media and communication. In *The Communication Crisis in America and How to Fix It*, my colleagues and I describe the growing use of what we define as geospatial media analytics to help journalists analyze data and map other geographic data to verify details and discover entirely new stories from computational data analysis. In this work we define media deserts as "a geographic locale that is lacking fresh, local news and information."[5]

The media deserts model (www.mediadeserts.com) assesses the code, content, and conduit levels of communication in geography:

Content: Is news and information being gathered and disseminated within the community?

Conduit: How does the communication infrastructure support community access through cellular and broadband channels, print, and online-only news platforms?

Code: Is the content created in such a way that it is accessible to local residents? Is it written in a language that is accessible to residents? Do algorithms and other online access points limit or constrain the accessibility and circulation of news?

My research and work focus on building our capacity for more and better news and information at the local level, but also developing new ways to connect with the people in our neighborhoods and put residents at the center of our journalism work. My methodologies are informed by social media, digital ethnography, and narrative mapping techniques that examine geospecific communities and monitoring digital and physical communications.

The Media Deserts Research Atlas, launched at Ohio University in March 2018, allows users to search by state, county, and zip code to find what media are operating on these multiple levels or what regulatory conditions might be affecting local access. Our goal is to help jump-start local conversations about building media capacity and helping residents create local solutions. I examine down to the zip code level (or ZCTA areas, which are the geographic equivalent of the postal system routes). I worked with my colleagues across disciplines from geography, public policy, and journalism to shape our research tool to raise awareness of the growing media deserts. The intent through this geospatial media analysis is to illuminate, inform, and support community information health that contributes to thriving, inclusive communities. Through a mixed-method, ethnographic approach, we are attempting to make visible new virtual spaces for news and information, community dialogue, and action. And design the new public square of physical and digital spaces where news and information fosters democracy in action. Specifically we:

- Learn about processes that grow and support community information health.
- Create products and relationships that support a thriving news and information ecosystem.
- Cocreate strategies for thriving, inclusive deliberation and dialogue.
- Support and mentor a community of practice dedicated to shaping healthy civic information spaces.
- Identify actions to amplify the activities in and outside of traditional newsrooms.
- Amplify the innovations and entrepreneurship in service to community information health.

- Begin to understand how engagement changes communities, the relationship between community members and journalists, and the field of journalism.
- Articulate new roles and responsibilities and new actors for creating and supporting thriving, inclusive community civic spaces for news and information and dialogue and deliberation.

The Media Deserts methodology is designed to monitor the changing local media environment and utilize the data and visualizations to create targeted interventions and solutions to ameliorate the desertlike conditions. To provide a more complete view of the complex physical and digital environments, the media deserts methodology uses a variety of audit tools: inventories and asset mapping, benchmarking, discovery processes, and some participative goal-setting and self-driven, collective self-representation. We move community stakeholders, journalists, and others to deepen their use of geospatial media analytics and community engagement practices to design news and information pathways. The Media Deserts Project makes visible these information flows and gaps, helping to facilitate the processes of coordinating actions and resources across contexts. These resources are particularly valuable to building community-based communication solutions that often need the support of multiple stakeholders in order to move initiatives forward. Since 2012, my approach has been to focus on bringing the whole system into the communication processes—governmental information, civic communication, emerging media innovations on social media platforms—and helping to grow sustainable, thriving media ecosystems customized to local conditions.

SOWING THE SEEDS OF CIVIC COMMUNICATIONS

One project, in rural southeast Ohio, lays bare the complexities of solving for the lack of local news and journalism. In order to begin the process of seeding media innovations in rural Appalachian media deserts, I made efforts to deepen our understanding of the locations. Any successful media innovation needs to be well suited for the locality, so I believe it is essential to develop a baseline understanding of the communities, the people, community assets, and the media landscape. The Media Seeds Project builds on my prior work in the region. Using Media Deserts Project data, as well as other topical datasets on opioid deaths and broadband access, we sought a variety of locales in southeast Ohio for our design efforts (figure 8.2). Our initial activities on the Media Seeds Project occurred between August 2017 and May 2018.

The Media Seeds Project in southeast Ohio allowed me to apply the research in media deserts to a specific geography and bring engagement

154   *Michelle Ferrier*

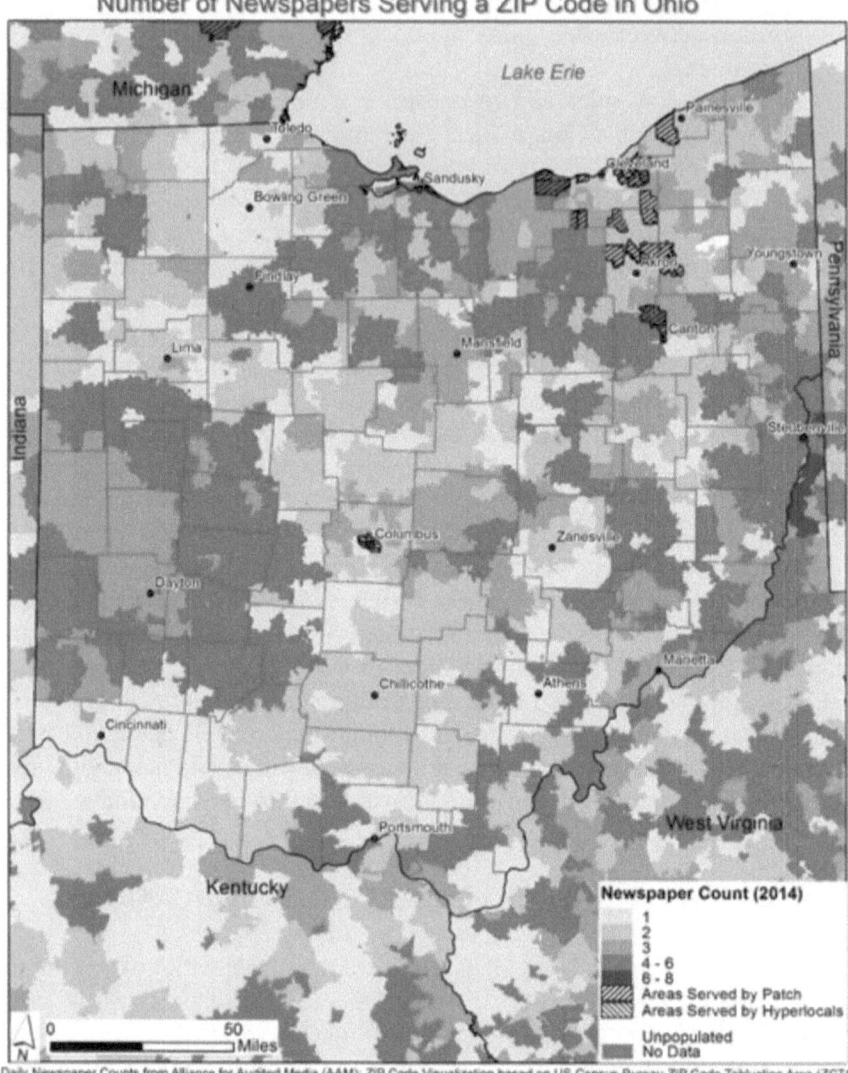

Figure 8.2. A multilayer map from the Media Deserts Project of Ohio from 2014, showing the Patch.com network of sites, other hyperlocal online news start-ups, and daily circulation newspaper organizations.

practices to my students in media and communication, community leaders, and others to help them cocreate news and information for the region. These knowledge audits took many forms from content analyses to focus groups, interviews, observation (digital and social), story collection, surveys, knowledge mapping, and sensemaking, to network maps of knowledge flows and resources. Our discovery process helped identify communities of interest as well as community residents and organizations interested in learning how best they might communicate with each other.

The project also tested the engagement principles, created out of my work with Journalism That Matters and journalists, to guide my work in turning deserts into fertile civic information oases. Since 2001, Journalism That Matters has brought together journalists, librarians, technologists, editors, artists, civic leaders, and others to examine civic communications in the United States and how journalism functions in a democracy. The Civic Communications Framework was developed in 2015 by Journalism That Matters while I was board president.[6] Our framework and principles emerged out of several gatherings hosted by Journalism That Matters since 2001: "To be a thriving, resilient ecosystem, communication needs to go beyond 'reporting' what is happening in the ecosystem to providing robust information and inclusive dialogue, fostering collaborative action that achieves community goals."[7]

The Media Seeds Project is grounded in invention—the cocreation of media tools and communication infrastructure in the heart of America's media deserts. Our operational principles were drawn from the work of Journalism That Matters and its creation of engagement principles for our southeast Ohio work:

Figure 8.3. Civic Communications Framework by Journalism That Matters.

1. Nothing About Us Without Us
2. Speak Truth to Empower
3. Listening Is Our Superpower

The approach is dialogic, ethnographic, and collaborative. For me, my sensitivity to local community issues is driven by my commitment to these Journalism That Matters engagement principles and are used as a touchstone to my ethnographic work and the work of my students. These principles became part of our community-based research practices and were especially important in our specific Appalachian context where we were cocreating with community residents, business owners, and civic leaders.

SOUTHEAST OHIO: DESERTLIKE ON MANY LEVELS

As the demographics for the region show, southeast Ohio residents represent some of the poorest residents in Ohio and in the country. Population is dispersed, clustered in small villages scattered throughout the foothills of the northern Appalachian mountains. These regions also lack broadband infrastructure and face other challenges such as access to health care, which complicate life in the region. Hard hit by the opioid epidemic, lack of jobs, and rising health and housing costs, regional leaders struggle with multiple issues to keep their communities alive. Economic development is critical and several nonprofits and the local university are attempting to build entrepreneurial ventures in the region and other strategies for economic vitality and sustainability.

Appalachian culture is known for its combination of self-reliance and support for members of their community, which are attributes that can support community-based innovation and development. However, this cultural commitment to the local community can also lead to suspicion of outsiders. The region of southeast Ohio has a history of resource extraction (coal mining, deforestation, hydraulic fracturing, and the storage of nuclear power waste) that was led by outsiders. Many Appalachian communities face deep and widespread poverty and devastated local boom-and-bust economies. Appalachian communities are more diverse than stereotypes dictate, but racism is still a substantial and visible problem in the region. As an "Affrilachian" or Black in Appalachia, I can personally attest to the racism and challenges to personal safety, while teaching journalism students how to do journalism better in today's diverse America.

In August 2017, Ohio University students located in the region of our work used digital ethnography methods to create county-level media audits. Using a variety of research and design methods, students deepened their analysis and understanding of the region and local communications ecosystems. The university is the main employer of the city and for some of the region. In this first phase of assessment, mapping, and monitoring, students used a variety of social media and online channels to map digital news and information flows in more than twenty southeast Ohio counties. We conducted deeper analysis in counties in southeast Ohio that had been identified as media deserts.

Students engaged in deep social monitoring and human-centered design practices to design and test communication strategies that explored how we might:

> "Foster and celebrate a greater sense of community or sense of place in the county."
> "Help communities affected by the health crisis to thrive."
> "Encourage dialogue and information sharing in our county. New pathways?"

We had four main goals:

1. Learn how to assess the assets of a region.
2. Learn ethnographic, dialogic, and engagement practices.
3. Cultivate/support local participation and connection.
4. And cocreate local news/information and communication strategies.

Students engaged with community members throughout the first year of the project, first through monitoring activities on social media, where they conducted a network analysis of social influencers, content, and key activities that drive engagement online. Students developed final reports of more than twenty counties in southeast Ohio that summarized health and news and information-related solutions based on communication audit and monitoring tools. Our deep, digital ethnographic work involved compiling information about the county, including demographic makeup, economy, education, housing, and civic sectors. Students mapped out the county's media landscape by investigating what media served the county and how residents used social media.

We also conducted a media survey of all households in our target communities using a direct mail postcard with a reply card delivered to each household in our region of study. We asked questions about the media diet of residents and their sentiments about their community and their personal engagement in civic activities. Several complained about the lack of access to fresh, local news and information. Others indicated that they are often left unaware of local events until *after* they have happened. In the comments box on the reply card, residents voiced their frustrations; for instance, "Daily newspaper comes delivered—sometimes late, sometimes not at all."[8]

Throughout the first year of community work, we centered our efforts on deepening our knowledge of the rural communities, building relationships with community members, and designing localized media tools with communities. Using human-centered design methods, interviews, workshops, and surveys, students worked with community members to imagine and design communication tools and strategies that might facilitate the circulation of news and information but also connect residents around issues such as health communication, community issues, and assets available in the region.

The detailed county-level weekly reports helped us examine the local media ecosystem for targeted interventions. Their digital ethnographic work resulted in a series of tools that may be used by community residents and provided insights into how we might cocreate solutions:

1. Community Information Needs Audit: Using the "Checklist for Community Information Needs in a Democracy," developed by Esther Thorson and Eric Newton, we examined each county on access to government records and media sources. Within each county report, students answer the audit questions on access to government data, media sources, etc.[9]
2. Digital Ethnography Report: Using Google Earth and Street View, students created a "walkaround" in the community, providing commentary about their observations from both street and ten-thousand-foot views of the geography.
3. Geography/Demography Report: We provided key demographic, geographic, and historic features of the region in the county reports that describe media sources in the area, recent news in print, broadcast and online, geographic markers, and other visual and narrative data.
4. Weekly Social Media Reports: These weekly summaries identify key influencers, news of the week, and observations about the community social sharing. Identified visual, textual, and thematic content from community conversations on Twitter (now X) and Facebook.
5. Community Dashboard: This social media directory, provided in .xls format, provides the names, address, and social media profiles of key agencies, organizations, and social media influencers discovered during our monitoring.
6. User Personas: We grouped our social media observations into ten user personas—personalities that are representative of the characteristics of social media users of the region.
7. Stakeholder Mapping: We identified communication sources and communication influencers in this visual communication mapping exercise.

8. Creative Matrix: We designed for community communication needs using different stakeholders and diverse media and communication tools.
9. Social Media Strategies for User Personas: News and Information: We specifically examined news and information more broadly, looking at key influencers and designed strategies for specific user personas. Students provided county-specific reports on user social habits, shared news/social content, influencers, and other social media of the region.
10. Social Media Strategies for User Personas: Health/Opioid Social Strategy: We provided a strategy for reaching residents with public health issue messaging and tools using online and physical strategies.
11. Local Media Brand Strategy: If local newspapers, radio, and other media existed in the county, the student reports provide recommendations for building the capacity using social tools.
12. Targeted Communication Survey: Zip code–specific surveys collected data about residents and their media habits. Questions also focused on community well-being indicators. Specific comments are captured in transparent images circulated back to the community.

In our project, we found that developing user personas was helpful because it uncovered different types of people in the communities who might seek out news and information. These user personas helped us think about what kind of content would be most useful for these different types of community members and also helped us develop specific tools and strategies for those groups. Additionally, we recognized the challenges related to technology, infrastructure, and broadband access in rural communities in southeast Ohio that prevent community members from having easy access to news and information. Identifying these issues and developing a deeper understanding of them allowed us to develop tools and strategies to make the community visible to itself and to outsiders in ways that are responsive to the local conditions.

START WITH LISTENING AND ENGAGEMENT

Out of our first year of work, we identified three communities in southeast Ohio for interventions. After completing the earlier work in asset mapping and digital ethnography to better understand the news and information needs of twenty different counties in southeast Ohio, our team selected three geographies for more targeted interventions. These areas are McConnelsville, Ohio (population 1,776); Chesterhill, Ohio (population 279); and Pomeroy, Ohio (population 1,790). McConnelsville and Chesterhill are both in Morgan

County; Pomeroy is in Meigs County. We examined our own goals and those of the community to answer these questions on the impact of our work:

1. How did we create and provide local news in a rural Appalachian media desert?
2. How did we cultivate and support participation from potential partners?
3. How did these activities dovetail with Journalism That Matters principles and our insights from our earlier work?
4. What else has emerged? How can these learnings inform the national conversation?

In addition to the general survey of residents, we cultivated close working relationships with community partners in all three geographies. The specific types of relationships varied in each geography, based on specific aspects of those local communities. In McConnelsville, Matt was deeply embedded in the community. He grew up in and currently lives in McConnelsville. As an embedded, local journalist, Matt was the centerpiece of the Media Seeds work there.

In Pomeroy, we partnered with the existing entrepreneurial economic development initiative (B-BEST), run by a local nonprofit organization, Rural Action. Media Seeds team members wrote profiles of some local businesses for ZipIt.News and continued to work with some local business leaders throughout the project. Pomeroy is trying to revitalize the downtown area and develop new businesses, so partnering with the B-BEST team made sense for us in this community. In Chesterhill, we partnered with both the mayor and a local village council leader, who acted as a champion for our project. Chesterhill is very small and is a culturally mixed location with an active Amish community as well as other White African American residents. Local community development includes the Chesterhill Produce Auction (supported by Rural Action and other local nonprofit organizations), where farmers and other local vendors sell their products to restaurateurs and other buyers from around the region.

In addition, we focused on the opioid epidemic in southeast Ohio and throughout the region. We engaged our local county health departments in thinking about direct mail and other solutions to reach residents with health-related information. The students and community members developed digital media strategies for health communication in these rural areas.

PRE- AND POSTSURVEY OF RESIDENTS

From the presurvey to the postsurvey results, residents rated information availability lowest of all of the community well-being indicators. Just 8.8 percent of residents on the presurvey rated a (5) on the statement, "When I make life decisions, information is readily available within my community." For the postsurvey, the percent of respondents who indicated a 5 was 11.7 percent. Residents ranked trust the next lowest on the community well-being indicator. On the community trust question, "Most people can be trusted," presurvey respondents indicated an 8.9 percent agreement with a 5 ranking. Postsurvey respondents edged higher with 19.8 percent indicating a 5 ranking. And while many respondents indicated they feel their community is safe, that they feel a part of the community, and that people are willing to help others in need, respondents themselves indicate they are not very engaged in their communities. Less than one-quarter of respondents (21 percent) indicate they are active in local organizations. Twenty-five percent indicate they have attended a local event in the past six months.

Respondents, when given space to voice their concerns in a comments section, pointed to the lack of broadband and cellular coverage, no access to computers, and other infrastructure issues that prevent them from accessing the news. Residents who are able to get broadcast news receive "local news" from West Virginia, across the Ohio River. Residents are very aware of the digital divide that leaves them uninformed and disenfranchised. One resident stressed the critical nature of this often taken for granted resource: "Get internet available to everyone/everywhere. My phone is like my master key."

If weekly newspapers exist, they are likely to be struggling and staffed mostly by stringers who have low or no pay. Existing local radio culls news from around the region and has limited or no local reporting. Projects that involve a combination of print and online media can be useful to reach a broad range of community members. However, given the lack of widespread internet access in the region, it is likely that much of the population will only see the print versions. For the rural communities we worked with, the digital divide is very real in the lives and minds of its residents.

We recognized that our taken-for-granted reliance on technology would limit our ability to effectively work in a media desert. Many residents in these communities do not have high-speed internet access, and even those who do experience frequent outages that can take days to resolve. We also learned about localized efforts to make broadband internet available through the region, and we shifted our work somewhat to help support our community partners' efforts. It also forced us to embrace multimodal media tools that do not require cellular service or Wi-Fi. Finally, we shifted our use of technology when the online platform we were initially using for the project closed down and we needed to move all the content to a new space. This prompted us to explore different online platforms for our project work.

Working with the principle of "Nothing about us without us" has been more difficult. Even though we developed productive relationships with key local stakeholders, the logistics of maintaining close collaborations with local stakeholders at three different locations was very challenging for community members and students. Both physically and digitally isolated, communication with stakeholders, residents, business leaders, and others was made more challenging by the lack of robust cellular and internet access. Additionally, engaging stakeholders in regular planning meetings via videoconferencing technologies was difficult. In these rural environments, many of the key community partners are people who are busily involved in many local activities, so they are stretched thin in terms of time and resources. Our listening work—through our visits, our surveys, our stories, and our conversations—amplified and made visible the rich, complex, frustrating, and fractured communication environment in the region.

The second stage involved three experiments: (1) a "homegrown" local journalist in McConnelsville; (2) postcards with local news sent directly to residents in McConnelsville, Chesterhill, and Pomeroy; and (3) an online local news platform open to residents of McConnelsville, Chesterhill, or Pomeroy to create their own profile and publish local news. The Media Seeds Project began implementing local news and information innovations in the summer of 2018.

Experiment #1: A Homegrown Local Journalist

Our first experiment directly explored one of the key principles of engagement from the Journalism That Matters community work: Nothing About Us Without Us. This experiment tested a "grow your own" approach to building news and information capacity in the region, a concern voiced by residents in the presurvey distributed in spring 2018 to households in the region. This approach followed the "media corps" model, developed by Michelle Ferrier, who was the project lead. The approach seeks to develop the skills and knowledge of a local resident to build the news capacity in the region. Similar efforts by Report for America to develop local newsroom capacity had raised concerns about how local is local—were embedded journalists "a local boy"? Research on the project had highlighted the difficulty of establishing trust and developing networks in a region that many embedded journalists did not call home.[10]

Matt, a resident of McConnelsville, was a student journalist training to build capacity for local government reporting in his town. He also was hired as a reporter for the long-standing weekly paper. Matt covered local city and village council meetings and wrote enterprise stories on issues affecting the two counties. Matt's stories were posted to the regional online platform ZipIt. News and to the weekly newspaper. Matt also worked for the local radio station but was not directly involved in creating or distributing news and information on the channel.

Experiment #2: Postcards Mailed Directly

Our second experiment tested two principles in the Journalism That Matters engagement model: Nothing About Us Without Us and Listening Is Our Superpower. From our asset mapping and digital ethnography work, we learned of the challenges residents experienced getting access to fresh news and information. From broadband access and cellular coverage, as well as news paywalls blocking local content, we found that the infrastructure was sorely lacking in providing access to the news and information that did exist in the region.

This experiment involved sending postcards with local news and information directly to residents in McConnelsville, Chesterhill, and Pomeroy by using the US Postal Service's Every Door Direct Mailing (EDDM) service. Through this service, we could select specific postal routes within zip codes to receive our mailing. The first postcard, our presurvey delivery method, invited residents to complete a survey of their "media diet" as well as to describe the kinds of news and information they needed. These postcards were visually appealing and had content that was specifically designed for the particular geography. Postcards contained teasers of local news stories and QR codes and website links to the full stories, posted on the ZipIt. News platform.

Experiment #3: Regional Online Platform Featuring Local News

Our goal was to build an inclusive communication tool to address the Journalism That Matters principle: Speak Truth to Empower. From our asset mapping and digital ethnography work, we learned that residents were not getting information in a timely fashion. They did not get notifications of local events or government meetings where they could get involved. We also discovered that local governments lacked transparency about when and how local residents could be involved in decision-making, effectively disenfranchising residents from participating in local democratic processes. Local communities lacked websites or communication tools to keep residents informed and engaged. No tools existed to discuss or educate the public about local or regional issues. Our rural communities lacked that virtual "public square" for deliberation and dialogue.

This experiment focused on engaging community residents in McConnelsville, Pomeroy, and Chesterhill in building and using a new online news resource to the region that was accessible, free, and allowed for residents to contribute by posting stories, events, and other information for the region. The ZipIt.News platform is powered by CommunityQ, a content management system that allows users to create a personal profile from which they can create and share content on the platform. The ZipIt.News website contained the full news stories that had teasers on the postcards. Initially, the website was populated with the county reports and local stories created by Ferrier's students during the 2017–2018 academic year. Media Seeds team members wrote news stories related to Pomeroy, Chesterhill, and McConnelsville and published them to ZipIt.News in September 2018, October 2018, January 2019, April 2019, and June 2019. These stories corresponded to the content shared on the postcards.

INSIGHTS INTO USING COMMUNITY-BASED CREATION PRACTICES

In our project notes, Matt, our homegrown journalist, describes the challenges of being in and of the community that you report on. He describes the shifts in long-standing community relationships as he engaged in this project work. We learned from our own roles as ethnographers and engaged cocreators about and with our communities. From our project diaries, a glimpse into our reflections on our work:

> Project Diary (Matt): Community Journalists play a role as public relations officer, promoter, advertiser and diplomat. A C-J has to walk a line between flamboyant and realistic; advocate and critic; credible and trustworthy; puppet and independent thinker. Easy to work with vs. blackballed. Ethics must be the backbone of every decision a journalist makes, entering ethics into every decision makes explaining your actions and looking into the mirror that much easier. Rollercoaster week of emotions has led me to realize that journalists do have to make a stand at times. Easy or not.

In this work, we began to develop an understanding of key insights that we believe may travel well into other projects using community-based creation practices. These insights are principles that are essential to community engagement and trust, the basis of a healthy, civic communications ecosystem.

#1. Consider Your Identity

To successfully enter a media desert, it is important to reflect on who you are and what relationship you have to the community. This means seriously considering what knowledge and experience you bring to the project, how others in the community are likely to see you, and how these things may limit the scope or pace of your work in the community. Having an outsider view of a community can be very useful because outsiders may see things and ask questions that uncover assumptions and allow for new ways of thinking. Recognize, however, the context-specific limitations one is likely to experience based on these competing identities.

#2. Listen Deeply

In addition to engaging in self-reflection, it is essential to learn about the assets and needs of the community. This deep listening builds on the principle "Listening Is Our Superpower" to emphasize the importance of learning as much as possible about the community before entering. We call this listening deeply because it requires doing more than gathering basic demographic information to really get to know the heart and soul of a place and its residents. Listening deeply can help you become a more competent communicator in the community. Practicing this kind of listening helped us challenge our preexisting assumptions about people and places that could have prevented us from developing good working relationships with community members.

#3. Make the Invisible Visible

Discover the factors that affect the capacity for community members to connect to themselves and others (for example, geography, history, technology, temporality, politics, demographics, culture, and power). Many rural communities are invisible to people outside of the community as rural America is stereotyped in particular ways. But even within the communities themselves, events and assets are often unknown because local news and information is not consistently and easily available. To seed media deserts with high-quality news and information, it is important to understand what factors obscure information and what impacts community members' ability to connect to one another.

#4. Embrace Serendipity

When doing this work in rural locations, it is useful to expect the unexpected. Of course having a plan is important, but given how much travel and technology are central to working in rural locations, planners should be willing to let go of best laid plans to work with the unexpected. Being flexible and responding to changing weather, internet connectivity problems, travel difficulties, or changing schedules is essential. It is not useful to treat these unanticipated events as challenges that prevent project work. Instead, we learned to take a mindset where we were open to learning from people and places we encountered.

#5. Treat Every Community as Unique

Finally, it is important to design tools that are consistent with and build from what you learn during the deep listening. From an outsider perspective, rural communities might look the same. But the specific assets and needs vary widely, and successful designs are based around those specific assets and needs. In our project, one community had specific needs related to improving communication between government officials and community members. Another community's needs centered on the local business community. The size of the communities also became a criteria in determining priorities. A village of five hundred residents has very different needs than a community of five thousand. Existing media entities also played a role in how residents viewed their news consumption and needs. Collaborating with local partners helps to keep the designs well grounded in the assets and needs of that community, but it is also important for designers to be mindful of how the innovations address the unique, specific characteristics of each locality.

INSIGHTS INTO OTHER PROJECTS ENGAGING LOCAL COMMUNITIES

Out of our community work, we developed five insights that may be applicable to other projects engaging local communities:

#1. Design for the Realities of the Region

Rural communities have local assets but also face constraints related to infrastructure, geography, and culture. Innovations should be designed to fit these realities. Many rural communities have insufficient communication infrastructure, which can have a significant impact on a project's success. As noted previously, cell service and internet access are not consistently available in many areas throughout southeast Ohio. This means that many people get their news and information from print, radio, and television sources.

#2. Attend to Journalists' Emotions and Inner Life

How do you hold both intimacy and objectivity at the same time? We learned that to build rapport and engagement you must be present. As a local resident in a small town, Matt struggled to make an impact with his reporting work and move his community to action. Even with tenuous and real social connections, Matt was still an outsider. This work can be isolating and emotionally difficult. Journalists need preparation and tools to manage emotional dynamics. For example, embedded journalists can feel overwhelmed and isolated because they occupy a unique role in the community and can face significant hurdles to doing the work. Providing a support network with others working in similar settings might mitigate some of the feelings of isolation.

#3. Recognize Limits and Public Perceptions of Existing Local Media

Local media are embedded in cultural and political institutions. Any new innovation will enter into that cultural and political context. Small town politics have deep roots, with a small number of people holding a concentration of local power. This has clear potential for corruption of the media. In our project we found that many community members distrusted local media, which they criticized for a lack of transparency. Local media also have some structural issues that can be problematic. Paywalls, which are common, prevent the circulation of information to larger audiences. Local papers that only present after-the-fact reports of events do not fully serve the public. In our project we saw some local media sources that underpaid, or simply did not pay, the workers. All of these exacerbate the public distrust of the media. It became clear to us that just because some local media exists does not mean they serve the public good.

#4. Anticipate That Innovations May Disrupt Existing Power Structures

Change is difficult and can be threatening to local leaders, who may resist or challenge your work. It became apparent to us that our project was disruptive. The communication innovation we promoted in this rural media desert challenged the status quo and was seen as threatening to people in power. Although this might not always be the case in other geographies, project leaders should anticipate that innovations could be met with resistance. An isolated, embedded journalist does not have the social capital to effectively manage this disruption, especially if that journalist lacks support from existing local media. It would be useful to find ways to navigate the power system and proactively address the potential for resistance.

#5 Enlist a Local Champion, Even If the Journalist Is from the Community

Supportive local partners play an important role in the project's success. This role is different from what journalists can do alone. Ideally the project will involve collaboration between journalists and local community members at all stages of the work, from inception through implementation. In Chesterhill and in Pomeroy, we were piggybacking on the social capital of trusted people and business leaders. The project had more success in the communities of Chesterhill and Pomeroy, where Media Seeds had local champions.

TAKING THE LEARNINGS DEEPER

The Media Seeds Project work took place within significant political and cultural challenges to creating news and information innovation in rural Appalachian media deserts. Although we did not begin this project with the goal of disrupting local power systems, it became clear that media innovations were disruptive and seen as threats by both local politicians and owners of local media. We felt firsthand the importance of understanding and appreciating geography and collectively creating a sense of place.

It is also important to design for rural geography. Distances between rural communities can be sizable, and any project that involves multiple communities will require a substantial amount of driving. Road quality can vary and terrain can block signals and create challenges for travel and mobile communication.

Finally, it is essential to develop a deep understanding of local culture and learn to work within that culture. The rural region of southeast Ohio has predominantly conservative political leanings and an aging population that is not as computer literate and media savvy as people living in more urban environments. Communities have their own calendars, such as in Chesterhill, where town activity centers around the Chesterhill Produce Auction. Although there are some local activists working for social justice and progressive community members working for economic development, many of the communities can be insular, homogeneous, and suspicious of outsiders. A robust civic communications ecosystems requires developing a shared vision. That can be especially challenging in the rural environment, especially if working across different towns. But it's important to engage in deep listening, collaboration, and dialogue with community stakeholders to create the community vision.

Through this kind of deep engagement, journalists can engage in civic communication projects that enable community members to share their own narratives and cocreate local solutions.

The Media Deserts Project and our work in Media Seeds demonstrated the critical need for journalists to develop enhanced skills around dialogic practices, listening, hosting, collaborating, and engagement practices. Moving from journalist to community weaver requires journalists to reorient themselves to local voices and needs in order to adjust traditional practices in meaningful ways. Said another way, we avoid focusing on the presence or absence of a newspaper as an indicator of healthy communities to reframing the issue around community information needs and designing by, for, and with people and their geographies. Journalism—and the news and information we produce—in service to communities that thrive. As described in Journalism That Matters's Civic Communications Framework,

> We see our task as not reimagining and reinventing journalism but rather imagining and inventing inclusive, generative communications ecosystems that foster thriving, resilient communities—what we call *"civic communications."* With community at its heart, it makes room for all voices to be heard, all peoples to be seen, and residents to be informed and in action on issues of importance to themselves and their communities.[11]

This Media Seeds and Media Deserts Projects work are articulating new practices for journalists as "community weavers" to add to the journalistic canon. Honoring the voices and stories of communities requires deep engagement. Deep engagement builds trust. But this engagement need not be at odds with the aims and goals of journalism. Counter to this belief, engagement engenders deeper trust by bringing diverse voices into the media and communication processes and attending to a whole systems view. Ultimately, these new geospatial media analytics and digital ethnography practices will help journalists and other media workers to cultivate a communications ecosystem with their communities to support democracy and a thriving, local civic life.

NOTES

1. Richard J. Tofel, "It's Important Not to Look Away from the News Deserts Problem," *Second Rough Draft*, Substack, last modified March 21, 2022, accessed March 21, 2022, https://dicktofel.substack.com/p/its-important-not-to-look-away-from.

2. According to Michelle Ferrier, "The FCC has a critical role to play in the allocation of public resources and in ensuring a media infrastructure that serves all communities," Ferrier said. "My hope is that through policy interventions at the federal level

and entrepreneurship interventions at the local level, we can address the inequities in the media system." Michelle Ferrier, "Michelle Ferrier Contributes to FCC Research on Community Information Needs," Today at Elon, July 31, 2012, https://www.elon.edu/u/news/2012/07/31/michelle-ferrier-contributes-to-fcc-research-on-community-information-needs/.

3. Mark Lloyd and Lewis A. Friedland, eds., *The Communication Crisis in America and How to Fix It* (London: Palgrave Macmillan, 2016), vii.

4. This is not unlike the US Department of Agriculture's food desert map created in 2011 to examine the local foodways and access to fresh food.

5. Michelle Ferrier, Gaurav Sinha, and Michael Outrich, "Media Deserts: Monitoring the Changing Media Ecosystem," in *The Communication Crisis in America and How to Fix It*, 215–32. See also Michelle Ferrier, "The Media Deserts Project: Monitoring Community News and Information Needs Using Geographic Information System Technologies," paper presented at the AEJMC Midwinter Conference, University of Oklahoma, February 2014.

6. Peggy Holman, Yve Susskind, Michelle Ferrier, Mike Fancher, and Stephen Silha, "Journalism for Democracy and Communities: A New Framework," May 2017, Journalism That Matters, https://medium.com/journalismthatmatters/journalism-for-democracy-and-communities-a-new-framework-b537e28fb32b.

7. Holman, Susskind, Ferrier, Fancher, and Silha.

8. Laura W. Black and Michelle Ferrier, "Media Seeds: Fresh News in an Appalachian Media Desert: What We Learned," Journalism That Matters, July 21, 2019, https://medium.com/journalismthatmatters/media-seeds-fresh-news-in-an-appalachian-media-desert-5720aa417503.

9. Esther Thorson and Newton Thorson, "Indexing Community Information Needs in a Democracy: A Checklist," January 2008, http://www.docstoc.com/docs/164567409/Checklist-for-Community-Information-Needs-in-a-Democracy.

10. Christine Schmidt, "Is He a Local Boy? Is Report for America Building Trust within the Communities It Serves?" Nieman Lab, May 6, 2019, https://www.niemanlab.org/2019/05/is-he-a-local-boy-is-report-for-america-building-trust-within-the-communities-it-serves/.

11. Holman, Susskind, Ferrier, Fancher, and Silha.

Chapter 9

The Problem-Solving Solutions Journalism Model

Treating News Audiences as *Problem Solvers* in *Solutions Journalism*

Serena Miller, Soo Young Shin, and Jennifer Cox

Historically, journalists working at traditional news media organizations have not provided information on solutions to problems or ways the public may act to address community problems due to a concern their audiences may view them as biased. Given the state of unrest and uncertainty heavily felt by many people in the world, we argue news organizational leadership should rethink and experiment with the restructuring of news content to assess whether varying their news content structures yield more positive audience psychological and behavioral engagement. Journalists often perform well at alerting the public to crises, political conflict, and social unrest. A daily barrage of such negative information garners audiences' attention, yet the problem is such news also results in audiences experiencing unhealthy emotions (for example, freeze state, anger, helplessness) because humans are biologically hardwired to protect themselves by scanning environments for signs of danger.[1] The news media's generation of public outrage toward societal events motivates some people to act, but the news media should be wary because audiences also describe the news media as harmful, intolerable, and negative, contributing to readers feeling overwhelmed, distrustful, apathetic, and disempowered when faced with issues of geographic and humanitarian concern.[2]

In this chapter, we explain how the news media should continue to alert people to problems (that is, dangers, risks, and threats) despite concerns about the negative nature of news, but they should add one additional content component—problem-solving efficacy. Perceived self-efficacy, for example, is among the strongest predictive concepts that explains whether people positively respond, including act, when faced with negative news or events.[3] The extended parallel processing model (EPPM), rooted in the fear message appeals and protection motivation literature, posits communicators (that is, journalists) should provide both *threat* and *efficacious* information if they care about fueling positive and healthy responses to negative news such as tragedies, risks, and crises. EPPM, applied mostly in health campaign research, summarizes a content structure that hypothetically encourages public awareness and action. People first evaluate both the severity of a threat and their susceptibility of being affected by the reported threat and then they may either perform the suggested problem-solving actions (that is, danger control processes) or respond emotionally with anger, disgust, or sadness if they feel a lack of efficacy (that is, fear control processes) following exposure to content messages.[4] Ideally, an individual's perceived efficacy is stronger than their concern of a threat to encourage a positive response. Traditional news media journalists, however, emphasize the presentation of news through a problem frame, encouraging reactions rather than actions even though they may hope audiences may do something about the problem.

The public's negative perceptions of the news media could hypothetically be swayed in a more positive direction if the news media understood the power of efficacious information. We argue the Solutions Journalism Network (SJN) team could augment the solutions journalism approach by teaching people to communicate more about the efficacy of individuals and institutions to encourage solutions' engagement.[5] Solutions journalists defend the value of the practice by asserting it leads to both audience psychological and behavioral engagement,[6] with research showing it influences perceptions of psychological empowerment, engagement intentions, and story trust among readers.[7] Work, however, remains to examine the validity of assumptions whether solutions journalism spurs positive change in communities.[8]

We seek to support SJN by discussing the augmentation of the solutions journalism rigors framework by putting forth the Problem-Solving Solutions Journalism Model, a content model that provides guidance on how to structure content to serve people with a desire to respond to problems. We argue solutions journalists could serve their audiences better by sharing information that signals their problem-solving efficacy and treating solutions news as knowledge. In the present solutions news content model, however, news sources, often solution stakeholders, try to persuade readers (spectators) of the solution's value likely to increase its acceptance.[9]

In this chapter, we review the research on problem-solving, solutions journalism, and EPPM with the intent of presenting logic behind the selection of concepts we argue represent the Problem-Solving Solutions Journalism

Model. Thus, we use theoretically and practically informed literature to build a framework intended to serve the practice of solutions journalism. Methodologically, we employed a content analysis[10] of solutions journalism articles to quantitatively assess the extent solutions journalists followed the practices suggested in our proposed content model: (1) problem definition, (2) solution goal, (3) solution evaluation, and (4) problem-solving efficacious information. We content analyzed 555[11] text-based solutions journalism articles filtered by SJN leaders from the Solutions Story Tracker database to get a baseline of solutions journalists' performance. To accomplish this we first provide an overview of solutions journalism, followed by a discussion of the problem-solving model. We conclude with a discussion of the positive implications of the application of this model.

SOLUTIONS JOURNALISM

The Solutions Journalism Network (SJN) is an independent, nonprofit organization that advocates for the practice of solutions journalism by providing global educational training and resources for journalists to incorporate this approach in their newsrooms. Rather than endlessly reporting on the failures of society (and leaving someone else to fix it), solutions journalism signals to readers that solutions to problems do exist through their rigorous reporting on responses to problems. The SJN gained news organizational support and respect due to the rigorous structure of the practice[12] and continues to gain acceptance based on responses from 211 global news media publishers, finding 73 percent of them perceived solutions journalism will be important in combatting news fatigue and avoidance.[13] The SJN, trainers of the solutions journalism practice, teach journalists to abide by four rigors when crafting solutions journalism content: limitations, evidence, how-to, and insights. Solutions journalists practice an investigative approach by reporting on the weaknesses and strengths of a solution. Journalists are advised to evaluate a solution by investigating a solution's *limitations* and *evidence*, while the *insights* rigor is the inclusion of knowledge that offers broad views about human behavior and descriptions of how society could be made to work better.[14] Journalists that abide by the *how to* rigor provide instructional-like information that guides readers on how to enact the solution. Based on the present solutions journalism approach, journalists critically evaluate a solution, or problem-solving efforts of a group, and disseminate that information to readers.

The problem is that solutions journalism adopters may unconsciously treat readers as passive recipients or solutions journalism spectators. Solutions journalism readers want the news media to facilitate local community involvement, but they are unable to locate ways to engage with solutions in news content.[15] The controversy related to the desired level of involvement of readers is a historical debate. Beginning in the 1920s, journalist and political commentator Walter Lippmann and American philosopher John Dewey, an influential scholar on problem-solving, debated the functions of journalism in democracy including the role the public should play in responding to problems. John Dewey believed the news media should encourage involvement in public affairs through reflective inquiry and active agency because he conceptualized the public as a group of people who recognized a problem and organized to addressed it.[16] Lippmann's libertarian views in the twentieth century, however, dominated the news media's stance toward constructing news in which bodies of experts act on the behalf of people. Lippmann's philosophy toward informing the public empowered journalists because it held that they were experts in prioritizing information to be shared with the public.[17] The objectivity approach stemmed from journalists' desire to align their reporting practices to mimic the scientific method such as verifying information and citing expert sources, while avoiding appearances of bias such as empathetic communication, issue advocacy, or journalistic opinion.[18] Some critics have claimed Lippmann's approach toward the public, treating them as incapable spectators, resulted in the disconnect between journalists and the public.[19] The inclusion of news information that encourages engagement in public problem-solving was and is still a rare occurrence because journalists perceive providing information on opportunities for action a violation of the objectivity principle.[20] Deeply rooted norms, routines, and resources explain to some extent why journalists emphasize residing in the role of mediator between the experts and the public rather than empowering community residents to work alongside experts. The ingrained historical norm of objectivity (that is, detachment toward issues and people) continues to be an influential journalistic principle leading to the exclusion of engaged components in news content despite public calls for journalists to increase their community involvement and report news from a more representative lens.[21]

The solutions journalism reporting approach may be presently limited because it may result in audiences simply reacting to solutions by evoking positive psychological perceptions rather than audiences actually participating in the solution or using the information to launch or refine a solution elsewhere. Research on solutions journalism reveals people may not feel the need to act after reading a solution's article, and thus, we argue solutions journalists should include information about the problem to secure their attention[22] and report on the response (that is, solution's effectiveness), but they should also recognize impact that problem-solving efficacy likely has on influencing public action and confidence. Wenzel, Gersen, and Moreno found focus groups participants who read solutions journalism content felt the problem was addressed and did not warrant their attention because solution news stories "glossed over the problem."[23] EPPM research explains that if *perceived response efficacy* (that is, the message recipient's perception that a response [that is, solution] addressed the threat) is high and perceptions regarding the likelihood of a threat are low, people will dismiss the message (that is, news content) because they perceive the problem has been adequately addressed.[24] Thus, solutions journalism leaders and researchers may need to conduct a more critical review of a solution's content structure to isolate what content aspects influence people to feel good and what aspects influence them to behaviorally respond if they care about behavioral engagement.

Journalists would likely frame content differently if journalists supported Dewey's notion that publics are groups of people who are collectively able to address problems facing their communities and society. Journalists could help stakeholders not only decide whether a solution is feasible for their community, but they could also communicate member's capabilities of addressing problems. In the problem-solving literature, a public is a group of people with varying degrees of activity or passivity who decide whether to participate often based on relevance and confidence. Active members are people who want to work toward a problem resolution.[25] Problem-solving and EPPM perspectives nestled within the solutions journalism approach could result in empowering readers to address society's problems. The problem-solving literature summarizes the information structure people require to cognitively and behaviorally enact the problem-solving process, while the EPPM provides evidence on the importance of consuming efficacious information to encourage people to confront challenging situations. Solutions journalism is an ideal approach to consider for the inclusion of efficacious information. The existing structure of solutions news content somewhat aligns or could align with the theoretical premise of EPPM when journalists report on both a problem and a solution in a single news unit. EPPM encourages communicators to balance *threat severity and susceptibility* components with *response and self-efficacy* to influence prosocial behavior. Solutions information likely communicates to readers the *response efficacy* of a group because solutions journalists are encouraged to evaluate and present evidence of a solution's effectiveness for audiences, yet we do not know whether solutions reporters present readers with solutions information through a *problem-solving efficacious* lens communicating that readers may also serve a role in problem-solving. Most of the four solutions journalism rigors serve readers and align with how one should communicate problem-solving information based on the problem-solving literature. But only one of the proposed solutions journalism content rigors signals to individuals and groups they themselves are efficacious and capable—the *how-to* rigor. We recommend solutions journalists communicate information that not only informs readers about the solution but also reflects to what degree they are informationally supporting readers' potential capacity to learn, adopt, or refine a solution.

We organize bodies of literature to show how the SJN could expand its solutions approach by manifestly recognizing people and institutions as capable problem solvers. We use problem-solving scholarship to conceptually and empirically describe ways that journalists could structure content to support readers' desire to become problem solvers. In Lippmann's passive audience approach, an expert evaluates the solution's success and the news media disseminates that knowledge. The sources try to persuade others (spectators) of the solution's value encouraging audiences to be reactive rather than active in problem-solving behaviors. The Problem-Solving Solutions Journalism Model summarizes our intent to engage and support the SJN. Experimental research shows solutions journalism generates inspiration for involvement.[26] We, however, do not know if solutions journalism contains components that aid them in becoming involved in the problem-solving process.

PROBLEM-SOLVING SOLUTIONS JOURNALISM MODEL

We align the solutions journalism approach with the problem-solving literature to demonstrate how solution journalists could both inspire and teach audiences how to respond to problems. People faced with problems seek information and then evaluate whether they are able to respond to a problem. Problem-solving often involves higher-order thinking skills such as abstracting, reasoning, evaluation, and visualization. Problem *case-based reasoning* is one approach in which experts or nonexperts apply knowledge learned in another situation to their problem.[27] A problem is "an unknown entity in some situation (the difference between a goal state and a current state),"[28] while problem-solving is "cognitive processing directed at achieving a goal when no solution method is obvious to the problem solver."[29] Solutions journalism content could be classified as applied knowledge that informs people about how to address problems such as homelessness, recidivism, water pollution, or food insecurity, for example. Solutions journalists, as communicators, present readers with at least one case detailing how other people have responded to a problem. The problem-solving process involves identifying the problem, defining the problem, searching for solutions, implementing a solution, and evaluating a solution's effectiveness.[30] People, especially nonexperts (that is, people with little problem-solving experience in a particular context), typically first search for information when problem-solving and they could employ news stories (or cases) to help them navigate unfamiliar problem spaces and identify experts to help them address a problem.[31] Stakeholders could learn how to apply a solution's knowledge to different but similar contexts by reading about other cases. Insights extracted from solutions journalism news content could help future problem solvers produce positive outcomes, yet it is unknown whether or how solution's news knowledge is applied in real-world contexts.

We present a prescriptive content model informed by EPPM, problem-solving, and solutions journalism literature that demonstrates how journalists could support the development of learning and engaged communities by reporting how individuals and institutions may join a solution or learn from a solution. Scholars most often view the solving of problems as a sequenced set of operations.[32] The Problem-Solving Solutions Journalism Model houses concepts argued to be fruitful for supporting problem-solving process: (1) problem definition,[33] (2) solution goal,[34] (3) solution evaluation,[35] and (4) problem-solving efficacious information.[36] Solutions journalists could structure their stories by presenting readers with these content elements if their desire is to support the problem-solving capacities of their readers.

Problem Definition

Problem articulation is the first step in any problem-solving model because stakeholders must define the problem before they can generate ideas on how to solve it. The problem solver extracts information to try to understand the *problem space*, which is a representation of the structure and context of the problem.[37] In an example story about a solution to blood shortages, the reporter clearly stated the problem:

> It is an open secret that in Nigeria, blood is not always available at the point of need, and sometimes has to be sourced by relatives of individuals who need it. Many gaps exist in the blood supply chain, from inadequate infrastructure for storage, to the high costs of screening. The most challenging gap is finding willing, unpaid blood donors who can donate to either people in need instantly, or to health facilities who have the equipment to screen and store the blood for transfusion to patients.[38]

It would be difficult to collectively proceed if stakeholders do not agree upon the boundaries of the problem according to the problem-solving literature,[39] while EPPM states audiences may not be motivated to act if journalists do not present them with threat information. Thus, a problem must first be articulated and constructed before one is able to identify solution options or activate existing knowledge to address a problem.

We expected solutions journalists would communicate a problem in solutions articles.[40] Walth, Smith Dahmen, and Thier found 97 percent of seventy-three sampled solutions stories identified a social problem. The articulation of the problem is and should be an essential component in solutions journalism, but the problem was rarely identified as an outlier. We found the majority (83.2 percent) of solutions news articles included information about the problem (see figure 9.1). Only 6.1 percent of articles, however, included a negative outlier statistic as evidence of the severity of a problem as in this example, "The country's third-largest city isn't its most dangerous (several smaller cities, such as New Orleans, St. Louis and Detroit, have higher murder rates), more total murders happen in Chicago than in any other American city: 764 in 2016, up sharply from 485 in 2015."[41] We did not analyze the structure or framing of the problem beyond the inclusion of a negative outlier,

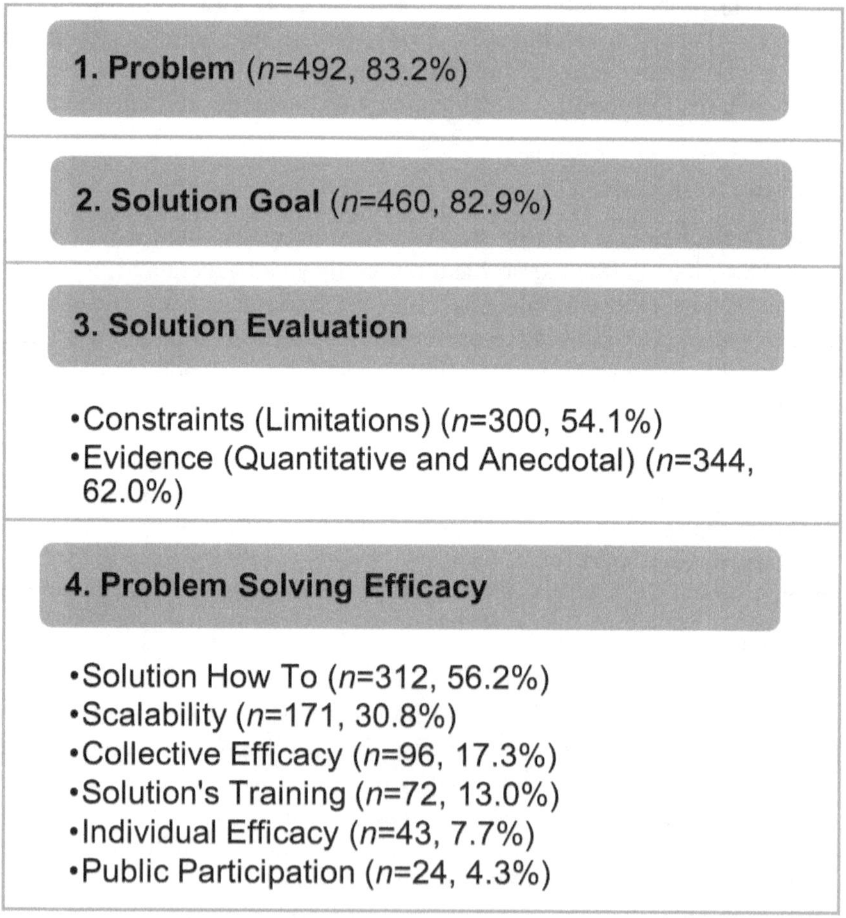

1. Problem (n=492, 83.2%)

2. Solution Goal (n=460, 82.9%)

3. Solution Evaluation

- Constraints (Limitations) (n=300, 54.1%)
- Evidence (Quantitative and Anecdotal) (n=344, 62.0%)

4. Problem Solving Efficacy

- Solution How To (n=312, 56.2%)
- Scalability (n=171, 30.8%)
- Collective Efficacy (n=96, 17.3%)
- Solution's Training (n=72, 13.0%)
- Individual Efficacy (n=43, 7.7%)
- Public Participation (n=24, 4.3%)

Figure 9.1. The Problem-Solving Solutions Journalism Model and Content Analysis Findings.

but future research should evaluate both the presentation of the concreteness and the urgency of it to evaluate whether and what problem message components influence behavioral engagement intentions.

Solution Goal

Problem solvers reduce the cognitive load by identifying goals that enable them to craft problem-solving action steps. A problem with no clear solution must be transformed into a goal state to direct problem-solving behaviors.[42] Complex problems often require multiple solution iterations with different goals and strategies before problems are substantially addressed. Goals, a motivational concept, provide clear objectives that guide people in addressing nonroutine and ill-defined problems.[43] For example, *Politico*'s reporting of a group therapy solution included this goal statement: "It aims to help young men like these learn impulse control—to think more slowly as a way of avoiding the reflexive anger that has led to the deaths of so many young people in Chicago—and learn skills and values that will guide them to productive lives after they graduate."[44] We found most (82.9 percent) solutions news articles communicated solution goal information, which means stakeholders communicated to journalists their solution goals and journalists shared that information with audiences.

Solution Evaluation

Limitations (Constraint Recognition)

According to SJN, the limitations rigor in solutions-oriented news should point out the uncertainties, costs, constraints, or side effects of the implemented solutions. The communication of limitations informs readers the extent a solution is replicable elsewhere by detailing the setbacks implementors faced.[45] Journalists could note areas of resistance to communicate the barriers affecting the solution's implementation as shown in this example: "Elsewhere, there remains resistance from both sides. When CUNY tried to help New York City's high schools better prepare their students for college, Logue recalled, they were stymied by the sheer number of schools and by university faculty who prefer to set their own standards for the students they accept into their courses."[46] *Constraint recognition* is also a concept housed within the Situational Theory of Problem-Solving.[47] In the problem-solving literature, *limitations* are conceptually referred to as *constraints* and problem solvers identify the negative factors that may affect the solution's implementation. The Situational Theory of Problem-Solving is a model that summarizes the communicative actions associated with problem-solving. Constraint recognition predicts lower motivation for communicative problem-solving efforts such as information search, selection, and transmission. Perceived obstacles such as expertise, resources, or participants associated with implementing a solution influence whether one proceeds toward a solution. We found slightly more than half (*n*=300, 54.1%) of solutions articles reported the constraints or limitations of a response. This finding suggests there is collective room for improvement for journalists who support this approach.

EVIDENCE

SJN teaches journalists to provide evidence of a solution's effectiveness and defined *evidence* as observations that provide justification concerning the effectiveness of a response.[48] Stakeholders, researchers, or experts assess the performance of a solution. Problem-solving scholars conceptually refer to *evidence* as *evaluation*, while EPPM literature refers to it as *response efficacy*. Solutions journalists may incorporate quantitative evidence by presenting data about how a population was affected by the implemented solution (for example, "Lending circle participants average a 168-point increase in their credit score and decrease their debt after 11 months, according to reports from the Mission Asset Fund."[49]) or share anecdotes of direct positive experiences associated with the solution (for example, "'I am wicked, I didn't go to prison for stealing apples. . . . I was a violent person; I would get into lots of fights and riots inside.' . . . He says 'The Actor's Gang programme teaches you how to control your anger and emotions.'"[50]). We found solutions journalists provided quantitative or anecdotal evidence (that is, response efficacy) of a solution's effectiveness in 62 percent of articles. This information is critical for people to cognitively process whether they will be able to overcome challenges and whether it is worth the investment to employ that solution in another context.

Problem-Solving Efficacy

Human behavior, including problem-solving, is often motivated by efficacy beliefs. Bandura stated, "efficacy beliefs influence whether people think erratically or strategically, optimistically or pessimistically."[51] EPPM states negative perceptions of the news media will be reduced if they recognize how only problem-framed stories result in perceived inefficacy and a lack of control. Bandura's identification and development of the self-efficacy concept provided notable evidence that efficacy perceptions influence people's motivations, reactions, and behaviors.[52] *Problem-solving efficacy* is the positive communication of people's capacity to address problems such as signaling readers' ability to handle or adapt their behaviors to correct a problem. People's problem-solving confidence influences whether they avoid or approach problem-solving.[53] David Bornstein, a cofounder of the SJN, stated, "We need to balance news about problems and possibilities *so that people can engage with reality with some sense of agency.*"[54] Readers may become overwhelmed, defensive, dismissive, or paralyzed by a problem, such as a natural hazard, if they only receive information about potential threats, or they may dismiss the severity of the problem if only efficacious information is presented because people will perceive the problem does not require their attendance.[55] Thus, solutions journalists should include both problem and efficacy information in a news unit. A survey of two thousand Americans by the international nonprofit More in Common and the American Press Institute found 87 percent of respondents desired "information on problems in society in order to solve them," while 63 percent wanted journalists to report on solutions as well as problems.[56] Research suggests reading solutions journalism may result in increased self-efficacy perceptions when compared to reading nonsolutions content,[57] while one researcher did not find a relationship between reading solutions news and self-efficacy perceptions.[58]

We did not assess self-efficacy perceptions following the consumption of content, but we manifestly evaluated whether solutions journalists *communicated* problem-solving efficacious information. Gans argued the news media hinders public participation because they do not treat them as capable change agents.[59] The inclusion of efficacy communicates the public's agency in addressing problems themselves. We, however, did not expect solutions journalists would communicate problem-solving efficacy information to a great degree due to professional norms and a lack of training. In media sociology studies, *mobilizing information* was one of scholars' first conceptual attempts to study the extent that journalists informationally communicated ways people could act on issues of personal concern.[60] News mobilizing information included business phone numbers, public meeting times, information on how to volunteer, and contact information of officials, for example. News professionals, however, rarely include mobilizing information.[61] Journalists do not provide details such as dates and times of events because they view them as "dull details" and their inclusion has been viewed as a violation of the objectivity standard.[62] Mobilization is a goal-oriented activity intended to address a problem, and it should not be viewed as an advocacy framed concept in which groups organize to voice their dissatisfactions with institutions.[63] Lemert stated mobilizing information was meant to provide information for people who want to act but who are not aware of how to proceed.[64] Lemert and Ashman argued the exclusion of this information edged out outside viewpoints and discouraged people from actively participating as members of their community.[65]

Along with this history, solution journalists strive to not appear they are advocating for a solution. Many journalists accept the practice because it reflects an investigative approach toward journalism.[66] Solutions journalism focuses on the reporting of an existing solution and journalism that *advocates* for a particular solution is not classified as solutions journalism. Journalists are taught to carry out evidence-based reporting on a solution while they are instructed to not advocate or promote an existing solution to their readers.[67] This emphasis assumes audiences will instead evaluate a solution. Solutions journalism leadership understood that it had to confront journalists' initial assumption that solutions journalism meant that they were advocating for a solution. In one survey of US journalists, only approximately a quarter believed their role was to point people toward possible solutions.[68] The teaching that solutions journalism should be rigorous may explain the resistance related to informing people about their abilities to solve problems due to the fine line between advocating for a solution and treating people as capable problem solvers.

Efficacy information is essential to motivate people to act. We present an expansion beyond the mobilizing information conceptual perspective by encouraging journalists to provide more than information on how to participate in solutions but also present efficacious information based on both EPPM and the problem-solving literature. The proposed *problem-solving efficacy* manifest construct is represented by six content variables. Problem-solving efficacy is enacted if a journalist includes any one of these pieces of information, but we seek to promote the inclusion of more than one of these efficacy components in news content: (1) how-to, (2) scalability of a solution, (3) collective efficacy, (4) individual efficacy, (5) solutions training, and (6) participation opportunities.

SOLUTION HOW-TO

The solution search process involves creating procedural steps.[69] The SJN recommends solutions journalists to follow the how-to rigor in which they communicate the concrete steps taken to respond to a problem. For example, an article about an accessible and equitable health care solution provided readers with some details about their solution's procedures:

> In Nigeria, women often carry the burden of using family planning commodities and Beji PHC was not an exception. However, the PHC staff members devised an approach early in 2018 where the husbands of pregnant women who came for antenatal sessions were invited to come for talks. Mrs. Musa took the time to explain the benefits of family planning in a one-on-one session, after which

the male laboratory technician in charge of the laboratory explained how family planning works using anatomical models of the male reproductive organ and a male condom. They also made family planning services available every day. This ensured that anyone could walk into the PHC to access the family planning commodities discretely.[70]

A detailed how-to section by journalists may encourage others to replicate, adapt, or modify the solution in another context.[71] We found a little more than half (n=312, 56.2%) provided such information. The methodological steps carried out to respond to a problem help readers determine whether they themselves could perform those steps in another context or whether they could recruit an expert to perform them.

Given the nature of problem-solving in that some people are not qualified to implement a solution, we examined whether expertise was necessary. Domain-specific experts are often needed to address ill-structured, complex, or unfamiliar problems due to their abstract-thinking strategies and knowledge. Experts understand how to construct mental models and diagrammatic representations to cognitively process a problematic situation. Domain-specific knowledge, or schemas, enable experts to recognize the similarity of problems and modify problem-solving procedures to their problem context. Novices, on the other hand, are limited in their perceptual ability to recognize patterns because they interpret situations based on isolated and concrete aspects of a case.[72] We found 88.5 percent of solutions required some domain expertise. Thus, journalists tend to rely on solutions experts likely because experts understand how to cognitively address problems. We also examined the leading sponsors of solutions and found the leading solution's implementors were groups such as nonprofits (31 percent), businesses (19.3 percent), nonlocal government (16 percent), local government (15 percent), and health care (8.6 percent). Even if community members do not possess the expertise, skills, or experience to address a particular problem, nonexperts could hypothetically work alongside experts to assist them with solutions tasks. Thus, problem-solving can be a shared responsibility.

Scalability

A limitation of a solution is that readers would view a solution as being only relevant to the article's context. Scalability information directly communicates that knowledge and lessons learned could be used to implement a response to a problem elsewhere. Thus, scalability communicates informational usefulness by telling readers how solution's knowledge could be applied in another context. We found solutions journalists were somewhat likely to mention scalability (n=171, 30.8%).

COLLECTIVE AND INDIVIDUAL EFFICACY

Journalists could provide information about people's abilities to solve problems. Perceived collective efficacy is defined as "people's shared beliefs in their collective power to produce desired results."[73] Collective efficacy represents the "performance capability of a social system as a whole,"[74] emphasizing the collective actions that groups (that is, organizations, marginalized groups, nonprofits) may take in communities. Journalists could highlight the role that groups play in supporting the continuance of the solution such as in this example featuring reporting on a fistula care center solution: "Community and religious leaders . . . create awareness through health promotion drives, leveraging on their highly respected positions in their communities. They, working alongside centres like Gesse, can help ensure that women like Umaima and Bilkisu have the knowledge of and the access to healthcare centres close to them when they are ready to give birth."[75] On the other hand, individual efficacy involves the journalist communicating how individuals could help to address a problem. In this example, the journalist detailed one role individuals could take to prevent an infection, "Trachoma can be prevented through ensuring proper personal and environmental hygiene. Therefore, people are urged to keep their faces clean by washing with soap and water every day and avoid sharing handkerchiefs and towels. People are also urged to dispose of waste (including feces) properly, so as to minimize presence of flies, which transmit the disease."[76] Thus, journalists could mention actions or efforts groups or individuals could perform to continue responding to a problematic situation. Content analytic work shows journalists overemphasize threat information and disregard communicating information about people's ability to mitigate a threat.[77] We found solutions journalists rarely highlighted people's collective efficacy ($n=96$, 17.3%) or individual efficacy ($n=43$, 7.7%), suggesting that journalists avoid writing about people's capabilities of solving problems. Journalists should reflect whether their work communicates problem-solving efficacy because if it is not present in content, readers may engage in denial or fear coping strategies instead of positively behaviorally responding to the article.

SOLUTIONS TRAINING

The news media can demonstrate how readers are co-learners rather than spectators of problems and solutions. Solutions trainees are likely community members affected by the problem or people with a similar background of those being helped by the solution. Sponsors often recruit local community members to combat participant resistance to the solution, but this information could also signal to readers they could seek training if they wanted to help. We found few articles mentioned people unaffiliated with the solution participated in solutions training ($n=72$, 13%).

PUBLIC PARTICIPATION INVITATION

The news media has the power to combat people's feelings of helplessness by informing them of a solution's participation opportunities, which is the heart of the mobilizing information concept.[78] The news media may reinforce divisions or a sense of helplessness among the population if they do not recognize that news consumers and institutions have a role in the problem-solving process. Participation does not mean encouraging people to deliberate about a topic or advocate for a solution but rather providing people with participation information that informs individuals and institutions of different possible paths of action related to the enacted solution. Participation opportunities encourage acceptance and education of the solution. In a story about a library project, the public was notified they could participate in that solution: "Borrowers can also attend practical skill-sharing events including mending meet-ups, repair parties and DIY classes. People can volunteer their time to become a 'host,' 'thing fixer,' 'ambassador' or 'skill sharer.'"[79] The communication of public participation opportunities was low ($n=24$, 4.3%), which is not surprising given the cognitive nature of the problem-solving process or how there is often inequality in power between the problem solver and the people affected. People motivated to solve a problem are often housed together in organizational units tasked with addressing domain-specific problems.

The public, however, wants to be notified of participation opportunities to feel less powerless when facing problems.[80] Participation opportunities could include well-defined tasks because engaged scholarship literature shows that cooperating and working together to solve a problem leads to increased acceptance and support of a solution.[81] Journalists may promote perceptions of inequality and powerlessness by situating problem-solving in the realm of an individual expert.[82] Problem-solving models often not only require higher mental functions but coordination and participation as well. Overall, solutions journalism and university education training along with continued influence of the objectivity norm will likely influence whether and how solutions journalism is practiced.

CONCLUSION

In service of a solutions journalism approach, we present a research-informed framework that could advance solutions journalism. Problem-solving involves the identification of a problem and its context, and restructuring that situational knowledge learned from the previous problem-solving efforts and applying that knowledge to another problematic context. Dewey argued people need useful, problem-solving information, and the news media could be a primary source that facilitates these actions.[83] The beauty of solutions journalism is it naturally aids in the problem-solving process because people often seek to locate solutions and generate ideas when there is no obvious solution to a problem. They not only cultivate awareness of solutions but also communicate methods for solving problems and inform people about opportunities to participate. Solution journalists, proponents of problem-solving knowledge transfer, represent the public, and readers of their work could learn how other stakeholders handled challenges in an accessible way, helping them to evaluate whether reported solutions are worthy of their resource investment.

Journalism helps orient people to what is going wrong in the world around them, yet journalism could do more help orient them toward becoming problem solvers. The proposed content model supports community resilience by communicatively detailing not only the ways the public could positively respond to adverse events but affirming readers are capable change agents. In 2015, *Nieman Reports* quoted the Center for Civic Media's Ethan Zuckerman stating that he perceived solutions journalists should inform audiences on how to positively act, yet he speculated solutions journalists would avoid doing so to distance themselves from the appearance of advocacy.[84] People need to know whether they can do something about a problem—and, ideally, some guidance on how. A recognition that audiences may also serve a role in problem-solving would mean that solutions journalism would include both solutions and an audience-framed perspectives. Tactical efficacy support information such as providing information on volunteer opportunities or communicating about the applicability of a reported solution is not advocacy but rather valuable and useful information for readers. Thus, solutions journalists could hypothetically support community well-being even more by communicating that people can resiliently participate in problem-solving by reviewing not only exemplar or innovative solutions to problem cases but informing readers of the public's role in addressing these cases. Researchers should test the assumptions of this research-informed structure by varying content elements of solutions journalism. The separation of content elements moves solutions research beyond the comparing problem and solutions stories in experiments into a more nuanced direction that isolates content elements that will help us understand what aspects influence psychological engagement and what content aspects influence behavioral engagement.

Future research should also examine the solution idea generation and news gathering stages to assess how journalists conceptualize solutions journalism and identify story ideas. One suggestion often put forth by SJN trainers is that journalists should focus on the positive performance of an organization or geographic area. SJN's positive outlier recommendation, however, was rarely employed by journalists ($n=10$, 1.8%). Social norms or data journalism training may explain the minimal use of this recommendation, but we encourage the continued emphasis of highlighting positive performers to educate people about what people have done to address a problem. The solutions story generation and news crafting phases could add more training modules to help journalists locate and examine such data (perhaps a collaboration with the Investigative Reporters & Editors or National Institute for Computer-Assisted Reporting nonprofit), and, of course, more research in the story-generation phase would serve people who want to understand the solutions journalism practice more deeply.

Overall, the Problem-Solving Solutions Journalism Model is intended to move the needle of solutions journalism beyond psychological engagement toward community action. We overviewed content elements that support problem-solving action. We do not expect all efficacy elements be placed in a news story, but it is intended to encourage solutions journalists to consider whether they have provided enough information to encourage people to use this knowledge elsewhere.

NOTES

1. Pamela Shoemaker, "Hardwired for News: Using Biological and Cultural Evolution to Explain the Surveillance Function," *Journal of Communication* 46, no. 3 (1996): 32–47; Kim Witte, "Putting the Fear Back into Fear Appeals: The Extended Parallel Process Model," *Communication Monographs* 59, no. 4 (1992): 329–49.

2. Jürgen Habermas, *The Structural Transformation of the Public Sphere: An Inquiry into a Category of Bourgeois Society* (Cambridge, MA: MIT Press, 1989); David Merritt and Maxwell McCombs, *The Two W's of Journalism. The Why and What of Public Affairs Reporting* (Mahwah, NJ: Lawrence Erlbaum, 2004); Mariska Kleemans, Rebecca N. H. de Leeuw, Janel Gerritsen, and Moniek Buijzen, "Children's Responses to Negative News: The Effects of Constructive Reporting in Newspapers Stories for Children," *Journal of Communication* 67 (2017): 781–802; Mikko Villi, Tali Aharoni, Keren Tenenboim-Weinblatt, Pablo J. Boczkowski, Kaori Hayashi, Eugenia Mitchelstein, Akira Tanaka, and Neta Kliger-Vilenchik, "Taking

a Break from News: A Five-Nation Study of News Avoidance in the Digital Era," *Digital Journalism* 10, no. 1 (2022): 148–64; Andrea Wenzel, Daniela Gersen, and Evelyn Moreno, "Engaging Communities through Solutions Journalism," *Columbia Journalism Review* (April 26, 2016), https://www.cjr.org/towcenterreports/engagingc ommunitiesthroughsolutions journalism.ph.

3. Hyehyun Hong, "An Extension of the Extended Parallel Process Model (EPPM) in Television Health News: The Influence of Health Consciousness on Individual Message Processing and Acceptance," *Health Communication* 26, no. 4 (2011): 343–53.

4. Erin K. Maloney, Maria K. Lapinski, and Kim Witte, "Fear Appeals and Persuasion: A Review and Update of the Extended Parallel Process Model," *Social and Personality Psychology Compass* 5, no. 4 (2011): 206–19; Witte, "Putting the Fear Back into Fear Appeals."

5. Katherine N. Kinnick, Dean M. Krugman, and Glen T. Cameron, "Compassion Fatigue: Communication and Burnout toward Social Problems," *Journalism & Mass Communication Quarterly* 73 (1996): 687–707.

6. Kyser Lough and Karen McIntyre, "Journalists' Perceptions of Solutions Journalism and Its Place in the Field," *ISOJ Journal* 8, no. 1 (2018): 33–52; Ella Powers and Alex Curry, "No Quick Fix: How Journalists Assess the Impact and Define the Boundaries of Solutions Journalism," *Journalism Studies* 20, no. 15 (2019): 2237–57; Wenzel, Gersen, and Moreno, "Engaging Communities through Solutions Journalism."

7. Kleemans, de Leeuw, Gerritsen, and Buijzen, "Children's Responses to Negative News"; Villi et al., "Taking a Break from News"; Kathryn Thier, Jesse Abdenour, Brent Walth, and Nicole Smith Dahmen, "A Narrative Solution: The Relationship Between Solutions Journalism, Narrative Transportation, and News Trust," *Journalism* 22, no. 10 (2021): 2511–30; Xin Zhao, Daniel Jackson, and An Nguyen, "The Psychological Empowerment Potential of Solutions Journalism: Perspectives from Pandemic News Users in the UK," *Journalism Studies* 23, no. 3 (2022): 356–73.

8. Susan Benesch, "The Rise of Solutions Journalism," *Columbia Journalism Review* 36, no. 6 (1998): 36–39.

9. Powers and Curry, "No Quick Fix."

10. We designed manifest content analysis measures by reviewing literature and pretesting the variables. In quantitative content analysis research, scholars seek to operationalize any latent content variable at a more manifest level. Coders coded the presence or absence of each variable; however, several variables were rarely present in content leading us to employ an intercoder reliability statistic to assess rare event variables (that is, negative outlier, individual efficacy, collective efficacy, public participation invitation) during the formal intercoder reliability stage. Gwet's coefficient AC was applied as the standard to these four variables instead of Krippendorff's alpha. Gwet's is recommended in cases in which the variable received low intercoder reliability, high percent agreement, and low variable presence. For intercoder reliability, a doctoral student and one professor author independently conducted three rounds of pilot tests on articles not included in the sample. For formal intercoder reliability, eighty-one articles were randomly selected for the first round of formal intercoder

reliability and sixty-two articles for the second round. The full coding protocol is available upon request.

11. United States (*n*=232, 41.8%), Europe (*n*=208, 37.5%), and Africa (*n*=115, 20.7%).

12. Lough and McIntyre, "Journalists' Perceptions of Solutions Journalism and Its Place in the Field."

13. Nic Newman, "Journalism, Media, and Technology Trends and Predictions 2023," *Reuters Institute*, 2023, https://reutersinstitute.politics.ox.ac.uk/sites/default/files/202301/Journalism_media_and_ technology_trends_and_predictions_2023.pdf.

14. Solutions Journalism Network, "Ten Questions to Inform Your Solutions Journalism," *The Whole Story* (September 25, 2017), https://thewholestory.solutionsjournalism.org/the-ten-noble-questions-f7b97d137135.

15. Wenzel, Gersen, and Moreno, "Engaging Communities through Solutions Journalism."

16. John Dewey, *The Public and Its Problems* (New York: Holt, 1927).

17. Walter Lippmann, *Public Opinion* (San Diego, CA: Harcourt, Brace, and Company, 1922).

18. Lough and McIntyre, "Journalists' Perceptions of Solutions Journalism and Its Place in the Field"; Sue Robinson and Katy Culver, "When White Reporters Cover Race: News Media, Objectivity, and Community (Dis)trust," *Journalism* 20, no. 3 (2019): 375–91; Karen McIntyre, "Solutions Journalism: The Effects of Including Solution Information in News Stories about Social Problems," *Journalism Practice* 13, no. 1 (2019): 16–34.

19. Merritt and McCombs, *The Two W's of Journalism*.

20. Serena Carpenter, "How Online Citizen Journalism Publications and Online Newspapers Utilize the Objectivity Standard and Rely on External Sources," *Journalism & Mass Communication Quarterly* 85, no. 3 (2008): 533–50; Lindsey H. Hoffman, "Is Internet Content Different After All? A Content Analysis of Mobilizing Information in Online and Print Newspapers," *Journalism & Mass Communication Quarterly* 83, no. 1 (2006): 58–76.

21. Robinson and Culver "When White Reporters Cover Race."

22. Kevin Wise, Petya Eckler, Anastasia Kononova, and Jeremy Littau, "Exploring the Hardwired for News Hypothesis: How Threat Proximity Affects the Cognitive and Emotional Processing of Health-Related Print News," *Communication Studies* 60, no. 3 (2009): 268–87.

23. Wenzel, Gersen, and Moreno, "Engaging Communities through Solutions Journalism," 15.

24. Witte, "Putting the Fear Back into Fear Appeals."

25. James E. Grunig and Todd T. Hunt, *Managing Public Relations* (New York: Holt, Rinehart and Winston, 1984); Kirk Hallahan, "Enhancing Motivation, Ability, and Opportunity to Process Public Relations Messages," *Public Relations Review* 26, no. 4 (2000): 463–80.

26. Kleemans, de Leeuw, Gerritsen, and Buijzen, "Children's Responses to Negative News"; Wenzel, Gersen, and Moreno, "Engaging Communities through Solutions Journalism."

27. Agnar Aamodt and Enric Plaza, "Case-Based Reasoning: Foundational Issues, Methodological Variations, and System Approaches," *AI Communications* 7 (1994): 39–59.

28. David H. Jonassen, "Toward a Design Theory of Problem Solving," *Educational Technology Research and Development* 48, no. 4 (2000): 65.

29. Richard E. Mayer and Merlin C. Wittrock, "Problem Solving," in *Handbook of Education Psychology*, ed. Patricia A. Alexander and Philip H. Winne (New York: Routledge, 2009), 287.

30. Welleskey R. Foshay and Jamie Kirkley, "Principles for Teaching Problem Solving," *PLATO* (1998), https://www.researchgate.net/profile/WellesleyFoshay/publication/262798359_Principles_for_Teaching_Problem_Solving/links/579fc46b08aec29aed214834/Principles-for-Teaching-Problem solving.pdf.

31. Mary L. Gick, "Problem Solving Strategies," *Educational Psychologist* 21, nos. 1–2 (1986): 99–120.

32. Jonassen, "Toward a Design Theory of Problem Solving."

33. *Problem definition measure*: A problem is an unknown entity in a situation in which the goal state is different from the current state. A journalist or source that communicates how a present state is unfavorable or employs statistical information as evidence of the unacceptable state (93.7%, α=.76, Gwet's AC1=.91). *Negative outlier*: an outlier is an unusually high or low quantitative figure that notably stands apart from the average. An unfavorable (negative) statistic provides evidence regarding the severity of a problem (88.9%, α=.53, Gwet's AC1=.86).

34. *Solution goal measure*: The aim of a solution following the application of it such as the intent was to reduce crime, prevent deaths, increase student reading scores, increase charitable donations, etc. (95.2%, α=.83, Gwet's AC1=.95).

35. *Evidence measure*: The presentation of data or empirical observations that show the effectiveness of at least one solution. For anecdotal evidence (85.9%, α=.72, Gwet's AC1=.72), coders were instructed to record it as present if the journalist cited human sources that discussed the effectiveness or direct impact of a solution on them. For quantitative evidence (87.3%, α=.75, Gwet's AC1=.75), coders evaluated whether the journalists cited or provided numerical data associated with the effectiveness of a solution, such as studies or statistics associated with the solution. *Limitations measure*: the journalist's recognition of constraints, perceived obstacles, or weaknesses related to the implementation or maintenance of at least one solution to a social problem (92.1%, α=.83, Gwet's AC1=.85).

36. *Problem-solving efficacy measures*: (a) *How-to measure*: Information that details how a specific person or group carried out the solution by providing tactical information or steps on how a solution sponsor implemented the solution. How-to must be technical or concrete instructions that provide explicit guidance and instructions on how to implement the reported solution (84.1%, α=.70, Gwet's AC1=.72); (b) *Domain expertise*: This variable assessed whether domain-specific knowledge or expertise was applied to implement the focal solution such as relying one someone with training, skills, education, or expertise to implement or assist with a solution (91.5%, α=.70, Gwet's AC1=.88); (c) *Scalability*: the journalist or a source addressed whether or how the solution could be implemented beyond the context reported in the

article. Examples included highlighting how a solution could work with other community members, geographic regions, or similar institutions (85.7%, α=.71, Gwet's AC1=.69); (d) *Collective (positive) efficacy*: the journalist or a source recommends actions that institutions, social systems, or groups could take on their own to address or mitigate a problem or threat. This variable reflects the expressed confidence or plans of other institutions in performing certain activities related to the suggested solutions in the future (85.7%, α=.60, Gwet's AC1=.79); (e) *Solutions training*: solution leadership or a sponsor trains unaffiliated people to become active participants in the solution (88.9%, α=.76, Gwet's AC1=.85); (f) *Individual (positive) efficacy*: a news source or journalist expressed a positive belief or opinion in individuals' abilities or capacity to address problems or threats in the future (90.5%, α=.60, Gwet's AC1=.79); and (g) *Public participation invitation*: the sponsors or stakeholders associated with the focal solution explicitly encourage public participation (that is, people not currently involved with the solution) to participate in the reported solution. This information could include an invitation for public action, involvement, or comments by including information such as the time and the place of public information sessions, volunteer sign up opportunities, etc. (92.1%, α=-.03, Gwet's AC1=.91).

37. Gick, "Problem Solving Strategies"; Marshall Scott Poole and Michael E. Holmes, "Decision Development in Computer-assisted Group Decision Making," *Human Communication Research* 22, no. 1 (1995): 90–127.

38. Bashar Abubakar, "Meet Your Match: J Blood Artificial Intelligence Connects Blood Donors to Receivers in the FCT," Nigeria Health Watch, December 13, 2019, https://nigeriahealthwatch.medium.com/meet-your-match-j-blood-artificial-intelligence-connects-blood-donors-to-receivers-in-the-fct-f5af76086b4e.

39. Poole and Holmes, "Decision Development in Computer-assisted Group Decision Making"; Mike U. Smith, "A View from Biology," in *Toward a Unified Theory of Problem Solving: Views from Content Domains*, ed. Mike U. Smith (Mahwah, NJ: Lawrence Erlbaum, 1991), 1–19.

40. Brent Walth, Nicole Smith Dahmen, and Kathryn Thier, "A New Reporting Approach for Journalistic Impact: Bringing Together Investigative Reporting and Solutions Journalism," *Newspaper Research Journal* 40, no. 2 (2019): 177–89.

41. Erick Trickey, "Group Therapy Is Saving Lives in Chicago," *Politico*, September 21, 2017, https://www.politico.com/magazine/story/2017/09/21/chicago-violence-crime-psychology-cognitive-behavioral-therapy-215633/.

42. Jonathon Gutman, "A Means-End Chain Model Based on Consumer Categorization Processes," *Journal of Marketing* 46 (Spring 1982): 60–72.

43. Mayer and Wittrock, "Problem Solving."

44. Trickey, "Group Therapy Is Saving Lives in Chicago."

45. Solutions Journalism Network, "Ten Questions to Inform Your Solutions Journalism."

46. Jon Marcus, "A Solution as Obvious as It Is Rare: Making High School Graduate Ready for College," *The Hechinger Report*, August 18, 2016, https://hechingerreport.org/solution-obvious-rare-making-high-school-graduates-ready-college/.

47. Jeong-Nam Kim and James E. Grunig, "Problem Solving and Communicative Action: A Situational Theory of Problem Solving," *Journal of Communication* 61, no. 1 (2011): 120–49.

48. Solutions Journalism Network, "Ten Questions to Inform Your Solutions Journalism."

49. Nicole Hayden, "Poor Credit Is a Barrier to Affordable Housing. Lending Circles Are a Tool for Those in Poverty," *Desert Sun*, February 14, 2020, https://www.desertsun.com/story/news/2020/02/14/coachella-valley-loan-program-aims-break-poverty-cycle/4547059002/.

50. Kate Bissell, "Actor's Gang: How Tim Robbins Has Cut Reoffending Rates," *BBC News*, March 14, 2016, https://www.bbc.com/news/magazine-35786775.

51. Albert Bandura, "Exercise of Human Agency through Collective Efficacy," *Current Directions in Psychological Science* 9, no. 3 (2000): 75.

52. Albert Bandura, "Self-Efficacy Mechanism in Human Agency," *American Psychologist* 37 (1982): 122–47.

53. Lynda L. Butler and Donald Meichenbaum, "The Assessment of Interpersonal Problem Solving Skills," in *Assessment Strategies for Cognitive Behavioral Interventions*, ed. Philip C. Kendall and Steven D. Hollen (New York: Academic Press, 1981), 198–225.

54. David Bornstein and Tina Rosenberg, "If We Can Report on the Problem, We Can Report on the Solution," *New York Times*, November 11, 2021, https://www.nytimes.com/2021/11/11/opinion/fixes-solutions-journalism-lessons.html.

55. Kim Witte, "The Role of Threat and Efficacy in AIDS Prevention," *International Quarterly of Community Health Education* 12, no. 3 (1992): 225–49.

56. More in Common and the American Press Institute, "Americans Seek Stories of Solutions and Inspiration from the Media," *More in Common U.S. Newsletter*, March 10, 2023, https://moreincommon.substac k.com/p/americans-seek-stories-of-solutio ns?utm_source=substack&utm_medium=email&mc_cid=18acd442 9f&mc_eid=a2e d5f635d.

57. Alexander L. Curry and Keith H. Hammonds, "The Power of Solutions Journalism," *Engaging News Project/Solutions Journalism Network*, 2014, https://mediaengagement.org/wp-content/uploads/2014/06/ENP_SJN-report.pdf; Alexander L. Curry, Natalie Jomini Stroud, and Shannon McGregor, "Solutions Journalism and News Engagement," *Engaging News Project*, 2016, https://mediaengagement.org/wp-content/uploads/2016/03/ENP-Solutions-Journalism-News-Engagement.pdf; Michelle Gielan, Brent Furl, and Jodie Jackson, "Solutions-Focused News Increases Optimism, Empowerment, and Connectedness to Community," *Institute for Applied Research*, 2017, https://michellegielan.com/wp-content/uploads/2017/03/Solution-focused-News.pdf; Zhao, Jackson, and Nguyen, "The Psychological Empowerment Potential of Solutions Journalism."

58. Karen McIntrye, "Constructive Journalism: The Effects of Positive Emotions and Solution Information in News Stories" (doctoral diss., Chapel Hill, NC, The University of North Carolina at Chapel Hill, 2015).

59. Herbert J. Gans, "What Can Journalists Do for American Democracy?" *Harvard International Journal of Press/Politics* 3, no. 4 (1998): 6–12.

60. James B. Lemert, Barry N. Mitzman, Michael A. Seither, Roxana H. Cook, and Regina Hackett, "Journalists and Mobilizing Information," *Journalism Quarterly* 54, no. 4 (1977): 721–26.

61. Hoffman, "Is Internet Content Different After All?"; Lemert, et al., "Journalists and Mobilizing Information."

62. Lemert et al., "Journalists and Mobilizing Information," 725; Hoffman, "Is Internet Content Different After All?"

63. Charles Payne, "Ella Baker and Models of Social Change," *Signs* 14, no. 4 (1989): 885–89.

64. James B. Lemert, "News Context and the Elimination of Mobilizing Information: An Experiment," *Journalism Quarterly* 61, no. 2 (1984): 259–62.

65. James B. Lemert and Marguerite Gemson Ashman, "Extent of Mobilizing Information in Opinion and News Magazines," *Journalism Quarterly* 60, no. 4 (1983): 657–62.

66. Lough and McIntyre, "Journalists' Perceptions of Solutions Journalism and Its Place in the Field."

67. Powers and Curry, "No Quick Fix"; McIntyre, "Solutions Journalism: The Effects of Including Solution Information in News Stories about Social Problems."

68. Jesse Abdenour, Karen McIntyre, and Nicole Dahmen, "Putting Broadcast News in Context: An Analysis of U.S. Television Journalists' Role Conceptions and Contextual Values," *Electronic News* 12, no. 3 (2018): 179–93.

69. Foshay and Kirkley, "Principles for Teaching Problem Solving."

70. Bashar Abubakar, "A Tale of Two PHCs in Niger State: Accessing Equitable Healthcare From Beji to Maito," *Nigeria Health Watch*, July 23, 2019, https://articles.nigeriahealthwatch.com/a-tale-of-two-phcs-in-niger-state-accessing-equitable-healthcare-from-beji-to-maito/?amp=1.

71. Daria Sukharchuk, "What Makes a Successful Solutions Journalism Story?" *International Journalists' Network*, October 30, 2018, https://ijnet.org/en/story/what-makes-successful-solutions-journalism-story.

72. Laura R. Novick and Miriam Bassok, "Problem Solving," in *The Cambridge Handbook of Thinking and Reasoning*, ed. Keith J. Holyoak and Robert G. Morrison (Cambridge, MA: Cambridge University Press, 2005), 321–49; Jan Maarten Schraagen, "How Experts Solve a Novel Problem in Experimental Design," *Cognitive Science* 17 (1993): 285–309; Smith, "A View from Biology."

73. Bandura, "Exercise of Human Agency through Collective Efficacy," 75.

74. Bandura, "Self-Efficacy Mechanism in Human Agency," 469.

75. Bashar Abubakar, "Beyond Surgery: Gesse Centre's Innovative Approach to Fistula Care in Kebbi," *Nigeria Health Watch*, April 23, 2019, https://articles.nigeriahealthwatch.com/beyond-surgery-gesse-centres-innovative-approach-to-fistula-care-in-kebbi/.

76. Lillian Namusoke Magezi, "Mass Treatment Helps Uganda to Eliminate Trachoma," *New Vision*, August 14, 2018, https://www.newvision.co.ug/news/1483474/mass-treatment-helps-uganda-eliminate-trachoma.

77. Michele K. Olson, Sarah C. Vos, and Jeannette Sutton, "Threat and Efficacy in Television News: Reporting on an Emerging Infectious Disease," *Western Journal of Communication* 84, no. 5 (2020): 623–40.

78. Kathryn S. Quick and March S. Feldman, "Distinguishing Participation and Inclusion," *Journal of Planning Education and Research* 31 (2011): 272–90.

79. Lucy Purdy, "Library of Things: Borrow Power Tools, Ukuleles, and Ice Cream Makers Alongside Books," *Positive*, May 10, 2018, https://www.positive.news/society/library-of-things-borrow-power-tools-ukuleles-and-ice-cream-makers-alongside-books/.

80. Wenzel, Gersen, and Moreno, "Engaging Communities through Solutions Journalism."

81. Andrew H. Van de Ven, *Engaged Scholarship: A Guide for Organizational and Social Research* (New York: Oxford University Press, 2007).

82. John A. Meacham and Nancy Cooney, "The Interpersonal Basis of Every Day Problem Solving," in *Everyday Problem Solving: Theory and Application*, ed. Jan D. Sinnott (Santa Barbara, CA: Praeger, 1989), 7–23.

83. John Dewey, "Experience and Education," in *The Kappa Delta Pi Lecture Series* (New York: Macmillan, 1963).

84. John Dyer, "Is Solutions Journalism the Solution?" *Nieman Reports*, June 11, 2015, https://niemanreports.org/articles/is-solutions-journalism-the-solution/.

Chapter 10

Media Monopolies and News Making

An Analysis of How Media Conglomeration Affects the Marketplace of Ideas

Cayce Myers

Mainstream media has undergone a litany of criticisms in the 2020s. It is the source of political polarization, fake news, news bias, sensationalism, and a general decline in the intellectual discussions in American society. In fact, the 2023 Edelman Trust Barometer, a global annual trust analysis, found that media and the government are viewed as primary sources of misleading information. Journalists were found to be one of the most distrusted institutional leaders, along with government leaders and CEOs.[1] This analysis is ironic; mainstream media has never been more accessible, faster, or more pervasive in US history. American society has never had as much information as it has today, yet because overall media content quality has declined many Americans greatly distrust the sources of that information.

News making is inextricably intertwined with news business. In the 2020s, the mainstream news in the United States is a mixture of traditional and new media. Radio, television, and newspapers still have a presence in the media landscape. However, they have been replaced by and supplemented with digital outlets, notably social media. Because of this, news information is more diffused and, as a result, more susceptible to manipulation and disinformation. This has created a real distrust of media by American viewers. According to Gallup, in 2022 only 34 percent of Americans trust the media, with Democrats far more likely to trust the media (70 percent) than

Republicans (14 percent).[2] High levels of trust in the media is quite low, with only 7 percent of the US adult population, Republicans and Democrats, saying they have "great trust," compared with 38 percent of adult Americans have "no trust" in newspapers.[3]

Media conglomeration is potentially a big part of the reason this distrust in media is so high. Viewpoint diversity in mainstream US media is low, in part because large companies own so much of the US media. Looking back to 1983, media ownership in the United States was more diversified with around fifty companies owning approximately 90 percent of all media outlets. By 2012, that number had shrunk significantly to only six companies owning 90 percent of outlets.[4] Today, that number has changed again because of the introduction of new media, such as streaming services, but large media conglomerates still dominate the ownership in US outlets.

How did mainstream media get to where it is today? How did the media go from having figures such as Walter Cronkite of CBS News, who was voted the most trusted figure in the United States from 1973 to 1995, to having media and journalists viewed as primary sources of disinformation in 2023?[5] What can be done to restore mainstream media into a place of prominence and trust within the United States? In this chapter, I provide some answers to these questions by examining the US laws and policies that have allowed mainstream media to be controlled by a clique of large corporations. This chapter begins with an examination of the current viewership trends in mainstream media and demonstrates how audience segmentation has presented unique problems to the business model of news. Next, I explore the increased conglomeration of ownership of US mainstream media companies and analyze the ownership regulations and antitrust laws that have allowed this growth. In the next section I share my analysis of how media conglomeration impacts the marketplace of ideas, particularly in a political context, and present contemporary criticism of the impact concentrated media ownership has on news production, the rise of fake news, and the homogenization of information. I conclude with suggestions on how this can be addressed, namely by consumers, and how the media marketplace largely reflects consumer taste.

Of course, the overriding question of this chapter and book is about "fixing" mainstream media and is rooted in an underlying assumption about media. That is, that media today has some type of inherent flaw that has caused distrust, and that if this flaw were addressed there would be some type of workable solution. Examining the laws regulating business mergers and acquisitions for media companies, I show that regulating the size and conglomeration of media does not have the effect of improving media quality. Instead, it is up to the consumers of media to demand better content, and it is the responsibility of an informed citizenry to fix what is wrong with American media today.

DEFINING MAINSTREAM MEDIA: A BLURRED LINE

Understanding the current problems in mainstream media is rooted in the business of news. Mainstream media is typically thought to be the broadcast and print media that represent the so-called traditional media of the 2020s. However, mainstream media today is not a clear-cut term. In a 2021 study, Pew Research found that mainstream media varies among American media consumers with mainstream status fluctuating between outlets. For example, broadcast and cable outlets, such as ABC, CNN, and Fox News, are overwhelmingly identified as mainstream media. So are print outlets such as the *New York Times* and even the more tabloid *New York Post*. However, online outlets such as Huffington Post, Buzzfeed, Newsmax, and Breitbart are not.[6] Looking at this analysis, mainstream media appears to be identified more with outlet typology (broadcast/cable/print) than political viewpoint. However, in terms of identity the mainstream media has credibility issues with a majority of Americans with 56 percent agreeing with the statement, "Journalists and reporters are purposely trying to mislead people by saying things they know are false or gross exaggerations."[7] Within mainstream media there is sharp criticism for so-called left-wing news. For example, Laura Ingraham of Fox News and host of the *Ingraham Angle* referred to the mainstream media as the "political wing of the Secret Service" in a monologue in March 2021.[8] Despite the political identity of some mainstream media, I do not identify mainstream media as a political ideology but as popular media outlets, including traditional print, broadcast, and cable, as well as digital and social media.

A complicating factor in the identity of mainstream media is social media. Social media has traditionally been thought of as separate from the more established mainstream media. That is because social media began as an individual user experience in which personal accounts shared content. However, in 2023, most, if not all, so-called mainstream media outlets have a presence online and are active in social media content production. In fact, consumers of mainstream media content frequently gain access to the content through social media, and the traction mainstream media has is amplified by the sharing of content on social media. In that sense, speaking about social media as distinct from mainstream traditional media ignores a reality about current media use. Mainstream media is represented on social and vice versa. So in speaking about the issues of mainstream media, particularly in viewpoint diversity, I have included both traditional and social under the umbrella term of "mainstream media."

MEDIA CONSUMPTION: BLENDING TRADITIONAL AND SOCIAL MEDIA

The current issues in mainstream media are in some ways born out of the consumer use of specific mediums. Broadcast and print media have undergone a decline in viewership in the past thirty years, which has significantly changed their content and impact in US society. Conversely, social media have proliferated in the past twenty years, with social media use being a form of media that has increased among all major US age demographics.[9] As a result, when discussing the decline of mainstream media, that discussion is centered on traditional media, that is, print, broadcast, and radio. However, that is only part of the story. Social media has revolutionized how content is produced and consumed. Mainstream media is highly impacted by social media, and the Centre for Economic Policy Research (CEPR) finds that social media, for example, Twitter (now X), frequently serves as an agenda-setting medium for traditional media coverage.[10] Discussing the current reality of mainstream media requires an analysis of both social and traditional media. These two halves of the whole of mainstream media present stark contrasts. Understanding both categories of media is essential to understanding why media conglomeration works the way it does and why, as a whole, mainstream media has become a more homogenized and concentrated voice in news content.

Broadcast news is an area where viewership has increasingly declined for the past forty years. In 1980 the big three network news programs on CBS, NBC, and ABC ranged in evening news viewership from 12.6 million (ABC) to 15.9 million (CBS).[11] Compare that with April 2023 where the big three networks are in a heated ratings battle for evening news ratings with the winner garnering a viewership of just over 7.9 million, half of the total of the top evening news in 1980.[12] The decline of newspapers in the United States presents one of the most significant and stunning examples of the change in media in the twenty-first century. In a 2021 study, Pew Research found that weekly newspaper readership was at a low of just over twenty-four million estimated readers in 2020, down from a high of over sixty million readers from the 1960s to the early 1990s.[13] Gone are the days when a large city would have newspaper competition between two or more dailies. Most newspapers today are owned by a handful of companies, with half of the major US daily newspapers (382 out of 672) owned by just seven companies.[14] This conglomeration also represents a trend in the newspaper business where certain areas have become so-called news deserts, where there is no newspaper covering local issues. As a result, 200 counties in the United States have no newspaper, and 1,540 have only one newspaper. This has only become a compounded problem with the limitations of COVID-19 pandemic restrictions, which have resulted in problems, both in reporting and readership, for local newspapers.[15] Online newspaper subscriptions and advertising revenue have also made newspapers a less lucrative business. According to the Associated Press in 2022, newspapers continue to die at a rate of two per week, with newspaper revenue overall decreasing by more than half, $50 billion to $21 billion, from 2006 to 2022.[16]

Print, cable, broadcast, and radio all have another aspect in common. They have all experienced a significant decline in employees. In 2008, there were approximately 114,000 newsroom employees in the United States inclusive of all journalists, editors, and videographers in a cross-section of media including broadcast, print, radio, and cable. By 2020, that number was 85,000, a 26 percent decline.[17] This trend bears out in recent college graduates who are journalism majors. According to Georgetown University's Center for Education in the Workforce, only 15 percent of journalism majors find early career employment as news analysts, reporters, or correspondents.[18]

In contrast to traditional media, news consumption on social media has proliferated. A Pew Research study in 2021 shows that half of all Americans get their news from social media, with only 9 percent of Americans not using social media for news ever.[19] Of the social media platforms nearly one-third of Americans use Facebook for their source of news with YouTube coming in at second place at 22 percent. Democrats are slightly more likely to get news using social media, but Republicans do regularly use social media for news.[20] However, social media continues to have high levels of distrust in society. According to the 2023 Edelman Trust Barometer, social media is distrusted by a majority of people globally.[21]

This perception of distrust presents a unique divide between journalists and nonjournalist news consumers. Journalists have much higher rates of social media use than nonjournalists, with 94 percent of journalists using social media in their jobs regularly with Twitter being the primary platform in 2022 (prior to Elon Musk's takeover of Twitter).[22] The use of social media has residual effects on news content with journalists' use of social media informing news coverage, story ideas, leads, and news context. The CEPR, a pan-European nonpartisan nonprofit, found that this reliance on social media by journalists can create a distorted news process in which journalists misconstrue public sentiment and distort facts.[23] There is some recognition by journalists that social media may actually harm the news reporting process with the Medill Media Industry Survey finding that 90 percent of journalists think social media gives a bad mix of news and early 80 percent think social media has adversely impacted news content.[24]

Notwithstanding that criticism, social media and mainstream news have a symbiotic relationship with social media being used regularly by mainstream news outlets and their journalists. As of the writing of this chapter in 2023, the *New York Times*, @nytimes, has fifty-five million Twitter followers and has had a presence on the platform since 2007. CNN Breaking News, @cnnbrk, also enjoys a strong following on Twitter with sixty-four million followers. This type of social media presence is not limited to Twitter or to news organizations. Journalists who work in the mainstream media frequently have large followings on social media and are major influencers in trending news stories on social media. For example, Rachel Maddow of MSNBC and Anderson Cooper of CNN rank as some of the most followed journalists on Twitter. However, on the list of most followed journalists also include non-US broadcast journalist celebrities including Carlos Loret de Mola, a *Washington Post* contributor and former host of a morning show on Mexican multimedia network Televisa.[25] This use of social media for journalists is something that is part of brand management for the individual journalist. Doing it well means building credibility while also developing a following for content at mainstream news outlets. There are risks as well as rewards, however, as journalists on social media face public backlash toward their work and even their personal lives in what has been termed "dark participation" of citizen journalists and nonjournalist social media users.[26] Newsrooms have become more involved in regulating these individual accounts, noting that journalists' social presence reflects on the branding and reputation of the news outlet. This has led to some consternation of journalists who think these in-house regulations restrict their individuality and even their personal journalistic brand.[27]

Despite these disagreements, what is evident is that traditional media, or so-called mainstream media, and social media enjoy a synergistic relationship. Understanding how to address the issues in mainstream media requires a new conceptualization of news that embraces the multimedia aspect of news creation and communication. Looking at mainstream news' decline on its traditional platforms, for example, television or print, tells only part of the story of news. Social media content is populated by mainstream news, and mainstream news content is frequently generated by and populated with content from nonjournalists, citizen journalists, and garden variety social media users.

CONGLOMERATION AND DEREGULATION OF MEDIA OWNERSHIP: VIEWPOINT DIVERSITY VERSUS REGULATION

Conglomeration is the by-product of two intertwined events. The first is the massive deregulation of the broadcast market in the 1980s through the 2000s. The second is the increased competition news outlets have experienced in the past forty years. Media conglomeration has controversial results. Some argue that concentrated media ownership creates a lack of viewpoint diversity and separates media from local interests and control. Critics of this philosophy argue that within the past thirty years of conglomeration viewpoint diversity really is not an issue. If anything, larger corporations are able to produce content that has increased diversity of views because large companies have the resources to support talent that can provide a variety of perspectives.[28]

From the 1920s to the 1990s, the US government supported heavy regulations on radio and television based on the spectrum scarcity, a concept that meant the literal scarcity of frequencies were finite and had to be carefully managed. This rationale was a major force within broadcast regulation, and its philosophical approach to regulation can be seen in laws such as the Radio Act of 1927 and the Communications Act of 1934.[29] The underlying philosophy of spectrum scarcity was the basis for many ancillary issues in broadcasting content unrelated to licensing, such as the Fairness Doctrine, which required broadcasters to provide equal time for public issues. The US Supreme Court even held that this concept of equal time was constitutional under the First Amendment because of the unique power and scarcity of broadcast.[30]

Beginning in the 1940s, the FCC embraced the linkage between viewpoint diversity and media conglomeration without looking specifically at the relationship between media ownership and viewpoints.[31] The underlying philosophy between media ownership and diversity was that conflicting views that enhance robust debate in the political sphere in the United States are supported by limiting the conglomeration of media. That philosophy is rooted in the FCC values of competition, localism, and diversity, which are separate but intertwined concepts that ensure a robust multisided debate in the broadcast marketplace that is reflective of communities.[32] This philosophical approach was known as the convergent hypothesis, which argued that concentrated ownership reduces viewpoint diversity because of the inherent nature of media conglomerations. By the 1970s, the FCC went further in its analysis of conglomeration creating rules about newspaper and broadcast crossover. In 1975, the FCC restricted common ownership of a newspaper and a broadcast station (either television or radio) within the same media market. There were also rules that capped market ownership in broadcast, and a dual network rule that banned major networks (for example, Fox, CBS, ABC, and NBC) from ever merging. For example, there was a national television ownership rule that banned any one company from owning an aggregate television market of more than 39 percent, and an outright ban of any network from having any stake in program syndication. Courts upheld these regulations primarily because of studies that seemed to support the convergent hypothesis, with little concern over these studies' validity. For example, the newspaper broadcast crossover rule was challenged by the American Newspaper Publishers Association in a case that ultimately was decided by the US Supreme Court. In its decision, the issue of the relationship between viewpoint diversity and ownership was largely dismissed by the court. Citing the "elusive concepts" of diversity and media ownership the US Supreme Court did not agree that the underlying concepts of viewpoint diversity and conglomeration were questionable.[33]

This attitude toward media conglomeration changed with the 1996 Telecommunications Act, a landmark law that fundamentally altered the news media landscape.[34] The act removed national ownership rules for radio stations but retained local market restrictions, such as limiting a licensee ownership to a set number of stations depending on market size.[35] Similar caps were removed for broadcast television allowing companies to own an unlimited number of television stations so long as the aggregate ownership did not exceed 35 percent of the television market in the United States. That was later raised to 45 percent and again reduced to 39 percent with the rationale that group ownership actually increased program quality for media consumers.[36] The act also limited the number of television stations owned in a given market initially requiring at least eight stations to remain if a company owned two stations in that market. That rule also was eliminated later in 2017 under the opinion that local conglomeration allowed local markets to be better served by broadcasters. Cross-media ownership, the ownership of television and radio stations, was also revised under the act. In 2009 the US Court of Appeals of the DC Circuit struck down the cross-ownership rules regarding cable companies owning broadcast stations.[37] By 2017, the FCC removed all cross ownership rules for newspaper-broadcast and radio-television citing the growth of multiple sources for local news. The US Supreme Court in 2021 upheld this change in *FCC v. Prometheus Radio Project*, citing that the FCC's rationale for the removal of the rule was not arbitrary or capricious under the Administrative Procedure Act.[38]

After the implementation of the Telecommunications Act of 1996, federal courts reversed several regulations on broadcast station ownership. The Court also moved away from the concept of convergent hypothesis, embracing an economic legal theory from the Chicago School of Economics and promoted by economist Robert Coase, Judge Richard Posner of the US Court of Appeals for the Seventh Circuit, and Judge Guido Calabresi of the US Court of Appeals for the Second Circuit. The Chicago School focused on microeconomic consideration in legal application, specifically in issues surrounding antitrust. This legal philosophy argued that when examining conglomeration there must be a cost-benefit analysis for consumers, and that in many respects conglomeration had benefits for consumers including lower cost and greater access to goods and services. Within broadcast conglomeration this economic theory of law gained traction, particularly with the influential Judge Posner, Judge Frank Easterbrook, and Judge Robert Bork of the Seventh Circuit. Judge Posner applied aspects of this theory to a 1992 case *Schurz Communications, Inc. v. FCC* involving viewpoint diversity and media ownership.[39] Other cases followed suit. In 2001 the US Court of Appeals for the DC Circuit struck down the so-called vertical limit on the number of channels owned by affiliated programmers.[40] A year later, the DC Circuit struck down a regulation, known as the local ownership rule, that required common ownership to only exist in markets where there were at least eight independent voices.[41] In that case the court struck down the ban on broadcast stations and syndication rules based on the fact the FCC could not articulate how the rule advanced viewpoint diversity.

Recently, the issue with the FCC and cable operators has focused on cable operators' decision on which cable outlets they will carry. The FCC can intervene in some situations where the cable operator demands financial interest in the outlet, demands exclusive rights to carry, or discriminates against nonaffiliated networks.[42] These carry issues have even given rise to cases where there an intersection between cable carry and alleged racial discrimination.[43] Still, cable and broadcast regulation continues. Must carry rules that require cable providers to carry broadcast stations are still required for all but the smallest cable providers, and the requirement has been upheld twice by the US Supreme Court.[44] As technology has progressed in the digital era, this must carry rule for digital broadcast, which can have multiple channels in addition to its main channel, presents a unique application of the must carry rule. Currently, the FCC states that the digital must carry only applies to the main broadcast channel rather than all the channels.[45]

In the current environment, although the media convergence theory has some devotees, it has been largely debunked by scholars and jurists. As legal scholars Daniel Ho and Kevin Quinn point out in their analysis of viewpoint diversity, the convergence hypothesis is "tautologically true that if two media outlets merge, one 'voice' is lost."[46] However, that loss of voice is much more complex. Ho and Quinn argue that there is a concept of "monopoly diversification," which posits that uniformity of news in most mainstream news outlets in a centrist viewpoint may be used to attract the majority of consumers.

However, that may not be the actual goal of any firm. Instead, the monopoly of news outlets may create diversification in order to attract consumers into segmented markets, therefore creating viewpoint diversity.[47] While Ho and Quinn's analysis may be true in some sense, it does not explain the emergence of diversity of news content in the fractured news market. Diversity of viewpoint does not emerge in mainstream news content. Rather, there have been an increase of news content, mainly conservative in different digital spaces, namely podcasts and social media. For example, after being fired from Fox News, Tucker Carlson released a nearly three-minute video on his Twitter account on May 9, 2023. In less than one month, that video had 133 million views.[48] Even though this video is a small clip on social media, it does demonstrate where the competition for mainstream news might emerge. Figures such as Carlson, and other media figures such as former Fox News anchor Megyn Kelly, have name recognition and cache that can take viewers away from mainstream news platforms, such as Fox News. This means that market segmentation for viewers becomes further fractured, causing news outlets to focus on niche programming that does not approach the political center.

ANTITRUST AND BIG TECH

Compounding this issue of media conglomeration is the large, established multibillion dollar social media companies and search engines known as Big Tech. Accounting for $7.17 trillion, or 18.35 percent of the total capitalization of the S&P 500, Big Tech (Amazon, Apple, Google, and Facebook) purchased over five hundred different companies since 1998.[49] As a result, they represent one of the largest segment of wealth and control over communication in the world. Critics argue that this conglomeration of Big Tech, similar to the conglomeration of media, represents a challenge to viewpoint diversity and adversely impacts the content and organization of information. Unlike broadcast and cable news, the legal approach that would address the rise of social media is antitrust law. Created in the late nineteenth century, antitrust laws in the United States attempt to regulate the market for the benefit of consumers. The idea behind the traditional approach to antitrust law is that consumers benefit when there is a robust marketplace of choices and that monopolies actually harm consumers and business in general because of the anticompetitive environment they create.

The Sherman Act, passed in 1890, was the first attempt to regulate monopolies by federal statute.[50] This law prohibited unreasonable mergers and acquisitions of businesses, but it leaves the decision of what is unreasonable to federal courts. An early application of the Sherman Act was in 1911 with the landmark case of *Standard Oil Co. of New Jersey v. United*

States. Controlling nearly 90 percent of US oil refineries, Standard Oil used its position in business to force favorable business treatment, specifically railroad pricing. Finding for the United States, the US Supreme Court held that section 2 of the Sherman Act had a minimum threshold for violation that required the government to show that there was the use of a monopoly to facilitate anticompetitive conduct.[51] Later Congress passed the Clayton Antitrust Act of 1914, commonly referred to as the Clayton Act, which permitted lawsuits by individuals who were harmed by entities engaged in anticompetitive behavior.[52] That same year Congress passed the FTC Act, which created the FTC as an administrative agency and tasked the organization to enforce laws promoting competition and antitrust.[53]

Antitrust as a concept also underwent philosophical changes since the enactment of the Sherman, Clayton, and FTC Acts. The ability of a company to compete within the marketplace is at the core of these statutory protections. The primary consideration in these laws is the ability of the consumers to have agency in their purchase decisions and have the ability to gain access to options in their purchasing choices. Two schools of thought have been at odds in the development of antitrust law, the Harvard and Chicago Schools, and the legal acceptance of these antitrust philosophies has guided courts' decisions. The Harvard School, established by a group of Harvard legal-economic scholars including Donald F. Turner and Phillip Areeda, viewed mergers, acquisitions, and other conglomerations as presumptively illegal because such agreements enhanced market power. This view was accepted by federal courts and agencies during the 1960s through the 1970s. Using this antitrust philosophy, little attention was paid to the benefits conglomeration could have on consumers, especially in terms of lowering prices.[54]

In response to the Harvard School, the Chicago School of antitrust emerged with proponents including Judge Robert Bork. Unlike the certitude of the Harvard School, the Chicago School looked at more nuanced issues such as consumer rights. Judge Bork saw antitrust as a legal mechanism that was in place to promote efficiency of markets.[55] For the Chicago School, the intervention into the market only occurred when anticompetitive practices were threatening consumer welfare. The core belief in the Chicago School was that markets can self-correct and that Harvard School interventionists did not have the level of insight to see that intervention in markets yielded bad results for consumers. By the 1980s, the Chicago School effectively won out over the Harvard School with a new strain of antitrust cases citing the underlying philosophies of market self-correction and consumerism.[56]

Big Tech in the 2020s has largely been kept intact because of the prevalence of Chicago School legal philosophy. Challenges to the size of Big Tech corporations do occur, as is the case in 2023 when the US Department of

Justice (DOJ) sued Google for monopolizing digital advertising technology under the first and second sections of the Sherman Act.[57] However, monopolizing content in a way where consumers cannot make a choice is a different story. Cases against Big Tech have not led to large breakups of companies. The closest case in antitrust law to dismantling a Big Tech company came in 1998 with the case *United States v. Microsoft Corporation* where the DOJ claimed Microsoft forced PC manufacturers to use Internet Explorer instead of Java or Netscape in its original manufacturing in violation of the Sherman Act.[58] While the US District Court for the District of Columbia held that Microsoft violated the Sherman Act and had to split into two separate companies, the Court of Appeals for the DC Circuit overturned the District Court's decision. Microsoft later settled with the DOJ without having to break into two companies. This decision in Microsoft foreshadowed how Big Tech would be evaluated under antitrust law. Corporations that include Apple, Alphabet (Google), Meta (Facebook and Instagram), and Amazon continue to grow and thrive in the current marketplace. While the European Union Commission has investigated the monopolistic aspects of Google search apps and Microsoft Teams, the US government has not been so eager to follow suit. Perhaps part of the reason is the research on antitrust intervention has borne out that intervention, much like the Chicago School advocates profess, does not translate into product innovation.[59]

HOW TO FIX MAINSTREAM MEDIA: QUESTIONS AND A POSSIBLE SOLUTION

Examining the laws of conglomeration begs the question: Can the law "fix" what is wrong with mainstream media? We have seen how issues of viewpoint diversity and antitrust have largely not been able to "fix" issues of content or bias. The fragmentation of media has led to increased niche programming and a general decline in the once dominant sphere of broadcast and cable news as well as newspapers. It is also important to note that there is no solution to any media problem that will create a new reality of news that reverts back to the predigital era. It is also worth pointing out that when there was a "most trusted man" in America, there was still media bias, even by him. To address the issues in news content today requires an acknowledgment of the current technological reality of news delivery. In the section that follows I present three questions and answer them both from a legal and practical standpoint, ultimately concluding that while the law does have a role in correcting some of the problems in twenty-first-century media, the responsibility of fixing the problems ultimately lies with us as the consumers.

Could Antitrust Lawsuits or Ownership Regulations Fix Traditional Media?

Potentially yes, but it may come at a large unintended price. Antitrust laws and regulations on ownership of media are meant to preserve the competitive marketplace. By not legally permitting media oligopolies, there is an increase of diverse ownership and, as a result, the potential for greater viewpoint diversity. Traditional media have become less diverse in ownership in broadcast since the Telecommunications Act of 1996, and the increase of large newspaper chains has certainly created a reality in print journalism where there is no true newspaper competition today between dailies. This conglomeration of newspapers has also created an economic reality where news as a commodity is packaged in a way that is shared across outlets, creating a lower need for journalists and other newsroom personnel. Perhaps the marketplace of ideas would be well served to enforce more stringent antitrust laws and refining broadcast ownership rules to allow for less market share being owned by a single company.

Despite the potential of this solution, the reality would likely be less news content. The reason for this is the traditional news business has undergone such changes that individual medium ownership would likely be not economically viable. The decline in viewers and readers coupled with the change in advertising revenue means that broadcast outlets and newspapers as a business requires conglomeration to work as a business model. The day of owning a successful newspaper or broadcast station as a single entity is largely over, and this is why conglomeration, for better or worse, is likely the reason these stations and newspapers can survive. There are some alternatives, such as running newspapers more or less as a philanthropy, for example, Jeff Bezos and the *Washington Post*, or nonprofit newspapers sponsored by donations and grants. However, these types of newspaper structures are limited and have their own inherent limitations surrounding funding and potential bias.

Could Antitrust Lawsuit or Ownership Regulations Fix Large Online Media Companies?

Potentially yes, but it depends on what the competition does. The dominance of social media and other large online companies, such as Alphabet, has a major impact on what information people see. Antitrust could break large social media conglomerates, for example, Meta, into smaller companies. This would obviously increase competition. However, the question here is what would result that actually improves the news experience of users. Smaller social media companies could then emerge and tailor their algorithm and community standards to show people different information.

There is the potential that breaking large media companies, for example, Meta, Microsoft Apple, and Alphabet, into smaller components would lessen their power in controlling the flow of information. For example, Google controls much of the way information is organized because it controls over 80 percent of the global search market share.[60] There is also algorithmic dominance of companies such as Meta (Facebook) who use data analytics to control what information people receive. That coupled with community standards, those formalized rules of social media, also regulate what information a person can actually see on social media. Regulation in this area could remove the position of some companies such as Alphabet (Google) from its superdominance in communication control and organization. New companies could emerge to compete in the social media sphere, creating an increased viewpoint diversity and, as a by-product, a different user experience. This would not, however, change the policies or approaches of other social media companies. The net result would likely be the dominance of the giant online social media corporations would remain, but with slightly less dominance than before.

WHAT CAN FIX MAINSTREAM MEDIA?

News is a reflection of society's demands. Whether it be Sunday morning political talk shows or tabloid-style entertainment programming, the media gives consumers ultimately what they want. After all, the news business is a business that relies on customers to consume its product. For mainstream news that product is content, and the content relayed by mainstream media is a reflection of two dichotomous entities—newsworthy information and audience taste. In striking the balance between these two forces, news is broadcast, printed, or circulated on the internet. And it is this consumption of this manufactured content that informs our ideals, aspirations, opinions, thoughts, votes, purchases, attitudes, and behavior. Given these high stakes and big impacts of news, understanding what is right or wrong with the process is important.

Although the causes of contemporary problems in American society are difficult to precisely identify, what is clear is media, mainstream or otherwise, has an impact. In fact, the press as a whole plays an important role in representing, defining, and changing American identity and culture. As media and pop historian Michael Schudson states, it is the press that is the "representative carrier and construer and creator of modern public consciousness."[61] However, the media is not a unidimensional communicator. It both speaks to and hears from society at large. Social media, if anything, has increased that two-way communication. In his groundbreaking analysis of public opinion published a century ago, Edward Bernays pointed out that the press (pretelevision, pre-internet, and pre–social media) was an institution that was highly influenced by and affected by the public's sentiments.[62] It represented the public's interests and reflected that in the work it produced. News was a reflection of what readership demanded. That, of course, makes sense, even in today's vastly more complex media world, because news is a business. It relies on consumers of media to ensure its success, and while business models have changed and continue to evolve, it is the readership and viewers that still determine what is going to be watched, heard, or reposted.

That leads us to the question of what really can be done to "fix" the mainstream media. As I have argued throughout this chapter, the idea that there's a mainstream versus nonmainstream media is hard to justify because there is such an interconnectedness between media outlets, journalists, and consumers of news. Looking at issues of conglomeration, it is hard to imagine there is a cure-all. After all, the media issues today are complex, and the law is not always the best mechanism to ensure change. It is true that if media ownership laws changed, there would be a different media landscape. Perhaps that would ensure more accountability and more viewpoint diversity. Certainly it would lessen the power of the small clique of large media companies dominating the news. However, would these changes really result in real beneficial changes in media consumption? Would American news consumers really have greater insights into the complex issues facing society? Would there be a change for the better of society? In my opinion, not likely.

The reason I think that is based in what Schudson and Bernays said: media reflects society. Consumers of media in many ways control what the media says because they control what is consumed. Change would only occur if consumption changed. We have seen that with the demands of partisan cable news, the rise of talk radio, and the choices on social media of who gets followed and who does not. Although there are mechanisms in the law that can lead to more outlets and more voices, it is ultimately up to the consumers of media to decide what is going to be listened to. The analysis of antitrust law shows that media monopoly does not necessarily create new outlets or perspectives. If anything, regulations requiring the breakup of media companies may actually stifle media viewpoint diversity. The "problem" of mainstream media is frequently rooted in bias. Because of that, news consumers must go to new sources of content to find news that has a different perspective. This, in turn, may have an effect on mainstream news itself, as losing viewers to digital media, for example podcasts and social media accounts, may create a corrective response to win back audience share. These newer news sources also enjoy a confidence mainstream media does not. For example, the Pew Research Center found that 87 percent of podcast listeners expect the content to be "mostly accurate."[63] All of these statistics and history of media also present a new question: Should mainstream media be fixed? There is increasing evidence that the answer to that is no, because mainstream media today is evolving in a way where streaming content, digital outlets, and social media are replacing it. Perhaps the real problem of mainstream media is that it has outlived its purpose, and the present US news consumer no longer has a need for its type of content because other alternatives are available.

The media in America has evolved dramatically since the founding of this country from the partisan press of the eighteenth century, to the penny press of the early nineteenth century, to the sensationalist muckrakers of the early twentieth century, to the influencers of the twenty-first century. Those trends in media were made in large part by changes in technology and changes in society. All of those iterations of the press received widespread readership and widespread criticism. So, in many ways, fixing the media is an oft repeated refrain in American history, and one that will likely continue.[64]

That may lead many readers to think I have no solutions to offer, only ponderous observations, typical of any academic analysis. However, there is one way to fix the media permanently, for the better, and with little to no legal intervention: the marketplace. Consumers dictate what is offered to them by having expectations. The mainstream media's news content is no different than any other item in the marketplace. It is consumed because the public decides to consume it. Journalism is undergoing a radical transformation in the 2020s as once sacred news concepts, such as objectivism, have given way to a more advocacy-based journalism that is "trustworthy."[65] That change in approach will inevitably change the type of news that is consumed. However, the true test of whether that type of news gathering and writing will be accepted is if the public permits it. Laws regulating media, business, and power can produce good results. They can cure some symptoms of problems. However, fixing the media in the twenty-first century lies within us to determine what is going to define "modern public consciousness."[66]

NOTES

1. "Edelman Trust Barometer Global Report," Edelman.com, accessed April 20, 2023, https://www.edelman.com/sites/g/files/aatuss191/files/2023-01/2023%20Edelman%20Trust%20Barometer%20Global%20Report.pdf.

2. Megan Brenan, "Americans' Trust in Media Remains Near Record Low," Gallup, November 17, 2022, accessed April 19, 2023, https://news.gallup.com/poll/403166/americans-trust-media-remains-near-record-low.aspx.

3. Ibid.

4. Michael Corcoran, "Twenty Years of Media Consolidation Has Not Been Good for Our Democracy," BillMoyers.com, September 28, 2016, accessed April 20, 2023, https://billmoyers.com/story/twenty-years-of-media-consolidation-has-not-been-good-for-our-democracy/. At the time this statistic was provided mergers and acquisitions changed the percentages. However, the larger narrative that a few companies control a vast majority of media remains true.

5. "Cronkite Podcast: The Most Trusted Man in America," Journalism History, July 19, 2020, video, https://journalism-history.org/2020/07/19/cronkite-podcast-the-most-trusted-man-in-america/.

6. Elisa Shearer and Amy Mitchell, "Broad Agreement in U.S.—Even among Partisans—on Which News Outlets Are Part of the 'Mainstream Media,'" Pew Research Center, May 19, 2021, accessed April 19, 2023, https://www.pewresearch.org/fact-tank/2021/05/07/broad-agreement-in-u-s-even-among-partisans-on-which-news-outlets-are-part-of-the-mainstream-media/.

7. A. Meek, 2021, "Fewer Americans than Ever Before Trust the Mainstream Media," January 5, 2021, accessed June 1, 2023, https://www.forbes.com/sites/andymeek/2021/02/20/fewer-americans-than-ever-before-trust-the-mainstream-media/.

8. Samuel Chamberlain, "Laura Ingraham: Mainstream Media Acting as 'Political Wing of the Secret Service' for Biden," *Fox News*, March 12, 2021, accessed April 19, 2023, https://www.foxnews.com/media/laura-ingraham-biden-media-political-secret-service.

9. Pew Research Center: Internet, Science & Tech, "Social Media Fact Sheet," April 5, 2023, accessed April 20, 2023, https://www.pewresearch.org/internet/fact-sheet/social-media/.

10. CEPR, "Social Media Influences the Mainstream Media," July 9, 2022, accessed April 19, 2023, https://cepr.org/voxeu/columns/social-media-influences-mainstream-media.

11. Pew Research Center's Journalism Project, "Network TV: Evening News Ratings Over Time by Network," July 9, 2015, accessed April 19, 2023, https://www.pewresearch.org/journalism/chart/network-tv-evening-news-ratings-over-time-by-network/.

12. A. J. Katz, "Week of April 3 Evening News Ratings: ABC World News Tonight Marks Another Week at No. 1 Despite Decline," Adweek.Com, April 11, 2023, accessed April 19, 2023, https://www.adweek.com/tvnewser/week-of-april-3-evening-news-ratings-abc-world-news-tonight-marks-another-week-at-no-1-despite-decline/527868/.

13. Pew Research Center's Journalism Project, "Newspapers Fact Sheet," January 9, 2023, accessed April 19, 2023, https://www.pewresearch.org/journalism/fact-sheet/newspapers/.

14. The seven companies are: Advance Local Publications (22), Alden Global Capital Venture Capital (56), Chatham Asset Management (30), Gannett Co., Inc. (250), Hearst (23), Lee Enterprises (90), and Tribune Company (10). The Future of Media Project, "Index of Seven Big Owners of Dailies," n.d., https://projects.iq.harvard.edu/futureofmedia/index-seven-big-owners-dailies.

15. Center for Innovation and Sustainability in Local Media, "News Deserts and Ghost Newspapers: Will Local News Survive?" The Expanding News Desert, June 22, 2020, accessed April 19, 2023, https://www.usnewsdeserts.com/reports/news-deserts-and-ghost-newspapers-will-local-news-survive/.

16. David Bauder, "US Newspapers Continuing to Die at Rate of 2 Each Week," AP News July 1, 2022, accessed April 19, 2023, https://apnews.com/article/journalism-united-states-39ef84c1131267233768bbb4dcaa181b.

17. Mason Walker, "U.S. Newsroom Employment Has Fallen 26% Since 2008," Pew Research Center, April 8, 2022, accessed April 19, 2023, https://www.pewresearch.org/fact-tank/2021/07/13/u-s-newsroom-employment-has-fallen-26-since-2008/.

18. CEW Georgetown, "Stop the Presses: Journalism Employment and the Economic Value of 850 Journalism and Communication Programs—CEW Georgetown," December 8, 2022, accessed April 20, 2023, https://cew.georgetown.edu/cew-reports/journalism/.

19. Mason Walker, Katerina Eva Matsa, and Sara Atske, "News Consumption Across Social Media in 2021," Pew Research Center's Journalism Project, September 20, 2021, accessed April 19, 2023, https://www.pewresearch.org/journalism/2021/09/20/news-consumption-across-social-media-in-2021/.

20. Ibid.

21. "Edelman Trust Barometer Global Report."

22. Mark Jurkowitz and Jeffrey Gottfried, "Twitter Is the Go-to Social Media Site for U.S. Journalists, But Not for the Public," Pew Research Center, August 29, 2022, accessed April 19, 2023, https://www.pewresearch.org/fact-tank/2022/06/27/twitter-is-the-go-to-social-media-site-for-u-s-journalists-but-not-for-the-public/.

23. CEPR, "Social Media Influences the Mainstream Media," July 9, 2022, accessed April 19, 2023, https://cepr.org/voxeu/columns/social-media-influences-mainstream-media.

24. Local News Initiative, "Journalists Give Thumbs Down to Social Media," February 9, 2022, accessed April 19, 2023, https://localnewsinitiative.northwestern.edu/posts/2022/02/09/medill-social-media-survey/.

25. "The 2022 State of Journalism on Twitter," Muck Rack, May 18, 2022, accessed April 20, 2023, https://muckrack.com/blog/2022/05/18/2022-state-of-journalism-on-twitter.

26. Jacob Nelson, "A Twitter Tightrope without a Net: Journalists' Reactions to Newsroom Social Media Policies," *Columbia Journalism Review*, December 2, 2021, accessed April 19, 2023, https://www.cjr.org/tow_center_reports/newsroom-social-media-policies.php#Upholding%20traditional%20notions%20of%20%E2%80%98objectivity%E2%80%99.

27. Ibid.

28. Daniel Ho and Kevin Quinn, "Viewpoint Diversity and Media Consolidation: An Empirical Study," *Stanford Law Review* 61, no. 4 (2009): 781–868.

29. Radio Act of 1927, Pub. L. No. 632 (1927); Communications Act of 1934, Pub. L. No. 73–416, 48 Stat. 1064 (1934) (codified at 47 USC §151 et seq.).

30. Red Lion Broadcasting v. FCC, 395 US 367 (1969). The Fairness Doctrine would eventually be rescinded in 1987 with changing nature of communication and the rise of cable.

31. Natl'l Citizens Comm. For Broad v. FCC, 555 F2d 938 (DC Cir. 1977).

32. 2002 Biennial Regulatory Review—Review of the Commission's Broadcast Ownership Rules and Other Rules Adopted Pursuant to Section 202 of the Telecommunications Act of 1996, 18 FCCR 13, 620, 13,627 (2003).

33. FCC v. National Citizens Committee for Broadcasting (NCCB), 436 US 775, 796 (1978).

34. Telecommunications Act of 1996, Pub. LA. No. 104–104, 110 Stat. 56 (1996).

35. This size limitation is five stations in a market with up to fourteen stations, six in a market with fifteen to twenty-nine stations, seven in a market with thirty to forty-four stations, and eight in a market with more than forty-five stations. No owner can own more than half the stations in a given market if lower than fourteen.

36. Stuart Brotman, "Broadcast Regulation," in *Communication and the Law*, ed. W. Wat Hopkins (Sylvan Springs, AL: Vision Press, 2023), 151–70.

37. Fox Television Stations v. FCC, 556 US 502 (2009).

38. FCC v. Prometheus Radio Project, 592 US ___ (2021).

39. Schurz Communications, Inc. v. FCC, 982 F.2d 1043, (7th Cir. 1992).

40. Time Warner Entertainment Co. v. FCC, 240 F.3d 1126 (DC Cir. 2001).

41. Sinclair Broadcast Group v. FCC, 284 F.3d 148 (DC Cir. 2002).

42. Matt Jackson, "Regulating Cable Communication," in *Communication and the Law*, ed. W. Wat Hopkins (Sylvan Springs, AL: Vision Press, 2023), 171–97.

43. Comcast Corp. v. National Association of African American Owned Media, 289 US ___ (2020). In 2020 the US Supreme Court heard a case involving cable provider Comcast's refusal to carry the Entertainment Studios Network (ESN), the only 100 percent African American owned cable channel outlet. ESN sued Comcast alleging the decision not to carry its channels were part of racial bias. In a unanimous decision the US Supreme Court held that in order for a claim like this to go forward ESN had to establish that racial discrimination was the primary reason for Comcast not carrying ESN

44. Turner Broadcasting System, Inc. v. FCC, 512 US 622 (1994).

45. Jackson, "Regulating Cable Communication," 179.

46. Ho and Quinn, "Viewpoint Diversity and Media Consolidation: An Empirical Study," 795.

47. Ibid.

48. @TuckerCarlson (Tucker Carlson), "We're Back," Twitter, May 9, 2023, 4:42 p.m., https://twitter.com/TuckerCarlson/status/1656037032538390530.

49. Iman Ghosh, "Which Companies Belong to the Elite Trillion-Dollar Club?" Visual Capitalist, October 26, 2021, accessed April 19, 2023, https://www.visualcapitalist.com/which-companies-belong-to-the-elite-trillion-dollar-club/.

50. Sherman Act, Pub. L. No. 51–647, 26 Stat. 209 (1890) (codified as amended at 15 USC §§ 1–7).

51. Standard Oil Co. of New Jersey v. United States, 221 US 1, 140 (1911).

52. Clayton Act, Pub. L. No. 63–212, 38 Stat. 209 (1890) (codified as amended at 15 USC §§ 12–27).

53. Federal Trade Commission Act, Pub. L. No. 63–203, 38 Stat. 717 (1914) (codified as amended at 15 USC §§41–58).

54. Thomas Piraino, "Reconciling the Harvard and Chicago Schools: A New Antitrust Approach in the 21st Century," *Indiana Law Journal* 82 (2007): 346–409.

55. Robert Bork, "Legislative Intent and the Policy of the Sherman Act," *Journal of Law & Economics* 9 (1966): 7–48.

56. Piraino, "Reconciling the Harvard and Chicago Schools," 352; Reiter v. Sonotone Corp., 442 US 330, 343 (1979).

57. Department of Justice, Justice Department Dues Google for Monopolizing Digital Advertising Technologies, https://www.justice.gov/opa/pr/justice-department-sues-google-monopolizing-digital-advertising-technologies.

58. United States v. Microsoft Corp., 253 F.3d 34 (DC Cir. 2001).

59. Sruthi Thatchenkery and Riitta Katila, "Innovation and Profitability Following Antitrust Intervention against a Dominant Platform: The Wild, Wild West?," *Strategic Management Journal* 44, no. 4 (2023): 943–76, https://doi.org/10.1002/smj.3470.

60. Statistam, "Global Search Engine Desktop Market Share 2023 | Statista," February 24, 2023, https://www.statista.com/statistics/216573/worldwide-market-share-of-search-engines/.

61. Michael Schudson, *The Power of News* (Cambridge, MA: Harvard University Press, 1995, 37).

62. Edward Bernays, *Crystalizing Public Opinion* (New York: Boni and Liveright, 1923).

63. Sara Atske, "Podcasts as a Source of News and Information," Pew Research Center's Journalism Project, April 18, 2023, accessed June 1, 2023, https://www.pewresearch.org/journalism/2023/04/18/podcasts-as-a-source-of-news-and-information/.

64. David Sloan, *The Media in America: A History* (Sylvan Springs, AL: Vision Press, 2020).

65. Kathryn Towey, "How to Produce Trustworthy News without 'Objectivity'— Cronkite News Lab," Cronkite News Lab, February 16, 2023, accessed April 19, 2023, https://cronkitenewslab.com/digital/2023/01/26/beyond-objectivity/.

66. Schudson, *The Power of News*, 37.

Chapter 11

Reporting on Low Voter Turnout Is a Self-Fulfilling Prophecy

Katherine Haenschen

News articles and segments articulating low voter turnout are all too common during and after local elections. Take, for example, these recent headlines published in March and April 2023:

> "Tampa Mayor Jane Castor Bemoans Low Turnout So Far in City Election."[1]
> "Quiet Day at the Polls for Milford's Annual Town Election."[2]
> "Turnout, Enthusiasm Remained Low for Mableton's Historic Runoff Elections."[3]
> "Low Turnout in Denver Election."[4]

Such reports do more than inform—they actively dissuade citizens from voting by creating a descriptive norm of low participation. This chapter explores the impact of reporting on low voter turnout and its negative consequences to democratic society. First, I review the literature on social norms, both injunctive and descriptive. I then argue that by reporting on low turnout, the news media inadvertently creates a descriptive social norm of nonparticipation. Descriptive social norms refer to the perception of what people are generally doing and have been shown to exert tremendous power on individuals. In fact, descriptive norms are often more influential than injunctive norms, or what a person "should" do, in shaping behavior. Based on social science research, news reports that emphasize low turnout may unintentionally give the impression that "no one" is voting and further suppress turnout.

Local reporters need to *stop* reporting on low turnout and *start* setting an agenda that local elections are important by profiling election workers and voters and by presenting deeply reported pieces about the candidates and issues at stake. Emphasizing the importance of an election and encouraging people to vote is in keeping with the social norm that voting is one's civic duty in a democracy. By leaning into this social norm, the news media can stop depressing turnout and start inspiring voters to participate.

THE POWER OF SOCIAL NORMS

Humans are social animals, and when presented with evidence of what other humans are doing, we tend to follow the herd—even when it goes against what we are "supposed" to do. The culprit are social norms, the oft unwritten rules that govern human behavior. Norms form within groups of people and are shaped by cycles of repetition and reward: follow the norm, and other members of the group will heap praise. Break the norm, and one can expect some form of social sanction—a reprimand, a shaming look. Bruce Rind and Daniel Benjamin[5] argue that external or extrinsic concerns about public image matter more than internal concerns about self-image in fostering adherence to norms. This is because other peoples' opinions about one's behavior can inspire in the subject the two most social emotions: pride and shame.

Norms have the power to shape socially desirable behavior through compliance and conformity. Robert B. Cialdini and Noah J. Goldstein distinguish between these two by defining compliance as acquiescence to a request and conformity as "the act of changing one's behavior to match the responses of others."[6] Ergo, while norm *compliance* consists of simply going along with what one is asked or expected to do, norm *conformity* can be thought of as a social act—a behavior change driven by an individual's expected reaction of others within a social network. Social theory further distinguishes between injunctive norms, or what one *should* do in a situation, and descriptive norms, or what we perceive a critical mass of others to be doing.[7] When used strategically, both injunctive and descriptive norms can shape behavior—for better or worse. Generally, however, descriptive norms of what many people are doing are more powerful in shaping human behavior than injunctive norms spelling out what an individual *should* do in a given situation.

This phenomenon of emphasizing descriptive norms to change behaviors is well documented across the social sciences. For example, messages emphasizing high rates of compliance with social norms have been able to increase recycling, reduce littering, and reduce energy consumption.[8] These studies show that the descriptive norm ("everybody's doing it") needs to emphasize compliance with the injunctive norm ("you should do it") for it to be effective. Mess up the combination, and the message does not always work. Several experiments attempting to reduce energy use found that when individuals were sent postcards showing that their consumption was below the neighborhood average (that is, lower than the descriptive norm), they actually *increased* their usage to match the descriptive norm—unless a smiley face was added to the mailers, reinforcing the injunctive norm to save energy.[9] Descriptive norms do not need to constitute a majority (over 50 percent) to shape behavior—they simply need to cue that enough individuals are doing something to provide perceived license to others. One study conducted at a Petrified National Forest was intended to reduce people taking pieces of petrified wood home. Signs emphasizing the rate at which tourists took forest artifacts with the injunctive norm not to steal actually resulted in an increase in theft by creating a perception that the behavior was widespread—perhaps more so than people had assumed.[10]

SOCIAL NORMS AND VOTING

Voting is an extremely strong social norm—doing one's civic duty is often cited as one of the key obligations of life under democracy. Norm-based messages have proven effective at increasing voter turnout. Mailers emphasizing the need to do one's civic duty were able to increase voter turnout by 1.8 percentage points relative to receiving no mailers.[11] Messages that create a descriptive norm of high turnout have been shown to increase intent to vote and validated turnout; messages emphasizing low turnout are not as effective.[12] Another study found that mailers emphasizing prior low turnout were shown to actually reduce participation in a current election.[13] A mailer sent to Latino voters reporting that while 90 percent of young Latinos intended to vote, only 20 percent actually voted in the previous election reduced turnout by 2.4 percentage points among the target population relative to a mailer without the 20 percent statistic.

Taken as a whole, the research is clear: telling people that turnout is high makes them more likely to vote. Conversely, telling people that turnout is, will be, or was low makes them less likely to vote or say they intend to. Emphasizing the descriptive norm of high participation increases compliance with the injunctive norm that everyone should do their civic duty and vote.

NEWS REPORTING ON LOW TURNOUT

And yet every time local elections roll around, the news media reports on low turnout. A search of the open-source tool Media Cloud for "low voter turnout" and "election" among 258 US news outlets across the entirety of 2021 shows a steady stream of depressing stories. Figure 11.1 shows the number of stories published per day ostensibly reporting on low turnout.

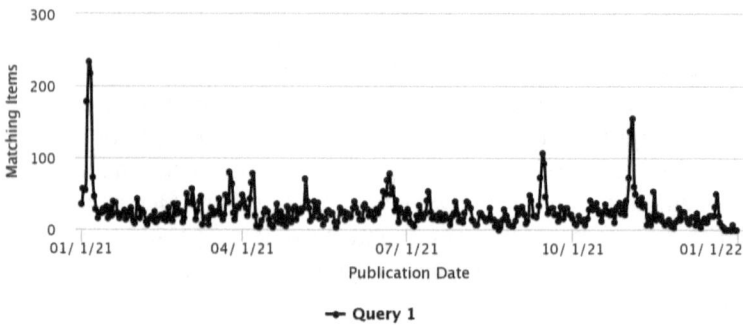

Figure 11.1. Number of News Articles per Day that Include Both "Low Voter Turnout" and "Election" Generated Using MediaCloud.org.

Spikes in these terms tend to occur on—wait for it—local election days! The first notable spike is January 5, 2021, during the US Senate runoffs in Georgia. To the right of the timeline are spikes on Tuesday, September 14 (a major primary election date), and on November 2–3, 2021, when many state and local elections were held. Stories meeting these criteria amounted to 0.269 percent of all news stories published in 2021. That may seem like a small share, but it amounts to roughly two to three of every one thousand news articles published in the entire year, creating a descriptive norm of low election turnout. That is a lot of emphasis on low turnout!

Or consider these headlines from the 2023 Chicago mayoral race. For context, embattled incumbent Lori Lightfoot faced a fleet of challengers on the February 28, 2023, ballot (Kam Buckner, Chuy Garcia, Ja'Mal Green, Brandon Johnson, Sophia King, Roderick Sawyer, Paul Vallas, and Willie Wilson). No candidate received a majority, so the top two vote-getters, Johnson and Vallas, moved on to the April 4, 2023, runoff. There were major differences between the candidates on issues of public education and crime, with Johnson prevailing 52.2 percent to 47.8 percent.

Turnout in the first round was a fairly robust 35.85 percent in February and 38.7 percent in the runoff, which is actually pretty strong for a local election that did not coincide with the November congressional election calendar. Yet the headlines frame the election as a low-turnout affair:

"'Slow and Sleepy' Chicago Voting Totals on Par with February Election Turnout"[14]

"Low Overall Turnout for Runoff Elections, Despite Increase in Early Voting"[15]

"Chicago Voter Turnout: Only 35% of Chicagoans Turned Out to Vote in Runoff Mayoral Election"[16]
"Chicago Voters Dismayed by Low Turnout in Mayor's Race: 'It's a Shame'"[17]
"Anemic Voter Turnout Means Few Decide Who Rules You"[18]

Ironically, some of the articles actually do a good job at providing more nuance and pointing out positive aspects of turnout, despite the headlines emphasizing nonparticipation. One piece in the *Chicago Sun-Times*, with the headline, "Chicago Voters Dismayed by Low Turnout in Mayor's Race: 'It's a Shame,'" talks up how young voters aged eighteen to twenty-four increased their participation from February to the April runoff, though noting that their turnout still lagged behind older groups, as it does in nearly every election over the past few decades, raising the question of whether the lag is newsworthy in and of itself. The reporters also quote a voter who disliked both sides but "said it was her obligation to vote in the mayoral race," underscoring the social norm of doing her civic duty.

Others lean hard into the descriptive social norm that no one is voting. Take this segment from ABC7:

> With early voting, mail-in ballots, drop boxes and extended voting hours, voting as never been easier and more accessible in Chicago, yet, only 35% of city residents voted in Tuesday's runoff election. "I didn't get a chance to vote on Tuesday . . . I was too busy," said Chicago resident Eric Fox, when asked why he didn't vote Tuesday. "I just didn't, no particular reason. Sorry y'all," said another resident.[19]

The story goes on to emphasize how turnout is even lower in Latino areas.

Of particular concern is the predilection of public officials and top election administrators to emphasize low turnout. The director of public information for the Chicago Board of Elections Max Bever told reporters, "It's looking like a slow and sleepy Election Day." His quote made the headline for WTTW, the local PBS affiliate.[20] This trend is also present in reporting from Tampa Bay ("Tampa Mayor Jane Castor Bemoans Low Turnout So Far in City Election") and Champaign, Illinois ("Close Champaign Co. Races Finally Have Winners, Clerk Disappointed in Low Turnout"). These leaders are part of the problem, because they give the news media an easy way to emphasize low turnout; instead, the media might ask why these offices are not engaging in scientifically informed best practices to promote turnout or working to move their local elections to co-occur with November general election ballots.

STOP REPORTING ON AND EMPHASIZING LOW VOTER TURNOUT

News programs need to stop emphasizing low turnout. By reporting on low voter turnout, the news media creates a descriptive social norm of nonparticipation. This becomes a self-fulfilling prophecy, in which voters decide not to bother participating because "no one's doing it." At worst, emphasizing low turnout rates will depress participation.[21] At best, describing low turnout fails to impact participation in either direction,[22] so what's the point? This goes beyond journalists and reporters to the copyeditors laying out the paper and the web producers and digital producers who prep content for the web. Stop writing headlines emphasizing low turnout!

One argument in favor of emphasizing low turnout often takes the form of "fewer people voting means that your vote counts more toward the outcome!" This perspective is rooted in the rational choice model of voting suggesting that people vote when the perceived benefits outweigh the costs.[23] However, this model ignores the myriad psychological and sociological pressures that motivate individuals to vote in the face of clear odds that their one vote will not be determinative.[24] I am not suggesting that reporters lie and claim that voter turnout is high when it is not—for one thing, that does not seem to work either! Mailers with descriptive norms emphasizing high turnout did not increase participation in a low-salience electoral context,[25] perhaps because telling people "voter turnout is high" when they are not hearing about it from people they know does not ring true. Norms need to be salient within one's network to be powerful.

And, of course, reality presents a challenge here. Voter turnout in elections other than presidential and congressional elections in even-year Novembers tends to be much lower than 50 percent. This is unfortunately by design—in choosing to hold local elections on dates other than the traditional November Election Day, policymakers are ensuring lower turnout. Research shows that moving local contests to national election dates substantially increases participation in them;[26] many scholars have called for such reforms.[27]

So local news media should not report on low turnout because at best it will have no impact on motivating voters and at worse may encourage people to stay home. What are reporters to do instead?

WHAT SHOULD LOCAL REPORTERS DO?

If they cannot report on low turnout, what can reporters do instead? First, set the agenda and frame the election as important to the community rather than "sleepy." Keep the election front of mind for the audience, with constant reporting about the upcoming decision. Run stories that emphasize elements of local contests that will boost confidence in elections, namely profiling the individuals involved—voters, election workers, *and* candidates—and emphasizing the injunctive norm of doing one's civic duty.

Some of these strategies draw from an approach known as solutions journalism, which is broadly understood by practitioners and scholars alike to refer to "news reporting about how people are responding to social problems."[28] Solutions journalism differs from traditional reporting practices by focusing on problems and their solutions and can be character driven, focusing on how individuals are addressing a problem in meaningful detail.[29] Such stories often quote members of the public beyond typical experts. Solutions-framed journalism also produces greater positive affect and higher intentions to take positive action than traditional negatively or catastrophically framed reporting.[30]

START SETTING THE AGENDA TO VOTE

The news media plays a tremendous role in determining *what* people think about and *how* they think about it through two key functions: agenda setting and framing. Agenda setting is defined as "the process of the mass media presenting certain issues frequently and prominently with the result that large segments of the public come to perceive those issues as more important than others."[31] More news coverage makes an issue seem more important to the audience. In this manner, the media tells its audience what matters, what to care about. Local news outlets need to report on the *importance* of the election and what is at stake for the community. Draw clear distinctions between candidates to help voters make an informed choice. This can be done objectively, without any bias, through interviews with candidates and analysis of the statements they make to endorsing organizations, prior votes cast, or other evidence.

Rather than depicting elections as low-turnout, humdrum affairs, the media needs to frame them as important. Robert M. Entman's definition of media framing is helpful here: "To frame is to select some aspects of a perceived reality and make them more salient in a communicating text, in such a way as to promote a particular problem definition, causal interpretation, moral evaluation and/or treatment recommendation for the item described."[32] The existing pattern of emphasizing low turnout frames elections as decidedly unsexy, low-salience affairs. If no one's voting, why should anyone care? Indeed, ample work suggests that the twinned functions of agenda setting and framing can impact how voters see themselves and their role in elections and determine whether they are motivated to participate. In their book *Votes that Count and Voters Who Don't*, Sharon E. Jarvis and Soo Hye Han conduct a seven-decade (!) content analysis of news articles about voters. Their conclusion?

> Reporters used the word vote prominently between the years 1948 and 1968 but gradually gave more attention to the term voter later in the analysis. The shift from discussions of the vote—which was depicted as "sought after" and "counting"—to greater attention to the voter—which was subjected to thin personalization and often cast as marginalized and isolated from the political game—devalued the general meaning of electoral participation in coverage.[33]

A subsequent survey experiment and set of focus groups finds that when the news portrays voters as active or playing a role, participants were more likely to value voting, and express more positive sentiment toward elections and trust in the media, compared to when the news frames electoral outcomes as preordained based on polling results.

Other work in this vein argues that the traditional media (and the political actors that attempt to shape it through public relations efforts) results in citizen alienation and a lack of interest in elections.[34] One interesting study explores how this coverage impacts adolescents during their period of political socialization—in short, how it shapes individuals as they approach age eighteen and their first opportunity to vote. They find evidence that the news media's agenda-setting function "serves as a critical intrinsic process in political socialization contributing to the crystallization of political predispositions, which lead to electoral participation" among young people.[35] Now think about how the media often portrays younger voters: often as less likely to participate, if not ignored all together.[36] What kind of political socialization is that?

Several examples of successful agenda setting can be found in Texas-based publications. A recent piece published by Dallas-area ABC affiliate WFAA titled "Everything North Texans Should Know About the Upcoming May 6 Elections" focuses on the importance of the elections, the races on the ballot, and provides logistical information to voters. It does not use the phrase "turnout" once.[37] Phrases such as "North Texans already have another big voting day coming up on the calendar" and "cities will still have ever-important city council seats up for grabs" emphasize that the election matters.

The ABC affiliate in Beaumont, Texas, has another great example in the run-up to the May 6, 2023, election. The article, titled "Political Expert Stresses Importance of Voting During Upcoming Joint Municipal and School Board Elections," starts off by stating, "Officials are stressing how important it is for residents to register to vote and have their voices heard during the upcoming elections."[38] The piece goes on to detail the races on the ballot and issues at stake. Again, it does not mention turnout or set expectations that it will be low.

Another piece from the nonprofit news outlet *The 19*th profiles gun safety advocates and talks about how important the issue is to American voters ahead of the 2024 election. The article, "Americans Want Change on Guns. It Could Shape the 2024 Election," profiles activists and candidates seeking to enact gun control legislation and frames the issue as important to voters through the use of opinion polling and examples of the endless scourge of mass shootings.[39] The article does not refer to turnout at all; instead, the author Errin Haines, the publication's editor-at-large writes, "The issue could be especially motivating for the Democrats' base: women, young people and voters of color."

START PROFILING THE PEOPLE INVOLVED

There are plenty of people who are participating in local elections who deserve more attention: candidates, election workers, and voters. Although candidate profiles are already common, these segments give voters information about the stakes of an election and help them make an informed decision. Indeed, prior turnout experiments show that when voters in local elections are mobilized, they subsequently seek out information to determine which candidates best support their views.[40]

Next, profile election workers and people who work the polls. Show how they are trained and detail the procedure of voting: signing in at the poll book, using the voting machine, receiving an "I Voted!" sticker. Profiling competent poll workers has the added benefit of increasing trust in elections and perceptions of democratic legitimacy. As prior work shows, "The enthusiasm election workers have for their job is crucial to maintaining trust in the system and creating a connection with the citizen-customer."[41] News stories can also engage with the volunteers working outside the polls to find out what motivates them, why they chose to participate, and what kind of experiences they're having.

The article "Trainings Give Poll Workers Tools for Free, Fair Elections" published in *The Daily Journal*, an outlet in Johnson County, Indiana, provides a great example. Reporter Noah Crenshaw profiled Marcia Whited and her family, who have been serving as poll workers for over a decade. The piece goes on to describe their training and procedures:

> During the roughly two-hour training, poll worker trainees learned how to check in poll workers, how to set up election equipment, and got a chance to practice

checking in voters themselves. The county hosts five trainings for poll workers, with local political parties spreading the word to those who may be interested in taking part.[42]

The reporter also quotes Whited, stating, "We run into so many people that we know, and it's none of our business as far as how they're voting, but we're glad that they're out to vote," which also helps to create a descriptive norm of participation.

Finally, profile voters at the polls to create a soft descriptive norm of participation, regardless of actual turnout rates. Why are people voting? What issues matter to them? Show an array of citizens diverse in terms of age, gender, race, and region, and offer a range of motivations for participating. Heap praise upon these people for doing their civic duty, to help induce a bit of norm conformity. However, *do not* include images of long lines at voting locations, as research shows that news stories depicting lines reduce stated intent to vote among viewers.[43] Instead, consider reporting on how quick and easy the process is, showing voters moving efficiently through the polling location.

START FRAMING NUMBERS IN A POSITIVE MANNER

Another avenue for reporters consists of emphasizing the raw number of people who voted rather than the percentage. Perhaps descriptively large numbers of voters will convey a descriptive norm of participation. Reporters might also favorably compare turnout in a present election to a similar one in the past, to convey higher relative turnout. These are all avenues of potential experimentation worthy of future research to determine how reporters can talk about the numeric aspects of turnout without also creating a descriptive norm of low turnout.

Take this selection of turnout tweets from Matt Largey, a reporter at KUT, the NPR affiliate located in Austin, Texas, on the campus of the University of Texas at Austin. Largey regularly reports on turnout on local elections. One interesting feature of Texas elections is a widespread early voting period, in which voters may cast ballots in person for approximately twelve days prior to Election Day. Early voting turnout is often used as a barometer for overall turnout.

The tweets in table 11.1 2a and 2c, sent during the 2016 general election and 2021 local election, emphasize that turnout is not only high, but (potentially) record-breaking! This is a great way to frame turnout—especially in the May election, when the overall percent turnout is not particularly high (it reached 22.6 percent). 2b is a mixed bag. The tweet emphasizes overall

Table 11.1. Selection of Tweets by KUT Reporter Matt Largey Discussing Turnout in Local Elections

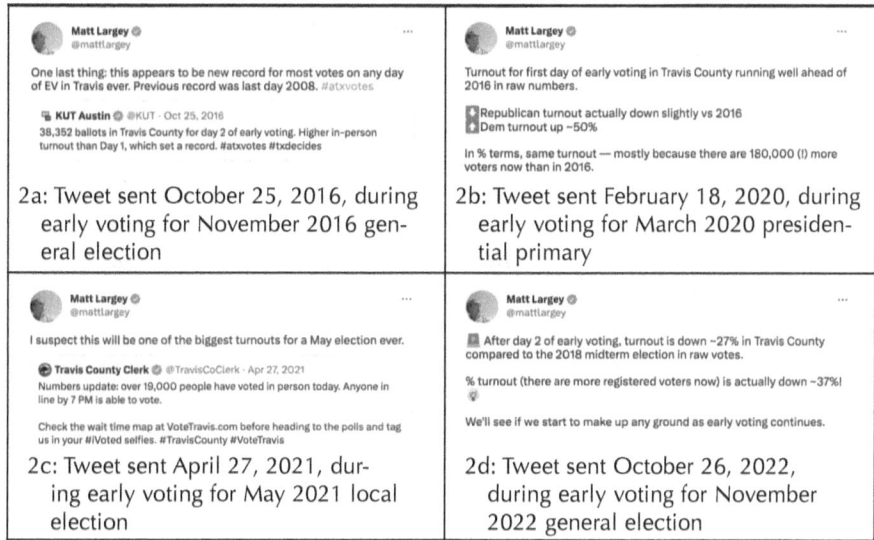

2a: Tweet sent October 25, 2016, during early voting for November 2016 general election	2b: Tweet sent February 18, 2020, during early voting for March 2020 presidential primary
2c: Tweet sent April 27, 2021, during early voting for May 2021 local election	2d: Tweet sent October 26, 2022, during early voting for November 2022 general election

higher turnout in the 2020 primary relative to 2016 primary terms of raw numbers, which is good. Largey also notes lower turnout among Republicans and higher among Democrats without offering context about the relative competitiveness of the 2016 and 2020 primary contests. He also notes that there are more voters, which impacts percent turnout figures. Finally, 2d in the 2022 midterms talks about how turnout is down relative to 2018 in both raw numbers and percentage participation, which might start to contribute to a descriptive norm of nonparticipation.

START EMPHASIZING THE NORM OF CIVIC DUTY

Finally, reporters can emphasize the injunctive norm of doing one's civic duty *without* emphasizing low turnout. Invoking the need for voters to "do their civic duty" triggers what Alan S. Gerber and Todd Rogers describe as the "psychological benefit from following the injunctive norm of voting."[44] The desire to be seen as compliant with this norm explains why so many voters overreport their own turnout.[45] One field experiment that tested the power of the injunctive norm that everyone should vote found that nonvoters were 20 percent more likely to not answer the door for a postelection survey about whether they voted.[46] These voters did not want to lie, nor did they want to admit to failing to adhere to the injunctive norm. Reporters can emphasize this norm in their reporting, particularly when profiling voters, thanking them for doing their civic duty.

Another avenue of investigative reporting outside of the election cycle is to ask lawmakers and local election officials what they are doing to move local elections to co-occur with November general elections or whether election clerks are using scientifically proven best practices to increase turnout. Lawmakers who oppose moving local elections often do so because they prefer to campaign in a low-turnout scenario, likely because they perceive it to be more favorable to their campaign prospects: fewer voters means a smaller budget and an electorate they may feel more comfortable with. That is no reason not to change it—if politicians cannot appeal to a majority of voters, why should they hold their office? Similarly, ample evidence suggests that local election administrators can send mailers, text messages, emails, and other missives that will increase the likelihood of individuals voting.[47] Reporters might engage in finding out if these tactics are being pursued, and if not, why?

FINAL THOUGHTS: REPORTING ON LOW TURNOUT SERVES NO PURPOSE

Reporters are not covering low turnout in an intentional effort to suppress turnout; a good-faith interpretation suggests that reporters are earnestly trying to alert the public to a social conundrum. However, their efforts may inadvertently make the problem worse. These potentially deleterious effects are a by-product of the influence of descriptive social norms. I agree that low turnout remains a problem and commend reporters for caring enough to want to address it. Yet the conundrum remains: reporting on low turnout can have the unintended consequence of making the problem worse!

I encourage reporters to think through what purpose it serves to emphasize low turnout: What information is this giving their audience other than to let them know that their community is not engaged? Telling audiences that turnout is low will not inspire participation and may even depress related attitudes about confidence in elections or democratic legitimacy—after all, if so few people vote, how can the winners be considered to represent their constituency at large? Such reports may further alienate and disengage the very public they are designed to awaken.

Reporting on low turnout—*particularly during an ongoing election*—does not serve anyone. Yes, journalists have an obligation to dig into the causes of lower participation, be it inconvenient election dates, a lack of competitive races, underfunded campaigns, or elected and election officials who are not adopting necessary reforms that are known to boost turnout. But perhaps the best time to report on these topics is not during the "hot phase" of an election but rather the other ten months of the year.

Instead, local news outlets can lean into the power they hold to set civic agendas in their communities by covering the issues and people involved in an election, framing numbers in a positive manner, and emphasizing the norm of doing one's civic duty, all without talking about "low turnout." Many outlets are already doing this, by profiling candidates, poll workers, and voters, and quoting people talking about doing one's civic duty. This is great work, and social science suggests it will have an ameliorative effect. Let us see more reporting that can increase turnout and fewer reports of nonparticipation.[48]

NOTES

1. Charlie Frago, "Tampa Mayor Jane Castor Bemoans Low Turnout So Far in City Election," *Tampa Bay Times*, March 7, 2023, https://www.tampabay.com/news/tampa/2023/03/07/tampa-mayor-jane-castor-bemoans-low-turnout-so-far-city-election/.

2. Tom Benoit, "Quiet Day at the Polls for Milford's Annual Town Election," *Milford Daily News*, April 5, 2023, https://www.milforddailynews.com/story/news/politics/elections/local/2023/04/05/milford-ma-town-election-low-turnout-decide-town-school-races/70069809007/.

3. Ryan Zickgraf, "Turnout, Enthusiasm Remained Low for Mableton's Historic Runoff Elections," *Atlanta Civic Circle*, April 19, 2023, https://atlantaciviccircle.org/2023/04/19/turnout-enthusiasm-remained-low-for-mabletons-historic-runoff-elections/.

4. 9news.com, "Low Turnout in Denver Election," 9News Denver, April 5, 2023, https://www.9news.com/video/news/politics/elections/low-turnout-in-denver-election/73-30cb9061-5a49-4e88-98bb-08b5a4b38ec1.

5. Bruce Rind and Daniel Benjamin, "Effects of Public Image Concerns and Self-Image on Compliance," *The Journal of Social Psychology* 134, no. 1 (1994): 19–25.

6. Robert B. Cialdini and Noah J. Goldstein, "Social Influence: Compliance and Conformity," *Annu. Rev. Psychol.* 55 (2004): 606.

7. Cialdini and Goldstein, "Social Influence," 591–621.

8. Hunt Allcott, "Social Norms and Energy Conservation," *Journal of Public Economics* 95, nos. 9–10 (2011): 1082–95; Robert B. Cialdini, "Crafting Normative Messages to Protect the Environment," *Current Directions in Psychological Science* 12, no. 4 (2003): 105–9; Robert B. Cialdini, Raymond R. Reno, and Carl A. Kallgren, "A Focus Theory of Normative Conduct: Recycling the Concept of Norms to Reduce Littering in Public Places," *Journal of Personality and Social Psychology* 58, no. 6 (1990): 1015.

9. P. Wesley Schultz, Jessica M. Nolan, Robert B. Cialdini, Noah J. Goldstein, and Vladas Griskevicius, "The Constructive, Destructive, and Reconstructive Power of Social Norms," *Psychological Science* 18, no. 5 (2007): 429–34.

10. Robert B. Cialdini, Linda J. Demaine, Brad J. Sagarin, Daniel W. Barrett, Kelton Rhoads, and Patricia L. Winter, "Managing Social Norms for Persuasive Impact," *Social Influence* 1, no. 1 (2006): 3–15.

11. Alan S. Gerber, Donald P. Green, and Christopher W. Larimer, "Social Pressure and Voter Turnout: Evidence from a Large-Scale Field Experiment," *American Political Science Review* 102, no. 1 (2008): 33–48.

12. Alan S. Gerber and Todd Rogers, "Descriptive Social Norms and Motivation to Vote: Everybody's Voting and So Should You," *The Journal of Politics* 71, no. 1 (2009): 178–91; Gregg R. Murray and Richard E. Matland, "Mobilization Effects Using Mail: Social Pressure, Descriptive Norms, and Timing," *Political Research Quarterly* 67, no. 2 (2014): 304–19.

13. Lauren D. Keane and David W. Nickerson, "When Reports Depress Rather than Inspire: A Field Experiment using Age Cohorts as Reference Groups," *Journal of Political Marketing* 14, no. 4 (2015): 381–90.

14. Matt Masterson and Erica Demarest, "'Slow and Sleepy' Chicago Voting Totals on Par with February Election Turnout," WTTW, April 4, 2023, https://news.wttw.com/2023/04/04/slow-and-sleepy-chicago-voting-totals-par-february-election-turnout.

15. CBS Chicago Team, "Low Overall Turnout for Runoff Elections, Despite Increase in Early Voting," CBS Chicago, April 5, 2023, https://www.cbsnews.com/chicago/news/chicago-runoff-elections-turnout-early-voting/.

16. Sarah Schulte, "Chicago Voter Turnout: Only 35% of Chicagoans Turned Out to Vote in Runoff Mayoral Election," ABC7, April 6, 2023, https://abc7chicago.com/chicago-voter-turnout-2023-mayoral-election-voting-results-in/13096289.

17. Emmanuel Camarillo, Violet Miller, and Kaitlin Washburn, "Chicago Voters Dismayed by Low Turnout in Mayor's Race: 'It's a Shame,'" *Chicago Sun-Times*, April 5, 2023, https://chicago.suntimes.com/politics/2023/4/4/23670053/voters-cast-ballot-chicago-mayoral-runoff.

18. Charles Selle, "Anemic Voter Turnout Means Few Decide Who Rules You," *Chicago Tribune*, April 11, 2023, https://www.chicagotribune.com/suburbs/lake-county-news-sun/opinion/ct-lns-selle-voter-turnout-st-0411-20230410-lku5lknmxvhsjpd4nbqylsncwy-story.html.

19. Schulte, "Chicago."

20. Masterson and Demarest, "Slow."

21. Keane and Nickerson, "When Reports Depress Rather than Inspire," 381–90.

22. Murray and Matland, "Mobilization Effects Using Mail," 304–19.

23. Anthony Downs, "An Economic Theory of Political Action in a Democracy," *Journal of Political Economy* 65, no. 2 (1957): 135–50.

24. See, for example, Betsy Sinclair, *The Social Citizen: Peer Networks and Political Behavior* (Chicago: University of Chicago Press, 2012).

25. Costas Panagopoulos, Christopher W. Larimer, and Meghan Condon, "Social Pressure, Descriptive Norms, and Voter Mobilization," *Political Behavior* 36 (2014): 451–69.

26. Zoltan L. Hajnal, Vladimir Kogan, and G. Agustin Markarian, "Who Votes: City Election Timing and Voter Composition," *American Political Science Review* 116, no. 1 (2022): 374–83.

27. Zoltan L. Hajnal and Paul G. Lewis, "Municipal Institutions and Voter Turnout in Local Elections," *Urban Affairs Review* 38, no. 5 (2003): 645–68; Melissa Marschall, and John Lappie, "Turnout in Local Elections: Is Timing Really Everything?" *Election Law Journal: Rules, Politics, and Policy* 17, no. 3 (2018): 221–33.

28. Karen Elizabeth McIntyre and Kyser Lough, "Toward a Clearer Conceptualization and Operationalization of Solutions Journalism," *Journalism* 22, no. 6 (2021): 1558.

29. Solutions Journalism, "What Is Solutions Journalism?" *Medium*, March 6, 2017, https://medium.com/@soljourno/what-is-solutions-journalism-c050147bb1eb.

30. Deise Baden, Karen McIntyre, and Fabian Homberg, "The Impact of Constructive News on Affective and Behavioural Responses," *Journalism Studies* 20, no. 13 (2019): 1940–59.

31. Renita Coleman, Maxwell McCombs, Donald Shaw, and David Weaver, "Agenda Setting," in *The Handbook of Journalism Studies* (New York, NY:Routledge, 2009), 167–80; Maxwell McCombs, "A Look at Agenda-Setting: Past, Present and Future," *Journalism Studies* 6, no. 4 (2005): 543–57.

32. Robert M. Entman, "Framing: Toward Clarification of a Fractured Paradigm," *Journal of Communication* 43, no. 4 (1993): 51–58. Additionally, according to Jim A. Kuypers, frames "are located in the communicator, the text, the receiver, and the culture at large. Frames are central organizing ideas within a narrative account of an issue or event; they provide the interpretive cues for otherwise neutral facts." Jim A. Kuypers, "Framing Analysis," *Rhetorical Criticism: Perspectives in Action*, ed. Jim A. Kuypers (Lanham, MD: Lexington Books, 2009), 182.

33. Sharon E. Jarvis and Soo-Hye Han, *Votes that Count and Voters Who Don't: How Journalists Sideline Electoral Participation (Without Even Knowing It)* (University Park, PA: Penn State Press, 2019), 9.

34. David Weaver, "Media Agenda Setting and Elections: Voter Involvement or Alienation?" *Political Communication* 11, no. 4 (1994): 347–56.

35. Spiro Kiousis, Michael McDevitt, and Xu Wu, "The Genesis of Civic Awareness: Agenda Setting in Political Socialization," *Journal of Communication* 55, no. 4 (2005): 756–74.

36. Dianne G. Bystrom and Daniela V. Dimitrova, "Rocking the Youth Vote: How Television Covered Young Voters and Issues in a 2004 Target State," *American Behavioral Scientist* 50, no. 9 (2007): 1124–36.

37. Paul Wedding, "Everything North Texans Should Know about the Upcoming May 6 Election," WFAA, April 19, 2023, https://www.wfaa.com/article/news/local/vote/voting-guide-everything-should-know-about-may-6-election-north-texas/287-f5e48a1a-5e84-483d-a661-8b636d895571.

38. Kayla Choates, "Political Expert Stresses Importance of Voting During Upcoming Joint Municipal and School Board Elections," KBMT, March 28, 2023, https://www.12newsnow.com/article/news/politics/elections/political-expert-stresses-importance-of-voting-during-upcoming-joint-and-municipal-school-board-elections/502-94d660e6-0d57-461c-8633-974820f1ab98.

39. Errin Haines, "Americans Want Change on Guns. It Could Shape the 2024 Election," *The 19th*, April 20, 2023, https://19thnews.org/2023/04/the-amendment-errin-haines-gun-control-election-2024/.

40. Victoria A. Shineman, "If You Mobilize Them, They Will Become Informed: Experimental Evidence that Information Acquisition Is Endogenous to Costs and Incentives to Participate," *British Journal of Political Science* 48, no. 1 (2018): 189–211.

41. Amanda D. Clark, Christina S. Barsky, and Monica A. Bustinza, "Heavy Lifting: Emotional Labor and Election Administration," *Administration & Society* 55, no. 2 (2023): 308–25.

42. Noah Crenshaw, "Trainings Give Poll Workers Tools for Free, Fair Elections," *The Daily Journal*, April 17, 2023, https://dailyjournal.net/2023/04/17/trainings-give-poll-workers-expertise-needed-to-help-voters/.

43. Kathleen Searles and Christopher Mann, "Election Coverage that Shows Generic 'Long Line' Images May Discourage Voting, New Research Finds," NiemanLab, November 7, 2022, https://www.niemanlab.org/2022/11/election-coverage-that-shows-generic-long-line-images-may-discourage-voting-new-research-finds/.

44. Gerber and Rogers, "Descriptive Social," 181.

45. Robert F. Belli, Michael W. Traugott, Margaret Young, and Katherine A. McGonagle, "Reducing Vote Overreporting in Surveys: Social Desirability, Memory Failure, and Source Monitoring," *The Public Opinion Quarterly* 63, no. 1 (1999): 90–108.

46. Stefano DellaVigna, John A. List, Ulrike Malmendier, and Gautam Rao, "Voting to Tell Others," *The Review of Economic Studies* 84, no. 1 (2016): 143–81.

47. For example, see Neil Malhotra, Melissa R. Michelson, and Ali Adam Valenzuela, "Emails from Official Sources Can Increase Turnout," *Quarterly Journal of Political Science* 7, no. 3 (2012): 321–32; Lisa A. Bryant, Michael J. Hanmer, Alauna C. Safarpour, and Jared McDonald, "The Power of the State: How Postcards from the State Increased Registration and Turnout in Pennsylvania," *Political Behavior* (2020): 1–15; Barry C. Burden and Jacob R. Neiheisel, "Election Administration and the Pure Effect of Voter Registration on Turnout," *Political Research Quarterly* 66, no. 1 (2013): 77–90.

48. The author thanks Meg Heckman and reviewers for their feedback on this chapter.

Chapter 12

Democracy-Destroying Practices of the American Mainstream News Media and Their Potential Solutions

Jim A. Kuypers

By the time of World War II, Americans were already concerned about what they had learned in Europe about fascist and communist control of the news media. In response to this growing awareness, the Commission on Freedom of the Press, later known as the Hutchins Commission, was established to address problems in journalism. In 1947 the commission published *A Free and Responsible Press* in which it argued that media ownership was too concentrated and that unpopular ideas did not get fair hearing. It concluded that "freedom of the press was in danger."[1] The commission proposed five guidelines to enhance press performance, asserting that the press had an obligation to serve the society in which it operated. This idea of press service, alive still today, was a mix of both objective and activist standards for press performance:

First, the press must provide "a truthful, comprehensive, and intelligent account of the day's events in a context which gives them meaning."

Second, the press must serve as a "forum for the exchange of comment and criticism."

Third, the press must project "a representative picture of the constituent groups in society."

Fourth, the press must assume responsibility for "the presentation and clarification of the goals and values of the society" in which it operates.

Fifth, the press must provide "full access to the day's intelligence."[2]

In a large sense, the Hutchins Commission's report reflected not only a Golden Age of objective journalism, but also an emerging activist voice, as seen particularly in the fourth point, presenting and clarifying the goals and values of society.

In 1956, Fred S. Siebert, Theodore Peterson, and Wilbur Schramm published *Four Theories of the Press*, which is still instructive today.[3] The four press types they identified were:

The Libertarian, which is a market driven, commercial operation. News outlets are free to publish what they like. Attacks on government are both allowed and encouraged.

The Social Responsibility, in which the press has an obligation to society to temper the freedom to publish anything in order to help society better itself. The media and government are partners in creating a civil society.

The Authoritarian, in which government control assures that the media serve the interests of the state. The media are not allowed to publish anything that could undermine the authority of the state or offend existing political/ideological values. Control is maintained by government censorship and punishment.

The Soviet, in which, theoretically, the press operates in solidarity with workers. In practice, this is simply authoritarian. One might today replace this with the Communist Chinese model, updating for technological control over its population.[4]

Siebert and his colleagues, following the Hutchins recommendation, felt that "the power and near monopoly position of the media impose on them an obligation to be socially responsible."[5] They introduced beginnings of a progressive standard, arguing that journalists should "serve society" rather than merely report news,[6] thus movement toward a socially responsible press.

The American press has traditionally been seen as libertarian, with a gradual movement to social responsibility. It is a combination of the two today, with an *overwhelming* socially responsible element in political reporting, something slowly building since the late 1960s.[7] One noticeable way this has manifested itself is through the increase in reporter interpretation over presentation of facts, thus increasingly less time devoted to soundbites and increasing amounts of time devoted to the commentary of journalists.

Between 1968 and 1988, for instance, soundbites from presidential candidates on evening news fell from 43.1 seconds to 8.9 seconds,[8] with today this average at just 8 seconds. Print space devoted to original utterances have shrunk during this time as well.[9] This alone gives journalists extraordinary power to convey their interpretation of issues and events[10] and is just one example of journalistic movement from libertarian to social responsibility. Unfortunately, as journalists move from reporting to interpreting, coupled with their growing acceptance of social responsibility and advocacy,[11] we see a perfect storm brewing, and a transformation of the American model of news production from essentially libertarian into an authoritarian model of the press.[12] And it is this argument I wish to advance in this chapter, and will do so in four sections: the political composition of the press; journalists' world views and moral judgments expressed in news stories; the implications of all of this; and, finally, some solutions to repair the damage being done.

THE POLITICAL COMPOSITION OF THE PRESS

In 2002 I discovered that over 90 percent of mainstream news media newspapers used the same frames on any given controversial issue or event.[13] How could this be? One could certainly point to the widespread use of news services such as the Associated Press and Reuters and argue that they contribute to the consistency pointed out earlier; however, we must also look to the concept of *groupthink*. Reporters have a shared value system that predisposes them to see and report news remarkably the same; this shared value system facilitates a monolithic ideological voice, thus the results seen above. So to better see the genesis of this shared value system and how it impacts reportorial practice, let us look briefly at the ideological makeup of the mainstream American press, which is, *as a group,* overwhelmingly Democrat, liberal, and progressive.[14]

This ideological situation is long-standing, beginning with a leftward shift in the 1950s from more balanced newsrooms.[15] By the early 1990s, party affiliation was 50 percent Democrat, 37 percent Independent, and only 4 percent Republican,[16] with over 60 percent of journalists describing themselves as liberal, and only 15 percent leaning right.[17] Nationwide at that time, however, party affiliation was 33 percent Democrat, 33 percent Independent, and 30 percent Republican, with roughly 20 percent of Americans, regardless of party affiliation, describing themselves as liberal, 40 percent describing themselves as moderate, and 40 percent describing themselves as conservative, numbers that are similar still today.[18] Of note is that in *political activities*, the ideology is liberal as well. For example, the percentage of journalists voting for the Democrat candidate for president has, since the 1960s, consistently hovered between 75 percent and 80 percent, and this percentage is even higher among national-level journalists. In terms of political donations, during the 2016 presidential election, almost 90 percent of the journalists surveyed gave exclusively to Democrats, and another survey found that of those journalists who donated to the presidential race itself, 96 percent gave money to Clinton, with contributions to Trump approaching only 3 percent.[19]

Such figures represent the newsroom environment, yet educational experiences play a role in journalist development as well. Neophyte journalists are essentially exposed to one ideological perspective while in school, and this plays a role in the formation of journalist groupthink.[20] As reported in one study from 2019:

> Although general trends . . . show that [conservatives] are almost non-existent in higher education, with only 9% of college professors identifying as conservative or conservative leaning, the trends are even more concerning when we look at party affiliations . . . in the . . . majors . . . where journalists earn their degrees. . . . [Here] the number of Republicans on average approaches zero. Keep in mind that the number of Americans who lean toward or identify as Republican is around 40%, plus or minus a few percentage points.[21]

As stated by reporter Lara Logan just before the 2020 pandemic, "85 percent of journalists are registered Democrats [and] are left or liberal. . . . [And] we've become political activists in a sense, and some could argue propagandists."[22] Thus new journalists are steeped in liberal and progressive culture throughout their schooling and then they step into newsrooms overwhelmingly dominated by progressive thought as well.

Be this as it may, some will suggest that just having progressive politics does not necessarily mean that journalists inject it into their reporting.[23] Yet the evidence is overwhelming that they do:[24] we have journalists' self-admissions that they allow their politics to influence their reportorial practices;[25] we know that they see themselves as having an advocacy role, through self-admissions, open advocacy,[26] and the exposés (such as Project Veritas secretly recording the president of CNN conspiring to hurt conservatives and promote a liberal political point of view);[27] we have stunning journalistic collusion demonstrated by like-minded liberal/progressive journalists in groups such as JournoList, Cabalist,[28] GameJournoPros,[29] JournoList 2,[30] as well as demonstrably anti-conservative reporting.[31] All of this leads to a disjunction between journalists and the public they are to serve.

WORLD VIEWS INFORMING THE FRAMES AND MORAL JUDGMENTS OF JOURNALISTS

One can go beyond surface evidence, self-admission, exposes, etc. and look even deeper for ideological bias injected into reporting. From what I have discovered when investigating the worldviews and motivations of journalists I find that, as a group, they are *incapable* of accurate reporting on political news given their current, monolithic ideological composition. In this section I share insights gleaned from three major studies I have conducted. In two I looked for worldviews as expressed in news stories, and in the other I looked at the moral foundations of journalists as expressed in news stories.

Worldviews

In terms of worldviews, I used the work of Kenneth Burke, specifically motivational analysis, which allows one to look for deeply unconscious worldviews. I examined first the nomination acceptance speeches of Donald J. Trump and Hillary Clinton[32] and then performed a similar analysis of the mainstream news media coverage of those speeches.[33] Through Burke's work we can discover unity, or shared views of reality of the world, what Burke would call being consubstantial, and also to discover points of disunity, or inconsubstantiality, points where worldviews and shared notions of reality diverge. When comparing the reporting of the mainstream news on Trump and Clinton, I found it wholly *in*consubstantial with Trump but wholly consubstantial with Clinton's thinking, with the worldview she expressed in her speech.

In short, the worldview of the journalists as expressed in their *actual reporting* matched almost exactly that which Clinton expressed in her speech. However, this was not the case with Trump, whose worldview he expressed in his speech was not conveyed but contested. What this means is that the reporting of Trump's speech failed to convey its tone and essence and was presented as divisive and contentious—it did, after all, present values and a worldview diametrically opposed to those reporting upon it. As Walter Lippmann shared, "Since my moral system rests on my accepted version of the facts, he who denies my moral judgments or my version of the facts, is to me perverse, alien, dangerous."[34] Clinton's speech, on the other hand, was conveyed in a laudatory manner, presented as unifying and natural and simply as "a good."

That the worldview expressed by Clinton and the press are so close in composition is cause for concern. The tendency would be for those consubstantial with each other to see reality in similar ways, and with the press, to report the same as true. Thus, the very way that the press sees the world prevents it from fairly and accurately covering both candidates. The lens (worldview) through which it is viewing the candidates, and by extension I would argue all political elements, is enormous in its power to select, reflect, and deflect our attention from one aspect of reality toward another. These worldviews are composed of "terministic screens," and they are "indicative of the internal thinking of the communicator" and affect the very "nature of our observations."[35] Thinking of terministic screens, "whatever terms we use . . . constitute a . . . kind of screen [and this screen] directs [our] attention to one field rather than another."[36] The screens we hold induce us to see the world in a particular way or to direct our attention toward or away from certain elements. Or put another way by Burke, *"many of the 'observations' are but implications of the particular terminology in terms of which the observations are made."*[37] This works in part because "even if any given terminology is a *reflection* of reality, by its very nature as a terminology, it must be a *selection* of reality; and to this extent it must function also as a *deflection* of reality."[38] In summation, such strong consubstantiality between Clinton and the press would *naturally* lead the press to pro-Clinton coverage on issues and events. Thus, even while she was an extremely unpopular primary candidate, we do see in later studies that she received far less negative coverage than did Trump during the general election.

The press was thus consubstantial with Clinton's worldview, one whose values are also consubstantial with both the Democratic National Committee's platform[39] and progressive politics.[40] Both their shared political leanings and shared worldviews contributed to this; that in as much as the press was consubstantial with Clinton it was working (consciously or not) on its own behalf in helping her and hurting Trump.

Moral Foundations Theory

We can see this same consubstantiality operating when we look at press coverage of Trump through the lens of moral foundations theory (MFT).[41] According to moral psychologist Jonathan Haidt, MFT starts with the premise that human nature is intrinsically linked with moral elements;[42] that is, we naturally view actions and events through a moral lens. MFT provides strong evidence that moral reasoning is generally not about discerning truth but used instead to support our "social agendas—to justify our own actions and to defend the teams" to which we belong.[43] There are five moral foundations analogous to five possible moral "tastes," each of which contains an opposite quality: care/harm, fairness/cheating, loyalty(ingroup)/betrayal, authority/subversion, sanctity/degradation.[44] Importantly, empirical research links these receptors to political leanings in individuals, with findings indicating that liberals operate with an increased sensitivity to some receptors, most notably care/harm, and decreased sensitivity to the others when compared with conservatives, who tend toward a balanced palette use.

According to Haidt, we are prewired for much of our moral sensitivities, which means that there is a certain innate aspect to our possessing moral sensibilities. These initial sensitivities are subsequently modified as we grow and mature, so we also *learn* our morality. The society in which we live influences us, as do our family, friends, experiences, and culture. *To the degree that this is true, we should find that the mainstream news media, as its own culture (and liberal/progressive in composition), would show signs of moral reasoning/judgments indicative of the liberal mind in its reporting.*

To further investigate this unconscious bias, I blended MFT with framing analysis to examine news coverage of four major policy announcements made by President Trump.[45] I looked for the frames used by Trump, and then looked at the mainstream news media reporting on those announcements to detect any differences. The results showed that the press simply failed to convey both Trump's framing and moral foundations as expressed through the speeches; they instead prioritized their moral foundations, ones, such as care/harm, that are empirically linked with liberal political beliefs. Put simply, the progressive ideology of the reporters permeated their reporting, so much so that they utterly failed to convey Trump's moral foundations, instead *imposing* their own. Interestingly, the reporting, both the framing and conveyance of moral foundations, was lock step with the framing and moral foundations as expressed by the Democrat and progressive critics that the press cited in its stories about Trump.

Summing up all of these studies, we see press reporting intimately aligned with what Democrats, liberal critics, and Hillary Clinton are saying. Their criticisms and policy ideas were never subjected to a critical reception, as were Trump's utterances. So striking was this that it appeared that the press has, consciously or not, subordinated itself to Democrat Party views, adopting *in practice* an authoritarian model of press functioning; meaning, the press voluntarily served the needs of the Democrat Party and printed little that would undermine that party's authority or standing or that would give offense to the existing political values endorsed by that party and its members.[46] This leads toward the conclusion that the press has, consciously or not, subordinated itself to those views, voluntarily adopting *in practice* a model of press functioning that seems to blend the old Soviet model and an authoritarian model of press production, one existing to support the power of the Democrat Party.[47]

These studies, along with decades long observations, lead me to agree with journalist John Nolte, who wrote: "Our national media now sees itself as part of the government, and as a consequence, the media's mission to hold institutions accountable has been dropped entirely in favor of relentless agenda-pushing"; and this goes a long way toward explaining its favoritism toward Democrats and progressive policy.[48] Supporting one side of an issue or policy while weakening or deprecating the other presents an incomplete picture to the general public; it is little better than propaganda. In addition, such reporting circumvents democratic processes and moves clearly into an authoritarian model of news production.

Understanding the political composition and worldview of the press in some ways explains how the press could willingly abrogate its social mandate as the fourth estate watchdog and morph into a new model of news production that is dangerously close to the authoritarian model Siebert and colleagues warned Americans about. The press today is acting not to support a robust Constitutional Republic but acting instead to advance its own partisan political beliefs over those of others. And this pushes it away from a libertarian or social responsibility model squarely into an authoritarian one. And this does have implications for the American Republic and its democratic ideals.

IMPLICATIONS FOR THE AMERICAN REPUBLIC

In *Partisan Journalism: A History of Media Bias in the United States*,[49] I demonstrated how the mainstream news media had, since the 1960s, morphed into a monolithic structure with politics congruent with those of the progressive left. I also pointed out the growth of an alternative press, one that represents conservatives as well as attempts at traditional objective reporting. As this alternative press grew, I reasoned, mainstream press journalists as well as progressive politicians would have to contend with oppositional points of view in print, on the airwaves, and online. So we were having a new competitive, although partisan, press. If we cannot have objectivity, let us at least have a competition of ideas. American Founding Father James Madison would have been pleased with that situation because he saw various factions as a sure guarantor of American democracy. So if we cannot have an objective press, let us have an adversarial press—not as adversaries with a particular president or politician but with each other, because the First Amendment—free speech—is far too powerful a protection to shield only part of the political spectrum.

Whereas I would have liked to have seen the response to this challenge from alternative news sources to take the form of a return to more objective reporting, the mainstream news response has been denial and a continuation of biased reporting. Here are a few, more recent, examples of this:

During the initial phase of the COVID-19 pandemic, the limited mainstream news media reporting on hydroxychloroquine was essentially neutral until President Trump praised it, whereupon coverage immediately turned negative, even with some evidence of its effectiveness.[50] After the Trump Presidency, the press tempered its criticism, with some elements now quietly saying hydroxychloroquine is beneficial. How many tens of thousands may have died because of the press politicization of its reporting here?[51]

During the 2020 presidential campaign, the mainstream news media's coverage of Trump was, as it was throughout his presidency, over 90 percent negative; candidate Biden, however, received 66 percent positive coverage, with reports now suggesting this positivity has only continued. To put this into perspective Trump received roughly five percent positive coverage; Obama received roughly 42 percent positive, and Joe Biden is receiving roughly 66 percent positive coverage.[52] It is no wonder that a majority of voters believe the press was and is biased against Trump.[53]

We also see this bias in action looking at the press suppression of facts. During the 2020 presidential campaign, for example, we witnessed the blatant omission of oppositional information. Stories that could hurt Biden with voters were minimized or withheld: His public admission of extorting the Ukrainian government by withholding military aid unless it fired the prosecutor who was investigating the company paying his son to be on its board;[54] or Biden's son's business dealings with Communist China; or, the content of Biden's son's laptop;[55] or the palpable lack of any in-depth questions of candidate Biden's proposed policies; or the withholding of stories and interviews that could hurt his position such as his radical anti-2nd amendment stances (gun control) should he take office.[56]

And we see this reportorial behavior continuing after the presidential election as well. For example, with credible accusations and evidence of voter fraud in the 2020 presidential election being actively discussed in the alternative press and in State legislatures across America,[57] the mainstream news media responded with the simple and oft repeated assertion that the election was "free and fair" even as almost 100 million Americans, including 20–30 percent of Democrat voters, believe it was not, and that the man who is now president is there fraudulently.[58] So, instead of addressing these concerns and investigating, the news media simply ignore it, and blithely calls those who have doubts about the validity of the election, "conspiracy theorists" who need to be re-educated,[59] even as before the election around 40 percent of Americans had "no confidence in American elections.[60] Today in 2022 only around "20% of the public say[s] it's very confident in the country's elections."[61] Our Federal Republic simply cannot properly function when almost a third of its population believe the highest office in the land was gained through fraud. And the news media's refusal to address this only exacerbates the situation and Americans' mistrust of them.

In the space after the election these examples continue ad nauseum, with the press favoring Biden and progressive interpretations of events, with even the press "objective" "fact-checkers" favoring Democrats. For instance, PolitiFact, during the first one hundred days of the Biden administration, "was nearly eight times more likely to fact check a criticism of Biden than they were to fact check a claim by Biden himself."[62] The *Washington Post* obsessively fact-checked President Trump for the slightest exaggeration, setting up a special unit to do just that, but then disbanded that unit of reporters after Joe Biden took office.[63] After months of suggesting to Americans that they could not trust the COVID-19 vaccinations being developed, ABC News, almost immediately after Biden assumed office, reversed itself and urged Americans to trust the vaccines.[64] And after railing against President Trump's rather reserved use of Executive Orders for several years,[65] ABC News actually praised Joe Biden for "aggressively pursuing executive orders" to obtain policy goals.[66]

Recall, too, that all during the summer and fall of 2020 in America that Black Lives Matter protests and riots were describe as "mostly peaceful," "Mostly a Protest," and "Not Generally Speaking Unruly," even when images of burning buildings were being displayed in the background, and over one billion dollars in damage was done.[67] The sympathy with leftist protesters and rioters even extended to the occupation by leftists of a federal building, and subsequent disruption of a confirmation vote for a Supreme Court justice nominee in 2018,[68] to throwing Molotov cocktails at federal buildings in Portland, and to the burning of cars, including the presidential limousine, to attacking police during Trump's inauguration, to protestors trying to burn down federal buildings with federal employees barricaded inside.[69] These were all reported as simply protests and either tacitly or actively condoned. On the other hand, Trump supporters entering the United States Capitol building was instantaneously labeled an armed insurrection, even as all the facts were as yet unknown.[70] Today we know that almost nobody was armed in any manner and that the FBI said no guns were confiscated.[71] And with foreign news outlets openly questioning[72] and even laughing at[73] Joe Biden's diminished mental capacities, the American mainstream news media's refusal to cover that during the election and up to the present day grows increasingly obvious.

Enter Big Tech

I mentioned earlier that the mainstream news was partisan, but that with the rise of the alternate news media, there was growing competition that could be a positive force in a free society. Unfortunately for the American polity, when one considers Big Tech such as Alphabet (Google, YouTube), Amazon, Meta

Platforms (Facebook, Instagram, WhatsApp), Apple, Microsoft (LinkedIn), other platforms, social media sites (TikTok, Twitter [now X]), and ISPs, the positive competitive dynamics are being forcefully attenuated. Many aggressively censor[74] and negatively label conservative news and many ideological narratives that they oppose,[75] all while allowing progressive messages, even some hateful ones advocating violence, to remain.[76]

Here are a few examples: the Twitter alternative, Parler, was deplatformed by its ISP for the crime of refusing to ban conservative thinking on allegations of election fraud in the 2020 American presidential election. Parler specifically links its free speech policy to that presently accepted as constitutionally protected speech. In short, you have Big Tech *in America* trying to destroy *an American free speech* social media site for using the US Constitution and its guarantees of free speech as its speech code. Yet Twitter,[77] whose new, as of November 2022, owner may or many not change company policy, continued to allow foreign despots such as Iran's Ayatollah Ali Khamenei a platform from which to spew hatred and threats of violence against Israel. It also allows Communist China's rulers to falsely accuse the United States for COVID-19, and also allows China to defend its genocide against over one million Uyghur Muslims,[78] but then actively discriminates against conservatives and helps liberals in America, as does Facebook.[79]

Some of the more obvious examples of these actions include Twitter locking the *New York Post* out of its account until it would retract its story on Hunter and Joe Biden's association with Communist China,[80] a move nothing short of extortion. Twitter permanently banned the undercover investigation organization Project Veritas for its exposes of powerful leftist groups and leaders.[81] And Twitter actually censored President Trump 625 times during his campaign while censoring Joe Biden not once,[82] and actively banned any discussion of election fraud in the 2020 election, as did YouTube,[83] with Facebook joining them by banning some and flagging other stories as "contested." Thus, any claim of a "contested" election was "contested" by Facebook. This censorship reached the point of absurdity when YouTube went so far as to ban the opening statement of President Trump's lawyer, who was testifying under oath in front of the US Senate's Homeland Security hearing on election fraud during the 2020 election.[84] YouTube still aggressively censors any discussion of COVID-19 vaccinations that in any way critiques their effectiveness, even to the point of censoring presidential candidates.[85] There was also the banning of the president of the United States from Twitter and subsequently Facebook. Consider that, if they can do this to the POTUS, which national leader or person can they not ban, as evidenced by the June 2021 banning of the President of Nigeria, with disastrous consequences.[86] Of note is that in the United States, almost all those banned by Big Tech are Republicans.[87] Concerning this suppression of free speech the

Intercollegiate Studies Institute wrote, "Welcome to the power of big tech. The tech giants . . . can shut down our ability to speak in an instant. The problem has grown so acute that America's FCC commissioner recently proclaimed that big tech 'now has more control over more speech than any institution in history.' Even prominent liberals are sounding the alarm."[88]

Such examples are signs of a rising authoritarianism, of voluntarily moving toward embracing a totalitarian one-party state. If a correct political value is not expressed, Big Tech can censor, deplatform, etc.[89] This is not how democracy flourishes but how totalitarianism is grown. As Frederick Douglass wrote, "Liberty is meaningless where the right to utter one's thoughts and opinions has ceased to exist. That, of all rights, is the dread of tyrants. It is the right which they first of all strike down."[90]

Importantly, the government did not compel this collusion between Big Tech and the mainstream news media; instead, with one-sided reporting and open attempts at censorship, both Big Tech and the mainstream news media willingly assume an authoritarian model of press operation: the MSMBT, with Big Tech in the supporting role. As Walter Lippmann wrote over one hundred years ago, "the press," and I would add now Big Tech, "threatens democracy whenever it has an agenda other than the free flow of ideas."[91] Moreover, when you have one political party aligned with the mainstream news media, which is aligned with Big Tech that controls much of the flow of information, we have a recipe for a totalitarian political system.[92]

In 2002 I wrote that, "by its political composition and its biased reportorial practices, the press not only breaks its own code of ethics, it functions as an anti-democratic institution since it undermines the very democratic ideals it professes to uphold."[93] The situation has only worsened since then. The mainstream news media and Big Tech are moving past being antidemocratic and into an authoritarian news media model of collusion,[94] with the press now *openly* taking sides in partisan political concerns, slowly rending the very fabric of the American Republic.[95] And these actions are not without consequences because democracy is fragile and cannot function and grow properly with the news media acting as an adjunct of a particular political party. As discovered by Gallup, Rasmussen, and others:

> Fifty-nine percent of voters agree that the news media are "Enemy of the People."[96]
> Over two-thirds believe the news media publish "fake news."[97]
> Only "16% of Americans have a great deal/quite a lot of confidence in newspapers; 11% have some the degree of confidence in television news."[98]
> "Voters don't trust news media fact checking."[99]

Seventy-two percent of Americans believe that "traditional major news sources report news they know to be fake, false, or purposely misleading."[100]

Only 17 to 23 percent of Americans rate journalists high or very high in ethical standards.[101]

There are, unfortunately, many more such surveys, with even foreign news outlets now reporting on the issue,[102] all of which suggest the same disheartening conclusion: *the American mainstream news media, in terms of political reporting, is seen as partisan, unethical, untrustworthy, and is contributing to an increasing sense of partisanship and distrust in American institutions.* As Michael Goodwin wrote, "there is a national crisis of confidence in all media."[103] Loss of trust in any institution weakens that institution's ability to perform its job. In the case of the press, how can it function properly as a watchdog when so many Americans distrust it? Such mistrust in the very institution that is supposed to be a trusted, impartial source for information from which to make political decisions only leads to poor decision by voters and opens the way to authoritarian rule by one party. As the Hutchins Commission concluded: "The tremendous influence of the modern press makes it imperative that the great agencies of mass communication show hospitality to ideas which their owners [and journalists] do not share. Otherwise, these ideas will not have a fair chance."[104]

STRENGTHENING REPORTING IN THE REPUBLIC: SOME SOLUTIONS

There are ways to begin addressing this dangerous malady. First, the public should demand, and the press should embrace, viewpoint diversity in newsrooms. As an institution the mainstream press possesses negligible variety of thought. The few nonleft political sources given voice in the mainstream news media have those voices made insignificant by the collective weight of hegemonic mainstream press thought. Healthy variety and competition cannot come from just alternate news sites (which the mainstream news media and Big Tech are actively trying to suppress) but must arise from ideological diversity in mainstream news media newsrooms. Given that over 90 percent of mainstream news media journalists are left of center,[105] newsrooms must burst the confirmation bias bubble by hiring those who are not liberal, particularly editors at first, and return to a notion of a press that serves the people rather than the political interests of the press. For it is only within the newsroom crucible, with coworkers of differing political ideologies working together to produce an objective news report, that we can arrive at a fairer, more accurate, and democracy-nourishing product for the American Republic. In a free society, it is simply not the role of the press to effect partisan change but to provide *complete, accurate details, within an unbiased context, so that the people may make informed political judgments.*

Second, the public should demand antitrust legislation to break up the corporate consolidation of news outlets and also Big Tech. Alphabet (Google, YouTube), Amazon, Meta Platforms (Facebook, Instagram, WhatsApp), and other news-owning organizations all should be broken up. As of 2016, fifteen billionaires own almost all of America's news media.[106] In 1983, 90 percent of media was owned by fifty companies; by 2012, 90 percent was owned by six: Time Warner, Walt Disney, Viacom, Rupert Murdoch's News Corp, CBS Corporation, and NBC Universal.[107] The best defense against a tyranny—whether of ideas, products, or people—is competition. Liberals have dominated the news media for more than forty years, and now when we see the rise of an alternative press, and nonliberals making good use of social media, both the mainstream news media and Big Tech engage in censorship and attempt to cancel their competitors and maintain their monopoly in both product and ideology. As expressed by Anthony George, "Social media is the technological lynch-mob of the 21st century. They can try you with no jury . . . cancel you, get you fired . . . they can banish you into exile, simply because you post something."[108] Such behavior is simply antidemocratic, and over 57 percent of Americans now desire more government regulation of technology companies.[109]

Third, the public should demand Section 230 protections be modified[110] to continue protecting small start-up companies, but also so that Big Tech companies who own and run social media networking sites are compelled to treat them as what they have evolved into: part of the public sphere. Toward the end of 2020, Supreme Court Justice Clarence Thomas argued that "Section 230 declares that social media platforms are not 'publishers,' which means that they cannot be held liable for content posted by their users. Some industry analysts have suggested that platforms should be responsible for certain content on their platform, and for the censorship of content from their platforms, an act that makes them a publisher instead of a platform."[111] Big Tech social media sites such as Twitter and Facebook, given their near monopoly status, should be treated legally as the public sphere in terms of freedom of speech. In America this means that their rules for free speech must comport with that established for any public space. Thus, no censorship based on political point of view; no censorship based on the whims of CEOs, something the new owner of Twitter, Elon Musk, has publicly promised. Other countries have begun the fight, with both India and Australia pushing back hard against Big Tech's "digital colonialism."[112] The European Union is pushing back as well in the area of Big Tech's (Google in particular) self-serving manipulation of information.[113]

Fourth, alternate news and social media sites must take steps to protect themselves from deplatforming. For example, the Twitter alternative, Parler, which specifically links its free speech policy to that presently accepted as American constitutionally protected speech, was deplatformed for the crime of refusing to ban conservative commentary on allegations of election fraud in the 2020 American presidential election.[114] Yet had it used decentralized server networks, such as the social media site Mastodon does, it could not have been so easily cut off. Decentralization will help prevent sites from being shut down on a political whim. The alternate press is in danger from this, just as are alternate social media sites. Recently we have seen calls from CNN, for instance, to ban Breitbart News and even Fox News. Facebook and Twitter censored and ultimately deplatformed the president of the United States and are in some ways calling for destroying alternate venues for free expression such as Parler, Gab, and MeWe.[115] Decentralization by alternate venues will help check the enormous power of the news media and Big Tech.

To conclude, we have reviewed the political composition of the press and its worldviews that reflect this composition. We have also seen how moral judgments flow from these political points of view, the implications of the press and Big Tech actions, and gone over some solutions. There is no easy path, but America must reform its news media and Big Tech practices soon or risk losing its democracy.

NOTES

An earlier version of this chapter was presented as a keynote address at the Media in America, America in Media: International Online Conference, March 25, 2021, Lublin, Poland; a condensed version of that presentation is published as "The Destruction of Democracy: American Mainstream News Reportorial Practices Today," *Res Rhetorica* 8, no. 4 (2021): 140–51.

1. For a good summary of this commission's work, see David Shedden, "Today in Media History: In 1947, The Press Reported on the Hutchins Commission Report," Poytner, March 27, 2015, https://www.poynter.org/reporting-editing/2015/today-in-media-history-in-1947-the-press-reported-on-the-hutchins-commission-report/. See also Edward C. Pease, "The Hutchins Commission: An Historical Perspective: Philosophical Underpinnings of Free Expression in Society," *Introduction to Mass Comm*, March 21, 2010, https://masscomm1500.blogspot.com/2010/03/hutchins-commission-historical.html.

2. All quotes: The Commission on Freedom of the Press, *A Free and Responsible Press* (Chicago: University of Chicago Press, 1947), 20–21.

3. Fred S. Siebert, Theodore Peterson, and Wilbur Schramm, *Four Theories of the Press* (Urbana: University of Illinois Press, 1956).

4. See Xiao Qiang, "Xiao Qiang: Digital Authoritarianism in China Undermines Democratic Values," YouTube, April 29, 2021, https://www.youtube.com/watch?v=szAQ61dEeuo&ab_channel=Forum2000; Alex Matthews, "China's Lack of Press Freedom Causes Problems for the World," *Deutsche Welle*, April 21, 2020, https://www.dw.com/en/chinas-lack-of-press-freedom-causes-problems-for-the-world/a-53198195; "One Country, One Censor: How China Undermines Media Freedom in Hong Kong and Taiwan," Committee to Protect Journalists, December 16, 2019, https://cpj.org/reports/2019/12/one-country-one-censor-china-hong-kong-taiwan-press-freedom; Journalists Without Borders ranks China 177th out of 180 countries for press freedoms. See the 2020 world press freedom index at https://rsf.org/en/ranking.

5. Siebert, Peterson, and Schramm, 5.

6. James L. Aucoin, "The Re-emergence of American Investigative Journalism, 1960–1975," *Journalism History* 21 (Spring 1995): 8. Also see Warren Breed, "Mass Communication and Sociocultural Integration," in *People, Society, and Mass Communications*, ed. Lewis A. Dexter and David Manning White (New York: Free Press, 1964), 183–201, quotation on 191.

7. The extent of this shift is debatable; yet there are numerous examples, and even journalists and academics openly calling for it. For example, see Carolina Are, "Q&A with Anita Varma About Journalism that Builds Solidarity," *Humanitarian Research News Network*, June 15, 2020, http://www.hnrn.co.uk/qa-anita-varma-journalism-solidarity. Or consider Robert Niles's statement: "I'm glad that some professors are teaching advocacy journalism. We get into this field to raise some hell and make things right. Let's never forget that—let's embrace it." Robert Niles, "Why We Need Advocacy Journalism," *Online Journalism Review*, December 20, 2011, http://www.ojr.org/p2042/.

8. Daniel C. Hallin, "Soundbite News: Television Coverage of Elections, 1968–1988," *Journal of Communication* 42, no. 2 (1992): 5–24; Center for Media and Public Affairs, "Journalists Monopolize TV Election News Study Finds Less Air Time, Shorter Sound Bites for Candidates," October 30, 2000, http://www.cmpa.com/election2004/JournalistsMonopolize.htm.

9. This shrinking soundbite is both on "television and in the newspaper." Thomas Patterson, "The News Media: An Effective Political Actor?" *Political Communication* 14, no. 4 (1997): 452

10. It also allows for deceptive editing as well. See this example provided by a conservative media watchdog site: "Watch: Major News Outlet Deceptively Edits Reporter's Interaction with FL Governor Ron DeSantis," *Resist the Mainstream*, April 5, 2021, https://resistthemainstream.org/watch-major-news-outlet-deceptively-edits-reporters-interaction-with-fl-governor-ron-desantis. For an explanation of how alternate news sites contest mainstream news framing and editing, see Steven D. Cooper,

Watching the Watchdog: Bloggers as the Fifth Estate (Spokane, WA: Marquette Books, 2006).

11. Martin Gurri, "Slouching Toward Post-Journalism," *City Journal*, Winter 2021, https://www.city-journal.org/journalism-advocacy-over-reporting; Jim A. Kuypers, *Partisan Journalism: A History of Media Bias in the United States* (Lanham, MD: Rowman & Littlefield, 2014).

12. Some mainstream news media journalists have noted this shift, calling contemporary American political reporting a "threat to Democracy." Bernard Goldberg, "Journalism Has Become a Threat to Democracy," *Bernardgoldberg.com*, October 19, 2020, https://bernardgoldberg.com/journalism-has-become-a-threat-to-democracy/.

13. Jim A. Kuypers, *Press Bias and Politics: How the Media Frame Controversial Issues* (Westport, CT: Praeger, 2002).

14. See the 1992 Freedom Forum–sponsored poll of 1,400 journalists at http://www.freedomforum.org, and "A Deep Dive into Party Affiliation," *Pew Research Center*, April 7, 2015, https://www.pewresearch.org/politics/2015/04/07/a-deep-dive-into-party-affiliation/0. For an historical overview, see "Media Bias 101," Media Research Center, January 2014, https://www.mrc.org/sites/default/files/uploads/documents/2014/MBB2014.pdf. See, too, Barbara Oakley, "Why Most Journalists Are Democrats: A View from the Soviet Socialist Trenches," *Psychology Today*, August 3, 2009, https://www.psychologytoday.com/us/blog/scalliwag/200908/why-most-journalists-are-democrats-view-the-soviet-socialist-trenches.

15. Kuypers, *Partisan Journalism*.

16. This lopsided party affiliation continues when one moves beyond Washington. See the Freedom Forum–sponsored poll above.

17. Kuypers, *Partisan Journalism*; see also Hadas Gold, "Survey: 7 Percent of Reporters Identify as Republican," *Politico*, May 6, 2014, https://www.politico.com/blogs/media/2014/05/survey-7-percent-of-reporters-identify-as-republican-188053. *Investor's Business Daily* editorially stated, "Even among 'financial' journalists . . . '58.47% admit to being left of center.' With only 4.4% of the total that lean right-of-center." Of note is that during the mid-1990s charges of liberal bias became widespread and journalists began to describe themselves differently: by mid-decade "only 22% of the press considered themselves liberal, 5% conservative, and almost two-thirds, 64% now considered themselves moderate." Editorial, "Media Bias: Pretty Much All of Journalism Now Leans Left, Study Shows," *Investor's Business Daily*, November 16, 2018, https://www.investors.com/politics/editorials/media-bias-left-study/. Molly Hemingway, "Another Survey Confirms Journalists Are Overwhelmingly Liberal," *The Federalist*, May 7, 2014, https://thefederalist.com/2014/05/07/another-survey-confirms-journalists-are-overwhelmingly-liberal/.

18. "A Deep Dive into Party Affiliation," *Pew Research Center*, April 7, 2015, https://www.pewresearch.org/politics/2015/04/07/a-deep-dive-into-party-affiliation/.

19. See Federal Election Commission Campaign Contribution Data, https://www.fec.gov/campaign-finance-data/presidential-campaign-finance-summaries/; Kuypers, *Partisan Journalism*, especially chapter 8.

20. For overviews of university faculty ideology, see Ashley Thorne, "Ideology and Disparity in College," National Association of Scholars, August 28, 2009,

https://www.nas.org/blogs/article/ideology_and_disparity_in_college; and Samuel J. Abrams, "Why Colleges' Liberal Lean Is a Problem," *The Chronicle of Higher Education*, March 5, 2017, https://www.chronicle.com/article/why-colleges-liberal-lean-is-a-problem. And for an investigation touching upon the impact of "group think" in the sciences, see David Randall and Christopher Welser, "The Irreproducibility Crisis of Modern Science: Causes, Consequences, and the Road to Reform," National Association of Scholars, April 9, 2018, https://www.nas.org/reports/the-irreproducibility-crisis-of-modern-science/full-report; for a case specific, although generalizable to higher education in general, see Natalie L. Kahn, "'An Endangered Species': The Scarcity of Harvard's Conservative Faculty," *The Harvard Crimson*, April 9, 2021, https://www.thecrimson.com/article/2021/4/9/disappearance-conservative-faculty/.

21. Michael Horning and Jim A. Kuypers, "Media Bias and Talking of War," *Vietnam: Veterans for Factual History* (Spring 2019).

22. Samantha Chang, "Lara Logan: The Media, Who Are 85% Democrat, Have Become Propagandists and Liberal Activists," BizPac Review, February 19, 2019, https://www.bizpacreview.com/2019/02/19/cbs-news-reporter-lara-logan-the-media-85-dems-have-become-propagandists-and-liberal-activists-725319/.

23. For an overview of the tension between objectivity and activism in journalism, see Michael Blanding, "Where Does Journalism End and Activism Begin?" Nieman Reports, August 21, 2018, https://niemanreports.org/articles/where-does-journalism-end-and-activism-begin; David Carr, "Journalism, Even When It's Tilted," *New York Times*, June 30, 2013, https://www.nytimes.com/2013/07/01/business/media/journalism-is-still-at-work-even-when-its-practitioner-has-a-slant.html.

24. See Kuypers, *Partisan Journalism*; Kuypers, *Press Bias and Politics*; Abe Aamidor, Jim A. Kuypers, and Susan Wiesinger, *Media Smackdown: Deconstructing the News and the Future of Journalism* (New York: Peter Lang Publishing, 2013) for numerous examples of this.

25. Bernard Goldberg, "No Liberal Bias in the Media? Who Is Chuck Todd Kidding, Besides Himself?" *The Hill*, August 16, 2021, https://thehill.com/opinion/campaign/567748-no-liberal-bias-in-the-media-who-is-chuck-todd-kidding-besides-himself/.

26. For instance, CBS news posting on Twitter instructions for how one can oppose a newly enacted state law: Tim Graham, "CBS 'News' Deletes Tweet Advocating How Companies Can Oppose Georgia Republicans," *NewsBusters*, April 4, 2021, https://www.newsbusters.org/blogs/nb/tim-graham/2021/04/04/cbs-news-deletes-tweet-advocating-how-companies-can-oppose-georgia.

27. For examples of these exposes, see David Limbaugh, "Project Veritas Strips CNN Naked," Townhall.com, December 4, 2020, https://townhall.com/columnists/davidlimbaugh/2020/12/04/project-veritas-strips-cnn-naked-n2581024; and "WATCH: CNN's Brian Stelter Confronted Over Explosive Videos Released By Project Veritas," Daily Wire, April 17, 2021, https://www.dailywire.com/news/watch-cnns-brian-stelter-confronted-over-explosive-videos-released-by-project-veritas.

28. Jeffrey Goldberg, "Meet the New Journolist, Smaller than the Old Journolist," *The Atlantic*, blog post, July 21, 2010, https://www.theatlantic.com/national/archive/2010/07/meet-the-new-journolist-smaller-than-the-old-journolist/60159/.

29. Milo, "The E-mails that Prove Video Games Journalism Must Be Reformed," *Breitbart*, September 18, 2014, https://www.breitbart.com/europe/2014/09/18/the-emails-that-prove-video-games-journalism-must-be-reformed/.

30. Charlie Nash, "'JournoList' 2 Revealed, over 400 'Left-of-Center' Members," Breitbart, June 28, 2018, https://www.breitbart.com/tech/2018/06/28/journolist-2-discovered-over-400-left-of-center-members/.

31. For a few examples, see https://www.breitbart.com/the-media/2023/05/16/pbs-newshour-negatively-covers-congressional-republicans-85/; Evan Siegfried, "Media Bias Against Conservatives Is Real, and Part of the Reason No One Trusts the News Now," *NBC News*, July 29, 2018, https://www.nbcnews.com/think/opinion/media-bias-against-conservatives-real-part-reason-no-one-trusts-ncna895471; Sally Zelikovsky, "The Enemy of the People," *The American Spectator*, November 15, 2018, https://www.americanthinker.com/articles/2018/11/the_enemy_of_the_people.html; Kuypers, *Press Bias and Politics*, 214–16; Kuypers, *Partisan Journalism*, esp. chapter 11. Although from a right-leaning site, here are some interesting comparisons of different coverage of similar topics based on political party: https://www.breitbart.com/the-media/2023/05/16/pbs-newshour-negatively-covers-congressional-republicans-85/.

32. Jim A. Kuypers, "The Presidential Nomination Acceptance Speeches of Donald Trump and Hillary Clinton: Terministic Screens and Antagonistic Worldviews," in *Political Campaign Communication: Theory, Method and Practice*, ed. Robert E. Denton Jr. (Lanham, MD: Lexington Books, 2017), 141–68.

33. Jim A. Kuypers, "News Media Framing of the Donald J. Trump and Hillary Clinton 2016 Presidential Nomination Acceptance Speeches: Terministic Screens and the Discovery of the Worldview and Bias of the Press," in *The 2016 American Presidential Campaign and the News Media: Implications for the American Republic and Democracy*, ed. Jim A. Kuypers (Lanham, MD: Lexington Books, 2018), 101–32.

34. Walter Lippman, *Public Opinion* (Digireads.com, 2011), 58.

35. Kenneth Burke, *Language as Symbolic Action, Essays on Life Literature and Method* (Berkeley and Los Angeles: University of California Press, 1968), 46.

36. Burke, *Language as Symbolic Action*, 49.

37. Burke, *Language as Symbolic Action*, 46.

38. Burke, *Language as Symbolic Action*, 45.

39. This refers to the 2016 platform, although I would say also with the 2020 platform. "Party Platform: The 2020 Democrat Party Platform," Democratic National Committee, 2020, https://democrats.org/wp-content/uploads/sites/2/2020/08/2020-Democratic-Party-Platform.pdf.

40. Kuypers, "News Media Framing of the Donald J. Trump and Hillary Clinton."

41. Jim A. Kuypers, *President Trump and the News Media: Moral Foundations, Framing, and the Nature of Press Bias in America* (Lanham, MD: Lexington Books, 2020).

42. Jonathan Haidt, *The Righteous Mind: Why Good People Are Divided by Politics and Religion* (New York: Pantheon Books, 2012), xiii.

43. Haidt, xiv.

44. Haidt has suggested a "provisional" sixth foundation, liberty/oppression.

45. Kuypers, *President Trump and the News Media*.

46. On this issue David Harsanyi wrote that the mainstream news media was now "an overtly partisan media, exemplified by CNN, which has dropped any pretense of fairness and become an organ of the Democratic Party." "CNN's Bias Is Now Beyond Laughable," *New York Post*, January 16, 2020, https://nypost.com/2020/01/16/cnns-bias-is-now-beyond-laughable/.

47. Others have noticed this as well; for instance: Adam Ford, "Here's Washington Post Coming Through with Some North-Korea-State-Media-Level Biden Worship," *Not the Bee*, Mach 7, 2021, https://notthebee.com/article/wapo-coming-through-with-north-korea-state-media-level-praise-for-biden.

48. John Nolte, "How the Political Media's Corruption Destroyed America's Most Crucial Institutions," Daily Wire, November 7, 2016, https://www.dailywire.com/news/how-political-medias-corruption-destroyed-americas-john-nolte.

49. Kuypers, *Partisan Journalism*.

50. Natalie O'Neill, "Hydroxychloroquine Rated 'Most Effective' Coronavirus Treatment, Poll of Doctors Finds," *New York Post*, April 2, 2020, https://nypost.com/2020/04/02/hydroxychloroquine-most-effective-coronavirus-treatment-poll.

51. J. D. Rucker, "How Many People Died Because MSM Told Them Not to Take Hydroxychloroquine?" NOQ Report, February 1, 2021, https://noqreport.com/2021/02/01/how-many-people-died-because-msm-told-them-not-to-take-hydroxychloroquine/.

52. Danielle Kurtzleben, "Study: News Coverage of Trump More Negative than for Other Presidents," NPR, October 2, 2017, https://www.npr.org/2017/10/02/555092743/study-news-coverage-of-trump-more-negative-than-for-other-presidents; Ian Haworth, "'Mario Kart' and 'Early Bedtimes': These 6 Headlines Show the Media's Worship of the Biden Administration," The Daily Wire, February 16, 2021, https://www.dailywire.com/news/mari-kart-and-early-bedtimes-these-6-headlines-show-the-medias-worship-of-the-biden-administration; Rich Noyes, "Study: Liberal Media Blasts Trump with 92% Negative Coverage, Biden Gets 66% Positive," *LifeNews*, October 27, 2020, https://www.lifenews.com/2020/10/27/study-liberal-media-blasts-trump-with-92-negative-coverage-biden-gets-66-positive/. My informal analysis of a random selection of one hundred mainstream news reports from the 2020 campaign found similar results.

53. Nolan D. Mccaskill, "Poll: Majority of Voters Believe Media Biased against Trump," *Politico*, October 19, 2016, http://politi.co/2el8Vgf. See also John Lott Jr., "The Media Just Can't Stop Lying About Trump," *The Hill*, June 16, 2018, https://thehill.com/opinion/campaign/393553-the-media-just-cant-stop-lying-about-Trump.

54. John Solomon, "Joe Biden's 2020 Ukrainian Nightmare: A Closed Probe Is Revived," *The Hill*, April 1, 2019, https://thehill.com/opinion/white-house/436816-joe-bidens-2020-ukrainian-nightmare-a-closed-probe-is-revived.

55. Joel B. Pollak, "Pollak: Mainstream Media, Big Tech Coverup Collapses with Hunter Biden Investigation," Breitbart News, December 9, 2020, https://www.breitbart.com/the-media/2020/12/09/pollak-mainstream-media-big-tech-coverup-collapses-with-hunter-biden-investigation-laptop/.

56. Garrett O'Leary, "Withheld Interview Exposes Depths of Biden's Anti-Gun Plans," February 12, 2021, https://www.americas1stfreedom.org/articles/2021/2/12/withheld-interview-exposes-depths-of-biden-s-anti-gun-plans.

57. I realize that this issue is contentious. The point is that a sizable percentage of Americans believe there was fraud and that fraud was being actively discussed in both nonmainstream media and in the state legislatures of the contested states and others such as Texas. For example, see how the alternative news media reported official State of Georgia Senate Committee Hearings on election fraud that were not well reported in the mainstream news: Zachary Stieber, "Georgia Senator: Coordinated Illegal Actions Appear to Have Taken Place During Election," *The Epoch Times*, December 21, 2020, https://www.theepochtimes.com/georgia-senators-coordinated-illegal-actions-appear-to-have-taken-place-during-election_3627176.html. YouTube censored news of the discussion: https://www.youtube.com/watch?v=8q9pOY4_qkE.

58. Surveys range from seventy-four million to one hundred million, with even a sizable number of Independents and Democrats believing there was voter fraud to elect Joe Biden. For example, Rasmussen Reports found that 20 to 30 percent of Democrat voters believe it "very likely" that the Democrats stole votes or destroyed pro-Trump ballots to ensure a Biden win. https://twitter.com/Rasmussen_Poll/status/1329741803025801217. See also "61% Think Trump Should Concede to Biden," *Rasmussen Reports*, November 19, 2020, https://www.rasmussenreports.com/public_content/politics/elections/election_2020/61_think_trump_should_concede_to_biden.

59. For example, see Sarah McCammon, "Combating Misinformation When a Loved One Is Caught in a Web of Conspiracies," NPR, January 30, 2021, https://www.npr.org/2021/01/30/959394083/combating-misinformation-when-a-loved-one-is-caught-in-a-web-of-conspiracies.

60. R. J. Reinhart, "Faith in Elections in Relatively Short Supply in U.S.," Gallup, February 13, 2020, https://news.gallup.com/poll/285608/faith-elections-relatively-short-supply.aspx.

61. Brittany Shepherd, "Americans' Faith in Election Integrity Drops: POLL," *ABC News*, January 6, 2022, https://abcnews.go.com/Politics/americans-faith-election-integrity-drops-poll/story?id=82069876.

62. Bill D'Agostino, "NewsBusters Explainer Video: How Fact Checkers Abuse Their Role to Boost Democrat Causes," *NewsBusters*, May 25, 2021, https://www.newsbusters.org/blogs/nb/bill-dagostino/2021/05/25/newsbusters-explainer-video-how-fact-checkers-abuse-their-role.

63. Shelby Talcott, "WaPo Fact Checkers End Trump 'False Claims Project,' No 'Plans' to Start One for Biden," *Daily Caller*, January 20, 2021, https://dailycaller.com/2021/01/20/washington-post-fact-checkers-end-donald-trump-project-no-plans-joe-biden-false-claims/.

64. As an example of cultivating trust; see P. R. Lockhart, "Experts Warn of Low Covid Vaccine Trust Among Black Americans," *NBC News*, December 11, 2020, https://www.nbcnews.com/news/nbcblk/experts-warn-low-covid-vaccine-trust-among-black-americans-n1250743. See also Kristine Marsh, "Hypocrites: ABC Urges Americans to Trust Vaccine Safety AFTER Spreading Anti-Vaccine Hysteria Before Election," NewsBusters, December 15, 2020, https://newsbusters.org/blogs

/nb/kristine-marsh/2020/12/15/hypocrites-abc-urges-americans-trust-vaccine-safety-after.

65. "Executive Orders," The American Presidency Project, March 18, 2021, https://www.presidency.ucsb.edu/statistics/data/executive-orders.

66. For example of negative coverage of President Trump using executive orders, here for delivering COVID-19 relief aid in August 2020, see Whit Johnson and Rachel Scott, *Good Morning America* [ABC News], August 9, 2020. For an example of positive coverage of Joe Biden using executive orders see George Stephanopoulos and Jon Karl, *This Week* [ABC News], February 7, 2021.

67. Sky News Australia, "BLM Riots Caused Over $1 Billion of Damage, 'Yet Media Says They're Mostly Peaceful,'" MSN, September 17, 2020, https://www.msn.com/en-au/news/australia/blm-riots-caused-over-241-billion-of-damage-yet-media-says-theyre-mostly-peaceful/ar-BB198RTB. See also, as examples, Tim Hains, "MSNBC's Ali Velshi Downplays Riot in Front of Burning Building: 'Mostly a Protest,' 'Not Generally Speaking Unruly,'" RealClearPolitics, May 28, 2020, https://www.realclearpolitics.com/video/2020/05/28/msnbcs_ali_velshi_downplays_riot_in_front_of_burning_building_mostly_a_protest_not_generally_speaking_unruly.html; and Tim Hains, "CNN Mocked for Reporting 'Fiery But Mostly Peaceful Protests' with Burning Riot in Background," RealClearPolitics, August 27, 2020, https://www.realclearpolitics.com/video/2020/08/27/cnn_mocked_for_reporting_fiery_but_mostly_peaceful_protests_with_burning_riot_in_background.html.

68. Ralph Ellis, "Anti-Kavanaugh Protesters Keep up the Fight, Even After He's Confirmed," CNN, October 6, 2018, https://www.cnn.com/2018/10/06/politics/kavanaugh-protests/index.html.

69. Paul Sacca, "Portland Rioters Barricade Door and Set Fire to ICE Building with Federal Agents Inside: 'Burn the Precinct to the Ground'!" TheBlaze, April 11, 2021, https://www.theblaze.com/news/portland-riot-ice-building-fire-antifa.

70. For instance, see Sarah N. Lynch, "Amid Setbacks, Prosecutors Abandon Some Claims in U.S. Capitol Riot Cases," *Reuters,* March 24, 2021, https://www.reuters.com/article/us-usa-capitol-arrests-justice/amid-setbacks-prosecutors-abandon-some-claims-in-u-s-capitol-riot-cases-idUSKBN2BG30C; Bryon York, "Byron York's Daily Memo: Developing Some Perspective on the Capitol Riot," *Washington Examiner*, March 4, 2021, https://www.washingtonexaminer.com/opinion/byron-yorks-daily-memo-developing-some-perspective-on-the-capitol-riot; and independent reporter Glenn Greenwald, "The False and Exaggerated Claims Still Being Spread About the Capitol Riot," Glenn Greenwald, February 16, 2021, https://greenwald.substack.com/p/the-false-and-exaggerated-claims.

71. Monica Showalter, "So Much for 'Armed Insurrection': FBI Official Says No Guns Confiscated at Jan. 6 Capitol Riot," American Thinker, March 4, 2021, https://www.americanthinker.com/blog/2021/03/so_much_for_armed_insurrection_fbi_official_says_no_guns_confiscated_at_jan_6_capitol_riot.html.

72. "Biden's Mental Health Concerns Increase After Walorski Gaffe," Sky News, October 11, 2022, https://www.skynews.com.au/world-news/bidens-mental-health-concerns-increase-after-walorski-gaffe/video/332db18f819ecec2abf3e8ff8444a4fd; Jack Davis, "News Host: 'Joe Biden Is Struggling with Dementia' and the Mainstream

Media Is Complicit in Hiding It," *The Western Journal*, February 21, 2021, https://www.westernjournal.com/news-host-joe-biden-struggling-dementia-mainstream-media-complicit-hiding/. See also Admin, "Australian News Mocks dailBiden's Lapdog Journalists at CNN for Pathetic 'News' Coverage," *Republican Daily*, June 15, 2021, https://republicandaily.net/2021/06/australian-news-mocks-bidens-lapdog-journalists-at-cnn-for-pathetic-news-coverage; Ben Johnson, "Foreign Media Skewer Joe Biden As 'Barely Cogent,' 'Bizarre,'" Daily Wire, July 3, 2021, https://www.dailywire.com/news/foreign-media-skewer-joe-biden-as-barely-cogent-bizarre.

73. "Joe Biden's Blunders Bring Sky News Australia Host to Tears," *Sky News Australia*, February 20, 2023, https://www.youtube.com/watch?v=WxXepkdJHko&t=215s.

74. See Jeff Poor, "FNC's Carlson: 'Never in American History Has There Been Press Censorship on This Scale,'" Breitbart News, January 27, 2021, https://www.breitbart.com/clips/2021/01/27/fncs-carlson-never-in-american-history-has-there-been-press-censorship-on-this-scale/. Consider also TikTok banning without explanation conservative Praeger University, which had millions of viewers. Praeger University Team, "BREAKING: TikTok Bans PragerU," email, April 7, 2021; or JW Player refusing to host PragerU's videos, saying they violate community guidelines but refusing to provide a single example, all while allowing progressive videos from The Young Turks and even Vice! to remain. LinkedIn canceled the account of the pioneer of mRNA vaccinations for questioning their safety for those under eighteen: Jack Phillips, "LinkedIn Deletes Account of mRNA Vaccine Pioneer Who Questioned Risks of COVID-19 Shots," *The Epoch Times*, July 2, 2021, https://www.theepochtimes.com/linkedin-deletes-account-of-mrna-vaccine-pioneer-who-issued-warning-about-risks_3884669.html. Facebook, too, has been exposed as intentionally censoring COVID-19 vaccination concerns raised by experts: "BREAKING: Facebook Whistleblowers Expose LEAKED INTERNAL DOCS Detailing New Effort to Secretly Censor Vaccine Concerns on a Global Scale," Project Veritas, May 24, 2021, https://www.projectveritas.com/news/breaking-facebook-whistleblowers-expose-leaked-internal-docs-detailing-new/.

75. This censorship is noted also by those in the industry. See Susan Crabtree, "Group of Tech Execs Takes on Social Media Censorship," RealClearPolitics, June 1, 2021, https://www.realclearpolitics.com/articles/2021/06/01/group_of_tech_execs_takes_on_social_media_censorship_145851.html. Consider also the liberal political composition of Big Tech employees, as in this example: Rani Molla, "Tech Employees Are Much More Liberal than Their Employers—At Least as Far as the Candidates They Support," *Vox*, October 31, 2018, https://www.vox.com/2018/10/31/18039528/tech-employees-politics-liberal-employers-candidates.

76. This also extends to the suppression or deletion of information that could challenge a preferred mainstream news narrative. See Jon Brown, "Facebook Quickly Scrubs Capitol Assailant's Facebook Page Praising Farrakhan as Jesus," Daily Wire, April 2, 2021, https://www.dailywire.com/news/facebook-quickly-scrubs-capitol-assailant-facebook-page-praising-farrakhan-as-jesus; or Tim Pearce, "Amazon Quietly Pulls Book on Transgenderism as Crackdown on 'Hate Speech' Continues,"

Daily Wire, April 14, 2021, https://www.dailywire.com/news/amazon-quietly-pulls-book-on-transgenderism-as-crackdown-on-hate-speech-continues.

77. Although acknowledging that the "left-wing censorship machine has it out for conservatives," it is too early to tell if Elon Musk's purchasing of Twitter will change its behavior. Ben Zeisloft, "Elon Musk Acknowledges Left-Wing Censorship Machine Has It Out for Conservatives," *Daily Wire*, November 4, 2022, https://www.dailywire.com/news/elon-musk-acknowledges-left-wing-censorship-machine-has-it-out-for-conservatives. For an early assessment of Musk's changes, see Michael Rectenwald, "Elon Musk's Twitter Gambit and What It Means to the 'Clique in Power,'" Mises Wire, April 26, 2022, https://mises.org/wire/elon-musks-twitter-gambit-and-what-it-means-clique-power.

78. L. Brent Bozell III, "Brent Bozell: Big Tech and the Scary Truth—If We Don't Have Online Freedom, Then We Are No Longer Free," *Fox News*, February 5, 2021, https://www.foxnews.com/opinion/big-tech-truth-online-freedom-free-brent-bozell.

79. Rebecca Downs, "Twitter Has Doubled Down on Punishing the Babylon Bee," Townhall.com, March 3, 2022, https://townhall.com/tipsheet/rebeccadowns/2022/03/22/twitter-has-doubled-down-on-punishing-the-babylon-bee-n2604899; Alec Schemmel, "STUDY: Facebook Lets Genocidal Communist China Influence Over 751,000,000 Followers," *NewsBusters*, June 2, 2021, https://www.newsbusters.org/blogs/free-speech/alec-schemmel/2021/06/02/study-facebook-lets-genocidal-communist-china-influence. See also, Jonathan Bucks and Daniel Bates, "Facebook 'Fact-Checkers' Could Be Politically Biased Themselves, Admits the Tech Giant's Vice-President Nick Clegg," *Daily Mail*, June 12, 2021, https://www.dailymail.co.uk/news/article-9679631/Facebook-fact-checkers-politically-biased-Nick-Clegg-admits.html. Such censorship began well before the 2020 election. See, for instance, Charlie Nash, "Facebook Censors Pro-Trump Page as Company Denies Censorship Before Congress," Breitbart News, July 17, 2018, https://www.breitbart.com/tech/2018/07/17/pro-trump-facebook-page-censored-same-day-platform-denies-censorship-of-conservatives/.

80. Bruce Golding, "How Tweet It Is: Twitter Backs Down, Unlocks Post's Account," *New York Post*, October 30, 2020, https://nypost.com/2020/10/30/twitter-backs-down-agrees-to-unlock-posts-account.

81. Brian Fung, "Twitter Permanently Bans Project Veritas Account," CNN, February 11, 2021, https://www.cnn.com/2021/02/11/tech/twitter-project-veritas/index.html.

82. Corinne Weaver, "Twitter Censors Trump and Campaign 625 Times, Biden Still Left Alone," NewsBusters, January 4, 2021, https://newsbusters.org/blogs/techwatch/corinne-weaver/2021/01/04/twitter-censors-trump-and-campaign-625-times-biden-still.

83. Such indiscriminate censorship exists even today. See, for example, Judicial Watch, "OUTRAGE: Youtube CENSORS Judicial Watch Election Video!," Youtube.com, May 16, 2022, https://www.youtube.com/watch?app=desktop&v=hkwyIv7girE&ab_channel=JudicialWatch.

84. Jack Phillips, "YouTube Removes Trump Lawyer's Opening Statement from Senate Committee Hearing," *Epoch Times*, December 20, 2020, https://

www.theepochtimes.com/youtube-removes-trump-lawyers-opening-statement-from-senate-committee-hearing_3626087.html. YouTube regularly censors points of view that counter its accepted political narrative; see, for instance, this example: https://www.frc.org/get.cfm?i=WA22C62&f=WU22C21.

85. Houston Keene, "YouTube Says It removed Jordan Peterson Interview of RFK Jr. for Violating Vaccine Policy," *Fox News*, June 19, 2023, https://www.foxnews.com/politics/youtube-says-it-removed-jordan-peterson-interview-rfk-jr-violating-vaccine-policy.

86. Emmanuel Akinwotu, "Nigeria Suspends Twitter Access After President's Tweet Was Deleted," *The Guardian*, June 4, 2021, https://www.theguardian.com/world/2021/jun/04/nigeria-suspends-twitter-after-presidents-tweet-was-deleted; Lela Gilbert, "Twitter Blocks and Bans in Nigeria," Family Research Council, June 7, 2021, https://www.frc.org/updatearticle/20210607/twitter-nigeria.

87. "Elected Officials Suspended or Banned from Social Media Platforms," Ballotpedia.org, March 20, 2023, https://ballotpedia.org/Elected_officials_suspended_or_banned_from_social_media_platforms.

88. "Is Big Tech a Threat?" Intercollegiate Studies Institute, February 24, 2021, https://www.bigmarker.com/intercollegiate-studies-inst/Is-Big-Tech-a-Threat.

89. A documentary exploring such censorship is found here: "Restricted: How Big Tech Is Taking Away Your Freedom," PragerU, September 29, 2021, https://www.prageru.com/video/restricted.

90. John R. Vile, "Frederick Douglass," *The First Amendment Encyclopedia*, February 2020, https://mtsu.edu/first-amendment/article/1763/frederick-douglass.

91. Walter Lippmann, *Liberty and the News* (Harcourt, Brace and Howe, 1920), 64.

92. With the release of the Twitter Files, there is even evidence now to suggest collusion between some in the federal government and Big Tech. See, for an example, Forbes Breaking News, "'Mr. Roth, I'm Going to Refresh Your Memory for You': Luna Confronts Ex-Twitter Executive," YouTube, February 8, 2023, https://www.youtube.com/watch?v=JZ2fV-XnLk0&t=2s&ab_channel=ForbesBreakingNews.

93. Kuypers, *Press Bias and Politics.*

94. Goldberg, "Journalism Has Become a Threat to Democracy."

95. I am not alone in this assessment. See Michael Goodwin, "American Journalism Is Collapsing Before Our Eyes," *New York Post*, August 21, 2016, http://nypost.com/2016/08/21/american-journalism-is-collapsing-before-our-eyes/; and John Nolte, "How the Political Media's Corruption Destroyed America's Most Crucial Institutions," Daily Wire, November 7, 2016, https://www.dailywire.com/news/how-political-medias-corruption-destroyed-americas-john-nolte.

96. "Media Still 'Enemy of the People,' Most Voters Say," Rasmussen Reports, May 23, 2023, https://www.rasmussenreports.com/public_content/politics/biden_administration/media_still_enemy_of_the_people_most_voters_say.

97. Sharyl Attkisson, "Americans Don't Trust the Media, and for Good Reason," *The Hill*, August 18, 2018, https://thehill.com/blogs/pundits-blog/media/347091-Americans-dont-trust-the-media-and-for-good-reason.

98. Megan Brenan, "Media Confidence Ratings at Record Lows" Gallup, July 18, 2022, https://news.gallup.com/poll/394817/media-confidence-ratings-record-lows.aspx.

99. "Voters Don't Trust Media Fact-Checking," Rasmussen Reports, September 30, 2016, http://www.rasmussenreports.com/public_content/politics/general_politics/september_2016/voters_don_t_trust_media_fact_checking.

100. John Concha, "Poll: 72 Percent Say Traditional Outlets 'Report News They Know to Be Fake, False, or Purposely Misleading,'" *The Hill*, June 27, 2018, https://thehill.com/homenews/media/394352-poll-72-percent-say-traditional-outlets-report-news-they-know-to-be-fake-false.

101. Jim Norman, "Americans Rate Healthcare Providers High on Honesty, Ethics," Gallup, December 19, 2016, https://news.gallup.com/poll/200057/americans-rate-healthcare-providers-high-honesty-ethics.aspx.

102. Saman Malik and Sarah Peterson, "How U.S. Media Lost the Trust of the Public," CBC [Canada], March 28, 2021, https://www.cbc.ca/news/world/media-distrust-big-news-1.5965622.

103. Michael Goodwin, "Goodwin: The New York Times' Long Descent from Credibility," *New York Post*, November 30, 2019, https://nypost.com/2019/11/30/goodwin-the-new-york-times-long-descent-from-credibility/.

104. The Commission on Freedom of the Press, 20–21.

105. The exact percentage is difficult to gauge, especially since the mid-1990s when journalists, responding to criticisms of bias, began to describe themselves as "moderate" and "independent." Nick Rokke, "John Stossel on Why the Media Are 90% Liberal," Palm Beach Research Group, September 4, 2018, https://www.palmbeachgroup.com/palm-beach-daily/john-stossel-on-why-the-media-is-90-liberal.

106. Kate Vinton, "These 15 Billionaires Own America's News Media Companies," *Forbes*, June 1, 2016, https://www.forbes.com/sites/katevinton/2016/06/01/these-15-billionaires-own-americas-news-media-companies/.

107. Katharine J. Tobal, "These 6 Corporations Own Most of the Media," https://www.exposingtruth.com/6-media-corporations-everything-watch-hear-read/.

108. Anthony George, "The Season of Consolidation," YouTube.com, June 7, 2021, https://www.youtube.com/watch?v=C0_M8qY9MDw&ab_channel=FirstBaptistAtlanta.

109. Megan Brenan, "Views of Big Tech Worsen; Public Wants More Regulation," Gallup, February 18, 2021, https://news.gallup.com/poll/329666/views-big-tech-worsen-public-wants-regulation.aspx.

110. "Big Tech Censorship Is a Problem, But More Government Involvement Is Not the Solution," FEE.org, January 6, 2022, https://fee.org/articles/big-tech-censorship-is-a-problem-but-more-government-involvement-is-not-the-solution/.

111. Ashly Gold, "Clarence Thomas Wants to Reel in Section 230," *Axios*, October 14, 2020, https://www.axios.com/clarence-thomas-wants-to-reel-in-section-230-fad81180-1f50-48a6-b638-f9386221f4f2.html; Tom Cioccotta, "Justice Clarence Thomas: Section 230 Protections for Big Tech Are Too Broad," *Breitbart News*, October 14, 2020, https://www.breitbart.com/tech/2020/10/14/justice-clarence-thomas-section-230-protections-for-big-tech-are-too-broad/.

112. Steve Turley, "India and Australia CRACKDOWN on Big Tech as 5 Oregon Counties Vote to SECEDE!!!," Youtube.com, February 25, 2021, https://www.youtube.com/watch?v=269hX0jGAbA&ab_channel=Dr.SteveTurley.

113. Robert Epstein, "10 Ways Big Tech Can Shift Millions of Votes in the November Elections—Without Anyone Knowing," September 26, 2018, https://www.theepochtimes.com/10-ways-big-tech-can-shift-millions-of-votes-in-the-november-elections-without-anyone-knowing_2671195.html.

114. Kim Lyons, "Apple and Google Face Pressure to Deplatform Parler Over Calls to Violence," MSN, January 8, 2021, https://www.msn.com/en-us/money/other/apple-and-google-face-pressure-to-deplatform-parler-over-calls-to-violence/ar-BB1cAzzJ; and Sonny Mazzone, "Parler's Antitrust Lawsuit Over Amazon Deplatforming Has Tough Road Ahead," *Reason*, January 15, 2021, https://reason.com/2021/01/15/parlers-antitrust-lawsuit-over-amazon-deplatforming-has-tough-road-ahead.

115. Audrey Conklin, "News-Sharing Social Media Site Rejects Censorship, Algorithms," *Fox Business*, October 31, 2020, https://www.foxbusiness.com/technology/moptu-social-media-censorship.

Index

Aamidor, Abe, 7
ABC News, 1, 197–98, 240
abortion, 117–18, 122
accepted truths, 63
accuracy, for fact-checking, 122–24
Administrative Procedure Act, 202
advocacy journalism, 7, 130, 209
African Americans. *See* Black Americans
agenda setting, for voting, 221–23
agriculture, 99
AI. *See* artificial intelligence
algorithmic content filtration systems, 60
AllSides.com, 57
AllSides Media Bias Chart™, 4, 57
AllSides Media Bias Ratings, 59
AllSides Technologies, 55, 65
Alphabet, 206–8, 240, 244
alternative news media, 1, 245
Amanpour, Christiane, 107–9
Amazon, 10, 23, 206, 240, 244
American Federation of Teachers, 111
American Newspaper Publishers Association, 202
American Press Institute, 15–16, 181
American Republic, 238–43
American Views 2022: Part 2, 56
Amish community, 160

Amusing Ourselves to Death (Postman), 55
anarchy, 64
And the Truth Shall Set You Free (Icke), 135
anti-Asian hate crimes, 132
antisemitism, 133, 136; Baldwin on, 134; great replacement theory and, 137–39; of Walker, A., 135
antitrust, 204–6; Clayton Antitrust Act, 205; law, 10; lawsuits, 207–8; Sherman Act, 10, 204–6
anti-Zionism, 136
Appalachia, 8, 147, 149, 153, 156–59
appeal: to nationalism, 96–98; to values, 93–95
Apple, 10, 208, 241
Arab Americans, 133
Arab-Israeli conflict, 140
Areeda, Phillip, 205
Aristotle, 42
Arizona State University, Walter Cronkite School of Journalism, 19–20
artificial intelligence (AI), 25
Ashman, Marguerite Gemson, 182
Asian Americans, 129, 132–33
al-Assad, Bashar, 116
Associated Press, 20, 112, 117, 233

Atlanta Journal-Constitution, 20
The Atlantic, 111
The Authoritarian (press type), 232–33
autonomy, 95

The Babylon Bee, 112
Baker, Brent, 6, 7
Baldwin, James, 134
Bandura, Albert, 180–81
Bankman-Fried, Sam, 99
banned books, 111–12
Baraka, Amiri, 136
Barrett, Amy Coney, 120–21
BBC, 20, 21, 58
B-BEST, 160
Bend the Arc, 114
Benjamin, Daniel, 216
Bennett, Naftali, 109
Berman, Emily, 120
Bernays, Edward, 209
Bever, Max, 219
Beyond Conflict, 60
Beyond Objectivity (Downie and Heyward), 31, 38, 43, 44–49
Bezos, Jeff, 207
Bhuiyan, Momen, 17
bias, 53, 195; confirmation, 58–60, 139; explicit, 15; filter bubbles and, 58–60; ideological, 25, 76; implicit, 15; increased, 19–22; liberal, 7, 48, 130, 247n17; media bias ratings, 4; partisan, 56–57; perception of, 4; polarization and, 57–58; political, 2, 6; progressive, 48; trust in news and, 15–16
bias fuel misinformation, 61–62
Bible, Christian, 90, 91
Biden, Hunter, 62
Biden, Joe, 57, 61, 109–11, 240–41
Big Tech, 10, 204–6, 240–45
Bing, 59
BIPOC (Black, Indigenous, and People of Color), 139
bird's-eye view and, 40–41

Black Americans, 7–8, 129–30, 136–37; tensions for, 131–35
Black Lives Matter (BLM), 62, 130, 240
Black nationalism, 134, 137
Black-on-Black crime, 130
Black Panthers, 135
Black Power, Jewish Politics (Dollinger), 137
"Blacks Are Anti-Semitic Because They're Anti-White" (Baldwin), 134
Bland, Bob, 136
BLM. *See* Black Lives Matter
Bork, Robert, 203, 205
Bornstein, David, 181
Bort, Ryan, 113
both-sides-ism, 19
"both-sides" reporting, 46
Breitbart, 197, 245
broadcast news, 198
Buckner, Kam, 218
Bullion, Stuart, 141
Bump, Phillip, 113
Burke, Kenneth, 235–36
Bush, George W., 71, 74
Buzzfeed, 14, 197

Cabalist, 234
Calabresi, Guido, 203
Cannon, Nick, 136
capitalism, 6, 87, 111; conscious, 91; entrepreneurship and, 99
Carlson, Tucker, 138, 204
Carmichael, Stokely, 78
Carroll, Kathleen, 20
case-based reasoning, 176
Catholic Church, 26
Cato Institute, 118
Cavuto, Neil, 112
CBN. *See* Christian Broadcasting Network
CBS Corporation, 244
CBS News, 196, 198
censorship, of news, 62
Center for Civic Media, 186
Center for Counter Digital Hate, 113

Center for Education in the Workforce, Georgetown University, 199
Centre for Economic Policy Research (CEPR), 198–99
Chadha, Kalyani, 16
Chang, Edward T., 133
change, linguistic, 48
Chavez, Cesar, 138
"Checklist for Community Information Needs in a Democracy," 158
chemical weapons, 116
Chesterhill Produce Auction, 160, 168
Chicago Board of Elections, 219
Chicago School of Economics, 202–3, 205
Chicago Sun-Times, 219
Chicago Tribune, 73
China, 98–99, 138, 141, 241
Christian Broadcasting Network, 89
Christianity, 90, 102–3
Christy, Alex, 6–7
Cialdini, Robert B., 216
citizen journalism, 54
citizens, transparency for, 17
civic communications, 153–56, *154, 155*
Civic Communications Framework, 155, 169
civic duty, 225–26
CLA. *See* College Learning Assessment
Clark, Dan, 110, 111
Clayton Antitrust Act (1914), 205
Cleaver, Eldridge, 135
Clemson University, 113
Clerwall, Christer, 18
clickbait, 61
Clinton, Hillary, 73, 116, 234–37
CNBC, 95
CNN, 1, 14, 112–13, 115, 140, 197, 200; "Facts First" campaign, 108; partisan bias and, 56–57; polarization and, 58
Coase, Robert, 203
collective efficacy, 184
collective intelligence, 24
collectivism, 87, 92

College Learning Assessment (CLA), 79
Collins, Paul M., Jr., 120–21
colonialism, digital, 244
The Color Purple (Walker, A.), 135
Columbia Journalism Review, 31
Comcast, 213n43
Commission on Freedom of the Press (Hutchins Commission), 23, 231–32, 243
commodification, of news, 88
commodities, 101
communication competence, 80
The Communication Crisis in America, and How to Fix It, 148, 151
Communication Policy Research Network (CPRN), 148
Communications Act (1934), 201
community-based creation practices, 164–66
Community Dashboard, 158
Community Information Needs Audit, 158
Community Notes (X), 24
CommunityQ, 163
compliance, 216
computer science, 25
confirmation bias, 58–60, 139
confirmation bubbles, 74
conformity, 216
conglomeration. *See* media conglomeration
conscious capitalism, 91
consolidation: media, 9; in news industry, 54
conspiracy theories, 123–24
constraint recognition, 179–80
consumption, of media, 198–200
content moderation systems, 64
controversy, public, 75–76
convergent hypothesis, 201
Coolidge, Calvin, 80
Cooper, Anderson, 200
Cooper, Stephen, 21
Court of Appeals, 202–3

COVID-19, 22, 123, 139, 141, 199, 239–41
Cox, Jennifer, 8–9
CPRN. *See* Communication Policy Research Network
Craft, Stephanie, 16
Creative Matrix, 158
credibility: for fact-checking, 122–24; recovering, 5
Crenshaw, Noah, 223
critical thinking, debate for, 75–78, *77*
Cronkite, Walter, 2, 196
Cronkite School of Journalism, 31
cross-media ownership, 202
cross-ownership rules, 10
crowdsourcing, 23–25
Cruz, Ted, 110, 120
cryptocurrency, 99
Cuomo, Andrew, 110–11
Curry, Alexander, 18

Daily Mail, 58
Daily Wire, 58
Dallas Morning News, 5
dark participation, 200
debate, 69; conclusion, 81; as critical thinking solution, 75–78, *77*; journalism strengthened by, 78–81; partisanship as problem for, 70–73; potential topics for, 81–82; rubric and evaluation form, 83–84; as solution, 74–75; speech evaluation form, 82–83
"Debate in Journalism Curriculum as a Solution to Ideological Normativity" (Voth), 5
debt forgiveness, 91
democracy, 97
Democratic National Committee, 236
Democratic Party, 58, 69, 72–73, 79, 196, 233–34, 237; *Roe v. Wade* and, 117–18; trust in news by, 13
democratic pluralism, 88
Department of Justice (DOJ), 205–6
DeSantis, Ron, 111–12, 115

descriptive norms, 216, 219–20
Deuteronomy 28: 43–44, 96
Dewey, John, 174–75, 186
digital advertisement revenue models, 54
digital colonialism, 244
"Digital Dissonance" (Gable and Warren, A.), 4
Digital Ethnography Report, 158
Digital News Report, 55
digital platforms, 54, 59–60
disagreement, 65
disclosure transparency, 16, 18
discursive complexity, 80
DOJ. *See* Department of Justice
Dollinger, Marc, 137
domain-specific knowledge, 183
Donnella, Leah, 137
double standards, 36
Douglass, Frederick, 242
Downie, Leonard, 19; *Beyond Objectivity,* 31, 38, 43, 44–49
DREAMERS, 130
Duke University, 62
DuVernay, Ava, 137

Easterbrook, Frank, 203
Eastern cultures, 92
East European Jews, 133
Ebenezer Scrooge (fictional character), 98–99
EDDM. *See* Every Door Direct Mailing
Edelman Trust Barometer, 195, 199
efficacy: collective, 184; individual, 184; problem-solving, 172, 180–81; response, 175, 180; self-efficacy, 9, 172
Eisenstein, Elizabeth, 26
election fraud, 61
Emerson, Ralph Waldo, 40
Emmerich, Susan, 90, 103
emotionalism, 55
emotional trust, 55–56
emotions: of journalists, 166–67; unhealthy, 171

Index

"Enemy of the People," news media as, 1
engagement, for media deserts, 159–60
Engelberg, Stephen, 34, 35
ENN. *See* Environmental News Network
Entertainment Studios Network (ESN), 213n43
Entman, Robert M., 221
entrenched journalism, 88–89
entrepreneurship, 99, 134, 148
Environmental News Network (ENN), 89
EPPM. *See* extended parallel processing model
equal time, 201
ESN. *See* Entertainment Studios Network
European Union, 244–45
even-handedness, 36
Evers, Medgar, 79
Every Door Direct Mailing (EDDM), 163
evidence measure, 180–82, 190n35
expert shopping, 118–21
explicit bias, 15
extended parallel processing model (EPPM), 9, 172, 175, 177, 180, 182

Facebook, 14, 59, 158, 241; fact-checking and, 112; Meta, 10, 206–8, 240, 244; as news source, 199
fact-checking, 6, 70, 107–8; accuracy and credibility for, 122–24; case selection for, 110–13; choosing sides and, 117–18; expert shopping and, 118–21; of facts, 114–15; leaning left/leaning right influences, 109–10; numbers for, 121–22; semantics and, 116; Trump and, 7, 74, 109, 114; *Washington Post* and, 109
"Facts First" campaign, 108
failed concept, 34
fair-mindedness, 36
fairness doctrine, 140, 201

fake news, 25, 195
false or misleading claims, 109–10, 113
Farmer, James, Jr., 77–79
Farrakhan, Louis, 134–36
fat shaming, 7
FBI. *See* Federal Bureau of Investigation
FCC. *See* Federal Communications Commission
FCC v. Prometheus Radio Project, 202
Federal Bureau of Investigation (FBI), 130–32
Federal Communications Commission (FCC), 10, 140, 147–48, 151, 169n2, 201, 203
Ferrier, Michelle, 8, 151, 162, 169n2
filter bubbles, 4, 54; bias fuel misinformation and, 61–62; confirmation bias and, 58–60; scope of understanding and, 60–61
Finkelman, Paul, 120, 121
First Amendment, 70, 73, 77, 81, 201, 238
Fisher, Mark, 46
Fletcher, Ryan, 15
Forbes, 58
foreign policy, 98
foreign relations, 91
Four Theories of the Press (Siebert, Peterson, and Schramm), 232
Fox Business Channel, 95
Fox News, 1, 14, 57–58, 112, 138, 197, 204, 245
Frankfurt School, 80

A Free and Responsible Press, 231

Freedom to Vote Act, 116, 118
free-for-all, informational, 64
free press, 5, 23, 70, 72–73, 81
free speech, 241–42
Freesus Patriot™ (X username), 111–12
fringe views, 59
FTC Act, 205
FTX, 99

Funke, Daniel, 119–20

Gab (social media platform), 245
Gable, John, 4, 55
Gade, Peter, 17
Gallup, 1, 4, 13, 55, 195, 242
GameJournoPros, 234
Gannett, 7, 129
Gans, Herbert J., 181
Garcia, Chuy, 218
Garcia-Ruiz, Emilio, 20
Garland, Merrick, 120–21
Gates, Bill, 99
gender, 119–20
generality, 36
Gen Z, 14
geographic information systems (GIS), 151
Geography/Demography Report, 158
George, Anthony, 244
Georgetown University, Center for Education in the Workforce, 199
Gerber, Alan S., 225
Gersen, Daniel, 174
GIS. *See* geographic information systems
Glasser, Ted, 46
goals, 179
"God and Country," 96
God's-eye view, 40–41
Goldberg, Bernie, 71
Goldberg, Jonah, 108
Goldberg, Whoopi, 139
Golden Rule, 37
Goldstein, Noah J., 216
good faith arguments, 65
Goodhart, Charles, 98
Goodwin, Michael, 243
Google, 10, 59, 206, 208
Google Earth, 158
Google News, 14
The Great Debaters (film), 77–78
great replacement theory, 137–39
Green, Ja'Mal, 218
Greenburg, Jack, 137

Greene, Marjorie Taylor, 119–20, 139
Greenwald, Glenn, 40
groupthink, 74, 233
The Guardian, 58

Habermas, Jürgen, 80
Haenschen, Katherine, 10
Haidt, Jonathan, 236–37
Hamill, Mark, 111
Han, Soo Hye, 222
Harvard School (of thought), 205
Harvard University, 73
hate crimes, 131, 132
HBCU. *See* Historically Black College and University
Hebraic scriptures, 90
"he-said/she-said" reporting, 46
Heschel, Abraham Joshua, 137
Heyward, Andrew, 19; *Beyond Objectivity,* 31, 38, 43, 44–49
highly centralized governments, 63
The Hill, 71
Historically Black College and University (HBCU), 75, 77
Hitler, Adolph, 131, 139
HIV, 130
Ho, Daniel, 203–4
Holocaust, 131, 135–36
Home Depot, 112
Horning, Michael, 2, 3
"How to Produce Trustworthy News without 'Objectivity'" (report), 20
how-to rigor, 175, 182–84
Hudson, Michael, 90, 98
Huffington Post, 197
Hunt, April, 114
Hurricane Ian, 115
Hutchins Commission (Commission on the Freedom of the Press), 23, 231–32, 243
hyperpartisanship, 69

Ice Cube (rapper), 136
Icke, David, 135
identity, consideration of, 164–65

ideological bias, 25, 76
immigrants, 129, 130; great replacement theory and, 137–39
impartiality, 36
implicit bias, 15
implicit nominal rejections, of objectivity, 44
impossibility argument against objectivity, 32, 33–34
inclusion, rules of, 87
independence, 45
Independent Party, 14, 58
Indigenous peoples, 91
individual efficacy, 184
individualism, 87, 91
informational free-for-all, 64
Ingraham, Laura, 197
Ingraham Angle, 197
inner life, of journalists, 166–67
Instagram, 60, 206
Institute for National Security Studies, Tel Aviv University, 136
integrity, journalistic, 55–56
intelligence: AI, 25; collective, 24
Intercollegiate Studies Institute, 242
interminority racism, 130
internet, 54
Internet Explorer, 206
invalidity, of argument, 38
Investigative Reporters & Editors, 187
Iran, 117, 241
Iraq War, 21
Islam, 134
Israel, 6, 109, 138

Jackson, Jessie, 136
Jacobson, Louis, 120
Jarvis, Sharon E., 222
Java, 206
Jenkins, Mandy, 15
Jewish Americans, 8, 90, 92, 102–3, 136; great replacement theory and, 137–39; non-Jews, 95–96; tensions for, 131–35
Jim Crow, 111

Johnson, Brandon, 218
Jordan, Barbara, 79
journalism and journalists: advocacy, 7, 130, 209; citizen, 54; debate strengthening, 78–81; emotions and inner life of, 166–67; entrenched, 88–89; extrajournalistic expressions of opinion and, 49–50; public trust in, 2; revenue-driven, 4; self-reflection for, 15; solutions, 173–76, 221; traditional notions of, 3; trust in news and, 14. *See also specific topics*
"Journalism's Essential Value" (Sulzberger), 31
Journalism That Matters, 155–56, 162–63, 169
journalistic integrity, 55–56
journalistic objectivity. *See* objectivity
JournoList, 234
jubilee, 87; discussion and implementation of, 102–4; entrenched journalism and, 88–89; law of, 90–91; nationalism and, 95–98; proposed solution of, 89–90; pursuit of wealth and, 98–104; values and, 91–95
Jubilee USA, 91

Karlsson, Michael, 16, 18, 22
Keane, Fergal, 20
Keller, Bill, 43–44, 47
Kelly, John, 139
Kelly, Megyn, 204
Kennan, George, 108
Kerry, John, 71
Kertscher, Tom, 110–11
Kessler, Glenn, 109, 118–19
Khamenei, Ayatollah Ali, 241
King, Martin Luther, Jr., 79, 137
King, Peter, 108
King, Sophia, 218
KKK. *See* Ku Klux Klan
Klein, Ezra, 19
Knight Foundation, 4, 16, 55, 73

Knorpp, William Max, 3
knowledge: domain-specific, 183; management, 149; sources, 90
"knowledge is power," 77
Koliska, Michael, 16, 19
Korean Americans, 130, 132
Ku Klux Klan (KKK), 78, 135
Kuypers, Jim A., 11, 21, 238

Largey, Matt, 224–25
Latinos, 129, 217
Lee, Michelle Ye Hee, 119
Lemert, James B., 181–82
Leviticus, 91; 25:14, 99; 25:15–16, 98; 25:17, 99
Lewis, C. S., 120
LGBTQ+, 129
liberal bias, 7, 48, 130, 247n17

The Libertarian (press type), 232–33

Libertarian model, of news production, 11
Licht, Chris, 140
Liebling, A. J., 141
Lightfoot, Lori, 218
limitations, 179–80
linguistic change, 48
Lippmann, Walter, 21–22, 174, 176, 235, 242
listening: deeply, 165; for media deserts, 159–60
Listening Is Our Superpower, 163, 165
local champion, 167–68
Local Media Brand Strategy, 159
local news, 161, 163–64; limits and public perceptions of, 167; trust in, 13
local ownership rule, 203
Logan, Lara, 234
longitudinal studies, 19
"Long Telegram" (Kennan), 108
Los Angeles Times, 5
Lowery, Wesley, 45; "A Reckoning Over Objectivity, Led by Black Journalists," 44; "A Test of the News," 31
low voter turnout, 10, 215; agenda setting for, 221–23; civic duty and, 225–26; conclusion, 226–27; emphasizing, 220; local reporters and, 220–21; news reporting on, 217–19, *218*; positive framing of numbers for, 224–25, *225*; profiling of people involved, 223–24; social norms and, 216–17
Luke 15:11–31, 98

Mabus, Ray, 119
Maddow, Rachel, 200
Madison, James, 238
Madoff, Bernie, 99
mainstreaming, 7, 129
mainstream media, 1, 8; defined, 197–98; fixing, 206–10. *See also specific topics*
Malcolm X, 79, 134, 137
Mallory, Tamika, 136
manifest content analysis measures, 188n10
Maras, Steven, 34
Marcus, Bernie, 112
market segmentation, 54
Marshall, Thurgood, 137
mass audience, 26
Mastodon (social media platform), 245
Mastrine, Julie, 59
McBride, Kelly, 16
McConnell, Mitch, 116, 118
media bias ratings, 4
Media Cloud, 217
media conglomeration, 195–96; antitrust and, 204–6; Big Tech and, 204–6; fixing mainstream media, 206–10; mainstream media defined, 197–98; media consumption and, 198–200; viewpoint diversity versus regulation and, 201–4
media consolidation, 9
media consumption, 198–200

"media corps" model, 162
media deserts, 8, 147–49, 169; civic communications and, 153–56, *154, 155*; community-based creation practices for, 164–66; engagement for, 159–60; listening for, 159–60; other projects for local communities, 166–68; pre- and postsurvey of residents, 160–64; in southeast Ohio, 156–59; technology in, 161; visibility of, 150–53
Media Deserts Project, 8, 150–51, 153, *154,* 168
Media Deserts Research Atlas, *150,* 152
media framing, 221
media ownership, deregulation of, 201–4
Media Research Center (MRC), 112–13
Media Seeds Project, 153, 160, 162, 168
Medill Media Industry Survey, 199
Meredith, James, 79
message cues, 19
Meta, 10, 206–8, 240, 244
MeWe (social media platform), 245
MFT. *See* moral foundations theory
Microsoft, 206, 208, 241
middleman minority, 133
Millennials, 14
Miller, Serena, 8–9
ministry of truth, 62–63
misinformation, 23–25, 53, 70; bias fuel, 61–62; solutions to, 62–64
mobilizing information, 181
modeling, 38
Mohammed, Warith Deen, 134–35
monopoly diversification, 203
Moore, Ignacio T., 120
moral clarity, 46
moral foundations theory (MFT), 236–38
moral judgments, 235–38
moral superiority, 20
More in Common, 181
Moreno, Evelyn, 174
Morstatter, Fred, 26
motivated research, 139
MRC. *See* Media Research Center
MSNBC, 14, 56, 113
Muhammad, Elijah, 134
Muhammad, Wallace Fard, 134
Mulder, Brandon, 120
Murdoch, Rupert, 244
Musk, Elon, 21, 199, 244
Myers, Cayce, 9–10

NAACP Legal Defense Fund, 137
Nader, Ralph, 71
Nagel, Thomas, 35–36
National Institute for Computer-Assisted Reporting, 187
nationalism, 95–98
National Negro Business League, 135
national news, trust in, 13
National News Council (NNC), 23
national values, 97
Nation of Islam, 134
natural language processing (NLP), 23, 25–26
Navy, US, 119
Nazi Germany, 139
NBC News, 116, 121, 198
NBC Universal, 244
Nee, Rebecca, 17
Netscape, 206
neutrality, 45
Newhouse, Neil, 107
New Left activists, 138
Newman, Nic, 15
news censorship, 62
News Corp, 244
news deserts, 198
news industry, 54
Newsmax, 57, 197
Newton, Eric, 158
New York City, 136
New York Post, 1, 197, 241
New York Times, 1, 5, 58, 73, 140, 197, 200
New York Times Book Review, 135
New York University (NYU), 19

Nichols, Tom, 111
Nieman Report, 186
1960s news industry, 54
1980s news industry, 54
Nixon, Richard, 74, 80
NLP. *See* natural language processing
NNC. *See* National News Council
"no-eye view," 40
Nolte, John, 237
non-Jews, 95–96
norms, social, 216–17
Nothing About Us Without Us, 162–63
NPR, 121–22, 137, 224
NYU. *See* New York University

Obama, Barack, 107, 116–17
Obamacare, 108
obesity epidemic, 130
objectivity, 3, 6, 20, 31, 87, 174; bird's-eye view and, 40–41; conceptual objections to, 34–35; conclusions, 47–50; crisis of, 45; critics of, 45–46; defined, 35–37; definitional objections to, 34–35; implicit nominal rejections of, 44; impossibility with, 33–34; "objectivity" (the word) and, 43–45; perfection with, 33–34; POA and, 37–40; problems in, 32; pseudo-objectivity, 45–46, 48; recommendations for, 47–50; Thompson and, 41–42; Truth Not Objectivity, 42–43
Objectivity (Rescher), 37
"Objectivity and Anti-Objectivity in Journalism" (Knorpp), 3
O'Brien, Soledad, 108
Offit, Paul, 121
Ohio, southeast, 156–59
Ohio University, 152, 156
The Onion, 112
online media companies, 207–8
only perfect objectivity (OPO), 38–39
Orenstein, Walter, 121
Orwell, George, 48

Ossoff, Jon, 111
outrage, public, 171
Overton Window, 59, 74, 80
ownership regulations, 207–8

Paladino, Carl, 139
Palestine, 109, 138
Palma, Bethania, 111–12
"pants-on-fire" rating, 111
Pariser, Eli, 4, 60
Parler (social media platform), 241, 245
participatory transparency, 16, 18
partisan bias, 56–57
Partisan Journalism (Kuypers), 238
partisan polarization, 4
partisanship: hyperpartisanship, 69; as problem for debate, 70–73
paywalls, 167
Pearl Harbor, 114
People's Republic of China, 138
P/E ratio, 100
perceived response efficacy, 175
perceived self-efficacy, 9, 172
Perdue, David, 111, 114
"perfection argument," 3
perfection argument against objectivity, 32, 33–34
perfect objectivity argument (POA), 37–40
Perry, Stephen D., 5–6
Peterson, Theodore, 232
Petrified National Forest, 217
Pew Research Center, 4, 71, 73, 198–99, 209; on abortion, 122; confirmation bias and, 58; filter bubbles and, 58; on partisan bias, 56; on trust in news, 13, 56
Phang, Katie, 111
philanthropy, 95
philosophy, 41
Plato, 21
Plotkin, Stanley, 121
pluralism, democratic, 88
POA. *See* perfect objectivity argument
podcasts, 209

polarization, 54, 61; bias and, 57–58; partisan, 4
political bias, 2, 6
political composition, of press, 233–34
Politico, 179
PolitiFact, 108, 110–11, 114, 116, 118, 120
poor representation, 7
Posner, Richard, 203
postcards, 163
Postman, Neil, 55
power: "knowledge is power," 77; of social norms, 216–17; structures, 167
presidential elections: of 2000, 69; of 2004, 71; of 2016, 69, 73, 107–8, 112, 123; of 2020, 61, 69
prima facie plausibility, 38
printing press, 26, 53
The Printing Press as an Agent of Change (Eisenstein), 26
problem definition measure, 177–79, *178,* 190n33
The Problem of Equity in Journalism (Keane), 20
problem-solving efficacy, 172, 180–81
problem-solving solutions journalism model, 171–72; collective efficacy and, 184; conclusion, 186–87; evidence for, 180–82, 190n35; individual efficacy and, 184; problem definition for, 177–79, *178,* 190n33; public participation invitation for, 185–86; solution evaluation for, 179–80; solution goal for, 179, 190n34; solution how-to for, 182–84; solutions journalism and, 173–76; solutions training for, 185
Problem-Solving Solutions Journalism Model, 172–73
problem space, 177
progressive bias, 48
pro-life laws, 109
property, 91–96; redistribution, 100–102
ProPublica, 34, 147
pseudo-objectivity, 45–46, 48

public controversy, 75–76
public opinion, 209
Public Opinion (Lippmann), 21
public outrage, 171
public trust, in journalism, 2
public welfare, 97
Putnan, Hilary, 40

Quinn, Kevin, 203–4

racial segregation, 77–78
racism, interminority, 130
Radio Act (1927), 201
Radio Television Digital News Association (RTDNA), 16
Rafferty, Jason, 120
Rasmussen, 1, 4, 242
rationality, 31
reasoning, case-based, 176
receptors, 90
"A Reckoning Over Objectivity, Led by Black Journalists" (Lowery), 44
Republican Party, 5, 58, 69–74, 79, 81, 195–96; *Roe v. Wade* and, 117–18; trust in news by, 13–14
Rescher, Nicholas, 37
Resnick, Paul, 24
response efficacy, 175, 180
responsibility, social, 11
Reuters Institute, 55, 138, 233
Reuters Institute for the Study of Journalism, 4
revenue-driven journalism, 4
Revers, Matthias, 17
Reyes, Yacob, 115
Rind, Bruce, 216
Roberts, Gary, 91
Roe v. Wade, 117–18, 122
Rogers, Todd, 225
Rolling Stone (magazine), 113
Romney, Mitt, 107–8, 117
Rosen, Jay, 19–20
Rosenstiel, Tom, 16
routines, 88

RTDNA. *See* Radio Television Digital News Association
Rural Action, 160
rural communities, 149, 165–66
Russia, 62, 107, 138, 142

San Francisco Chronicle, 20
Sarsour, Linda, 136
Sawyer, Roderick, 218
scalability, 183
Schramm, Wilbur, 232
Schudson, Michael, 208, 209
Schurz Communications, Inc. v. FCC, 203
science, 31; computer, 25; social, 215
Scrooge (musical), 98–99
self-admissions, 234
self-efficacy, perceived, 9, 172
self-realization, 95
self-reflection, 15
Selma (film), 137
semantics, 116
Senate, US, 74, 218–19
sensationalism, 53–55, 61, 195
serendipity, 165
"7 Persistent Claims about Abortion, Fact-Checked" (NPR), 122
sex, gender versus, 120
Shapiro, Ilya, 118
Sherman, Amy, 116
Sherman Act (1890), 10, 204–6
Shorenstein, 73
Siebert, Fred S., 232, 238
signalized event, 21
Silicon Valley Bank (SVB), 112
Situational Theory of Problem Solving, 179–80
SJN. *See* Solutions Journalism Network
slave workers, 97
slow news, 147
Smith Dahmen, Nicole, 178
Snopes, 111–12
socialism, 6, 87, 94, 111
social media, 1, 54, 157, 195, 197–200, 208–9, 241, 244–45; antitrust law and, 10; journalists on, 17, 49; as news source, 14; trust in, 72. *See also specific platforms*
Social Media Strategies for User Personas: Health/Opioid Social Strategy, 159
Social Media Strategies for User Personas: News and Information, 159
social norms, power of, 216–17
social responsibility, 11
The Social Responsibility (press type), 232
social science, 215
social theory, 216
Society of Professional Journalists, 15
solution goal measure, 179, 190n34
solutions journalism, 173–76, 221
Solutions Journalism Network (SJN), 172–73, 179, 181, 187
Solutions Story Tracker, 173
Soul on Ice (Cleaver), 135
source cues, 19
southeast Ohio, 156–59
Southern Illinois University–Carbondale, 140, 141
The Soviet (press type), 232
Soviet Union (USSR), 103, 141–42
Speak Truth to Empower, 163
Stakeholder Mapping, 158
Standard Oil Co. of New Jersey v. United States, 204–5
Street View, 158
Stroud, Natali, 18
Students for a Democratic Society, 138
Sulzberger, A. G., 31, 47
"Supplement to 2021 Hate Crime Statistics" (FBI), 131
supply chains, 98
Supreme Court, 117–18, 120–22, 201–2
Surowieki, James, 24
SVB. *See* Silicon Valley Bank
Sweden, 111
Syria, 116

Talmud, 135

Targeted Communication Survey: ZIP Code, 159
teaching, 97
technology: in media deserts, 161; news industry and, 54; trust in news and, 53
Technopoly (Postman), 55
Tel Aviv University, 136
Telecommunications Act (1996), 10, 202
Televisa, 200
television, 54, 55
"A Test of the News" (Lowery), 31
Thier, Kathryn, 178
Thompson, Hunter S., 32, 34, 41–42
Thorson, Esther, 158
Tibet, 138
TikTok, 60
Time Warner, 244
Timm, Jane, 121
TNO. *See* Truth Not Objectivity
Tofel, Richard, 147, 149
Tolson, Melvin, 77
Torah, 91
traditional media, 197, 207
Trafficked (TV program), 100
transparency, 2–3, 65; for citizens, 17; defining, 16–19; disclosure, 16, 18; participatory, 16, 18; trust in news and, 14, 16–19
"transparency box," 18
"transparent eyeball," 40
trans rights, 141–42
Tree of Life synagogue massacre (2018), 131
Trump, Donald, 107–8, 121, 123, 234–37, 240–41; fact-checking and, 7, 74, 109, 114; false or misleading claims of, 110, 113; on Hitler, 139; Nazi logo and, 114–15; partisan bias and, 56–57; semantics and, 116
trust in news, 53–54, 195; bias and, 15–16; conclusion to, 26; confirmation bias and, 58–60; declining, 55–56; by Democratic Party, 13; filter bubbles and, 58–62; flawed solutions for, 62–64; increased bias and, 19–22; informational free-for-all and, 64; new approach for, 64–65; partisan bias and, 56–57; polarization and, 57–58; by Republican Party, 13–14; solutions for, 22–26; transparency defined for, 14, 16–19
"Trust in the News" (Horning), 2
truth, ministry of, 62–63
Truth Not Objectivity (TNO), 42–43
Turner, Donald F., 205
Tuskegee Institute, 135
Twitter, 199–200, 241, 244. *See also* X

Ukraine, 138, 142
Ungar-Sargon, Batya, 44
unhealthy emotions, 171
Uniform Crime Report (FBI), 130
United Farm Workers, 138
United Nations, 91
United States v. Microsoft Corporation, 206
"Unite the Right" rally (2017), 137
universalizability, 36
University of Chicago, 138
University of Colorado, 60
University of Southern California, 148
University of Wisconsin–Madison, 148
Up from Slavery (Washington, B.), 135
USA Today, 114–15
USC Information Sciences Institute, 26
User Personas, 158
US Postal Service, 163
USSR. *See* Soviet Union

vaccine hesitancy, 62
Vallas, Paul, 218
values, 91–92; appeal to, 93–95; national, 97
Valverde, Mariam, 119–20
Venezuela, 111
vertical limit, 203
The View (TV program), 139

viewpoint diversity versus regulation, 201–4
Vos, Tim, 16
voter fraud, 251n58
voter turnout. *See* low voter turnout
Votes that Count and Voters Who Don't (Jarvis and Han), 222
Voth, Ben, 5
voting, 217
Vox, 132–33

Walker, Alice, 135
Walker, Scott, 110
Wallace, Julia, 20, 34
Wall Street Journal, 1, 73
Walt Disney, 244
Walter Cronkite School of Journalism, 19–20
Walth, Brent, 178
Warner Media, 57
Warren, Adriel, 4
Warren, Elizabeth, 110
Washington, Booker T., 134–35
Washington, Denzel, 77
Washington Naval Conference (1922), 114
Washington Post, 5, 46, 58, 118–19, 136, 200, 207, 240; fact-checking and, 109; on false or misleading claims, 113

wealth: gap, 92; pursuit of, 98–104
Weingarten, Randi, 111
Wenzel, Andrea, 174
West, Kanye, 131
Whitaker, Barbara, 112–13
Whited, Marcia, 223–24
White-on-White crime, 130
Wiley College, 75, 77–78, 81
Wilson, Willie, 218
Wilson, Woodrow, 80
The Wisdom of the Crowds (Surowieki), 24
Women's March, 136–37
Woodward, Calvin, 117
worldviews, 235–38
World War I, 114
World War II, 10, 101, 114, 231
Wuhan, China, 141

X (social media platform, formerly Twitter), 14, 21, 158; Community Notes, 24; confirmation bias on, 59; crowdsourcing on, 25; Freesus Patriot™ on, 111–12

Yahoo! News, 58
YouTube, 199, 241

ZipIt.News, 162–64
Zuckerman, Ethan, 186

About the Contributors

Abe Aamidor (MA Southern Illinois University) is a former multiple award-winning reporter at the *St. Louis Globe-Democrat* (now defunct), *The News-Gazette* (Champaign, Illinois), and *The Indianapolis Star.* He is the author, coauthor, or editor of several nonfiction books from quality publishers such as Indiana University Press and Routledge, including three college-level journalism texts. He is the author of *Don't Go*, a collection of short stories published by the Stephen F. Austin State University Press in 2022, as well as the novel *Letting Go*, published by the Permanent Press in 2018.

Brent Baker (BA George Washington University) is Steven P. J. Wood Senior Fellow and Vice President for Research and Publications at the Media Research Center (MRC). He has been the central figure in the MRC's News Analysis Division since the MRC's 1987 founding and in 2005 spearheaded the launch of *NewsBusters*, the leading blog on the right critiquing the news media. Each week he advises the *Washington Examiner*'s Paul Bedard in selecting a "Liberal Media Scream." For fifteen years, Baker oversaw the selection of the award nominees and "winners" for the MRC's "DisHonors Awards," presented at an annual gala. In a 2001 *Weekly Standard* magazine article, the magazine's executive editor, Fred Barnes, dubbed Baker "the scourge of liberal bias." Baker is the author of *How to Identify, Expose & Correct Liberal Media Bias*, a 1994 book that offers detailed explanations and suggestions for what the average citizen can do about media bias. Baker was coeditor of *And That's the Way It Isn't: A Reference Guide to Media Bias*, a 1990 book containing excerpts, reprints, and summaries of forty-five studies documenting the media's liberal bias during the 1980s.

Alex Christy (BA Western Washington University) is a native of Everett, Washington. He majored in political science and is currently a news analyst for the Media Research Center in Reston, Virginia, where he specializes in daytime cable, primetime, late-night talk show, and weekend analysis. His work has been cited in *Fox News*, the *Washington Examiner*, and several other outlets.

Jennifer Cox (PhD University of Florida) is associate professor of communication at Salisbury University. She is the author of *Feature Writing and Reporting: Journalism in the Digital Age*. Her teaching and research areas include multimedia, immersion, community, solutions and participatory journalism, and civic engagement. Before obtaining her doctorate, Cox worked as a reporter at newspapers throughout Florida, covering government, crime, education, and business, among other topics. She earned her bachelor's degrees from Appalachian State University, double majoring in journalism and public relations. She received her master's degree from the University of Alabama in community journalism.

Michelle Ferrier (PhD University of Central Florida) is executive director of the Media Innovation Collaboratory, an incubator for media and technology communication solutions. She is the founder of TrollBusters, an educational service for journalists experiencing digital harms. Ferrier is an internationally recognized, award-winning technologist, journalist, scholar, researcher, author, and speaker around technology and digital/online spaces. Her pioneering research mapping media deserts and monitoring and modeling digital harms has won her grant support from organizations like the Knight Foundation, Democracy Fund, and others. Ferrier has won international, national, and professional recognition including three silver 2022 Anthem Awards, the AEJMC Professional Freedom and Responsibility Award for press freedom work, and the Dewey Community Service Award from SXSW. Named a 2018 Top 10 Educators to Watch by MediaShift, Ferrier has led hundreds of presentations on engaged journalism and digital technologies and developed curricula in digital media, media innovation and entrepreneurship, and online journalism and collaborated with international organizations like the United Nations, OSCE, Article 19, and other professional organizations to ensure global press freedoms.

John Gable (MBA Duke University) is cofounder and CEO of AllSides.com and AllSidesForSchools.org. Throughout his career, he has been a builder of tools, teams, and companies that empower people and improve the world. Before his nearly thirty-year career in technology, he worked in Republican politics in the 1980s for Bush, McConnell, and the Republican National Committee. In the early 1990s, he switched to high tech where he led the product management team for Netscape Navigator, helped ship the first version of Firefox, and held executive and management positions with Microsoft, AOL Time Warner, Kavi Corp, and Check Point Software. His research interests include media bias, polarization, and the impact of technology on news. Gable's writing has been published in *USA Today*, *The Huffington Post*, *The Christian Science Monitor*, and *The Cook Political Report*. In 2017, Gable gave a TED Talk on freedom from filter bubbles. Most recently, Gable was invited to present his research on technology and transparency to the Select Committee on the Modernization of Congress.

Katherine Haenschen (PhD University of Texas) is assistant professor of communication studies and political science at Northeastern University. She is also a faculty affiliate of the Network Science Institute. Prior to academia, she managed political campaigns, voter registration efforts, and voter turnout organizations for eight years in Austin, Texas. Her research focuses on the intersection of digital media and political behavior. Prior published work explores the effect of Facebook ads, internet ads, text messages, and interpersonal Facebook messages on voter turnout and volunteer efforts. Her work has been published in the *Journal of Communication*, *Political Communication*, *Political Behavior*, and the *International Journal of Press/Politics*.

Michael Horning (PhD Penn State University) is associate professor of multimedia journalism at Virginia Tech where he is also an affiliate with Virginia Tech's Center for Human Computer Interaction. Before entering the academy, he was a general assignment news reporter for a community newspaper in southwest Virginia where he regularly covered government and politics. His research interest includes how emerging media technologies influence audience experience and response to news, and how such technologies shape journalistic practices. His published research examines topics as varied as how audiences responded to the use of YouTube in the 2008 election debates, how mobile devices impact audience interest in news content, and how journalistic norms and value influence political cartoonists' coverage of sensitive political topics. Horning is also recipient of the Association in Journalism and Mass Communication's top research award in new media and politics.

William Max Knorpp (PhD University of North Carolina–Chapel Hill) is associate professor of philosophy at James Madison University. His research interests include the philosophy of Charles Sanders Peirce, meta-philosophy, and relativistic approaches to metaphysics and epistemology, including their associations with illiberal politics. He is the author of, inter alia, "What Relativism Isn't," "Reflective Equilibrium and the Justification of Inferential Principles," "The Relevance of Logic in Reasoning and Belief-Revision," "How to Talk to Yourself: Kripke's Wittgenstein's Solitary Rule-Following Argument and Why It Fails," and "Richard Rorty's 'Strongman' Prediction and the Cultural Left." He is current president of the Virginia Association of Scholars.

Jim A. Kuypers (PhD Louisiana State University) is professor of communication in the School of Communication at Virginia Tech. He is the author, editor, or coauthor of sixteen books, including *Purpose, Practice, and Pedagogy in Rhetorical Criticism* (winner of the Everett Lee Hunt Award for Outstanding Scholarship) and *Partisan Journalism: A History of Media Bias in the United States* (a Choice Outstanding Academic Title for 2014). He is a former coeditor for the *American Communication Journal*. He is the recipient of the American Communication Association's Outstanding Contribution to Communication Scholarship Award, the Southern States Communication Association's Early Career Research Award, and Dartmouth College's Distinguished Lecturer Award. His research interests include political communication, meta-criticism, Burkeian dramatism, and framing analysis.

Serena Miller (PhD Michigan State University) is associate professor at Michigan State University, methodology associate editor for *Review of Communication Research*, and a former associate editor for *Journalism Studies*. Her earliest research focused on media sociology and news content characteristics, especially research areas such as news quality, alternative forms of journalism, and journalism education. Her quantitative and qualitative approaches addressed fundamental questions such as who should be classified as a journalist and what should be categorized as news. Her interests evolved toward meta-science, social science theory building, quantitative methods, public engagement, and targeting concepts in need of conceptual and empirical specification. She has taught broadcast journalism at Bloomsburg University; digital media at Arizona State; and mixed methods, theory building, scale development, engaged journalism, and visual communication at Michigan State.

Cayce Myers (PhD University of Georgia) is professor of public relations and director of graduate studies at the School of Communication at Virginia Tech where he teaches public relations, communication law, and communication theory. Prior to entering academia, he was an attorney in Georgia. He is the author of *Public Relations History: Theory Practice and Profession*, *Money in Politics: Campaign Fundraising in the 2020 Presidential Election*, and coauthor of the fourth and fifth editions of *Mass Communication Law in Virginia*. His research focuses on laws affecting public relations practice, public relations history and development, and campaign finance in US presidential elections.

About the Contributors

Stephen D. Perry (PhD University of Alabama) is professor of communication at Regent University and former interim dean of the Robertson School of Government. His most recent book, *Pro Football and the Proliferation of Protest: Anthem Posture in a Divided America* (Lexington, 2019), dealt with the need to listen to and respect communication from both sides of the anthem kneeling debate in America. He is the former editor of *Mass Communication and Society* and currently serves as executive editor of *Better Journalism and Artifact Analysis*. He edits *Communication Research Replication*. He has authored thirty peer-reviewed journal articles plus over two dozen book chapters. His current research interests include media history, religious communication, and peace journalism.

Soo Young Shin (MA Michigan State University) is a PhD candidate in the School of Journalism at Michigan State University. Employing both quantitative and qualitative research methods, she studies how news professionals engage with the public, as well as examining how audiences perceive news organizations and their practices. Her research and teaching are inspired and informed by her professional experience as a digital journalist and copyeditor in South Korea. She started her career at a media startup company and worked for fourteen years while it expanded its service areas into various platforms. Her teaching specialties include data journalism, data visualization, news reporting, business news, and journalists' digital media engagement strategies, including building their own brands.

Ben Voth (PhD University of Kansas) is professor of rhetoric and director of debate and speech programs at Southern Methodist University. He also serves as the Calvin Coolidge Debate Fellow. He has served a number of international institutions including the United States Holocaust Memorial Museum, the George W. Bush Presidential Institute, and the U.S. State Department in Rwanda. He serves as an academic evaluator for C-SPAN's official rankings of US presidents since 2021. He is the author of four academic books including *The Rhetoric of Genocide: Death as a Text* (2014) and *Debate as Global Pedagogy: Rwanda Rising* (2021), both of which won the American Forensics Association's top award for research monographs (The Daniel Rohrer Award). He published more than two dozen academic book chapters and peer-reviewed journal articles on a range of subjects, along with over one hundred public editorials on a range of political controversies. As director of debate and speech he has coached and directed more than fifteen world champions of speech and debate events such as parliamentary debate (2000), IPDA (2022), informative speaking, and team sweepstakes.

Adriel Warren (BA Belmont University) is a master's student at Austin Peay State University and the marketing assistant at AllSides.com. She currently serves as the nonfiction editor for Zone 3 Press. During her time at Belmont University, Warren was elected the editor-in-chief of the *Belmont Literary Journal*. She also served on a panel for the Women's Rhetoric Archival Research project in 2018. In 2019, she received a certification in book publishing from the Columbia Publishing Course at Oxford University where she completed a full-length prospectus for an academic press. Warren was also invited to present her research on the modernization of time and mobility at the 2022 Tennessee Philological Association Annual Conference. Her writing has been published in a volume of *Tennessee's Emerging Writers*.